HEAVENLY DAYS

HEAVENLY DAYS

RECOLLECTIONS OF A CONTENTED AIRMAN

By

Group Captain James Pelly-Fry DSO, RAF

CRECY BOOKS

First published in 1994
by Crécy Books Ltd

ISBN 0 947554 32 7

Printed and bound in Great Britain by
Hartnolls Limited, Bodmin, Cornwall

To my darling Arleen, who gave me such a blissfully long and happy married life and encouraged me to write these memoirs.

Now she can read all these pages again in Heaven.

'I've topped the wind-swept heights with easy grace,
Where never lark or even eagle flew;
And while, with silent lifting mind I've trod
The high, untrespassed sanctity of space,
Put out my hand, and touched the face of God.'

Extract from 'An airman's Ecstasy',
written by Pilot Officer John Gillespie Magee,
aged nineteen, of the Royal Canadian Air Force,
killed in December 1941 whilst flying a
Spitfire. From his book HIGH FLIGHT.

Acknowledgement

This personal account would never have been written but for the prompting to do so over many years by my family and friends. Finally I succumbed; and it has been nostalgic to recapture so many events, places, and personalities during the process of taxing my memory for detail to the hilt.

It could not have been pursued without the great encouragement and help over many months by my late wife Irène, my daughter-in-law Anna (who cleverly suggested the title 'Heavenly Days' – an expression of mine that seems to have much usage), and Charles Hall who produces such clever aviation sketches under his pseudonym 'Holly'. To them, and to others who offered many constructive suggestions, I give my heartfelt thanks.

'I must at the same time apologise to those whose names I have failed lamentably to include in the pages. They may be unrecorded; but certainly not forgotten'.

I hope that this account of an airman's experiences will prove an encouragement to others to enter the magic world of aviation that in my lifetime has progressed so very dramatically. It is a great challenge; and abundantly rewarding.

Bristol 1994

An Index of Chapters.

Chapter I

Early Days

The Chantry, Kings Langley, in the County of Hertfordshire, has a distinctly ecclesiastical ring about it. The encyclopaedia describes a chantry as an endowment for priests to sing mass for the founder's soul, giving visions of tonsured monks in prayer and harmonised male voices singing beautifully in a place of repose and contemplation. All this may well have happened in the distant past, but the early twentieth century had produced a change. The Chantry, with men of the cloth long departed, was now a cottage hospital and was the place of birth in 1911 of the writer. In 1948 I made my way to Kings Langley by Green Line bus and visited the Chantry. Sadly, there were no holy men's ghosts, no cottage hospital, not even a small wall-plaque to record earlier events of import. The Victorian building was now housing a Shell Petroleum Company Research Establishment.

My first five years were spent in Colombo, where my father was a tea expert in a merchant house and, as I grew older, certain events became etched into my memory. I remember clearly a huge Christmas tree that reached far up to the ceiling in our home at Rosemead Place; my father running out to pick up a fallen leaf on the beautifully kept lawn just before the judges in the 'Best garden in Colombo' were due to arrive. I also remember going up to the hills of Nuwara Eliya, the hot weather escape for those fortunate enough to leave the heat of Colombo. One Easter-time, I had the thrill of hunting for – and finding – those coloured eggs that bunny rabbits laid only for the good little boys to enjoy. I remember taking a small cup and tapping a rubber tree for its thick creamy liquid and then kneading it into a ball that later became firm and bouncy. Then came the day when the system prescribed that my younger sister Rosemary and I must 'go home' to England to be put to school. Go home indeed, as I saw it Colombo was my home! The night prior to sailing I spent in the Galle Face Hotel watching the beam of the lighthouse flashing into my bedroom – it was a misery. The following day, once on board, I watched all the activity as we moved out of the harbour and, to some extent, this softened the blow. My mother yet again had to make the journey and those weeks at sea, in reality, were periods taken out of her life, and pretty disagreeable at that. After a day or two at sea there was no fresh fruit or fresh milk available and of course no air conditioning.

In those days one of the tricks, when booking sea travel from England to the East, that both shipping agent and discerning passenger alike understood was to travel 'Posh'. This was supposedly the advantage, based upon the sun's location, of giving you a cabin on the shady side of the ship – Port Out, Starboard Home. I suppose that there was a degree of truth in the idea. If nothing else, it was to give the English language a new word.

After our arrival in England my grandmother and maiden Aunt May provided a home for us in Epping, Essex. My brother, my two sisters and I, a gap varying from four to six years between each of us, stayed at the house called Somerfield during the school holidays. In keeping with my grandmother's Quaker background (she was a descendant of Elizabeth Fry, née Gurney of Earlham Hall, Norwich), we children had a very healthy ration of the Bible, prayers at mealtimes and the complete treatment on Sundays. Of course there was no radio or television to distract us and the Sabbath, I have to say, was a misery of enforced inactivity. A surfeit of anything soon palls, and in later years inevitably came the reaction. Going to church, I almost blush to admit, is now for Special Occasions rather than the accepted and satisfying regular affair that it should be.

The days spent in Epping, the Quaker outlook notwithstanding, did have a profound effect on my future. It happened that there was, and still is, a fine RAF aerodrome nearby called North Weald. From the aerodrome, to my immense interest and excitement, small tubby biplanes used to fly overhead and I learned somehow or other that they were called Armstrong Whitworth 'Siskins'. They were single-seat fighters and their job was to attack and destroy any naughty foreign military aeroplanes or airships coming to England with evil intent. The Siskins used to fly over as a rule one at a time. Flying high up, which I guessed to be around 5,000 feet, they used to cavort about like the Indian Ocean dolphins that I saw on the sea voyage home. What kind of super men could these be, I used to ask myself? What very special skills and bravery was called upon to become one of those pilots? At the age of seven and with no Papa on hand to answer these kind of questions I could only marvel at the magic of flight. By some good chance I was able to get hold of materials sufficient to try my schoolboy hand at making a simple, stick-type, rubber-powered model aeroplane. At the age and with absolutely no background information to work on the model, when completed, was destined to be a non-flier; however it taxied fairly briskly along the road in front of the house. Its final fling, literally, was when I took it to the top room in the house, wound up the rubber motor, and launched it with gusto from an open window. Alas, no prizes for guessing that the attempt was a dismal failure. However, the impressive if inelegant Siskins had left their mark on my imagination.

Later on came my preliminary schooling at a convent in Worthing and the next stage in my education was that incorrect description of today, the public school. Not wishing to bore the reader with the usual catalogue of events, likes, dislikes and dramas that all too often come the way of school life I will relate just one vital event, and the one that very nearly put paid to any prospects of becoming a military aviator. I was inflicted with a distinctly nasty malady called mastoid fever, an infection of the bone in the inner ear region. The illness, to put it bluntly, was quite dreadful; but by sheer chance I was rescued by an ear, nose and throat specialist who happened to come down for the week-end to his parents home near the school. My mother had rented a cottage nearby, and Mr Hamlyn Thomas agreed to see me. By so doing he saved me from a certain operation of a nature that I was just too ill to comprehend. That excellent gentleman from Harley Street by his prompt treatment enabled me subsequently to qualify medically for entry into the Royal Air Force. When reading the application form many years later, it said 'if you have had an operation for mastoid, under no circumstance will your application be acceptable'. The illness and subsequent convalescence effectively denied me two school terms. That coupled with my father's death three years earlier in Colombo and my mother's meagre pension prompted me to suggest to her that I could help matters by abandoning my education there and then. She agreed, and I never returned; my school days were over and I was fourteen-and-a-half years old. However I had succeeded in some respects for I was Captain of the 'Colts' rugby football side, sometimes playing wing-threequarter for the first team, and won the *Victor Ludorum* for athletics. The year was 1926 and the next stage in my young life was to enter the big wide world. I did not particularly mind terminating my general education at such a tender age but what I missed very much was the loving care, guidance and companionship of a father who I only remembered effectively during one of his infrequent leave periods to England. I confess that when the news of his death from para-typhoid reached me it was difficult to show adequate sorrow. His early death, aged only fifty, made me realise that family separation due to a parent earning his living at the other end of the world was definitely to be avoided when I became an adult and had to choose a career of my own. In retrospect this policy greatly influenced the timing of my marriage prospects – not least the factor that a major war was to come – and is a contributory reason why I married at the age of thirty eight after all the dust had settled.

Looking back on the disagreeable aspects of school life such as the cold monastic setting; the quite awful food that some boys even smuggled in paper bags for later disposal; the limited freedom and the enforced participation in activities outside the classrooms – like cross-country running, there were pleasant and amusing aspects to remember. On one of those awful cross-country runs in the depths of Berkshire, sitting by the roadside half way up the hill from Woolhampton village, was my friend Count Yaraslov Potoki from Poland. From all accounts his family seemed to own a large portion of that now turbulent country, but here, with everything in life to look forward to as an adult, the poor fellow certainly did not look like the very wealthy heir to vast estates. With a look of resignation on his face and grappling with a foreign and difficult language he cried out "I can no more – it is too up!". I whole-heartedly agreed with his sentiments and in later years his description admirably fitted other equally disagreeable activities.

Of the senior personalities, suffice to mention only two. One was the remarkably tall and handsome headmaster, the Reverend Ignatious Rice OSB, known for a reason never discovered by the distinctly inappropriate name of 'Piggy'. He was a most excellent head of school and I will be forever grateful to him for his endeavours in persuading the RAF Selection Board that only a long illness prevented me from gaining a School Certificate, the prerequisite to being acceptable scholastically for a Commission. The other name engraved on my heart – but for a different reason – was the Maths master, Dr Harold Dereham. He was a mixture of the stern teacher in the classroom and an enthusiastic patron of the 'Bull Inn' at Woolhampton on the Bath Road. The Doctor taught us with an iron-hand-in-velvet-glove. If he disapproved of a boy's lack of concentration or his misdemeanours he would slowly walk up to the offender and in a clear voice that must have been heard all over Berkshire would bark out "Boy! I must tell you that the quickness of the hand deceives the eye".

For all the immediate disadvantages of being a boarder at Douai School, run by Benedictine monks from the abbey that formed the larger part of the handsome estate and with a sprinkling of outside professional staff, there is no doubt whatever that the system taught us all those most desirable tenets of behaviour, catholic attitudes in the pure meaning, a sense of what was called 'fair play', an understanding, (as far as was possible in our immature age,) of a belief in the Deity, and our trust in the Almighty. It was a balanced and reasonable view that society could survive only provided that all of us should understand that we were human beings each in his way dependant upon the other. How well were these sound and eminently practical attitudes brought out in the Services – and in my own case the Royal Air Force. Service life is a classic example of how a community can be organised and enjoyed by all the participants and in a way is an extension of village life that so many enjoy.

Fortunately the family move to Barons Court in London had many pleasant facets even though I was destined initially to go to work in the Accounts Department of the P & O Shipping Company. This was a temporary affair before I became old enough at the age of sixteen to go into the tea trade as my father and elder brother had done. The three years as an apprentice was extended to six due to the recession and all this time I was working away in East London for the princely sum of fifty shillings (£2.50) per month. It was instructive in some ways, but for me it was precious time wasted.

The tea trade, purely in terms of tasting the product (as in wine tasting) was much more of a skill than I had expected. Apart from countries of origin, where the climate, the altitude and the soil affect the tea bush to produce a different taste and strength that can be identified, each estate in each part of the world produces tea with distinct varieties of flavour. For example, Ceylon tea – Sri Lanka is the name today – entailed careful tasting every week of perhaps as many as three hundred different samples, each from a specific estate. In my time with Tetleys Archie Skinner was the Ceylon tea expert par excellence. He could remember precisely what the previous importation (of, say, seventy chests) was like. Having judged each one, he then advised the tea brokers the price, accurate to a farthing, that he was prepared to bid in the tea salerooms in Mincing Lane, London.

The attention to detail extended to blending teas to suit particular areas where the water prescribed matching the tea to give the best results to the customer. This specialised expertise even entailed shipping samples of water from the United States so that Tetley's teas could be blended appropriately. Tea blending is designed to maintain the quality and flavour of a particular brand. Prior to World War Two, it was normal to be able to buy from a discerning store like Jacksons of Piccadilly or Harrods a small box of tea, the contents of which came from a specific tea estate, perhaps with a romantic name like Nuware Eliya, Lovers Leap, or Doombagastalawa. In later times, unhappily, this selectivity seems to have been displaced by the mass-blended product with a trade name. Worse still, the habit, originated in the USA, of putting tea into little bags on the pretext of convenience, has to my mind spoiled the joy of tea drinking.

There were of course lighter moments in our training. One of the happenings in tea tasting is that occasionally a sample taken from a consignment of perhaps fifty chests of tea would have a supplementary if discreet flavour of something like mint, cabbage, or other vegetable matter. The expert detected it immediately, and the conclusion was that a foreign element had been allowed to mix in during manufacture on the tea estate. One of the apprentices was an amiable if gullible fellow whose leg was pulled whenever we thought it a good moment. Together with another conspirator I decided that the moment was ripe. Having a small batch of some half-a-dozen teas made up, I called out to Edwards and said "Taste these teas, Edwards. The fourth one is quite odd – it tastes just like eggs-and-bacon." Friend Edwards duly inspected the sample, sniffed it, and then took a spoonful. He paused, thought about it, and then took another sip. We awaited his considered judgement. He then said, "Yes, you have a point. However, I must say that although I can taste the eggs, I'm damned if I can taste the bacon."

During my tea apprenticeship I fortunately came across the aeromodelling scene and I also followed the activities of full-sized aviation by going to air displays and read avidly magazines called 'The Aeroplane' and 'Flight'. The former was graced, or perhaps a better word might be enlivened, by a forthright editor called CG Grey. His editorials frequently berating Government policy and the aircraft industry were master-pieces of succinct prose. One minor gem that sticks even after all these years have passed went something like this; 'An Indian gentleman called Man Mohun Singh set off in his Gipsy Moth from Lympne aerodrome in Kent to fly to India. His aeroplane was aptly called *Miss India* and this he proceeded to do successfully because he missed India altogether.'

In the absence of any opportunity to get into the aviation scene at an early stage of my young life, I made a bid to go for the next best thing which was aeromodelling. A chance purchase of a magazine called 'The Model Engineer' proved to be the starting point. In those days the magazine was the only publication of its kind that appeared on the bookstalls and it was devoted naturally to the model engineering activities and interests of its readers. Whilst in the main one read about steam engines, lathes, locomotives, power boats, modelling expertise and the like, every now and then a column would appear about model aeroplanes and gliders. Aeromodelling work it seemed was not considered to be proper 'model engineering' but fortunately the publisher Percival Marshal was catholic in his attitudes even though those model aeroplanes were powered by skeins of twisted rubber. Through 'The Model Engineer' magazine I now discovered two things that transformed my teenage life. One was Wimbledon Common, where model flying took place at the weekends, the second was the existence of a society formed in 1922 from the marriage of the Kite and Model Aeroplane Association and the London Model Aeroplane Society. It was called The Society of Model Aeronautical Engineers and founded by Mr AE Jones and Mr FJ Camm whose brother was Sir Sydney Camm of Hawker aircraft fame. It was granted in due course a Charter by the Royal Aero Club to control national aeromodelling in the UK. Through the years there is no doubt that the SMAE has done a splendid job and today the movement has become a very complex and international affair.

So Wimbledon Common it was for the new boy and on most Sundays I would take the bus from Kensington to Putney and then go on up the hill to the Common. Initially it was just to look, listen and learn, but it was not long before I made friends. As in other human activities, the subject matter is paramount. Class, trade, background, education, social status – all are subordinated to the interest of a common hobby. It is a most agreeable situation and no doubt it helped me in large measure by the simple fact that aeromodelling in those days was just about as inexpensive a hobby as one could find. The materials were not only minimal, the whole secret of success and enjoyment lay in two human assets – the brain and the hands. You 'thought it out', as they say now, and then you moved to the kitchen table, at a quiet moment, to construct what was in your mind's eye. As a young man this appealed to me and my shallow pocket immensely.

My new friends were charming and most helpful and soon there came a moment when I felt bold enough to try my hand. My first attempt, a stick-type seaplane of spruce, piano wire, and oiled silk, was constructed on the kitchen table. It was carried to the famous Round Pond in Kensington Gardens very early one morning when only the ducks were there to impede or prevent my experiments. After winding up the rubber motor it was placed on the water. It scooted briskly away but failed to take off and ended up, still on it's three floats, in the middle of the 250 yard diameter artificial lake. This necessitated a second dawn visit the following day to recover it after it had drifted ashore. I then tried some hand launches over the grass; it flew after a fashion for a few seconds at a time, but that was all. The learning curve was nil. Then in one of the issues of 'The Model Engineer' there appeared one day an article with drawings and sketches of a fuselage-type rubber-powered high wing monoplane. It was the brain-child of a nice man many years my senior called WE Evans. He was a timber merchant by profession and cheekily I used to refer to him as 'Good Evans'. In order to acquire building materials I visited a model shop in New Oxford Street where the mildly forbidding Mr AE Jones was pleased to let the young man buy the necessary items. Perhaps of some interest is that one day Mr Jones gave me the very first sample of balsa wood seen in England, saying that he had no use for such rubbish! I soon put it to work and in due course the model was constructed. It had a wing-span of thirty-six inches and a clever triangular section fuselage which made for lightness, that vital word in our vocabulary. On a memorable Saturday afternoon, clutching the box containing my new and precious venture into the realms of flight, I set off by bus for the Common. Upon arrival I had an awful feeling of bashfulness about producing my model for all to see. What would my new friends think if my model flying machine would prove to be a dismal failure? Oh well, nothing to it now; I was committed and the members were watching. 'Good' Evans looked on encouragingly. I took the model out of the cardboard box, strapped on the wing with rubber bands, fitted the rubber motor, checked to see that there were no warps in the flying surfaces, and wound up the propellor to about a fifth of the maximum turns that the rubber would accept. Now came the moment of truth – the hand launch into a light wind. To my joy, and no less to my complete amazement, the model 'flew out of my hand' and climbed up a little bit before settling down to a level flight – just like that! Soon the power eased off, the model put its nose down into a descending path, and then it made a soft landing on the grass. I was so astonished that I stood transfixed. The magic of flight had revealed itself to me visually although the principles involved were still something of a mystery.

That was the turning point in my young life. This flying business, I decided, was now for me. It seemed almost uncanny that a model aeroplane of my own construction had actually flown and what's more it had flown exactly as I had prayed it would. Once the high pulse rate and the exultations had become less apparent, to the encouraging noises from the other modellers I made further flights. For me, utter bliss was a model aeroplane that actually flew and I returned to my mother's house with the glad tidings.

The following years were a compound of continuing my tea apprenticeship (which I confess was interesting except that my thoughts were now elsewhere), coupled with devoting most of my spare time to aeromodelling. In the winter months I played rugby football for Rosslyn Park, the excellent London Club with its fine grounds at the Old Deer Park adjoining Kew Gardens. This enabled me to enjoy my favourite game and keep fit at the same time. 'The Park', as the club was called, fielded no less than eleven teams. Although I was asked later to play for the first team I turned down the offer for the good reason that I could not afford the expense of that kind of top class rugby and certainly not on an income of fifty shillings a month! So I was perfectly happy to play for one of the 'A' teams and my rugger playing friends were splendid fellows who usually offered me a lift by car to 'away matches'. When occasionally going by train and starting from Victoria Station there was the 'Windsor Dive' pub nearby where you could get a steak, kidney and oyster pudding plus a pint of real draught Bass for one shilling and sixpence the equivalent today of nine pence!

By dint of maximum enthusiasm and learning fast I suppose it is fair to say that my youthful talents for aeromodelling were developed at speed. Not least it was the help and encouragement that I got from the top names in the hobby like the famous pioneer, Colonel Claude Bowden that spurred me on and before long I was beginning to win contests. I had joined the SMAE my membership number being 139 and, at the age of seventeen, I was elected a member of the SMAE Council. We formulated the concept of the first-ever International Trophy – called the Wakefield and donated by Sir Charles Wakefield, boss of the Castrol Oil Company. After council meetings we used to go to the 'Club', Joe Lyons Corner House in Oxford Street and, over a coffee and a bun, out would come all those old envelopes the backs of which would be put to work designing the very latest in model flying machines. Of course debate was rife over wing sections, flight stability, free-wheeling propellors (very advanced!), new materials and so on. Amongst those usually present were Frank Houlberg, our Chairman; Mullins, the Hon Sec; my hero Ralph Bullock, perhaps the best aeromodeller of all for my money; Richard Langley, an engineer who was our competition secretary and official timekeeper and J van Hattum, known as the Dutch Spy when a student at de Havillands. When Juste van Hattum and I first met at the 1928 Model Engineer Exhibition in London he approached me with the classic "Mr Pelly-Fry, I presume?" Both of us had dared to become aeromodelling writers and understandably each thought the other to be at least in his thirties when in fact I was eighteen and he was two years older. Van, as he was called, was an excellent artist and drew all the line drawings and sketches for my articles. He subsequently joined the Dutch aircraft industry and finally became a lecturer in aerodynamics at Delft University. Nearly sixty years later he is my longest-known male friend and we still communicate regularly.

In 1927 the SMAE had the pleasure of welcoming Air Vice Marshal Sir Sefton Brancker as the new President, succeeding Dr AP Thurston. Sir Sefton, the Director of Civil Aviation, was a VIP passenger on the ill-fated proving flight by the Airship R101 in 1931 on the journey to India. A year earlier Ralph Bullock and I had accompanied him to Eton College, where the Air Marshal gave the boys a lecture. This was followed by a demonstration of indoor model flying where Bullock, in particular, captivated his young audience by flying his 'Feather-plane' – the wings and tail consisting of feathers hand-picked from a turkey provided by his friendly butcher. As a foretaste to the future, little did I dream that forty years later my son Jonathan would one day attend that famous school as a scholar.

My immensely absorbing hobby of aeromodelling went on without let-up. Apart from being a member of the British Wakefield Trophy team for five successive years and, on the sixth occasion I flew by proxy the first American entry by Gordon Light which for practical purposes, gained equal second place. On one occasion we went to the famous Brooklands motor-racing course with the Vickers Aviation Company aerodrome located inside the oval-shaped track. The Brooklands Flying Club had invited the Society to give some demonstration flights and the party travelled by train from London. We met two famous pilots, Jim Mollison and Amy Johnson, who took a great interest in our models. The Flying Club Chairman proposed that we have a competition, the winner to be given a prize of thirty minutes dual instruction in one of the club's de Havilland Moths. In the event I was declared the winner and soon afterwards I made my way back to Brooklands for my first flying lesson. It was not my first ever flight because that happened earlier when Van Hattum and I had five shilling's worth of joy-ride from the beach near Ryde, Isle of Wight in an Avro 504N. We were dressed – if that is the word – in swimming costumes! The Brooklands Club seemed to like our model flying so much that they invited us back the following year and once again young JP-F won the contest and flying lesson No 2 was given. Yet another visit was made to Brooklands and I almost blush to relate that the young man won for the third time. When arriving for this spell of 'dual' my instructor grinned and said "You know, young fellow, with your luck you should eventually go solo at this rate – if you live long enough to enjoy it!"

Another episode was during an 'away match' and this time the venue was the pleasant grass aerodrome at Hamble, near Southampton. Whilst the other members and I were engrossed in our favourite hobby a man walked over to us and watched the general activity. He made some comments and when this got us into conversation with him it was quite apparent even to such a newcomer as myself that he was very well informed about aeromodelling. Our visitor then said "By the way, my name is Roe – AV Roe". He was the famous aircraft designer and I could hardly believe my luck in meeting him. 'Mr Avro' invited us to tea at his house which was on the edge of the aerodrome and he proved a charming and excellent host. Soon after arrival and we were enjoying tea with cucumber sandwiches and biscuits – he knew my tastes almost to perfection – a man came into the drawing room. Our host said "I would like you to meet my Spanish guest – *Senor* Juan de la Cierva". Yet another thrill – we were meeting the famous designer of the Autogiro and *Senor* Cierva said that he had seen our models flying and congratulated us on our skills. At an opportune moment I asked him if he could explain the principles upon which Autogiros work, the reason being that I would like to try to make a flying model. He smiled, shrugged his shoulders and said "You know, I have no idea at all; I just experimented until I made it fly successfully". I am inclined to think in retrospect that there was perhaps a degree of truth in what he said because in the late twenties designers had limited knowledge of rotary-winged flight.

The year was now 1932 and I was about to 'come of age', a process by which in those days a young man reaching the age of twenty-one was considered old enough to take on his own responsibilities. My mother was the sole guiding light and she had very firm views about the activities and careers of her children. In my case, clearly at a dead-end where going overseas in the tea trade was concerned because the recession of the early thirties was still with us, an impasse had been created. By now, whether or not a job might arise for me in the tea trade, my gaze was firmly up into the sky – I wanted desperately to become a pilot. Maternal instincts told my mother that this was a wild and dangerous path to follow so until I reached the magic age of twenty-one (when supposedly I would become master of my own destiny), there was no option but to hold onto the apron strings of the Great White Chief. Even other senior members of the family raised their eyebrows and my very elderly Aunt May said "Well Jimmy, if you really must go flying, please remember to fly low and slow; it's safer that way".

After a lot of thought was given to the problem, the first positive thing that I did was to write to CG Grey, the editor of my favourite 'Aeroplane' magazine. To my surprise he not only replied to my letter he even suggested that I go and see him at his editorial offices in Piccadilly. Mr Grey's establishment was on the first floor and I could not avoid noticing mountains of papers, magazines and files all over his office. When my eyes focused on a roll-top desk equally festooned with the written word, sitting behind it was an angular-faced, grey haired man who was wearing a monocle. "Aha, my young friend, so you want to go flying, eh?" "Yes Sir, very much so". There was a slight pause whilst he gave me what novelists call a piercing look. "Well my friend, not so much 'what do you know' as 'who you know', eh?". "Sir," I replied, "I know a Dutch student called Van Hattum who is at de Havillands and he has introduced me to his friends and so I have been able to go to Stag Lane Aerodrome". "Good," said Mr Grey "You have made a start". He then went on to tell me that the only way to get associated with practically any activity, be it South American butterflies, skiing, male-voice choirs or even learning Ethiopian Amharic, was to get to know the participants. After that, doors would open. In my case the prospect of flying aeroplanes fell into two categories; either you got it for free, or you were lucky enough to be able to afford it. I did not have to try very hard to convince him that quite definitely I fell into the former category. CG Grey then said that my only course of action was either to join the Auxiliary Air Force – but that meant having a proper job – or putting in a bid to get into the Royal Air Force; all the evidence pointed conclusively to the second option. CG Grey was a splendid person; he was direct, logical and realistic. Not only was I delighted to be asked to go and see him; the visit taught me a lot about the right steps to take in this tough world, it also taught me that 'going to the top' was the best way to accomplish anything. As Air Vice Marshal Sir Edward Fielden many years later used to say, "Always speak to the organ-grinder – never the monkey".

I could now appreciate the situation much more clearly and with CG Grey's sympathetic interest to encourage me two problems arose. First of all I had to come to terms with my mother's attitude, which was no easy task. Then second was to set about ways and means of approaching the Air Ministry in the correct way; the whole business seemed to be one big hurdle but it had to be tackled. Fate meanwhile had ordained that my elder sister Betty had travelled by sea to Colombo and had met a young woman on the ship. A lasting friendship developed, not only between the two of them but soon after between the two families. Jean Coghlan's mother lived in South Kensington and she generously offered my mother the ground floor of her house as our new home. The basement flat at the time housed Group Captain AAB 'Tommy' Thomson who was serving in the Air Ministry and that strange element destiny now began to smile in my direction. Tommy Thomson and equally his wife Margaret were a splendid couple. He seemed so enthusiastic about Service life – 'the best Club you will ever belong to' – and he told me something about what life in the Royal Air Force was all about. For the first move, he told me to write to the

Personnel Department of the Air Ministry and apply for a short Service Commission and within days the application form was sent to me.

After examining it carefully, to my dismay I read about the scholastic standard required which was a School Certificate; so I sent a letter quickly to 'Piggy' explaining the situation and asked if he could help in any way. It seemed strange at the time to ask a Benedictine monk to sponsor me for joining one of the fighting forces! In spite of my ex-headmaster's efforts the reply that arrived from the Air Ministry was a terrible shock. My application was turned down 'with regret'. This was a big setback and understandably I was very depressed about it. Perhaps I was not the Super Man to fly military aeroplanes after all.

After work I made my way to the basement flat and told Tommy Thomson the sad news. His reaction was a compound of sympathy coupled with words of encouragement. "I can only guess", he said, "that the Selection Board has candidates with better educational qualifications to choose from; so naturally during the initial weeding-out process anyone like you with a possible weak mark in scholastic attainment – however explainable – would be crossed off the list".

All was not lost, however. A few days later, Tommy Thomson suggested a new line of approach and said that there were some other possibilities worth investigating. Apart from the Auxillary Air Force which I already knew about after my visit to CG Grey, another was the RAF Special Reserve, personnel of which were posted to twin-engined squadrons that operated every week-end from aerodromes such as RAF Manston. The problem here was that previous experience was desirable, if not mandatory, so on both counts and equally on the score of the need to have some kind of an income they were both non-starters so far as I was concerned.

The third possibility that he mentioned was one that I had never heard of before and was an organisation called the Reserve of Air Force Officers. The RAFO was essentially a reserve pool of ex-service pilots who had completed their time in regular squadrons and were available for recall, when necessary, back into the Royal Air Force. The whole point of telling me about the RAFO was that he had heard quite recently that the role of this organisation was going to be expanded by recruiting direct from civilian sources. To this end the plan was to set up three or four civil flying schools – perhaps on the lines of a flying club but with a Service overtone – and in this way attract young men who would be taught to fly at Government expense. (Subsequently, I could not escape the conclusion that the planners in London were obviously aware that sooner rather than later more pilots would be needed for a war and this way one way to get them started.)

Heartened by the information from Tommy Thomson, I sat down and wrote out another application to Adastral House. I did not mention anything about my earlier bid for a Short-Service Commission and this was on the basis that it is wise not to volunteer information unless it is specifically called for. The entry form duly arrived and once again I was given the support of my headmaster about my scholastic standard. This time, to my great satisfaction I was summoned for an interview. Perhaps they did not care so much now about that damned School Certificate? No matter, I had now reached the bottom rung of the ladder and my prospects were beginning to improve. Having reached the interview stage, two supplementary hurdles had still to be surmounted. The first was to cajole my mother into giving her blessing to the project as there was no point in deliberately upsetting family harmony however strongly I felt about my ambitions. In the event she must have resigned herself because she adopted an attitude of "Oh well, if you must – you must" and I assured myself that my case was no worse than a whole number of similar ones in other families.

The second hurdle was that I had to get approval from the director of Joseph Tetley & Son in charge of apprentices to have an extra two weeks holiday to be able to carry out the fifty hours flying training on the syllabus. With nervous apprehension I saw Mr Mackie and told him about my application to get a Commission in the RAFO and added that I had been selected for interview. Mr Mackie, impassively sitting behind his desk, pondered for a moment. Suddenly, he looked hard at me and with some displeasure said, "What on earth do you think you are doing, wanting to go flying when you ought to concentrate on the tea trade as a career?" There was a pregnant silence. He then said, "Not only do you want to go flying, you have the temerity to ask for the Company's time in the process. I have never heard of such nonsense." Knowing him as I did with his set ways it was almost a relief to discover that my forecast about his adverse reaction had been entirely correct and in a curious way this improved my morale as at least I could play the ball back into his court. "Sir, I am dismayed to hear you think so poorly of my bid to join one of His Majesty's fighting forces." Slight pause, during which I hoped that this pearl of youthful wisdom would make its mark. "Secondly, Sir, with the greatest respect, although I am naturally grateful to have the opportunity of being an apprentice in your Company, I cannot resist mentioning that my wages amount to the princely sum of fifty shillings a month. I am not contesting the amount as presumably that is all that you think I am worth."

I had the feeling that standing up to my boss was now beginning to get the score evened up slightly. He possibly appreciated that refusing my request (as I had yet to receive my Commission) was going to exacerbate the situation. He had been an old friend of my father in Colombo and he may have realised that nothing was to be gained by refusing my request. So after asking whether my mother had endorsed my plan and I, replying that she had, with reluctance he said "Oh very well, go off and do what you want to do." I thanked him and left his office but I thought little of his ungracious attitude even if he had good intent.

There was an aftermath to the disagreeable episode. Some weeks later, by which time I had completed my initial flying training course and was back in the groove of the tea trade and still awaiting a job overseas, Mr Mackie summoned me to his office. This time I was offered a chair and I sat there wondering what was to happen. He then said with deliberate brevity, "My son Kenneth wants to join the Royal Air Force and I thought that you could suggest what he should do". Heavens! My boss was now seeking my advice when previously he had thoroughly disapproved of my own aspirations. After all his strictures, this time the problem was on his own door-step.

I warmed to my subject with gusto. I told Mr Mackie that I thought it was a splendid idea but there was a world of difference in the two cases. Whereas I had taken the only option open to me, at least his son had the advantages of being a school-leaver at the right age and with the right scholastic qualifications so he was well placed to apply to become a cadet at the Royal Air Force College at Cranwell. It was by far the best way to make a career in the RAF and I was very surprised to discover that Mr Mackie had never heard of Cranwell. Not only did I act as an enthusiastic public relations man I was able subsequently to follow it up by arranging to take Kenneth up for his first flight in the RAF Flying Club's Gipsy Moth, registration G-AAEO. We took off from Hatfield on April 22nd 1934 – and father paid the bill. Ken Mackie succeeded in getting a cadetship to Cranwell. Both of us were about to start what we really wanted to do but the initial opposition was daunting. Success does not come to the faint-hearted.

Chapter II

The Tiger Moth

The two major hurdles having been surmounted, there came the great day when I rose early in our new London home and set off for my interview at the Air Ministry; the next stage in the battle to get flying was about to commence. To my surprise and relief the interview turned out to be a painless affair and the sensible questions asked by the selection board people produced quiet confidence in the applicant. I even had the feeling that they wanted me to pass the interview and I left with head high and a feeling of cautious optimism. The medical examination that followed seemed a straightforward affair, but as I discovered later this was nothing like as thorough as the one for a full-time regular Commission. I concluded that there was a big difference in the standard required between being a Tiger Moth pilot in the RAFO and an intrepid Service pilot of military aeroplanes in the regular Royal Air Force. Perhaps much more was required of a superman to fly a future £5,000 Hurricane rather than a £500 Tiger Moth? One day an official letter with 'On His Majesty's Service' on the envelope fell onto the doormat and it told me that I had been accepted as a Pilot Officer in the Reserve of Air Force Officers. It also told me that as I lived in the London area my flying training was to be at Hatfield at the de Havilland School of Flying. My sense of elation knew no bounds! At long last, apart from those thirty minute annual flying instruction periods at Brooklands, I was now going to be given a fifty-hour flying course. A major aspect of the whole affair included the happy thought that it was all going to be free. CG Grey was right, and I will always remember him.

In the first week of June 1933, I presented myself to the Chief Instructor of the de Havilland School of Flying, and this start to my flying career was enhanced by the fact that he actually knew that I was due to attend. Such organisation, such care in administration, such efficiency! I felt for the first time in my life that I was wanted.

The first close view of the flying school was exciting. Although I invariably arrived at least forty-five minutes before the prescribed starting time of 9.00 am, there were already twelve beautiful Tiger Moths neatly lined up on the asphalt apron. They were all spanking new with the civil registrations in lettered sequence starting with G-ACDA but with ACDD missing. With one of those co-incidences that I hope the reader will bear with, I discovered fifty one years later that Tiger Moth G-ACDC was portrayed in 1984 on the front cover of 'Aeroplane Monthly'. She was in the original colour of all red with Father Christmas in person flying over the snow-covered Surrey countryside and that same aeroplane was flown more than once by myself in 1933! She is now part of the Tiger Club's fleet at Redhill aerodrome.

Just before the appointed hour (the Services have an excellent system whereby personnel are expected to be 'on parade' five minutes before the deadline), various people had arrived on the apron. The flying instructors somehow were readily identified as indeed were the ground engineers. The rest consisted of some dozen young men who, like myself, looked very much like the proverbial 'new boys'. With happy if somewhat expectant looks on our faces, someone quickly mustered us and took us to an office where we identified ourselves. We were enrolled and were now identifiable pupils with the exalted rank of Pilot Officers in the Reserve of Air Force Officers. The Flying Club store-keeper soon issued us with those delicious status symbols of parachute, (each one fitted to the particular human frame like a bespoke suit), leather helmet, Gosport speaking tubes, goggles and overalls. Thus equipped to cope with the requirements of our pending aerial adventures, we then mustered in a room where Flight Lieutenant CA Pike, the Chief Flying Instructor, welcomed us as the first batch of pupils to the new school. Clem Pike was the most charming, enthusiastic and dedicated of men and was a superlative instructor – he just smoothly imparted to his pupils the feeling of self-confidence so necessary when tackling the initial complexities of learning to fly. Better even than that, as the days went by he showed us all that being a good pilot began from the moment that you approached your aeroplane. Everything was to be done smoothly, quietly, very thoroughly, and without any fuss. Those early days at Hatfield taught us all that flying was more than an acquired skill, it was the pursuit of excellence. As in childhood, first impressions become paramount. Clem Pike's imparted wisdom stuck and has forever remained. The other instructors, in perhaps varying styles, were equally effective. Flying Officer Eddie Fulford, my regular teacher, was down-to-earth and by-passed a lot of niceties. He kept you on your toes. Flt Lt RW Reeve, the Deputy Chief Instructor and an ex-Royal Flying Corps pilot, was quiet, confidence-making and competent. One felt that he knew exactly what kind of a budding pilot you were and thus you respected his judgement. Other flying instructors were Flt Lt Cox, Flying Officer Moon, Flt Lt French and Flying Officer King. All in all, we pupils could not have had better or more understanding teachers and they made the whole course seem so worthwhile and pleasurable.

On the sixth of June, 1933, page one of my pilot's log book has its first entry. Tiger Moth G-ACDE with Flying Officer Fulford and his pupil took off from Hatfield and the flight lasted twenty minutes. The entry records: 'taxying; straight and level flying'. No more. So the great business of learning to fly had begun. Eddie Fulford demonstrated how to taxi across the grass, gently swinging the nose from side to side to keep the blind-spot in front as clear as possible because the engine obstructed the direct view ahead, and thus the Tiger 'waltzed' carefully across the grass. Little did I know that the difficulty was to be compounded when, sitting in the cockpit of a Spitfire, the top of the Rolls Royce engine cowling looked for all the world like a 'worm's eye view' of a snooker table. Once the tail of the aeroplane lifted, then you were master of all you surveyed. After being shown how to keep the Tiger straight and level in flight, usually by the pupil lightly following the movements of the control column (or 'joystick'), then came the time for the instructor to say "Now let's go back to the aerodrome. Follow my actions whilst I make a circuit of the aerodrome and then the landing. Do not touch the controls". It was for all practical purposes really a demonstration short flight just to give the pupil the feeling and sensations of flying. But it was all a necessary initial foray into the air and I suppose that for all of us we were so absorbed, physically and mentally, that twenty minutes seemed like all morning. Although I already had received my 'baptism in the air' with the bathing-costume joyride and those thirty minute periods at Brooklands for three years in succession, I had decided to ignore those early experiences and imagine that I was now flying for the first time just like all the other pupils. The last thing that I wanted was to make the silly mistake that 'lesson one' was old news; and worse still, to say so. Experience later told me always to remember that each flight should be treated as your first one, each one a new experience, each one to be given the same concentration as if it was your first solo. One never stops learning in aviation; which I suppose is what makes it all so utterly fascinating and rewarding.

The summer days passed blissfully. I was given dual instruction regularly by Eddie Fulford and on occasion Flt Lt Cox or Flt Lt Reeve stepped in to fill the gap if Fulford was not available. I did not appreciate it at the time, but in retrospect the reason for 'changing horses' was as likely as not for the purpose of a 'second opinion' at the instructors' conference.

On Saturday, June 19th, 1933, Flt Lt Reeve said that he and I would fly in his own Tiger – G-ACDK and innocently I thought that this was by way of another trip of two or three circuits and landings. We climbed in, I was told to carry out the usual procedures, taxi out, and take off. All very routine stuff and by now we pupils were well used to it. Each time we tried to follow the same flight pattern as taught to us and we felt that we were becoming quite good at it. I carried out two complete circuits and landings, and being with a 'new' pilot and the Deputy Chief Flying Instructor at that I was more meticulous than ever. If nothing else I did not want to let Eddie Fulford down with a poor showing. In the event, all was well and both landings pleased me. Don Reeve then told me to taxy back to the starting point, turn the Tiger around into the 'ready to take off' situation, and then stop. This done, he then undid his straps and climbed out so I thought that perhaps something was amiss. Not at all; he stood by the rear cockpit, gave me a bit of a smile, and then said, "I am going to secure the front cockpit harness to keep it away from the dual controls. When I have done that, well, off you go on your own". He added "Just make one circuit and landing". With a wave of his hand and another reassuring smile he walked away. So this was the moment of truth; I was about to fly by myself for the first time! My senses were a compound of elation coupled with one of surprise that it was so unexpected. Thus it was that the pupil went through the drill and procedures, checked and rechecked everything, and took off on his first solo flight. I was conscious of two things; one was that no reassuring head was to be seen in front of me and the other was the sensation of Tiger Moth 'DK' getting airborne much quicker than usual. Of course! – it was that much lighter; I should have known. After the quicker than usual take-off, there was the well practised drill of climbing up to 800 feet, throttling back, turning gently across wind, turning again at the right moment onto the 'downwind' leg, and watching the aerodrome to time the next turn for the crosswind leg. At the estimated correct position, checking the wind sock once more, throttle back gently to allow the nose of the Tiger to go down and maintain fifty-five to sixty mph and the aircraft steered in a smooth descending turn at such a safe height that you could glide down onto the aerodrome should the normally trusty Gipsy Major engine falter. The first part of the approach was a smooth descent, perhaps weaving a little from side to side – no slide-slipping had yet been taught – until you are happy that you are correctly and safely positioned to cross the hedge comfortably at your intended spot. The final bit, the one that matters the most, is to get the aeroplane gently down to what is called a soft landing and then keep her straight by use of rudder until she comes to a stop. Finally, a check that it is clear ahead and behind before taxying smoothly to your starting point.

In the event, all went well. I suppose that as a pupil one is so accustomed to all those repetitive circuits and landings that the first solo may seem to be just another flight. Well, not quite so, I'm happy to say. There is the distinct feeling that you are on your own and whatever befalls, you are no longer relying on the instructor to rescue you. Everything is now up to you. I do not recollect any 'birdman' elation at all. The reality was that you were now doing precisely what you had been taught to do. Understandably, the wonderful sense of achievement comes when you step out of the aeroplane and walk away trying like the devil to look like Gregory Peck! It's a wonderful feeling. Once back to the parking area, after switching off, checking the essential items of good airmanship, and then releasing the Sutton Harness that kept you in your seat, I reported to Flt Lt Reeve. I wondered if he noticed that I was at least twelve inches taller? That charming man said "Well done; copperplate effort". We then went and had a cup of coffee. So now, after all the efforts, the stresses and strains of wiggling my way into aviation, I had at last flown solo. The Tiger Moth became my passion.

The whole adventure had taken 10 hours and twenty minutes of dual instruction followed by that five minute solo flight. In the afternoon at 3.20 pm another dual flight came about; this time in 'DC' for fifteen minutes. My progression to self pilotage had happened in two weeks and I confess that I felt well satisfied with events. When I returned home I was able to tell my family that for the first time there was a flying man to record on the family tree. Not much of a pilot so far, but big news just the same and even my mother, bless her, was seen to smile. The Great White Chief was pleased to show approval. It had been my biggest day.

The daily pattern of flying continued during the rest of the month and then into June and July. The extended time scale, due to periods of bad weather that was unsuitable for trainees, inevitably necessitated another request for extra time from Tetley's. I was not at all popular but grudgingly, Mr Mackie conceded. Perhaps by then he realised that I was a lost cause and anyway he was now taking an interest in aviation because of his son's application to go to Cranwell.

The flying training was now a mixture of continued dual instruction with Eddie Fulford in the front seat interspersed with an ever increasing quota of solo flying. The stalls, stall turns, spins (ugh!), and pretend forced landings (with Gipsy engine throttled back) that I had been shown prior to my first solo flight was repeated all over again. Additionally, that 'fighter boy' stuff called aerobatics entered my life. Although the Tiger Moth (as any old 'Tiggie hand' will endorse) was by no means the best of aeroplanes for this kind of aerial flight, if nothing else the nature of its design was such that most manoeuvres took quite a lot of practice to carry out well. I had to bully the poor machine into turning upside down when all it wanted to do was to fly respectably the proper way up. Equally, it was an excellent machine on which to learn because it had to be flown all the time. If your mind wandered and you began to admire those beautiful cumulus clouds, the next thing you knew was that either you had lost speed, lost direction, or lost height. You had to fly it properly all the time and that required concentration if you wanted to achieve a polished performance. Eddie used to say to me "You must be in charge and make the aeroplane do just what you want it to do – not the other way around". Perhaps the most admirable of the Tiger Moth's qualities was that it was so forgiving to a student pilot.

It would allow you to do the most stupid things – up to a point – and let you get away with it reasonably safely. No wonder after all these many years is the Tiggie spoken of with such affection and nostalgia. One amusing quip of many from Eddie was "Any landing you can limp away from is a good one". We learned about instruments, compasses, maps, navigation of a simple kind, engines and how to use them intelligently; I doubt that any of us had to be told anything twice.

The names of some fellow pupils remain in the memory. One chap called Bob Brittain was the son of Sir Harry Brittain, a prominent figure in his day. Bob was an energetic aviator and it was he who by clever organising succeeded in forming the RAFO Flying Club – later to widen its scope by changing identity to the RAF Flying Club. As a founder member, the Club's DH Moth, G-AAEO began to feature frequently in the pages of my pilot's log-book and by some careful salesmanship I managed to get most of my flying by the simple expedient of getting my passengers to pay the costs which amounted to one pound ten shillings per hour! In order to fly civil aircraft it was first necessary to obtain my civil Pilot's Licence, No 6031, together with The Royal Aero Club Certificate. Flying the de Havilland school Tiger Moths had a dispensation by virtue of their being classified as 'Service' aircraft. Michael Wight-Boycott was another pupil who like myself later became a regular RAF Officer. During the World War II war he distinguished himself by flying night fighters and in due course retired with the exalted rank of Air Commodore.

Within twelve months of going solo I had 100 hours logged and to add to the Tiger Moth I flew the new types of aeroplanes such as the Gipsy Moth, Moth Major, Miles Hawk, Puss Moth, Salmson-engined Klemm monoplane and finally the DH53 ultra-light 'Hummingbird' single seater fitted with a thirty-two hp Bristol 'Cherub' flat-twin engine. The DH53 was owned by a very charming fellow called Robert Somerset and just how I persuaded him with my limited experience to let me loose in his pet flying machine I will never know. My log book has reminded me of other long-forgotten incidents. One was an entry in which it seems that for the first time in my life I made the crossing of the English Channel. I ferried Moth G-AAIA from Berck aerodrome (Le Touquet) to Heston Airport. It was a solo flight in company with a Hillman Airways 'Dragon', but just how I got to Le Touquet in the first place, where the aeroplane was based, and how I contrived to get in yet more flying time is not recorded. It is interesting to consider now how the pilot of the Dragon would have helped me in the unhappy event that the Moth ended up with a splash into the sea as in those days there was no Air-Sea Rescue Service.

During the flying training period this story must include one of the pupils. Poor fellow, the reality was that in some respects his talents were limited. He got past the 'solo' stage, after which – like all of us – he moved on to short flights across country, the idea being to get us accustomed to fly well out of sight of Hatfield aerodrome. We were given aiming points either by flying 'out and home' or on a triangular map-reading course. As our budding aeronaut was a little limited in the art, his instructor gave him a short triangular course to carry out. "This should be a straight-forward one, Bloggins", said the instructor. "Fly to Welwyn Garden City, which you cannot miss, then south to Potters Bar where the railway will be a good guide as it runs all the way on your port side, and finally a short run back to Hatfield. A piece of cake". Our intrepid aviator set off, headed for Welwyn Garden City in fine style, and disappeared into the wide blue yonder. To our surprise he reappeared much sooner than expected, landed nicely, taxied in, switched off, and left the cockpit. "I'm surprised that you are back so soon", said his instructor, "Any problems?" Bloggins pondered a moment, then said "Well Sir, I got to Welwyn alright, turned starboard onto my new heading and set off for Potters Bar". A bit of a pause. "I soon picked up the railway and began to follow it as you suggested". Another pause; it seemed that he was wondering how to recount the next part of his story. "The trouble, sir, was that I found to my astonishment that the railway line disappeared into a tunnel. Well, I failed to find where it came out at the other end, so I had to pack in and come home!"

The scene at Hatfield was a party one fine evening at the Aero Club where I and some others had been invited to celebrate another first solo. Time passes all too quickly and pleasantly when the company is good and laughter prevails. After some time I became aware that the fellow who had earlier offered me a lift to London had departed and there was no other transport available. Someone said "Don't worry, no problem at all. Go to the guest house run by the School on the edge of the aerodrome. You enter by the small gate just beyond the hangars. It's nice and handy and it's very inexpensive for 'B & B'. Have another half-pint and off you go". I stayed on a little longer and then decided that bedtime was now for me and made my way out into the dark, heading for the hangars with a rising moon to help the night vision nicely. I followed the line of the boundary hedge and then found the little gate that I had been told was the rear entrance to the Guest House. When I reached the front door not a light was to be seen. No matter, I thought; after all, it's quite late. I pushed open the front door, walked into the hall and waited for someone to show up. There was complete silence. Oh well, nothing to it but to go up the staircase, find an empty bedroom, and get into a bed in my under-pants. In the morning people would be about and I could explain to whoever was in charge that I was a de Havilland flying school student – even if complete absence of kit might seem rather unusual. I awoke early after a good sleep and all I had to do was to get up, have breakfast, pay the bill and return to flying duties. Once downstairs and making appropriate noises to draw the attention of somebody in charge, from a back room appeared a young girl. It was soon apparent that she spoke no English; perhaps she was Hungarian, and my

Hungarian is, shall I say, limited. She seemed astonished that I was there at all and I was embarrassed because I could not communicate and explain the situation. So with a shrug of the shoulders, a happy smile and a handshake with the pretty young girl, I walked back to the aerodrome. To my astonishment I discovered later that I had stayed the night in the wrong house!!

Chapter III

Joining the Club

The second half of 1933, with those blissful days at Hatfield flying Tiger Moths, demonstrated the wisdom of CG Grey's philosophy that the only way to get associated with the world of flying was to get to know those connected with it. The golden opportunity of becoming a member of the Reserve of Air Force Officers was now having the desired effect. So instead of being what in Germany is described as a 'hedge guest' – one of those who watched from nearby and so did not have to pay the entrance charge – I was in the satisfactory position of being able to walk in, say 'hello' to anybody who I hoped would recognise me, and thus get that delicious feeling of 'belonging'. The first hurdle had now been taken and I began to get the feel of things. Confidence brings a degree of self-assurance and I could now talk the language of aviation (or so I hoped) and could say many of the things in aviation jargon that made you 'one of the chaps' – as my school days expression put it.

The combination of my student friends at the de Havilland Technical School coupled with membership of the Reserve of Air Force Officers now began to put me in the swim. The aeromodelling field had earlier brought into my life the 'Dutch Spy', Juste van Hattum. Through him, I went on to meet his house-sharing friends, John Longman (whose family publish books), Michael Barrington, and Olaf Thornton. They were a wonderful lot of young men – carefree in their way yet dedicated to the world of aviation. Between them they mustered not only talent but those desirable things called motor cars. I climbed, so to speak, onto the bandwagon.

It was now 1934 and I began to cast around to find ways and means of escaping from the City of London and the tea trade. Until something better cropped up there was no option but to travel each working day between Barons Court and Aldgate East on London's underground railway system. One day my chance of being in the right place at the right time and seizing the opportunities came along. I met a tall, good looking fellow of my age by the name of Dick Wrightson whose family were well-to-do shipping people. Dick had recently been bitten by the aviation bug and like me had learned to fly against the protestations of his family. He had recently teamed up with a commercial pilot called Richard Pearce. The two of them, Wrightson with his drive and financial muscle and Pearce with not much of the first commodity but lots of sound aviation expertise, seemed a good partnership. It was called, not surprisingly, Wrightson and Pearce. The air charter company was set up at Heston Airport, the new privately owned establishment called Airwork Limited set up by Sir Nigel Norman and Alan Muntz to provide facilities for the growing demand in private and commercial aviation. These two enterprising and charming men successfully operated perhaps the best private aerodrome of its type in Britain. Everything was neat and tidy and there was an atmosphere of efficiency and friendly cooperation. No wonder that it became the Mecca for private owners and commercial operators alike. Heston was also the headquarters of the Household Brigade Flying Club whose smart silver aeroplanes with their dark blue and red colours gave the scene a certain style and elegance.

Dick Wrightson and I soon struck up a friendship and I suppose that our mutual passion for aeroplanes, coupled with a comparable age group and compatible personalities made the next stage of my career an easy jump over the hurdles. I was taken on by 'Rigson and Pigson' (as the eternally quick-witted aviation people soon dubbed it) but in no particular capacity. I was to be a general dogsbody, office boy and a helper by pushing aeroplanes about. I was also the available pilot when my meagre experience permitted me, for example, to ferry a light aeroplane or act as crew in the DH 'Dragon'. Apart from the 'Dragon', W & P also had that delectable commodity, a DH Leopard Moth, successor to the Puss Moth that continued to be so popular with private owners. The aircraft servicing was done by the airwork ground engineers at Heston who also looked after the numerous privately owned machines. It all seemed to be a very nice and compact arrangement and all that was wanted was a good flow of customers. For me, I said 'goodbye' to the tea trade with token grateful thanks. I was now very happily working with aeroplanes, and earning three pounds per week.

One most enjoyable affair at Heston was the annual Air Day when all manner of aeroplanes would arrive to participate. Some flew in just out of interest or for social reasons, others to be demonstrated before an admiring audience. One visiting machine that I always remember seemed to arrive quite unexpectedly. It was the first of the new Hawker 'Fury's' which I still think was the most elegant and handsome of all the biplane fighters. It appeared 'from out of the blue' just like any dramatic appearance on stage of a superstar and the 'Fury' proceeded to give us all a scintillating demonstration of its talents. Just when I and all the other spectators were at a crescendo of enjoyment that beauty came round in the circuit, throttled back with all those lovely popping noises that an over-rich Rolls Royce

Kestrel engine makes, and then a thistle-down landing on the smooth grass.

When my most favourite aeroplane had taxied in, a white-clad figure left the cockpit, removed his helmet and Meyrowitz goggles and began to shed his flying clothing. Heavenly days! It was none other than Gerry Sayer – ace test pilot from the Hawker Aircraft Company.

The removal of his flying kit revealed that my hero was impeccably attired in a Savile Row pin-stripe suit. He neatly folded his flying gear, opened the small locker just behind the cockpit, stowed his kit, produced a bowler hat and rolled umbrella and then elegantly sauntered away. Fraffly good fun this flying game, eh what?

Undoubtedly one of the attractions of the thirties was the large number of interesting aeroplanes that were to be seen and it was the era of the de Havilland Company's products in particular. Although other manufacturers like Percival were now turning out some really good aircraft there is no doubt in my mind that the magic 'DH' was stealing the show. How the company contrived to use its undoubted talents in such a variety of types and then sell them so successfully must have been a compound of design skills allied to excellent marketing acumen. We were blessed with Gipsy Moths, Moth Majors, Puss Moths, Leopard Moths, Hornet Moths, Moth Minors, Fox Moths, Dragons, Rapides and of course the ubiquitous Tiger Moths. Some other types followed in due course, including 'big' aeroplanes like the DH86 Express Airliner and that most beautiful and elegant of all, the DH91 Albatross.

Wrightson & Pearce seemed to be getting enough jobs to do. Dick Wrightson, ever the press-on type decided one day that he wanted a big aeroplane. So what happened? He showed up at Heston with a 'Tri-motor Ford', with corrugated metal surfaces like the German Junkers aeroplanes. The Rigson and Pigson boys were now 'living above their station', but like all status symbols it looked distinctly impressive. Mixed up in all this activity and the outward evidence of success there was a strange element of contrast in the personal life-style of my charming boss. Although fond of what used to be called 'dollybirds', nominally he lived on his own in a flat in West London so he was about midway between Heston and his favourite Piccadilly area where good restaurants and clubs could be found. Heaven knows why he retained that flat because he always seemed to be staying elsewhere and on one occasion I went there only to find outside the door about a dozen milk bottles with the contents of course in progressive stages of old age. Another foible was that he tended to forget to change his personal clothing so he always looked the same as on every other day. At a suitable moment and hoping that I was not being too rude I suggested that another shirt (or whatever) would be a good idea. "I keep forgetting", he said, "I really must do something about it". A day or two later he arrived at Heston looking like a well-dressed gent from Clubland and understandably we all admired his turn-out. "What's happened?", I said. "I took your tip", he said "and went to Austin Reed's in Regent Street, undressed completely, and started all over again". When I asked him where was the fat parcel that should have contained all his old garments, he said "Oh, I left the whole damn lot behind in the shop; the assistant seemed quite surprised". Even his shoes were new.

An interesting contract that came our way was one of those 'wheeler-dealer' affairs that I was now beginning to learn about. A Canadian born fellow by name of Donald Campbell who earlier had been swanning around looking for opportunities arrived one morning with a proposal. It appeared that he had got wind of an unsatisfactory Fleet Street situation about the national daily newspapers frequently failing to get to Paris on time for distribution. In those days a company called William Dawson & Son used to despatch bundles of newspapers by train from Victoria Station and thence via the conventional sea-crossing to Paris. The packages had to arrive in good time for sale at all those familiar Parisian kiosks but the problem was that Wm Dawson's consignment all too often seemed to, shall we say, get 'misplaced' en route. In competition with Dawson was a French organisation called Hachette and both companies used the same transport system and the same timetable in the early hours. The snag was that Dawson's Fleet Street consignment was often found abandoned on a French country railway station and when forwarded on would arrive so late that they were slowly being squeezed out. Don Campbell now got on to the entrepreneurial trail and he obtained a contract to do something hitherto unheard of in the Fleet Street world – daily transport to Paris by air. I supposed that our high-pressure friend had already 'done his sums' and had come to the conclusion that his interests would best be met by making a deal with a small air charter company rather than with Imperial Airways, the official British air transport carrier of those days.

Dick Wrightson and Richard Pearce decided that this new enterprise had all the exciting prospects of being a money-maker and they took on the job. After the requirement had been examined carefully the plan evolved was to use the DH Dragon and begin the operations from Croydon airport. In that way, apart from technical considerations such as available night-flying facilities and so on, we thought that it would give us some publicity.

On a certain misty night, at about 0400 hours the Dragon stood on the apron in front of the famous terminal building and we waited for the arrival of the cargo. Soon a van appeared into the floodlit area and we loaded up, Bill Rimmer got into the cockpit, and the French agent plus his 600 lb load of English newspapers flew away into the night. The first stage of the operation had been carried out to our entire satisfaction and later that day Bill and the Dragon returned safely to Heston. A Dragon (or any of the big transport aeroplanes for that matter) usually took two and a half hours and sometimes more to make the London-Paris flight in the nineteen thirties.

As the days passed, the Dragon flew to Paris and back with fair regularity despite the weather factor and now a fantastic new pilot was employed. He was 'Biffy' Newman, perhaps the best commercial freelance pilot that it had been my privilege to associate with, and the new arrangement was that I would collect the newspaper cargo from Fleet Street where Wm Dawson & Son had their premises. My vehicle was a Chevrolet van; I had only just learned to drive so it was Tiger Moths first and then the Chevvy. I used to arrive at the collection point at 2.30 in the morning and wait for the bundles to arrive straight from the presses of the Daily Mail, Morning Post (now The Daily Telegraph), Daily Express, Daily Mirror, the Times, and whatever else besides. Assuming that no snags developed during printing and then delivery to the distributor, the bulky and heavy packages would be loaded onto the van and off I would go pronto to Croydon Airport. Soon after the night-service to Paris started we reverted to Heston where the landing fees were cheaper and in general Heston was the better bet. The journey from Fleet Street to Heston, using the Bath Road as it was then called (now the A4) was straight-forward and if you timed it right you could get all the numerous traffic lights showing 'green'. Just out of interest I timed myself on one occasion and the reader will probably not believe me when I say that it took me precisely seventeen minutes, door-to-door.

Upon arrival at Heston I and the nightwatchman would open the hangar doors and push the Dragon out into the night. The next job was to start up both engines, warm them up and check them on 'run up'. If all was well – as it nearly always was – I would go to the main building and alert the customs man. A sleepy 'Biffy' would then arrive from somewhere and he would see the Met man, sign a form, say 'cheerio' to our customs friend, and then we would get on board and go. There was none of all that modern and complex form-filling, clearance, briefing, and then getting constant instructions from the tower. In those days, you were master of your destiny and we liked it that way. Modern times prescribe that a safe and complex formula exists that does not rely on the intuitive piloting skills of the earlier days.

Those early trips to Paris never ceased to interest me as there was always something new to see, to learn about and to enjoy. Biffy's navigation – perhaps a better description was his complete and uncanny 'sense' about where we were – was illustrated early one morning. Dawn was breaking and we were rumbling along somewhere near the outskirts of Paris. The amount of cloud was now beginning to thicken to what used to be called 8/10ths – small gaps opening up which from our 1000 feet altitude gave us fleeting glimpses of the terrain below. I was as usual standing at the open door of the one-man cockpit and by then must have been the chap with the most co-pilot hours logged standing up. When the next cloud gap came along, I had a fleeting glimpse of the red rooftops of a small factory. Biffy glanced down, pondered a moment, and then said "That's OK; we will get to Le Bourget in five or six minutes". And so we did. Soon afterwards, sitting in his favourite bistro opposite the airport entrance having a *café noir et cognac* (even my French was coming along!), I asked him about those red roof tops and his comment was "just keep your eyes open and remember what you see; it all comes in handy sooner or later". For the aviation facilities of the period his kind of aerial navigation prescribed concentration, remarkable memory, and a sixth sense about the correct action to take. It was that telling new word – Airmanship. His example was to stand me in good stead later on, particularly when making those long night sorties in a Wellesley over inhospitable Ethiopia.

Apropos new aids to navigation, sparse though they were, one may be of interest. One day a man came to the office at Heston and told us that his Company had just produced a new prototype aircraft radio. Would we like to try it out? Someone said, 'Marconi'? "No", said the representative, "Plessey". "Plessey? Who the hell is that?". The man said that it was a new manufacturer from Essex who was trying to get into the aviation market. Dick Wrightson, ever the chap to have a try at anything, asked the fellow to install it in the Dragon; and so he did. It worked surprisingly well. One snag, though, was that with the trailing aerial dangling below, sometimes it would be left behind on a farmer's tree or other obstruction. The Plessey radio was a good new product to use, and Rigson and Pigson were instrumental in introducing the name Plessey to the aviation world.

A tragic event in the London-Paris newspaper run happened a few weeks after the service had started. Inevitably the French distributors also had to get into the air freight business and chartered a strange-looking French machine that operated out of Croydon and I remember meeting the amiable two-pilot crew early one morning at Le Bourget. Our problem now was that the 'enemy' aeroplane was a little faster than we were, and by starting from Croydon the Frenchmen had a head-start on the Dragon operating from Heston. It was only a few miles further to fly, but significant at around 100mph. To make up time I had to make the dash in the old van from Fleet Street pronto and perhaps Stirling Moss might have been proud of me! Usually we managed to get airborne first, and after that the race to Paris was on. Alas, early one morning our French rivals crashed soon after take-off from Croydon and both pilots were killed which left a nasty feeling in the pit of the stomach. Even when competing against each other aviation people always hate accidents and it could not but be otherwise when the common enemy was nature and the elements.

Although my time with Wrightson and Pearce had been remarkably rewarding and satisfying, (after all I had made a break into aviation at last with some kind of job,) I now pondered about the future. I realised that what I was doing was not a long-term career so I decided that the next move was to have another try at becoming a regular officer in the Royal Air Force.

I wrote a letter to Adastral House and said that I was so enthusiastic about Service life that I wished to apply for a Short Service commission. The main snag as I saw it was that it was likely that their Airships – they have Lordships in the Royal Navy – would turn me down for the good reason that they had already got me where they wanted me – in the Reserve. However the very heartening reply told me that I would be accepted provided I passed another interview and medical test and it was not long before both events came about. The interview was passed satisfactorily – one gets a bit of practise in these things! – but to my chagrin the doctors expressed doubts and I suspected that the reason was an aftermath of an influenza attack. Fortunately they told me to get fitter and come back again; once more I had to get up early and make the pre-breakfast run into Hyde Park, right around the Serpentine, and back home where I was now living in Gloucester Terrace, Lancaster Gate. How I hated those sorties! Each time I wanted to say, like my school friend the Polish Count, "I can no more; it is too up!" But that is not the way to a Short Service Commission. So all the awful running carried on and it must have paid off because the RAF doctors said that my lungs were now OK. Thank God there were no X-Ray checks in those days because many years later they found scars on my lungs the size of fifty-penny pieces.

I told Dick Wrightson what was afoot and he was glad if only for the reason that the Family Trust had told him that it was the end of his jolly aeroplaning game. He gave up W & P, and went back to shipping. When the Hitler war came he joined the Fleet Air Arm and alas! as happened to so many of those most excellent people he was shot down and lost at sea.

In between leaving my friends at Heston and reporting to RAF Uxbridge I decided that a short break would be welcome. An eighteen hour day, with those newspaper sorties to Fleet Street and Le Bourget and then the rest of the normal working day at Heston was beginning to take its toll. So I spent some weeks at home seeing a lot more of my family and friends and generally relaxing. One favourite place to visit was the Science Museum in South Kensington and a pleasant walk across Hyde Park took me to see all those fine exhibits, especially the aeronautical ones.

There was however one interruption to indolent freedom. In December 1934, Donald Campbell – our Fleet Street contact man who had been the catalyst for the newspaper runs to Paris – telephoned and said that he had the nicest little snip of a short-term job for me; so we met somewhere for coffee and he told me about it. It transpired that one of his close friends in the newspaper hierarchy had agreed to his novel idea of advertising the 'Daily Express' by flying over central London with an aeroplane fitted with neon lights on the undersurface of the lower wing. What he had done so far was to get hold of an AVRO 504 from Cornwall Aviation, complete with the owner pilot Capt Percival Phillips. The necessary modifications to the aircraft had been made by Rollasons of Croydon and in order to control the output of the propellor-driven dynamo mounted on the top centre-section an operator was needed to do this from the back cockpit. My friend suggested that I was just the chap for the job and I would get some more night flying experience. It was only a short evening's work from Monday to Friday and he would pay me the princely sum of three pounds per week. Well, I fell for this one. After all, more flying and more in the pocket cannot be bad?

I went down to Rollasons at Croydon where I saw the '504' festooned underneath with large neon letters proclaiming 'Daily Express'. Captain Percival Phillips told me that he had flight tested the aircraft with the man who had installed the gear and all was well. All that I had to do was to slide a knob back and forth on a control panel to keep the needle on the dial at the correct point. As airspeed variations affected the rpm of the dynamo, some form of voltage control had to be operated manually.

Don Campbell told me that the essential tactic of the operation was to time the flights when all the offices, factories, and especially the shops were being emptied by people going home from work. This meant that the period from 5.30 to 6.30 pm would give the best 'prime viewing time' as the television people would say today. I suggested that we leave Croydon at 5 pm – it was in winter and so it would be dark by then and would suit admirably. Summer-time night sorties would not have the same impact because most of the workers and shoppers would have left the streets. The choice of route? Again my suggestion was agreed. This was to cross the Thames at Vauxhall Bridge, fly on to Victoria – plenty of rail travellers there – turn left to keep well away from Buckingham Palace and then proceed in a big wide sweep clockwise around inner London before reaching Fleet Street where we would give the valued clients visual evidence of success. We expected that flying over the mecca of journalism would bring a chorus of delight to the 'Daily Express' Top Brass and probably chagrin from their competitors who would realise that they had missed out on a smart piece of publicity.

The outline route having been agreed by Capt Phillips, I realised that my Cornish skipper might not be as familiar as I was with inner London. After all, he was a joy-ride pilot and not a cockney taxi driver. I had lived in London long enough and had walked for miles and miles along its streets and parks to be a practical navigator. For the pilot, map reading in a 504 in darkness was too difficult to do successfully and as we had no voice communication the plan was that I would tap Capt Phillips on one shoulder or the other, thus signalling 'left' or 'right' as appropriate. A double tap meant straight ahead. It was simple and effective.

On the evening of January 30th 1935 we took off safely from Croydon aerodrome and the run over the grass with the strange load of electrics made it longer than normal. Away we went, heading north towards the Metropolis and the neon lights were glowing well in the darkness and seen easily from my cockpit by reflection from the gathering mist. The slip of paper with principal street names and master check points written on it (like Hyde Park Corner) had some of them underlined with my sister Betty's eyebrow pencil. She had to be cajoled into letting me use it and to this day that slip of paper is still tucked away safely in a scrap-album . . .

We reached the river Thames, turned to the left slightly and then began the sweep over the planned route. We flew over Kings Cross Station, Euston, Bishopsgate and then began the run down to Fleet Street – the key target. The fly-past was splendid and the pavements were crowded with hundreds of faces looking up at us. It could not have been better timed, and I had visions of the fliers subsequently being congratulated by our sponsors in the Daily Express board room. Towards the end of the run down Fleet Street I thought that Captain Phillips was being unduly intrepid in the noble cause of maximum exposure because we were gradually descending and getting much too low for comfort. We flew lower and lower and then made a turn unexpectedly to the left in a gentle curve back towards the river. I tapped the pilot's right shoulder to get us back on track, and nothing happened. I tapped again, and this time a gloved hand came up and gave me the unmistakable wave that meant 'no'. The next thing I knew was that we seemed to be unusually throttled back and were now passing the illuminated face of Big Ben almost at eye level. Well, I did not feel the need to get quite so close to see that it was just past seven o'clock. The timing was good but the flight path left a whole lot to be desired! The 504 recrossed the river, getting ever lower, and by now it was abundantly clear that something was amiss and we were definitely flying with some difficulty back in the general direction of Croydon. I began to look around to see what chances there might be of getting down somewhere, somehow, but the problem was that although sundry black spaces are obvious, parks and commons have obstructions like trees, telephone wires, fences and so on, to say nothing of people. Better that, I thought, than 'arriving' on a rooftop and then falling to the ground. Very soon after staggering past Wandsworth Common a smaller black area came up. Phillips made a left turn, what little power there was was turned off, and down we came from a damned low altitude in a constant sideslip. Then came the inevitable and distinctly frightening sound of crunching aeroplane, tearing fabric and general mayhem. We were down, the silence broken only by sizzling noises from up front and the sinister drip-drip-drip of petrol falling onto hot things like the exhaust manifold. It was a very nasty moment. The fuselage had turned over sideways and the port wings had assumed a semi-vertical, leading edge down, attitude. Poor old Avro 504K, registration G-EBVV, was looking a sorry sight and action clearly was to escape from the wreck before it burst into flames. I called out to Captain Phillips and his reply – clearly remembered, even after a long passage of time – was "Oh, my leg!" I called back and said that I would try to get him out but in order to do this I had to thread my way amongst all the rigging wires in the dark. Eventually I reached him, only to realise that even if I got him out of the cockpit, I would somehow have to heave him over the up-ended wings as we were boxed-in, so to speak.

Then I heard voices. Peering over the top of the wings I could see two figures in white. My mind, probably bemused by then, had strange thoughts that this was what happens immediately upon demise but in fact the white figures proved to be nurses. I called out and told them I could get the injured pilot out of the cockpit but not over the wing. Fortunately two men appeared and between us we managed to extricate Phillips from the wreck and onto a stretcher and away to safety. As I walked away with the two nurses towards a large building, the first thing that I wanted to know was where we had crashed. The reply made me smile, it seemed so apposite. "You are walking across the football ground of the Springfield Mental Hospital, Tooting". No sooner had I entered the hospital (after checking that Capt Phillips was getting necessary first aid) than a man came up to me and said that he was the hospital duty doctor and took me to his room. After explaining who we were, what we had been doing and where we had started from, I said that I did not know what had caused the crash. He then produced a bottle of whisky, poured out a large tot, added some water and gave it to me. Equally, he had one himself. He said it would be good for me although I had already told him that I was not injured. Although whisky was a completely new tipple in my experience I drank mine even if I did not particularly care for the taste but doctors know best. I now remembered that I must telephone to someone and say what had happened. Don Campbell's number was in my pocket and he was distinctly upset and dismayed to hear the news. We had crashed on the very first sortie and he had planned many more flights over other big cities. He said he would fetch me right away and take me home. In the meantime, whilst waiting for him my amiable doctor seemed only too anxious to have more tots of whisky and to prescribe one for his 'patient' too. After about the fourth one, still wearing my borrowed Sidcot flying suit, I asked to be shown to a bathroom in order to have a clean up, and for the first time knew that my face was covered in blood. What kind of a doctor had I encountered? The face in the mirror instantly convinced me that I was a casualty and I should never have taken a look as I had been doing alright up to that point. I returned unsteadily to the doctor's sitting room where yet another whisky was put into my hand and then at last Don Campbell arrived. I travelled home in a bit of a coma, the crash or the whisky causing it I knew not. When crossing Battersea Bridge I was violently sick and once safely back in Gloucester Terrace my sister wisely put me to bed where I slept until the following afternoon.

The next day 'the man from the Ministry' was on the telephone after the 'Times' had reported the crash. (JP-F in print in the top people's paper?

Clearly I was on the way up!) One obvious question the Ministry man asked me was how high we had been flying. Well now, I cannot be all that stupid, and so all I said was that as I was the man controlling the neon lights, I did not know. How could I have told him that I could clearly see the hands of Big Ben from eye-level?!

Capt Phillips had broken his leg and later returned to Cornwall. We never met again, but in 1980 a photo appeared in an aeromodelling magazine which showed a picture of Capt David Phillips alongside a flying scale model of an Avro 504 at Croydon that once belonged to his father. He was the son of my pilot, way back in 1935, and now flew DC 10s from Gatwick Airport. I could not resist writing to him and he answered my letter from the Caribbean, saying that it was a remarkable coincidence, 45 years later.

What had caused the crash? Capt Phillips said that after about thirty minutes flying he found that to maintain the required power he had to ease the throttle forward and this action became progressive. As by then we were well over half way round the route it seemed pointless to continue so he tried to get back to Croydon. From the centre of London, especially low down at night in a single-engined aeroplane, all escape routes look equally hopeless and to maintain height he was eventually at full throttle, but to no purpose. The answer to the riddle of engine failure was carburettor icing. The damp night air at just above freezing point was ideal for ice to form in the carburettor intake and '504' engines did not have the refinement of coping with this hazard. Capt Phillips and I were lucky to have escaped so lightly.

Chapter IV

New Horizons

The instructions about my appointment as an RAF regular officer told me that I had to report to the Royal Air Force Depot, Uxbridge, in the spring of 1935. On the appointed day, suitably dressed as an officer and gentleman to the best of my sparse wardrobe, I presented myself at the Guardroom where the duty Sergeant directed me to the Station Adjutant and he in turn told me which building I was to report to. Well, at least I had entered the Pearly Gates and soon I found myself in the company of the rest of the intake. The Officer-in-Charge and another character called Warrant Officer Nightingirl appeared. After the preliminary talk had been completed we were shown our rooms.

Then began all the business of being indoctrinated into the ways and customs of the Royal Air Force. Essentially it was all about Service life but nothing at all about our *raison d'étre*, as they say, of becoming lantern-jawed intrepid aviators winging our way to victory above the clouds. All that we were bullied into assimilating was drill, saluting correctly, marching on the square, lectures on tradition, something called Kings Regulations, leadership, morale and so on. In retrospect, it was tedious but essential because we all needed a starting point. Apart from the newness of it all, (and naturally the feeling that the sooner the fortnight of indoctrination was over, the better), some entertaining memories remain. Perhaps the best one was occasioned when the approved tailors, Messrs Gieves of Old Bond Street arrived to fit us out with uniforms appropriate to our new – if very lowly – status as Acting Pilot Officers on probation. One of the new aspirants was a tall, lanky, Canadian from some unheard of part of that big country. His name was John Kent. He was very amiable, very conversational, very much the nice guy from the Colonies. When his turn came to be measured for his uniform, the tailor said, "Now Sir, I will measure you for your Mess kit." Our friendly Canadian understandably said, "Hell, what's that?". Immediately one of our party – the usual clever charlie – told him that it was uniform worn for Mess dinner nights, the rig consisting of a 'monkey jacket' and very tight-fitting trousers or 'overalls' as we were to learn. When the Gieves tailor came to the point of measuring young Kent for his overalls, he knelt down, offered up the brass end of his tape measure, and in a deferential voice said, "Which way do you dress, sir?". When this singularly personal item of information had been clarified about the preference (or natural habit) about which way male attributes like to get adjusted for maximum comfort, quick as a flash our tall young friend said quite languidly, "Oh, just make my pants nice and baggy down to the knees!!" In 1940 Wg Cdr Johnny Kent became one of the famous Battle of Britain aces.

Another new-boy also came from Canada. It was from a place called Kamloops, British Columbia. John Fulton was the most likeable of people and we soon became firm friends. Whilst we were all comparing notes about how we set about joining the RAF and what happened in the process, Fulton told us about first being a policeman, then going to Boeings to fly, and finally he made an Atlantic crossing in a cattle boat to get to England. The description of his interview with the Selection Board was most entertaining. "There was a bunch of guys sitting behind a long table and I was on the other side. They asked some darn silly questions. When it came to the turn of the hombre with the big moostach, he said that my application told of my sporting activities. 'What sports,'? said the guy. 'Not really being a sporting type of person – but only wrote it in my application because I thought it was what they liked – I said that in Canada I hunted the moose and the wild caribou. Not true, but it was just what those guys wanted to know. I passed.' Needless to say he was instantly given the name of 'Moose' Fulton. After that fortnight at Uxbridge, we were dispersed to our various Flying Training Schools and so finally we were now actually going to get close to those flying machines. The party destined for No 3 Flying Training School travelled by train from Uxbridge to Grantham, up in the wilds of Lincolnshire. These were pastures new for me. Hitherto, I had never ventured any further North than the 1934 trip to Mildenhall to witness the start of the McRobertson England–Australia Air Race. From the railway station at Grantham we were transported by lorry to the aerodrome which was called, for reasons never discovered, RAF Spitalgate. It was situated a little to the east of Grantham and on the top of a small escarpment that was the start of the flatlands running all the way to the sea. With my new-found if limited experience of aviation, clearly this bit of England was splendid terrain for flying men; there were big fields and the land was as flat as a billiard table with no high ground to encounter in bad visibility or cloudy conditions.

To the east of the technical and domestic area were fine hangars, and then stretching away beyond them was a good grass aerodrome. There were virtually no obstructions anywhere around its perimeter and beyond that the vastness of the fields that Lincolnshire farmers used mostly for crops. East Anglia is well-known for its good record of sunshine and this was another good point for flying people in that the weather factor for students was another bonus.

We soon settled into our new quarters and our original Uxbridge numbers had been thinned out considerably because some had gone to No 2 FTS, Sealand, and yet others had to make their way by sea to No 4 FTS located at a place called Aboukir in Egypt, close to the Suez Canal. For us, and certainly for me whose previous home had been no better than a 'bed-sitter' for the past two years, the new way of life offered quite a change of life-style. I not only had a bedroom of my own, I even had the services of domestic staff. It seemed as though I was now living in a pleasant country house with no domestic chores to do, so the Officers' Mess therefore was a wonderful change. We were blessed with a big ante-room where there were leather chairs to recline in, newspapers and magazines in profusion, and a well appointed dining room.

The daily routine of flying school life consisted essentially of classroom work in the morning, flying in the afternoon – and then a switch-over in the following week and so we had a good spread of workload to keep us occupied. Inevitably those parades and rifle-drill periods were part of the curriculum but in less degree than at Uxbridge and it's fair to say that this subject was not exactly popular. However it had to be part of becoming one of the King's men.

On arrival at Spitalgate one problem presented itself to three students. Moose Fulton, Anthony Tinne and myself had already learned to fly and we had around 100 to 250 hours recorded in our log books; Moose in particular had about twice as much flying experience as I had. Tinne and I already had a RAF uniform which obviated the need to be fully kitted out at Uxbridge and both of us quite independently had discreetly removed our wings before presenting ourselves to our new masters. So what to do? The three of us, now that each had discovered that we had a common problem, had a discussion and it was quickly agreed that the best course of action would be to say nothing at all and just see what happened.

It was my good luck to have as a flying instructor a remarkably nice and excellent teacher called Flying Officer George Snarey. Soon after our arrival at the flying school, on April 3rd 1935 he took me up in an Avro Tutor, K-3407. The 'remarks' in the flight log kept in the office said quite simply, 'Passenger flying'. I enjoyed listening to F/O Snarey explaining some of the basic points of flying whilst I looked around and said nothing. From Lesson One, which was later called 'Air Experience', I progressed happily from one thirty minute flight to the next although the instruction included nasty things like a demonstration of spinning. The simulated forced landings done by my instructor by way of showing me some of the expertise and airmanship required were great fun and I was now beginning to like the Avro Tutor very much.

After less than three hours of dual instruction I inadvertently gave my secret away. When returning to the aerodrome circuit I was told to carry out the pre-landing drill. This was to fly to the correct point on the crosswind leg, throttle back, and commence the turn into wind before the final approach towards the edge of the aerodrome. Just before crossing the hedge he would call out the now familiar "I have control" when I would hand over and he would make the landing. This time the happy pilot made the prescribed circuit, checked the windsock (and said so, thus indicating that I had done it), got to the end of the downwind leg, turned to Port at the correct moment, and throttled back to lose height prior to the final approach. So far, so good. However, due to misjudging the wind strength or just plain getting it wrong, it was apparent that we were a little too high and thus not well positioned for the final approach. Concentrating on the job in hand, what does the pupil do? Quite from habit, I put the Tutor into a neat sideslip, forgetting that this item of instruction was yet to come. Snarey took over control in his normal way, landed, and we taxied to our allotted parking space. As we both got out I tried to look my usual happy self but this time with a touch of innocence becoming to the new-boy. Straight-away he said, "Pelly-Fry, I'm damned sure now that you have been flying before you came here. Am I right?". "Yes sir," I said. "I was in the RAFO at Hatfield and learned to fly on Tiger Moths". There was a slight pause. Dear George, he looked at me, grinned, and said "You're fired from the Junior Course." The next day I was taken to the Flight Commander's office. This is where deputy-god lived, god himself being the dreaded Chief Flying Instructor. Flight Lieutenant Ralph Lywood, Officer Commanding 'A' Flight, was a tall, good looking man with a military mien and trim moustache, every inch my idea of a leader and I had to reveal my secret for the second time. Fulton and Tinne had also incurred strong suspicions about their previous flying experience and the same thing happened to them. The following day Ralph Lywood sent me solo and all of us were destined to move from the Junior to the Senior Course. I was glad to stay a little longer in 'A' Flight, flying the very nice Tutor for another fifteen hours. All of us might have been promoted sooner except that we had to do a crash course of ground studies but we soon reached the standard required of students on the Senior Course. In early July 1935, the three promoted students presented themselves to their new Flight Commanders and I went to 'D' Flight where my instructor was Flight Lieutenant George Heycock who I was to meet again in later years.

The big disappointment was to find that 'D' Flight was equipped with an abomination called the Armstrong Whitworth 'Atlas' fitted with an Armstrong Siddeley radial air-cooled engine that sat out front in the fresh air. Heavens, what an awful lump of ugly flying machine it was to be sure. The controls were heavy and unresponsive and when the engine was throttled back the thing glided like an empty gin bottle; thank heaven I never had the trauma of having to make a forced landing in it. I endured the doubtful pleasure of putting in over forty hours flying in the 'Atlas' and was thankful when I said good-bye to them upon leaving Grantham in September 1935. The only satisfying reward was to get a flying assessment 'Above the average'; it must have been a consolation prize.

Moose Fulton had the luck of going to 'C' Flight and all the bliss of flying the Bristol 'Bulldog' which was quite a different aeroplane altogether. Curses on the fellow – he not only got a nice fighter-type machine to fly, he rubbed it in by getting that highly prized assessment, 'exceptional' recorded in his log book. There is no justice in this world; those damned Colonials always get better treatment than we ordinary Englishmen. Moose was not only a very excellent pilot, his knowledge of what goes into an aeroplane in an engineering sense was particularly good. Clearly his time at Boeings was not wasted. Inevitably, promotion of the three 'new boys' to the Senior Course caused the usual resentment from one or two students. One in particular, whose name I had better discreetly forget as I disliked from him the first moment, was quite incensed about it. Typical of the bully-boy, relishing every moment of pushing around the fellows junior to him, his overbearing manner to all the pupils in the Junior Course could no longer be meted out to us with impunity; we now also enjoyed the privileges, such as they were, of being Senior Students.

A very pleasant diversion from the routine at Spitalgate unexpectedly came about and was the aftermath of an episode some months earlier. One day at Heston Airport I saw two people wandering about on the apron. It was easy to see that their interest in the general activity was balanced by a degree of uncertainty as to what they were looking for or trying to do. I walked up and introduced myself to them, saying that I was one of the regulars at Heston and had a job there with an air charter company. Could I help in any way?

The gentleman was a robust figure wearing a pork-pie hat and his lady was dressed in elegant country clothes. When they spoke it was apparent that they were Americans. He said that he was Gilbert Miller and that his wife's name was Kitty, so we were off to a good start on a Christian name footing. The three of us wandered around and as we came to each aeroplane I told Gilbert who the manufacturer was and the type of aeroplane. I also gave him a rough idea of its capabilities and added my own comments in the process. We were now getting on very amicably and my new friends began to take more than a superficial interest in what they saw and what their young escort was telling them. I asked Gilbert Miller if he had any experience of private flying. "No, I just wanted to have a look around." When we walked away from the hangars he asked me for my telephone number which I innocently thought was a pleasant American custom and soon we reached the car park area where a Rolls Royce was waiting for them with uniformed chauffeur in attendance. As they drove away my impression was that they were very charming people; I was sorry to see them leave and I had enjoyed talking about my favourite subject.

A couple of days later, my sister Betty said that I was wanted on the telephone. "It's Mr Gilbert Miller's secretary." The American voice of the lady secretary told me that Mr Miller would like to take me to lunch and would I meet him at the Savoy Hotel Grill on Wednesday next at 12.30? Trying hard to keep my composure I said, "With pleasure!". Savoy Grill, for heaven's sake! It was certainly not on my list so far. The reason for the lunch *à deux* was soon revealed – my host said that he wanted to seek my advice and recommendation about buying an aeroplane! We discussed the matter at length and this naturally raised a number of queries. What did he want an aeroplane for? What kind of flying did he have in mind? Would he fly it himself and did he want a small or large aeroplane? Where did he propose to keep it – in England or America? Whatever the answers were did he have any idea at all of the extent to which he would use it? That last question was to be one that in later years became a 'must' in future similar conversations. It hinged upon that single word 'utilisation'.

Gilbert told me that he lived in New York but had a town house in London and also a place in Sussex. Clearly, he was a man of substance. I was astonished that he had elected to spend precious time having lunch with a young man to discuss aeroplanes when in all probability there were any number of people who would have given their eye teeth to have been in my chair. He told me that he was an impressario so his name had a familiar ring to it for at the time his very successful show, 'Tovarich' was running in London. This explained why he had an office full of secretaries in Jermyn Street; I visited it some days later and what a high-pressure business it was to be sure. Busy secretaries, animated visitors everywhere, telephones ringing incessantly – the full treatment of the theatrical world.

Gilbert Miller admitted that the general idea of buying an aeroplane was just a thought but he felt that it would give him the great advantage of allowing him and his wife to be free to travel as and when he pleased. Clearly I was preaching to the converted.

At the end of the excellent lunch my host asked if I would like a cigar to smoke with my coffee. Trying to look a man-of-the-world, I said "Yes, thank you", although I had never smoked before but the thought that 'I must keep up with the Yankees' passed through my mind. When the uniformed man arrived with a large trolly loaded with numerous boxes of cigars and exotic cigarettes like flat Turkish ones and Balkan Sobranies, I have to confess that Gilbert's young guest was in deep water and about to make an unholy mess of the whole ritual. So without further ado the man selected a cigar for me and exhibited his talent by sniffing and rolling it between finger and thumb, a trick indicative of the *cognoscenti* in these matters. Then he gave it to me and said quietly "when the lighted match gets close, suck gently". Oh well, I suppose there always has to be a first time and I have to admit that the expensive cigar tasted awful.

Gilbert Miller not only accepted my suggestion of buying a Stinson 'Reliant' which in my judgement was a splendid aircraft for his purpose, he bought two of them! One was kept in England and the other in America. One unusual aspect of all this was that he took my word about a suitable type of aeroplane without even going to see one but told his office to get busy and employ a pilot in the process.

The story now goes a stage further, not in London but in Lincolnshire. At Spitalgate one day I was told that Mr Miller's secretary wanted to speak to me on the telephone. She explained that the Millers were coming to Grantham for the week-end and would I please have Sunday lunch with their host and hostess? When I asked who it was the answer was "Lord and Lady Brownlow, at Belton Park."

On a memorable Sunday morning I set off for the stately home and fortunately was able to borrow the 3-litre Bentley that my pupil friend Michael Stevens used to let me drive on a cost-sharing basis. As I motored past the gates and then along the tree-lined drive leading to Belton, I was not sure whether I was feeling smug or just nervous. The visit and the lunch was wonderland. It was so pleasant that I nearly forgot to take my leave at the appropriate moment and once back at the flying school I tried to get my feet on the ground again. Some years later Lord Brownlow's name was frequently quoted by the press during the unhappy episode involving the late King Edward VIII and Mrs Wallis Simpson, later to become the Duke and Duchess of Windsor.

Another Gilbert Miller invitation came my way later on when I was asked for the week-end to their country home at Drungwick Manor, near Horsham; in the middle ages it was the summer residence of the Bishops of Chichester. The Millers had recently bought it and completely redesigned it internally. Prior to the visit I was asked to go to their Hill Street house in Mayfair, and from there the plan was to go to Heston and fly to Drungwick in the new Stinson 'Reliant'. It was an exciting prospect.

I took the bus to Marble Arch and then down Park Lane and got off at the Dorchester Hotel when a short walk brought me to the house. It is quite close to Shepherds, the pub that I was to get to know so well in wartime. There is, or was, a splendid Sedan chair inside which could tell a tale or two of happenings between one of my war-time fighter pilot friends and a long-haired dolly bird. Ho hum! But I digress. The house in Hill Street was extremely elegant and when my host and hostess appeared Gilbert looked at his watch, carefully noted the time and then after saying "Let's go" we all sped off to Heston in the Rolls at a brisk pace. Upon arrival the new Stinson, G-AELU, was ready to go and looking very smart indeed. It had taken Gilbert only a few weeks to get that aeroplane; I do so like people who make up their minds quickly and then press on with the action.

Frank Steinman was the American pilot and we got on board and the radial engine with its Hamilton 2-position pitch propellor started up smoothly. Once airborne, the 'Reliant' was just like riding in a big comfortable motorcar. With the wing on top everybody had a very good view ahead and below. Gilbert and Frank sat in front and Kitty and I were in the back; and very cosy it was too.

The 30-odd mile journey, during which I spotted Brooklands aerodrome on the starboard side, took less than twenty minutes and soon the handsome Drungwick Manor showed up with a landing area alongside that Gilbert had converted from fields into quite an acceptable small aerodrome. The landing approach into the prevailing wind was between two copses and quite adequate for a careful pilot.

For the first time I experienced the satisfying and sensible business of a private aeroplane owner arriving home by air and taxying up to the garden gate. There seemed to be something quite magical and yet so eminently practical about it. If this was the way that the flying machine was going to be used in future years by those who could afford it, then aviation certainly had a bright future. To date the answer is only a qualified 'yes' because all the well-known factors in modern times have in practise limited the wide use of privately-owned aircraft to countries like America where the distances, geography and the climate are favourable. At the annual American 'Fly in' at Oskosh, Wisconsin for example, it is normal for as many as fifteen thousand privately-owned aircraft to be seen on the ground! The week's activity is beautifully organised by the EAA, the Experimental Aircraft Association and shows what is possible.

Drungwick House was wonderful. It had been beautifully and tastefully decorated; Every guest had a complete suite. Gilbert and his wife were so pleased with their new country home (they both loved England) that they gave me a conducted tour. In my dressing room there was a fine wardrobe about ten feet long and Gilbert said "Just watch how the sliding doors operate; nice and easy". He moved one of them with his finger and it silently travelled along its ball-bearing track revealing inside a massive row of padded coathangers provided for the guest. Suspended in lonely isolation was the sum total of my own week-end outfit – one pair of grey flannel trousers!

The house stood in beautiful grounds with a well-kept lawn that led to the landing ground; beyond that the fields of Sussex stretched away to be seen and admired. Neatly positioned and accessible nearby was a row of five garages above which was accommodation for members of staff. The garden, with flower beds and shrubs neatly laid out, was a joy to the eye. Although not much of a gardening man myself I still have a vivid memory of some elegant plants in full bloom that I now know to be called lupins.

The week-end had started well. On Saturday morning the very beautiful and elegant lady that I had met at Belton Park appeared again. Her name was Mrs Condé Nast, a name familiar in the world of publications such as 'Vogue'. Almost the first thing that Gilbert said to her as she was greeted effusively was "Honey, guess what? We came down in my new airplane; house to house, it only took sixty five minutes. How's about that?" The gorgeous person smiled, and replied, "Gilbert darling, what's the fuss? I have just come down all the way by automobile – it took me ten minutes less time!"

I confess that I had reservations about how the week-end would go for me because I was in a different age group from everybody else but in the event all was well and the time passed far too quickly. There were six guests, all delightful and talented in their fashion and we dined and wined and played all manner of card games, some of which were quite new to me. We talked on many subjects and we played darts, the latter fortunately something that I knew about. On Sunday morning a clay-pigeon shoot was laid on which I thoroughly enjoyed and was a foretaste of things to come in later years. Fortunately, I have a good eye and perhaps unusually I can shoot left or right-handed as I am ambidextrous.

There is one snippet of the domestic scene that I cannot resist relating about a way of life that I have never come across since. Apparently it was the custom that guests in their suites only used a cake of soap once, and once only. Each time a guest visited the bathroom, there in all its splendour was a brand new bar of soap of exotic and finest quality. I was so intrigued by this extravagant attention to detail that I would make spurious and quite unnecessary visitations upstairs. I never beat the system and wonder to this day what happened to all those one-time-only expensive cakes of soap? It was a revelation to experience the American life-style of the very well-to-do and I recommend it heartily. All too soon came the time for dreaming to end and I had to leave on Sunday afternoon so that I could be in London in time to go on by train back to Grantham. By the greatest of luck the lovely Mrs Condé Nast offered me a lift in her Cadillac – ahem! After thanking my charming host and hostess as adequately as I could, I just had to add, "It seems to be quicker by car!" (We all need an alibi sometimes.) Dear Gilbert and Kitty; I will always remember their great kindnesses. The last that I saw of them was just before they set off from Croydon *en route* to Budapest. Later they travelled to Paris and then returned by sea to New York. With them was Kitty's father, Jules Bache, of Bache and Company, the New York stockbrokers of repute. In post-war years I spotted a mention of him in the Daily Telegraph which recorded that in his will Mr Jules Bache had bequeathed his art collection to the Metropolitan Museum of Fine Art, New York. Value? – a mere four million dollars!

The Flying Training course at Spitalgate ended in the late summer of 1935 and we now proudly wore RAF wings on our tunics, the valued symbol of being qualified pilots. The next stage was to disperse to our new appointments and we were happy to have crossed the first hurdle of our new careers and escape from the monastic atmosphere of a flying school. Now at last we thought that we were proper airmen and no longer fledgling pilots. How wrong we were because in flying the learning curve is endless. Moose Fulton, Tony Tinne, myself and three others were posted initially to RAF Station, Worthy Down, Hampshire but this was only an interim move; the personnel people had decided that we would later be sent out to Egypt to get converted onto twin-engined aircraft. Although sounding quite strange in modern days, apparently the idea behind this plan was that we would get very much more flying in a given time in Egypt in the winter months than we would normally enjoy in England. I should qualify this by mentioning that in those days bad weather flying expertise was nothing like that of later times; all that Service aircraft had then were simple instrument-flying facilities the like of which would make a modern pilot wince. Another factor was that there were few twin-engined Squadrons in England for us to go to, so perhaps it was no bad thing to send us abroad to learn to fly 'twins' under sunny Egyptian skies. In the meantime there was a gap to fill because the Air Ministry had to arrange a sea passage for us to Port Said.

So RAF Worthy Down became our temporary home and we were there for six weeks. It was a very happy and interesting introduction to Squadron life before going to the land of the Pharaohs. If the officers' Mess at Spitalgate had been like a country hotel, then Worthy Down was better still in all respects. I was allotted a splendid batman, the kind of mature fellow who did everything for you and for example used to say "Sir, are we playing tennis this afternoon or shall I prepare the shooting kit?" The Officers Mess, although of the old type as it was a World War One structure was very comfortable and I always remember my first sighting of the dining room at breakfast-time where on the long sideboard was a richly prepared feast of the culinary arts. In attendance was a steward attired in an impeccable white coat and chef's cap and he would invite you to inspect the whole array of dishes displayed for your delectation. If you fancied ham and scrambled eggs for example, he would order the latter from the kitchen and then ask you how many slices of York ham – on the bone, of course – that he could carve for you. We lived like princes. I cannot resist adding that all this very fine cuisine was made possible for the mess members and their friends for an extra messing charge of two shillings and sixpence per day. Equally, dining-in nights, in our new mess kit was a splendid affair and the transition from pupil to an operational bomber base was remarkable.

RAF Station, Worthy Down housed two famous night-bomber Squadrons; Nos 7 and 58. They were equipped with the Vickers 'Virginia', a birdcage of a monster that winged its way across the skies at all of 80 mph. They had to be skillfully flown to ensure that they landed uphill on the near side of the grass aerodrome that had a distinct hump in the middle; if you arrived at the downhill part, well you had problems because brakes were non-existent.

At first we were attached to 7 Sqdn, and then a longer period with 58 Sqdn. No 7 Sqdn was in the process of changing over to the new Handley Page 'Heyford', and it gave me the experience of four flights in the new addition to Britain's night bomber force. I sat during three trips in the second-pilot's seat and then one in the rear-gunner's position which was very cold! With 58 Sqdn we fared better and I managed to get almost 14 hours flying in Virginias including five trips solo. Being allowed so soon to fly off quite on my own in this lumbering twin-engined machine was an experience that I had not expected. On one night sortie with two regular squadron pilots, I asked if I could occupy the rear gunner's position in the tail . . . Some people will do anything for kicks. I got into the 'dustbin' affair with difficulty, strapped myself in, looked at the Lewis gun with curious interest and soon we were away into the night. That location in the back really was an eyeopener; it was extremely cold and draughty, isolated in every way from the front end and the whole contraption of the double tailplane and double rudder was constructed like a box-kite with singing wires, the thing swinging about just in front of you with every movement of the aeroplane. It made me wonder if the air marshals who ordained it had ever been for a ride in the back of their creation? It was awful! The only moments to break the discomfort and tedium came when I noticed that the upper set of twin elevators were within arms reach – provided you stood up; so of course I had to try. Undoing my harness – parachutes were stowed for air gunners – I stood up, got my hands on the trailing edge of the elevators and pushed upwards gently. At once the 'Ginny' began to climb followed by the Captain's arm movements in shadowy form that could just be detected winding away furiously on the big trim wheel. Then I did the reverse and pulled the elevators down. Again drastic action from the pilot, accompanied by two heads close together in earnest talk. When I let go they got wise to it whereupon two gloved fists were giving me distinctly naughty signals. I think my mess bill suffered badly afterwards!

Another Worthy Down tale concerns meeting my esteemed Commanding Officer, Wing Commander Moody at lunchtime in the Mess. After paying my respects that earned me a gin and tonic for showing good manners I told him that I had a complaint to make. "What's this about, Pelly-Fry?" Slight pause for greater effect. "Sir", I began, "I have to tell you that whilst flying your splendid bomber this morning, the bomber designed to go deep into enemy territory and strike terror into the hearts of the foe, something happened that made me ponder". Another pause. "You see, sir, I have to report that I was overtaken by a chap on a motorbike going along the Winchester–Andover road". End of conversation. I thought he ought to know. Later on he might possibly have told the Air

Commodore; I heard tell that there really was one, somewhere.

There is a story about a Virginia that caught fire on a night flight. The tail gunner, seeing the flames belching out from one engine and the two pilots up front getting out to parachute to safety wisely decided to do the same thing himself. At the official enquiry the Air Ministry wanted to know why the tail gunner with no communication at all with the Captain had bailed out without authority!

Those few weeks at Worthy Down were a wonderful start to what was to prove such a happy and rewarding career in the RAF. Although in reality we were no more than birds of passage – sorry, I could not miss that one! – we were treated as though we had been posted in the normal way for a squadron tour. The relationship between the pilot officers – now no longer on probation – and the more senior ranks above was a relaxed one; we were all treated like squadron brother officers. Going up the ladder to Squadron Leader and Wing Commander of course ordained formal behaviour at work (if you can call it work) but in the Mess it was just like home. This subtle and very pleasing way of life is precisely what makes serving in His (or Her) Majesty's armed forces so attractive. Furthermore, the system also extends down the line to the non-commissioned officers and the men. As a young Service devoted to the use of a completely new weapon of war, the flying machine, it was inevitable that a bond would be created at all levels. The officer, pilot or not, admired and respected the skills of the men under his command. They in turn, accepted the fact that you were in charge, however young you were. You were assumed to have 'something extra' and to use the talent correctly. Best of all, when we got to our regular squadrons 'your' aeroplane was by far the best, the shiniest, and the fastest of all. Your ground crew saw to that. It often happened in my later experience that the lads would work through the whole night if necessary to get the aircraft serviceable for the next day. All too often I would not know but the grins of satisfaction on their faces told me everything.

It was a happy chance that Worthy Down was commanded by my very first 'patron' – Group Captain 'Tommy' Thomson. He and his wife Margaret each in their fashion made everything function smoothly. Once again I could see the system by which the top man leads the way with style and competence and all the way down the line from the Squadrons, to the supporting services, to the doctors and to the padres everything and everybody completed the jig-saw puzzle smoothly. It was all very good experience to note, digest, and try to emulate in due course.

An Australian personality who joined us at Worthy Down was Pilot Officer Grant M Lindeman. He had been commissioned into the Royal Australian Air Force and then been transferred to the Royal Air Force on the sensible system by which each Air Force not only exchanged personnel, they also exchanged ideas. Lindy was destined to join up with the new-boys and be sent to Egypt for the conversion course and we had the rare sight of seeing his tall upright figure going about his duties in the dark-dark blue RAAF uniform of his parent Service. There was one change in his appearance however that was prescribed every few days and this was when it was his turn to be posted as the 'orderly Officer of the day'. For a reason or reasons best known about by the Air Ministry it was laid down that an officer on duty as Orderly Officer was required to wear RAF uniform even if he was commissioned in another air force and there came the first occasion when Lindeman was the orderly officer. Poor chap; there he was in a 'foreign' RAF uniform that he even had to purchase out of his own pocket.

P/O Jim Irens, a most amiable giant of a rugger player, boxer, mountain climber and all-round sportsman was there when Lindy appeared. Going up to him and giving him a friendly pat on the back, Jim said, "Lindy! dear boy; white-man's uniform today, eh?". It was just another of those bits of light banter that was received in the same way as it was given. After some weeks the time came to pack our few possessions and say good-bye to all those nice people at Worthy Down prior to the voyage out to Egypt. I looked forward to a winter cruise through the Mediterranean at government expense; now aged twenty-three I could barely believe my good fortune. It was certainly a change from tea tasting in the City of London.

Chapter V

Eastern Promise

Six young RAF officers set sail from England's shores in a fine ship called the SS *Orama*. She was one of the fleet operated by the Orient Line, a Company well-known and liked 'east of Suez' and with a tonnage of 20,000 tons she proved to be all that we could have wished for. Our cabins were well placed near the Promenade Deck and as we seemed to have what was called 'the run of the ship' the days ahead were promising. After leaving Tilbury Docks, London, in November 1935, we soon settled into shipboard life. For the time being, No 3 FTS and then the brief and pleasing weeks at Royal Air Force Station, Worthy Down, drifted away from our thoughts. Now, with new places to see and new things to do, everything was going well for us.

The first port of call was the island of Majorca. Perhaps 'call' is not really correct as in reality the ship anchored out in the bay where some passengers disembarked and all we saw of the island was a fine view of the city of Palma. Who could have guessed that many years later Majorca would become such a popular resort? In large measure this popularity was brought about by the development of civil aviation and what is now called 'The Package Tour'. In those days I doubt very much that the island had an air-strip, let alone an international airport. After Majorca we sailed on, steadily heading East. The cruise – at Air Ministry expense – seemed a kind of make-believe, but then travel by sea usually generates such flights of fancy. With no responsibilities, no chores, nice Mediterranean November weather, pleasant RAF companions, good living, and a good sprinkling of nice fellow-travellers, it seemed like a floating shangri-la. Even our own personal expenses on board, few though they were (like a gin-and-tonic before lunch!) were minimal. After ten or twelve days, Port Said came into sight, the entry point to the Suez Canal, although it was difficult to pick out as it lies at the end of a narrow peninsular from the coastline. So this was Egypt – the fabled land of the Pharaohs! Having picked up the pilot, we now glided gently past the famous statue of Ferdinand de Lesseps, the architect of the canal, which stands at the end of the long breakwater and the tugs gently nudged us to the allotted berth. To say that berthing was uneventful is a mis-statement. Long before we were close enough for that manoeuvre many small boats arrived and the water was invaded by Egyptian youngsters calling out something that none of us understood but seasoned travellers knew the form. You threw a silver coin overboard and right away one or more boys would swim down into the dark water and come up with it in his teeth. Try a copper coin, however, and they did not bother. They were no fools, those kids. In due course the passengers were allowed ashore, some of them to visit shops, some to go by train to Cairo and later rejoin the ship at Suez. Some, like us, to collect our luggage and say good-bye to our temporary ship-board friends on the voyage. I have a pleasant memory of an Australian mother and an attractive young daughter; we all had the feeling that the young girl was being trotted around the world on the sporting chance that a suitable marriage would come her way. For the young airmen, none of us had wedding bells in mind as that was certainly not the reason why we had been sent overseas. There was only time enough initially to get settled into the RAF way of life, a full-time occupation in itself. Of Port Said, we only had a fleeting impression; however, we certainly noticed that it was noisy, bustling and full of the opportunists that all sea ports seem to have. Even the *gulli-gulli* men who played such clever conjuring tricks had to be bypassed for another day. The shipping agent took us to the railway terminal, got us and all our kit safely installed, and away we went for the rail journey to Cairo.

The next stage of our journey was the 130 mile route that follows the Suez Canal to Ismailia and then along the entire Eastern side of the Nile Delta. Because of the new experience with the Egyptian State Railways I doubt that we noticed the dust, the dry air, and – dare I say it? – the flies! Egyptian flies, we were soon to find out are a very special breed – they love white skins from England. Finally we pulled into Cairo Main Station where amid all the bustle that accompanies any arrival at a terminus it was complicated because nearly all speech was in Arabic. Luckily we found an amiable and helpful porter who assured us in 'Cairo' English that he would 'get all trunks fixed-up pretty damn quick all same for Queen Victoria'. He was as good as his word and by some miracle of effort he assembled all the kit. By making a pool of such Egyptian cash as we had exchanged from sterling at Port Said he was paid off and the tip was probably all too generous, judging by his look of delighted surprise. Our Egyptian learning curve had now left the base line. Whilst we were re-checking everything and getting it away from the platform to the station entrance, five young men appeared who soon identified us by our pink faces and looks of bewilderment. They proved to be officers of No 216 Squadron – the unit that we had been posted to join. The spokesman introduced himself and then each one of his team in turn. He then said "Sorry only five of us could come to meet you; you see the rest are saying goodbye to our Adjutant, Paddy Bandon." He was Flight Lieutenant the Earl of Bandon and that name was going to enter my life later when he became a legend in the Royal Air Force. The journey to Heliopolis was our first by road transport in Egypt and quite an experience. The convoy of three privately owned cars and the luggage truck took us out of the city and along the five mile run to Heliopolis, the 'City of the Sun' created by a Belgian architect called Jaspard as a good residential area outside Cairo. It was beautifully laid out. It boasted a fine Roman Catholic Cathedral, a race course, good shops, a sporting club, and the elegant Heliopolis Palace Hotel. Additionally there were many fine villas and blocks of apartments. It had all been designed and constructed from scratch on virgin desert and was a classic example of good town planning. From Cairo to Heliopolis, parallel with the single road ran the rail track for what was described quite simply as 'The Brown tram'. This was the main passenger communications link and greatly in demand by those unlucky enough not to have a private car.

During the journey to Helio, (as it was called), I thought about the welcome that these fellows had given to us. They had made a point of coming in person to the railway station to meet us and they were apologetic that the Squadron efforts had to be divided because this fellow Paddy Bandon had to be cared for somewhere else. It was a foretaste of things to come and a typical example of the remarkable way in which 216 Squadron (and the sister squadron No 208, also based at Helio) conducted day-to-day activities where visitors were concerned. No wonder Group Captain. Tommy Thomson said that the Royal Air Force was the best club in the world.

When we arrived at the aerodrome, the winter sun was going down in a blaze of pale red, soon turning to the rapid twilight that became so familiar in the months to come. In this part of the world, with its dry air and clear visibility, sunrises and sunsets are spectacular and the night brings its attraction of a horizon-to-horizon vision of untold stars. Immediately upon arrival we were shown our rooms and after a quick tidy up we assembled in the Mess Ante-Room. The lay-out of the place was simple enough. It consisted of a single-storey building facing a nice garden with a small circular pond and fountain in the centre. Flanking the garden on two sides, thus forming two sides of a rectangle, were the two-storey living quarters, each level having a verandah to keep the rooms sheltered from the sun. I was allotted a room on the upper floor, facing East, and from there I not only saw the excellent view right across the sandy aerodrome into the distance, I also had the benefit of being able to see the sunrise. In the mess we met more members of the squadron and also members of No 208 Squadron, it's role being to cooperate with the Army. We were entertained well and after dinner we left to go to our rooms, unpack some kit, and then to sleep soundly in our new environment. It had been a long day, the first of many happy days to come in Egypt. The start could not have been more agreeable.

The following morning we walked across the top end of the roughly fan-shaped aerodrome to present ourselves at the office of the Adjutant of No 216 (Bomber Transport) Squadron – to give this distinguished unit its full title. I had already noticed the squadron badge; it was an eagle in flight, carrying a bomb. The motto, quite simply, was *Dona ferens*. With my earlier Latin indoctrination at school, coupled with a little classical experience – at last school work was being put to good use! – I realised that the motto was an abbreviation of the famous dictum *Timeo daneos quam dona ferentes* – 'I fear the Greeks most when they bring gifts'. So the 216 Sqdn motto became 'Bringing Gifts'. The message of course was plain but do Arabs understand Latin? Perhaps it should have been written in Arabic, like the famous one of No 14 Sqdn given by King Abdulla of Transjordan. This motto so appropriately reads "I spread my wings and I keep my promise".

Flight Lieutenant GR Montgomery was the Squadron Adjutant. The six of us stood like new-boys in front of the headmaster. He welcomed us to the unit, gave us an outline of the six-month course that was to come, and allocated us to 'A' Flight which had been chosen as the training flight. After the basic briefing he told us in unmistakeable terms what was expected of us, both in the Squadron and in the world of Egypt. In particular, he emphasised that Britain was not in charge of Egypt, we were there solely as friends, helpers, and advisors. It was Britain's job not only to liaise with them militarily as the circumstance prescribed, it was essential that our presence in Egypt was acceptable to the Egyptians. So please be warned, he said, that one stupid move by any of us to upset the balance of good relationship could only mean one thing – the offender would be on his way back to England pretty damn quick. Needless to say, we received the message.

The Squadron Commander at the time was Squadron Leader Philip Mackworth. For a reason unknown, the first ten months of my time with 216 Sqdn had a Squadron Leader in command when the post normally provides for a Wing Commander. Whatever his rank, the CO was the big boss so far as we were concerned. Philip Mackworth was a tall, good looking man. He was clearly a dedicated officer, and equally a very professional airman. One does not often have a two-year course Specialist Navigation officer in a squadron; all too often they are relegated, poor chaps, to navigating a headquarters chair and not an aeroplane by the stars. I was soon to experience the high degree of professional accuracy that Philip Mackworth expected of his young men.

The key men were Officer Commanding 'A' Flight – Sq Ldr Charles Horn; O/C 'B' Flight was Flt Lt Nixon, and O/C 'C' Flight was Flt Lt Leonard Cubitt. We reported to Charles Horn in 'A' Flight. Thus began our indoctrination into the mysteries of flying a remarkable device called a

Vickers 'Valentia'. First sighting of them gave me twin emotions. I did not know whether to weep or laugh with incredulity that such a transport aeroplane could ever have been invented, let alone be capable of flying. It really was the birdcage to beat all birdcages. In the event I put in 1000 hours of flying in them with no technical problems except once when I had to make a single-engine landing in Kenya onto an airstrip 6000 feet above sea level.

The 'Valentia' was a fat bi-plane troop carrier powered by two Bristol 'Jupiter' radial air-cooled engines that without any cowlings enjoyed the maximum amount of fresh air. Each engine turned a pair of two-bladed wooden propellors bolted together at the hub and in flight one could almost identify each blade, especially when throttled back for landing.

The fat fuselage, made of wood, was just like a tube with a cockpit at the front where the two pilots sat out in the open, like a sports car. The fuselage was designed to accommodate – if that is the word – twenty-two fully equipped troops. They sat on canvas covered full-length metal frames eleven to each side. With a full load the crew of fitter, rigger and radio operator squeezed into any available space not taken up by passengers. The tail was another Vickers box-kite contraption similar to that on the Vickers Virginia at Worthy Down. The only difference, (to me anyway,) was that you could not sit in the non-existent tail gunners dustbin and 'fly the aeroplane' by hand, operating the top set of elevators. Perhaps it was just as well. Just to complete the picture, the broad biplane wings were kept in position with the usual complex of struts and wires. It must have been a nightmare to set the whole thing up correctly, and so Airframe fitters in those days had a lot to look after.

As we were soon to discover during our first dual-instruction flights, the performance of the Valentia matched its appearance. Take-off speed was about fifty-five miles per hour, cruise (with luck) at ninety mph and land at fifty to fifty-five mph depending upon the load carried. The single-engine performance for those days was the same old story; you just descended gently in controlled flight not so very far removed from a glide with both engines throttled back. Thus, unless at a height like 5000 ft, it was really a matter of choosing the best spot within a small cone underneath to make a descent and a landing. Fortunately most of the Egyptian terrain was such that you had a sporting chance of getting down safely, even if something broke in the process. The great saving grace was that those Bristol aero engines were quite remarkably reliable. 'Allah be Praised' – as we now learned to say.

The flying training, with Sq Ldr Charles Horn in charge, was very thorough. Our Flight Commander was a hard and meticulous taskmaster whenever he checked us out and he terrified us with the standards expected. Equally so the instructors (who where not professional instructors but just experienced squadron pilots) were meticulous in the trouble that they took to get us up to Transport Pilot standard. We all learned a whole lot and not least about the magic word 'Airmanship'. My teacher was Sergeant Paddy Egan and just about as good a pilot as one could wish to come across. He had that certain way of imparting his skills, and the teaching stuck, never to be forgotten. Not surprisingly he later became a commissioned officer.

The weeks passed very happily. The six of us felt that we were now integrated (if temporarily) into 216 Sqdn and the way-of-life at Heliopolis. All too soon the six-month training period was now coming to an end. What would happen next? For three of us, it proved to be something close to our hearts because we were selected to remain with the Sqdn for a regular posting.

One memorable occasion was the great pleasure of being hosts to No 820 Sqdn of the Fleet Air Arm, who flew off from HMS *Courageous* in Alexandria and came to stay with us. The famous aircraft carrier was due to be given an overhaul, and whilst the Royal Naval Dockyard was engaged in these important tasks, 820 Sqdn, equipped with Blackburn 'Sharks' arrived at Heliopolis, there to withstand the rigors of shore-based life with the 'crabs'. The entire Station seemed to be present to see the sailors land on – I use the correct naval expression – and after a smart formation fly-past each aircraft got into a stream landing pattern and were soon down and taxying in to the Communication Flight apron. The sailors were due to stay with us for some eight to ten weeks.

We soon sorted out who was who amongst the naval crews and then our party were taken to the Officers Mess and the Sergeants Mess took care of their own guests. It was a nice Autumn morning and we got back to the Mess around mid-day. I presented my compliments to the Squadron Commander, Lieutenant Commander Robin Poole RN. I said "Sir, what is your pleasure?" He clearly liked that kind of question, and replied "Mine's a pinkers, thank you". Unhappily I did not know what that was, so had to ask. "Pink gin, old boy; if you don't know one, well it's a good occasion to find out". Two good pinkers for us, plus the same for the other sailors were laid on. I have to say that two or three drops of Angostura bitters rolled around a small pony glass, a slice of gin, and water to suit, is an excellent Naval custom and I have been practising the habit ever since. Three cheers for the Royal Navy! The Senior Service and the 'crabs' got on splendidly, and we all had a most enjoyable time. We flew in each other's aeroplanes and we had jolly parties together. It was just one of those inter-service affairs that one dreams about. When 820 Sqdn finally had to return to HMS *Courageous* it was difficult to know whether the dark blue or light blue chaps were the more sorry. For me, it was the beginning of a long association with the Royal Navy that I really enjoyed. We seemed to talk the same language.

By the end of March 1936, I had seventy-five Valentia flying hours, day and night, recorded in my log book. This was accomplished in four months. I was pleased about this and the old bus was doing us proud. Although some of the flying training by definition was in the Heliopolis area – all those endless 'circuits and bumps' – there were plenty of sorties to all manner of aerodromes and landing grounds, the latter often just a number and the location only known from previous knowledge and so it was intrepid stuff for the new boys. To go flying out into the desert with absolutely no landmarks to work on and then to find a place only identified as the one you wanted because of a few wheel marks in the sand was an experience. After that we ventured forth with an instructor to an oasis that had fascinating Eastern names like Siwa, Bahariya and Kuffra. One landing ground recorded in my log book was called Black Cone; I wonder now where that was?

In early March we were told that the squadron training course was over. 216 Sqdn had done its work and we were now qualified as 'First Pilot, Day; to carry crew only'. My RAF log book was beginning to look quite respectable with a total flying experience 250 hours. This did not include fifty hours flying in civil registered aeroplanes and I had the feeling that the Royal Air Force regarded the latter as boy's stuff – not proper flying.

One day all six of us were summoned to the Adjutant's office and Flt Lt Montgomery announced that there were three vacancies to be filled in the Squadron. Did any of us want to stay on? Moose Fulton, Jim Irens and I immediately volunteered and were accepted. The other three pilots Lindeman, Campbell-Voulaire and Casley were quite happy to go back to the UK, – particularly so my friend Grant Lindeman. Being an Australian, naturally he wanted the maximum time in England before his exchange period from the RAAF ended. For the three volunteers, well it seemed a wonderful opportunity to be accepted into such an excellent squadron and one that flew regularly all over Egypt, Palestine, Transjordan, Iraq, the Sudan, Kenya, Uganda, Tanganiyka and anywhere else in the Middle East on special missions. One does not get that kind of wide and interesting experience operating from the United Kingdom. Thus the Middle East and Africa became our aviation world.

On April 6th, 1936 I was moved from the erstwhile 'A' (Training) Flight to 'C' Flight. Now at last I had become a proper person in the squadron. I had escaped from the close and frightening scrutiny of 'Trader' Horn and Sq Ldr Nixon was my new boss. The new move brought new vistas and it was yet another step forward to the life of becoming one of the regular pilots in the squadron; My companions and I were no longer in transit. With the prospect of promotion to Flying Officer, not only stability but a satisfying feeling of acceptability came our way. After the months of instruction into the mysteries of being a member of a squadron – and of course all the required duties when holding a commission – the future showed great promise. My new Captain of aircraft and my ex-instructor was again Sgt Paddy Egan. Here in his primary role was the real professional; a dedicated, meticulous and enthusiastic airman. To watch him doing everything, from pre-flight ground examination to the precise and smooth way that he handled his aeroplane was an education in itself.

The RAF practise in those pre-war days was for each pilot to be allotted his own aeroplane, together with the ground crew. Although the system has long since changed to what might be called 'central servicing', with each machine just the next in line to be taken away from the maintenance unit and flown by the squadron's flight crew, the great advantage of the old plan was the very close affinity that existed between ground and air crew. It may not suit modern expertise, but it certainly developed RAF life in a squadron into a very personal and close knit affair. It was people that made the old system, – not the computer, – and it was so much nicer that way. The other attraction in terms of personalities was the good fortune of being associated with squadron members like Basil Paul, George Musson, (who later was a crew member in one of the long-range Wellesleys that made the Egypt-Australian world record flights in 1938); Leonard Cubitt, Dicky Richardson, and Ben Boult. There was also the capable equipment officer, Jacko Jackson, who provided the squadron with all our technical requirements and became one of my long-standing friends.

After a while two new characters appeared on the scene. They had been posted from No 4 FTS, based at RAF Abu Sueir and close to the Suez Canal town of Ismailia where the French Canal Company had its headquarters. Pilot Officers Freddie Milligan and Dicky Abrahams had arrived to enliven the scene. It would be embarrassing to both of them to give a profile sketch of these entertaining and talented fellows; suffice to say that their arrival contributed in no small measure to the continued reputation of 216 Squadron.

I cannot however let pass their lighthearted activities in one respect. During our time with 216 Sqdn, the Station at Heliopolis was graced with two outstanding personalities. After Group Captain Mackey as Station Commander came the redoubtable, very much decorated, and colourful Group Captain Raymond Collishaw, the Canadian ex-RFC fighter ace of WW1. The new commander of 216 Sqdn was equally renowned. He was Wing Cdr SG (Joe) Gardiner, also well decorated for exploits in the North West Frontier area of what is now Pakistan. Each of these senior and highly respected officers had a distinct style of speech, – an accent that one could identify and a choice of words and expressions that we all got to know. Our two young friends began to use their vocal talents to wicked purpose. Not only between themselves, but – worse still – they plied their skills on all and sundry. The telephone would ring and the voice at the other end would say, "Oh yeah, you see, Pelly-Fry, Station Commander here. I wish to see you in my office right away". "Yes sir". When I arrived, wondering what was afoot, I was told that the Station Commander had in fact gone to HQ in Cairo for a conference. On another occasion, complicating matters more, Freddie would telephone pretending to be Joe Gardiner. Dicky answering the call and sensing that it was not Joe but the wicked Milligan, would purport to be Raymond Collishaw at the Communication Flight about to fly one of the Fairey 'Gordons'. The reader can imagine the ensuing conversation! Inevitably sooner or later the real officer would initiate the call and speak to the mimic who would think that his chum was playing games again. This would happen in either direction. "Oh laddie, I want you to be in charge of airmens catering". The reply from the victim to his 'phoney' boss – or so he thought! – and the real boss's irate reaction can be imagined.

The general life of the Station went on blissfully, and integration at all levels was manifest. One element that was so very satisfactory was the happy relationship existing between 216 Squadron and 208 Army Co-operation Squadron. This harmony when two squadrons are based on the same airfield was due in very large measure to the personalities of the respective Squadron Commanders. 216 Sqdn had Philip Mackworth followed by Joe Gardiner. 208 Sqdn was most fortunately blessed with possibly one of the best Air Commanders that it has been my good fortune to know. His name was Sq Ldr WAD Brook. Bill Brook commanded a unit specifically designated to work with the land forces and 208 Sqdn's role was to provide the eyes and the air-strike capability of the army. The job in effect was to be the army's specialised private air force.

This role, still rudimentary in pre-war days, meant that the pilots had to get to know the thinking, the aims, and even the personalities of army personnel that they worked with. Bill Brook went out of his way to that end. He was frequently in the company of the soldiers and he went to great pains to explain the vital need for the army to understand what the military aeroplane could do – and equally importantly what the aeroplanes could not do – and to this end he got to know the generals, the brigadiers and the colonels. Conversely, he told his squadron pilots what the army expected of them. This vital liaison between army and air was almostly entirely due to Bill Brook. Everywhere I went, be it to the Turf Club, the Gezirah Club, the 11th Hussars, the 4th Hussars, the Irish Guards, or wherever, everybody would speak affectionately about 'that splendid fellow Bill Brook'. To complete the picture (and it is very much an essential facet of service life as I began to realise), Bill's wife, Jean (Jay to everybody) could not have been a better ambassadress. So here we had the perfect Service husband and wife team that without any doubt welded army and air together in the Middle East. It seemed to be a good omen for the future.

In retrospect – how easy it is to be wise after the event – the concept of uniting the three arms of the fighting forces, navy, army and air, into an interlocking organisation faltered to some extent in its purpose in the early stages of the 1939–1945 war. It has to be said that in some measure this was due to the ingrained attitudes of some of the top sailors and soldiers due to their lack of the right appreciation of the correct use of air power. Either they regarded the military aeroplane as something of little consequence or they could not bring themselves to accept that without it there was just no chance of success and therefore a guarantee of failure. The whole saga came in stages. First there was the head-in-sand attitude of 'I can do without aeroplanes'; stage two was air attacks received from the enemy – the hard way to learn. The third stage was "Where the hell is the RAF? – why weren't they overhead when we were being attacked?" Even though Bill Brook was accepted as a nice personality by the soldiers, the colonels probably thought of him as one of themselves but a bit eccentric because he went flying instead of riding a horse. In the event, in World War II many got it wrong in varying degree; the soldiers (and sailors but for different reasons) – because they were set in their ways and the airmen because they had the right concept of air warfare but could not always agree amongst themselves on how best to use this new and potentially devastating weapon carrier in specialised ways. On balance, the British were more right – maybe less wrong is more apposite – than any of the other warring countries. The 1939–45 war was the first time that the military flying machine in all its varying roles came into its own and demonstrated the simple if unpalatable fact that air power now dominated the conduct of war.

No 208 Sqdn was equipped with a purpose-designed Hawker 'Audax', and an admirable aircraft for the time – that is until we knew much better. This two-seater (pilot and observer), did a sound job within its capability. All the pilots liked it and it did what was expected of it. The Audax was flown over Egyptian skies by enthusiastic pilots like John Tomes, Capt Misslebrook of the Manchester Regiment, 'Pilot' Pope (who amongst other natural talents had a fine bass voice put to good purpose after dining-in nights in the Mess 'Male Voice Choir'), Patsy O'Grady, Tom Fazan, (another chorister), Tony Powell, David Hopper and Guy Adnams.

John Tomes was married to Joanne. This matrimonial circumstance was perhaps unusual for those times because the younger RAF officers were discouraged from marrying by the cunning expedient of denying them a marriage allowance until they were aged twenty-five. However, John and Joanne brushed aside this curious ruling with their typical elan. They were talented, imaginative, inventive, multi-lingual, and intellectual compared to us ordinary mortals. They were usually three jumps ahead of us. However I got on famously with them and subsequently I was very flattered to be asked to be god-father to their first son Ian who later became a soldier. John's father was a brigadier and his god-father was General Bernard Montgomery. Clearly I was on the fringe of being in good company.

Apart from the pleasant non-flying activities on the Station – like the dining-in nights, the guest-nights, the Sunday morning Pimm's parties, the sports days and the visitors from other RAF stations as far away as Bagdad, Amman, and Khartoum, – all of whom were invariably met upon landing, – there were the opportunities of easy access to a city like Cairo. It was something that no other RAF unit in the Middle East Command could enjoy. Being officers of the British armed forces we had automatic entree to the clubs and in retrospect I now realise just how fortunate we were in this regard. The Cairo Turf Club, the Gezirah Club (where you could play any game from polo to table tennis), the Heliopolis Sporting Club with its fine hard tennis courts, squash courts and splendid thirty-three metre swimming pool filled each week with artesian well water (so no nasty additives), all were there for the asking. Furthermore, the clubs offered a special rate of subscription for British officers. I cannot resist the now famous MacMillan line – 'We never had it so good!'

There were the attractions of a variety of shops, the hotels like the famous Shepherds, the restaurants including Groppi's coffee shop with its luscious cream cakes, some night clubs, and the general fascination of an international cross-section of people. In the latter context we noticed how multi-lingual they all were. In the Heliopolis Sporting Club, just outside the aerodrome and but a minute's walk away, during my regular visits to the swimming pool it was quite normal to hear everybody, children especially, talking to each other in French, Italian, Greek, Arabic, Maltese and English (sometimes!) all mixed up together in a babel of voices.

For activities over and beyond what social life had to offer in Cairo, including the visitations in winter of the 'fishing fleet' of young ladies from Britain trying their luck with eligible bachelors, – there were trips out into the desert, the Pyramids, the wonderful museums of Egyptian antiquity (where one could see for example Queen Nefertiti's exquisite sculptured head), and many activities to enjoy. John and Joanne Tomes used to organise 'treasure hunts'. The game would start with each car-load being presented with a sealed envelope that could only be opened after driving away from the start point for a minimum of one mile in any direction. Each clue, correctly interpreted, would lead to the next and so on to the finish. I was often enrolled as the reconnaissance man-cum-organiser. On one memorable treasure hunt things went delightfully wrong. One clue, correctly decoded meant 'go to Cairo main railway station and look for a fellow called *Abdul-abulbul-Amir*' named after the forces song of that name. Cars loaded with jolly competitors flooded to the station entrance, all the boys and girls leaping out and asking every man to be seen if his name was 'Abdul'. Understandably, most of them said '*Aiwah*' – yes. My arab porter clue-minder unfortunately had been sent off at the critical moment to offload a train. I got him back after a search and normality returned – at least for a while. Another clue, duly interpreted was the lion's enclosure in the zoo. I had forgotten that zoos, like any other public establishment, have closing times. The delay at the railway station caused late arrivals at the zoo entrance and the gates were shut. Quite undaunted, all competitors climbed over the railings to hunt for the next clue. It cost me many Egyptian *piastres* using such kitchen Arabic as I could muster to pacify the zoo attendants. "Ahah", they said, "*Maleesh* – never mind; its the mad *Ingleezi* again". I began to think that they quite liked our harmless eccentricities.

Apart from the kind of activities outlined, there were many others – perhaps too many to delve into in one chapter. From time to time, probably because we had the pleasure of entertaining visitors from other RAF units in far-away places, we would go into town for the evening. It might be discreet to say sometimes well into the night – it was those night clubs! Our favoured restaurant was Finnish's. It was German owned, very good, and inexpensive. We used to enjoy *Wiener Schnitzlen mit kartofflen*, a delicious dish usually washed down by the equally good *Heineken* draft lager. This popular Dutch beverage has attracted even greater popularity in recent times with that entertaining advertisement which proclaims that it reaches the parts that other beers cannot. For us, we started the habit some fifty years ago.

My first sortie into Cairo – the Brown Tram, naturally – required a prior visit to the Mess Office to cash a cheque. I remember that it was for the princely sum of three Egyptian pounds – in those days the equivalent to the pound sterling. Having collected the money, I went to my room and left it, why I do not know, on my dressing table. Upon my return from lunch, to my dismay it had gone. Oh well, once again that learning curve. Just to make an effort to try and do something, if only to pacify my chagrin, I called out for my Sudanese servant, Mohamad Ibrahim, to tell him of the matter. At least he would then know that I knew and thus it might not happen next time. "Mohamad", I started cautiously, "have you been to my room when I was having lunch?" "Yes, *Sahib*". The tall and impeccably attired Sudanese waited for the next question. "Did you see some money on my dressing table?" I wondered what he would say. "Yes, *Sahib*". That fact was established anyway. "Mohamad, it is not there now; where is it – have you anything to say?" The young officer was making miniscule progress, but at least he was trying. "*Sahib* – I have the money inside my *Ghalabia*", the garment like a white nightshirt universally worn in Egypt. "Why have you taken my money?" I was trying to look stern; Mohamad just smiled. "*Sahib*, I keep the money safe for you. Many bad people in these places". That splendid and loyal fellow for the next three years looked after me to perfection. He treated me as a nice uncle would care for a nephew, particularly where money and other valuables were concerned. For the record, his monthly pay was all of six Egyptian pounds. Every time I asked my 'banker' for perhaps five pounds this possibly to go into Cairo with friends, all too often he would shake his head, declare that it was too much, and give me only four pounds. Then the next day in the early morning he would see the small change on the dressing table, look at me drinking my tea, shake his head and say, "I told you so". He was just a wonderful man and friend who arranged to have my clothing marked "Belly Friday". When in due course I was posted away to a new job, each of us had difficulty in hiding our emotions. I do hope that he is now sitting on the right hand of Allah in Moslem Paradise.

On the sandy Heliopolis aerodrome, squadron flying continued unabated. 216 Sqdn was only one of two transport units providing essential work for the whole of the Middle East area. The other famous squadron, No 70, was based at RAF Hinaidi, just outside Baghdad. It made me ponder about the very thinly spread air capability in all respects for such a huge territory that the bosses in London thought sufficient for the job.

The days passed and there was more and more flying to record in our log books. I now began to range far and wide. Changes in senior appointments were taking place, like Sq Ldr Storrar; Sq Ldr Tubby Dawson (the very talented and charming man who in later years as an Air Marshal had 'Dawson Field' named after him out in the Jordanian desert), and Sq Ldr RT 'Taffy' Taaffe, later to command 223 Squadron equipped with Wellesleys.

On June the nineteenth, 1936, Sq Ldr Storrar made an entry in my log book. It read 'Certified 1st Pilot by day and night – the last word written in red! – under 216 Standing Orders on Valentia aircraft'. I now had 400 hours flying experience to achieve that milestone, and I confess that I was a happy fellow. Now at last I was a professional RAF air transport Captain. I was twenty-four years old.

Chapter VI

The Long Distance Squadron

In June 1936, just before qualifying as a Captain of Valentia aircraft, one of the squadron's special trips came my way. It was to fly Air Chief Marshal Sir Robert Brooke-Popham, Commander-in-Chief, Middle East Air Forces on a seven-day tour down to the Sudan and return.

Flying Officer George Musson was Captain of Valentia K-3169; I was second pilot and there was a crew of four. Apart from the Commander-in-Chief, the only other passenger was his personal assistant Flight Lieutenant TNT Stephenson, who was later to become an Air Vice Marshal. To provide some degree of comfort in the cabin, two large round-backed wicker chairs normally used overseas in officers' Mess Ante-rooms were installed. As the Valentia was a slow and cumbersome flying machine, particularly in hot-air turbulence when it was awful to be in the cabin, we planned to avoid where possible the high sun period. The take-off time of each day was therefore 0600 hours in the cool of the morning. The first night stop was made at Wadi Halfa, situated at the southern point of Egypt and just across the frontier in the Sudan. In post-war years the river Nile has been completely transformed by the huge new dam constructed downstream from Wadi Halfa and forming the 225 mile long Lake Nasser; a remarkable piece of engineering reaching North as far as Aswan. This lake has given Egypt much greater control of the vital waters of the famous river, something that the Pharaohs could never in their wildest dreams have thought possible.

Wadi Halfa in the thirties had a good and well run small hotel, the main reason for its existence being that this is the location where the northern end of the Sudan Railway system terminates. Going North by surface travel the passenger carries on to Aswan by the pleasant and leisurely paddle-boat. As one sits on deck at midday under an awning, the passing Egyptian scene could be scanned with interest and in comfort – desirably with a gin-and-tonic, slice of lime and properly iced. It was a painless way to travel. One remarkable feat by Italian engineers, occasioned by creating

Lake Nasser, was the complete removal to high ground – huge stone by stone – of the spectacular Temple of Abu Simbel. But I must go back to the thirties to Valentia air travel with 216 Squadron.

Day One out from Heliopolis at 0610 hrs required a refuelling stop at Assuit before flying on to Wadi Halfa. The flying time on the first day was six hours thirty minutes and the distance was a touch over five hundred miles. Ground speed – eighty mph! Looking back, (when today people grumble about 'taking forever to reach Antigua' – or wherever), the speeds of fifty years ago seem almost unbelievable, particularly to the younger generation. For us, it was the measure of it and we did not complain as we knew no better. I suppose in a way I should be pleased to look back on those low ground-speeds as if nothing else it filled my pilot's log book.

Wadi Halfa to Khartoum entailed a refuelling stop at a desolate place in the Northern Sudan called Atbara. This is the principle Sudan Railways main depot and coincidentally it is also the headquarters. Why the top railway men elected to live and work in such hot, arid, and unbearable conditions defeats me. I personally could think of nicer places in the Sudan, not that there is much choice in the biggest country in Africa at one million square miles; it just looks impressive in the atlas. I was reminded of the Arab saying, 'when God made the Sudan, he laughed'. We flew on to Khartoum in the morning and spent two nights there in reasonable comfort despite the summer heat. The C-in-C was the guest of the Governor General and the rest of us were well cared for by No 47 Squadron which had been the sole RAF unit for that huge country since 1927.

Khartoum was well laid out with tree-lined streets, good-looking houses with well watered lawns and tropical flowers, the excellent Grand Hotel, and a zoo where a number of animals roamed at will. The Sudan in those days was administered (almost unbelievably) only by about 130 talented young men from the British Foreign Office and the annual budget was somewhere in the region of ten million pounds sterling. The Sudan was a classic model of efficient administration by very few and competent people.

One of 47 Squadron's specialities was to convert from landplanes, the ubiquitous Fairey 'Gordon', to floatplanes during the wet season. The problem essentially was that the White Nile and the Blue Nile meet at Khartoum (where the battle of Omdurman was fought in 1898) and each river floods very badly at the end of the Equatorial rainy season. The fall from the southern Sudan right up to Khartoum, a distance of some 900 miles, is so very slight that the waters cannot follow the river beds. The result is that vast areas called the Sudd are flooded out. So in order to be able to alight at-all the Gordon float-plane came into its own and it must have made squadron life for those pilots quite interesting.

From Khartoum the Valentia party sped on – not exactly the best description – towards the Red Sea Hills and thence on to Port Sudan. This sea port is the only access to the Sudan from the Suez Canal and the Indian

Ocean and thus the point where everything from locomotives to sewing machines, *et al*, must pass through. It is hot, sticky and not exactly the best seaside resort in the world. For all that, the Red Sea Hotel was well run by smiling Sudanese, the sea fishing is excellent and the swimming pool almost too warm for pleasure. Any other diversions for guests were limited to the point of non-existence. After one night in Port Sudan, we set off again and the Red Sea route took us to a place with the attractive name of Hassa Lagoon, then on to Hurgada, and finally back to Heliopolis. The round trip went off without a hitch and it entailed thirty flying hours. Sir Robert was pleased and 216 Squadron had carried out yet another seven-day tour 'as to the manner born'.

It was now back to routine flying again, although in practise each was always different from the previous one. The squadron programme was more like the operations of an air charter company rather than scheduled services by the major airlines and so it was much more interesting that way. We visited landing grounds in Egypt, Sinai, Palestine and Iraq, although most of the jobs were within Egypt. Places like Mersa Matruh and Sidi Barrani – shades of Richard Murdoch and Arthur Askey from wartime BBC Radio days – and many other new places were added to my store of experience.

Some sorties were, so to speak, to nowhere at all. These were for the inspection of emergency landing grounds spread across desert routes and they were in reality no more than marks on our maps. The idea of maintaining them was that if for any reason an emergency landing had to be made, with luck the pilot could reach one of these desert airstrips and wait to be rescued.

One such sortie was to inspect those emergency strips that were dotted along the Sinai Desert from the Suez Canal to what is now Israel. There were perhaps five or six of them, evenly spread out and each one only identified, with luck, by wheel marks from an earlier visit. Having arrived at one of them we got out and prepared to walk over it to check for bad patches and then to deal with them. One of the lads meanwhile took out a number of four-gallon tins of petrol from the Valentia for refuelling and we then placed the empty ones at the boundaries when almost invariably (and understandably) the *bedouin* would make off with them soon afterwards. Meanwhile another airman would begin the time-honoured custom of tea-brewing. Whilst we were checking the strip, in typical desert fashion there appeared as though from nowhere a Ford touring car carrying two men. Both were in Egyptian Army uniform and both were wearing the tarboosh, the red headgear that looks like an inverted flower pot. The car drew up and the officers got out as I walked towards them. Dutifully I commenced with the time-honoured '*Salaam-alikum*' – 'good-day'. The driver, a tall and handsome man with suntanned appearance replied similarly. So far, so good. Using my best Arabic I began asking the usual polite questions about his health, that of his wife and children and his parents well-being, followed by the customary Arab offer of tea. As most of his replies only needed a brief 'yes', 'Allah be praised', and 'thank you', I thought I was doing well. However, my continued conversation soon dried up because my Egyptian Army friend then launched into Arabic that was quite beyond me. So to try and cover up my confusion I said slowly and clearly, "Please sir, do you speak English?" There was a slight pause whilst my friend looked quizzically at me. He then replied "Yes; I happen to be the Governor of Sinai!!" Damn! He was just as English as I was. He was Colonel Hammersley, successor to the famed Major Jervis Bey. The Colonel was kind enough to say that my Arabic was quite good but there was too little of it. It must have been one of those days.

The best was now to come. In the summer of 1936 the RAF decided to base a small unit in East Africa. The interesting thing about this move – but not properly appreciated by us at the time – was that our long-sighted planners in London must have had a strong hunch that things were beginning to look difficult in the world of international politics. Mussolini was up to his tricks in Eritrea, Hitler was beginning to sharpen his sword, so it was time for Britain to get moving. The very small unit sent to Kenya, believe it or not, was just five Fairey Gordons, and they had to be logistically supported to some extent by air. Where else but from Egypt, only a couple of thousand miles away? 216 Squadron automatically got the job. There now started a series of flights to Nairobi carrying whatever the requirement decreed. Our Cairo masters were quick off the mark; All of a sudden senior air staff officers in HQ Middle East Command began to form a queue to get onto the limited passenger list. After all, was it not essential that they go down to inspect this, that, and the other? But of course, and for us the more VIP's the better. Our job was to fly the aeroplane to Nairobi, stay until the staff officers had done their work, and then fly them back again to Cairo. My first run to Kenya proved in the event to be more than a single round trip.

In order to provide an air transport capability in East Africa to supplement the Fairey Gordons, Air HQ in Cairo now decided to base two Valentias at Nairobi. These aircraft were later to be exchanged complete with air and ground crews, with replacement aircraft from Heliopolis. In this way the technical aspects like engine changes prescribed in the maintenance manuals and personnel changes would give all concerned greater experience and so would fit nicely into the pattern and was a scheme that appealed to everybody. It was my good fortune to be selected to go as crew on one of the first aircraft. This was Valentia K-3169; 'W' – Willie, as it was called. (Valentias could not possibly be girls, could they? Not the ungainly shape that they were!) No less a person than my esteemed commanding officer of 'C' Flight, Philip Mackworth – decided to be Captain; after all, he had to lead the way and see us to our destination correctly. The other Valentia was commanded by Flt Lt Rudolph Taaffe; its number was K-3167; 'M' – Mike, and we set off for Nairobi on October 10th 1936. In the back of 'Willie' we had the stocky and military-moustached Wg Cdr George Bowen, the amiable Sq Ldr Allan Churchman, the dapper and erudite Sq Ldr John Whitworth-Jones, and the egregious and colourful Flt Lt Victor Streatfield – who was destined to be the commander of the 'Gordon' flight in Nairobi.

The speedy Valentias – ahem – had to make ten hops to reach Nairobi. The first leg was a short fifteen minute flight to RAF Helwan just south of Cairo where No 45 Sqdn was based and there to pick up Allan Churchman who lived nearby. It was the usual 216 sqdn service. We followed the well-worn route to Khartoum and for me beyond that it was new ground of many more stages including one across the equator to Nairobi. For some now forgotten reason an extra day at Wadi Halfa had been planned. Philip Mackworth, ever the dedicated ace navigator, planned to use the time to good purpose as we had a morning to spare. Before leaving Heliopolis he said, "When we get to Wadi Halfa I have a little navigation exercise for you to carry out. So go to the Map Section and pick up the necessary sheets to fly about 200 miles west of Wadi Halfa. I expect that the best scale you can obtain is one over a million – that's near enough sixteen miles to the inch". Naturally curious to know more I asked him what he had in mind, if only to do some preliminary work. He smiled. "The job you have to do is to navigate me out into the desert to find what in Arabic is called a '*bir*' ". There was a slight pause for greater effect. "A *bir*, Pelly, in case you don't know, is a hole in the ground. It's a water well used by the *bedouin*. If they can find it, why shouldn't you?" So I was on my mettle. The Flight Commander had decreed; and perhaps my promotion to Flying Officer would be influenced after the navigation test had been completed. When I got to the Map Section, after rummaging about in those large shelves that maps were stored in, the airman produced four sheets. We both looked at them with incredulity. Apart from the river Nile showing on the Eastern sheet – we had laid them out on the floor for checking the overlaps – the rest were almost completely bare of the map-markers art as nearly all were plain white paper! One small item that I remember so well was a dotted line running semi-diagonally across adjacent sheets and the caption said 'Thought to be the route taken by Prince Kemal el din in 1922'. Heavenly days, what a challenge for the new boy! Fortunately, I found one sheet with a '*bir*' or two marked on it but how accurately placed were they on the map? Philip Mackworth selected the one that he fancied and I remember that the dot on the map actually had a name alongside it. The day after our arrival at Wadi Halfa, 'W' Willie was refuelled, checked over by the ground crew who always flew with us, and clutching my nav. instruments and the maps that looked more like Atlantic charts than anything else we climbed in and off we went into the desert wastes. The Captain was at the tiller and he smiled enigmatically; this was fun for him. The only way to navigate under those conditions was to take continuous readings by drift sight, thus giving necessary course corrections to the pilot to keep flying 'down the dotted line' on the map. The initial work with the Course and Speed Calculator, estimating wind strength and direction and then all those readings of drift kept me busy. My Captain often used to ask me what the drift was. "Three degrees to Starboard, sir". He would put his head into the slipstream, look down searchingly into the desert scene, and then would say "Not so; it's two degrees to starboard". How does one cope with that kind of visual accuracy?

After some ninety minutes flying over the desert at the usual five thousand feet altitude for Valentias, I completed my navigation work and hoped for the best. "In five minutes, sir, we will be overhead and should be able to spot your hole in the ground". We droned on. Now was the moment of truth. I undid my seat belt, stood up and holding on to something handy I looked over the top of the windscreen and the short bulbous nose. "*El Hamdulillah*" – there was a hole in the ground! It could not be anything but the aiming point and I pointed energetically downwards. Philip Mackworth banked round, took a hard look, smiled, and gave me a thumbs-up sign. I had passed the test. Apart from the black hole, I could see faint camel-tracks going to the *bir* from different directions. I wondered who had made the hole, how the water was found in the first place, and how often it was used? I concluded that one has to become a bedouin to find out.

The following day the two Valentias left Wadi Halfa and headed south once again. On this stage of the journey we followed the railway track across the wilderness of flat desert to Atbara, the place in the middle of nowhere designated as the Sudan railways main base. The Nile now slowly began to drift away towards the West and disappear from sight before returning later to Atbara after making a huge loop in the process. It is a four-hour flight in a Valentia and we landed to refuel. After the usual night stop in Khartoum, away we went again – take off 0540 – into the Southern Sudan. Now this was to be the new experience for me and I expect for the rest of the party too. The target for the day was Juba, just before we would leave the Sudan at long last and it took three hops en route for refuelling. The most interesting part of the journey now was the appearance and character of the ground which was changing steadily from the cotton-growing 'El Gezirah' area (it means 'island' in Arabic and is conveniently situated between the two Nile rivers south of Khartoum) and so from the everlasting dirty light brown of the desert to a token green. The day's first touch-down at Kosti suddenly gave me the exciting feeling that 'this was Africa – the real Africa!' Some kind of coarse grass was growing in places and there were short bushy trees with spikes on them which were the thorn trees that I had read about. There was now a curious and unmistakable

African atmosphere which I had not experienced before and to prove that everything was for real, as they say, standing like a very thin and tall sentinel a short distance away was a human being. He was obviously a male and he was impeccably turned out as he was only wearing a spear. He stood like a stork on one leg, leaning on his spear and the instep of his other foot was placed conveniently against the knee of the leg in use.

I cannot resist relating a brief conversation at Kosti on a later occasion. In February 1937, I was heading North in a Handley Page 42 'Hannibal Class' after delivering a Percival Speed-Six 'Gull' to Nairobi, about which more later. The passengers included an amiable American couple and the gentleman was attired in light grey trousers, lumberjack shirt, Panama hat, two cameras, and a pair of binoculars. Quite soon about six of the *Dinka* tribe appeared and were all doing the one-leg-down-and-the-other-at-the-knee stance with his spear held at head height. All of them must have been 6 ft 6 inches tall. It helps, they say, when looking above the elephant grass. After gazing in wonderment at the splendid six, our friend walked up to the Captain and said "Say, Cap'n; how long do we stay?". Our skipper replied "Just long enough to refuel, sir. Have you an appointment in Khartoum, perhaps?" Slight pause. "No sir", said our friend from the New World. He gazed again at the *Dinkas*, admired their fine masculine appearance, winced visibly, and then said slowly, "If we stay here much longer my wife will think that I am dee-formed!!"

As the Valentia flew south the country beyond Kosti now unfolded. It became more lush, greener, and yet more green. Beyond Malakal (for refuelling), the Nile made its second big, wide sweep to the west before returning to meet us at Juba. This is the huge area known as the Sudd; the elephant country. Exceptionally tall grasses, a few trees and not much else. In the rainy season it is flooded knee-deep so it is no place for a picnic.

The Sudd is the area where in October 1937 General and Mrs Arthur Lewin had to make a forced landing in their Miles 'Whitney Straight' two-seat private aeroplane when flying back to their home in Kenya. It happened because of a silly navigational error compounded by running out of fuel. A big search from the air by 47 Squadron and civil aircraft in transit eventually found them, but the whole operation took eight days before a ground party could reach them. No 47 Squadron then flew them to Khartoum, for which splendid effort that included supply-dropping the General donated a magnificent silver replica of a Vickers 'Vincent' as an appreciation of the squadron's work. By chance I met the general in London not long after his ordeal and he gave me a detailed account of the whole affair. In his typical forthright way, he said that he was a bloody fool – it should never have happened if he had been more careful about his navigation and had heeded the suggestions of his wife who had known better.

Juba had a reason for its existence. The river boats put in there, as it is the highest point that is navigable and it was also the capital of Eastern Equatoria, at the southern end of the Sudan. The landing ground was more than adequate and the Juba Hotel in its fashion was good. It was certainly sufficient for a comfortable overnight stop and the Sudanese staff were ever smiling and helpful. I really began to admire and respect them, each one a carbon copy of my wonderful Mohammed Ibrahim at Heliopolis. One memorable sight at Juba that convinced me that the 'real Africa' had been reached was to see a lion cub outside the hotel. Well, it was not all that much of a 'cub' as he was bigger than a Great Dane. As soon as I put my RAF topee down on the ground, the better to take a photograph with my new *Leica* – pilot officers much be rich! – the playful and handsome king of the bush proceeded to tear my headgear to ribbons. If nothing else it was a good excuse not to wear that outdated piece of millinery for a while. RAF *topees*, thankfully, are impossible to replace in the southern Sudan and I had pleasant visions of saying to my commanding officer, "Sorry sir; a lion ate it!".

We moved on again in the morning and now we were flying over David Livingstone country with all those familiar geography school-book names. This was Uganda! We made a brief stop at Lira to refuel and it looked for all the world like an English country park with a tropical atmosphere about it as the District Commissioner came out to greet us. Compared to modern times, what a most excellent and dedicated job these British Administrators did for the Africans; they were cared for, they had a peaceful life and they were happy. It must make a lot of us ponder about all this so-called new freedom in Africa and cause poor David Livingstone to turn in his grave.

When we reached Kisumu on the shores of the huge Lake Victoria – I wonder why it's not now called Lake Mumbo Jumbo in *Swahili*? – we were in Kenya. At last we were in the destination country and the pulse began to quicken. To the east we could see, partly cloud covered, the slopes of the Great Rift escarpement, the beginning of the high country that is such a feature of East Africa. Now we had to get our planes high enough to fly over this last leg of the journey in safety and take us across the equator. The route by common aviation usage in those days was to take off and then climb up as fast as possible on an easterly course that would follow the general route of the railway that runs to a small township called Nakuru. It entailed flying at ten thousand feet and it also prescribed that the amount of cloud (normally *cumulus* but sometimes *cumulo-nimbus*) was such that you could see ahead to fly around them safely. In those days, with basic blind-flying instruments only and certainly no navigation aids – other than eyesight – it was a case of the pilot using his discretion, his experience, and common-sense. Once you had started your climb and could get a pretty good idea of what lay ahead you could then get the measure of it. The escape plan always was to make sure that your return to the starting point if necessary was not endangered by rapid cloud build-up. I suppose that one could call it one of inspired airmanship and if nothing else – and this particularly applied to transport aircraft – it was the Captain's decision; it was his good judgement and his personal skills that counted. There was absolutely no question of being advised or even instructed about what to do and how to do it from external sources. Even the radio operator with his long aerial dangling down underneath could only hope to communicate under favourable circumstance.

Fortunately, the run was straightforward; we had very little cloud to bother us, very good visibility, landmarks unmistakably identified, and so all went well. Not far below us now unfolded some of the best and most attractive parts of the earth's surface that I have seen. Averaging some 7000 feet above sea-level we saw forest, lakes, open grassed areas, that attractive rich brown soil, settlers farmhouses, African villages, crops, cattle, some game (although most of the game is found at lower levels,) and overall a vista that reminded me of the highlands of Scotland but on a very much grander scale. I fell in love with Kenya at first sight.

Nakuru to Nairobi follows the line of part of the Great Rift. We flew past Lake Elementita where there are hundreds of thousands of flamingos – a fantastic sight – the big Lake Naivasha, over the N'gong Hills, and then a gentle downhill run to Nairobi. We had arrived! The 2,500 mile trip from Heliopolis had taken almost twenty-eight flying hours – thus we had made an average speed of eighty-nine mph. It had been a fascinating journey and very soon I learnt to say *safari* – the Swahili word which sounds better. The magic of East Africa was about to make it's inroads to my heart.

Chapter VII

The Kenya Scene

Nairobi as a city and the capital of Kenya was really an accident of fortune. Although there may once have been a small African settlement there, the reality is that when the British constructed the railway connecting the new harbour of Mombasa with the hinterland the job was very largely done by men willingly imported from the Indian sub-continent because the Africans were not too well disposed to get onto the payroll. The construction work halted temporarily at Nairobi, and the next stage of pushing into the much higher country and then on to Lake Victoria required a pause and lots of reconnaissance to find the best route. Inevitably it developed from a kind of Roman Camp into a settlement, then a small town, and finally a city. Dr David Livingstone would have been delighted.

Wilson aerodrome, named after the enterprising lady who pioneered civil aviation in East Africa, proved in later years to be too small for the new breed of commercial aircraft so the aviation authorities chose Embakasi, further out from Nairobi and on a greatly improved site for an international airport. In the interim, just before the Hitler-Mussolini war, the RAF decided to set up their own base and Wilson Airport returned to its original civil aviation role. The military aerodrome was destined to be located to the North East of Nairobi, and was named Eastleigh for a reason only known to the planners. In 1937 it was no more than a piece of African real estate so the curious choice of an English name remains a mystery.

Upon arrival at Nairobi we were taken to our Mess quarters, the senior men to the wood-constructed officers' Mess and the Sergeants and the airmen to their similar accommodation. By definition, it was small and compact because the requirements for RAF personnel to look after and fly a handful of small aeroplanes was no more than one expects. The addition of the small 216 Sqdn Detachment did not affect the accommodation requirement very much as it amounted to four officers and ten other ranks. The staff officer contingent was taken to the New Stanley Hotel in Nairobi, including Sq Ldr John Whitworth-Jones who was destined to become the commander of the Kenya unit. Flt Lt Rudolph Taaffe was in charge of the two Valentias and Flt Lt Victor Streatfield took over the five 'Gordons'. That therefore was the composition of the senior team and it seemed to be a pretty good one and our new CO John Whitworth-Jones had the attributes that one hopes for in a commanding officer.

After an evening spent with the handful of officers already stationed in Nairobi who consisted of pilots, one equipment officer and a doctor, we had our first night's sleep at 5,400 feet above sea level. I slept like a contented baby and soon discovered that living at high altitude suited me admirably. I awakened with the wonderful clear air of Kenya in my lungs and began the day in high expectation. With the usual service-way of jolly happenings, at breakfast time eight of us sat down to the table. "Well now", our Scottish Flt Lt Doc Blair said, "Kenya scrambled eggs; guess how many eggs in that fine dish?" Before we were allowed to help ourselves, our answers varied from eight to twelve "All wrong, my friends. The answer is – just one!" It was an ostrich egg and it was, shall I say, rather strong and fruity. That evening it was a leg of ostrich for dinner, a foretaste of many new culinary and other experiences to come. The day-to-day life in Kenya, as I came to discover, is full of variety and interest but for the present it seemed to be a start of a wonderful dream.

To an airman, the flying over this part of Africa was quite unlike anything that I had experienced before and there was a special quality about it that made it unique. The geography was on a grand and spectacular scale and furthermore there was complete variation and contrast of terrain and climate. With Nairobi as a starting point, to the North and West the ground climbs up majestically ever higher to the Abadare mountains and the Mau Escarpment. Some eighty miles further to the North is Mount Kenya, 17,000 ft high, snow covered, and almost exactly on the equator. No wonder the people who live within sight of it hold it in the highest esteem as a god-like vision.

In the high country, with a constant weather factor influenced by the two annual rainy seasons, one called 'the little rains' and the other 'the big rains', there are a great number of mountain streams that originate on the high slopes and travel downhill to feed (among others) the great Tana river and its sister the Athi river. Both eventually reach the Indian Ocean and in the process they help to make everything grow.

Going North beyond the mountain ranges and with Mount Elgon (14,000 feet) to the West dividing Kenya from Uganda as a prominent boundary mark, the ground now begins to fall away. The area changes colour from the lush green of Central Kenya to the green-brown and finally the brown-and-black semi-wilderness towards Lake Rudolf and beyond. The lake is 1200 feet above sea level, 150 miles long north to south and some twenty miles wide in places. It abounds with fish like the big 250 lb perch (called Aigle in the Nile) and twenty-foot crocodiles that lie in wait for anything that moves. In one place on the Athi River two notices say simply 'Beware of the crocodile' and 'Please do not disturb Hippo'.

The other remote areas of Kenya stretch away to the North East towards Ethiopia and Somaliland of which the most distant habitation is called Mandera set up in the fork separating the three frontiers. It is a 500 mile flight from Nairobi; just a boy's run in a Valentia at a hoped-for speed of ninety mph! Understandably, travellers going up to this very remote area by surface transport are either compulsive or crazy and how the British administrators maintained their equilibrium in this area of Colonial rule is still a mystery to me. I suppose that reading a four-week old copy of the London Times helped, in its fashion.

To continue the Kenya picture, 125 miles due south is Mount Kilimanjaro, just inside the country once called Tanganiyka and predictably changed to Tanzania by the new rulers who seem to know better. Kilimanjaro, thank heaven, is still Kilimanjaro and it is the highest point in all Africa at 19,340 feet. My splendid fellow officer Jim Irens climbed both Kenya and Kilimanjaro, he was that kind of chap. I still have one of his Kenya Colony maps to the scale of one over two million (say, thirty-two miles to the inch) and printed upon linen. The Services in those days knew how to treat us well where maps were concerned. However, perhaps understandably the maps were not too accurate or complete. Jim Irens' amended map has an eighty mile stretch of road track moved an average of twelve miles further south and it also has the land marks of two prominent hills marked in our own designated annotation. No prizes for guessing what a nicely rounded pair of shapely hillocks, suitably spaced, were called!

Finally the Kenya coastline along the Indian Ocean. It is almost 300 miles long, and with the port of Mombasa at the southern end it boasts a wonderful run of white sandy beaches, tropical vegetation, coconut trees swaying like languid dancers in Bali, and beautiful flowering trees and shrubs. There are many dreamy places like Malindi where the small Lawford's hotel is blissful and one swims nude in clear blue-green water a few steps away from your *chalet* called a *boma*. A beautiful and loving partner always completes the picture, certainly for chaps like me. Airmen will be airmen!

Geographical eulogies apart, Kenya was blessed with an abundance of excellent assets like wonderful climate, Alpine air, the wild game, and superb natural products like fruit, cereals and vegetables the like of which cannot be found elsewhere in that part of the world. It made a great change from Egyptian circumstance where all too often everything tasted mundane, colourless, tough, or all three. Kenya added up to the feeling that I was now in some kind of earthly paradise and the thought of being able to stay for some months was very exciting. I found the Africans to be very pleasant; they had a happy disposition, a nice sense of childish humour, and industrious in their fashion when the occasion demanded. They responded well to a caring master, someone who made them feel that they had a role to fill. Never did I or my contemporaries get the impression that they wished the white man should go away. All that, alas, came later when something called nationalism was fed into them by ambitious politicians of their own kind. The subsequent tragedy of the African scene makes old-hands like myself weep; it now seems to be a continent falling apart at the seams.

Apart from the Africans like those majestic *Masai*, the *Kikuyu*, the handsome *Turkana* up north, and many others – after all, Kenya is 225,000 square miles in area and has a large number of indigenous tribes – the Crown Colony had introduced in the early twentieth century the white-skinned element. There were the Government administrators who worked wonders and were an excellent and enthusiastic breed of men. There were the Railway people who operated such a splendid system; the fine Regiment of the Kings African Rifles; the police; and not least the white farmers who grew everything in the way of crops like coffee, tea, sisal, and pyrethrum for insecticides. They also raised superb imported cattle for beef and dairy produce.

One farm of 30,000 acres that was devoted to cattle and dairy produce lay some thirty-five miles south/east out of Nairobi towards Machakos. There lived the Percival family – father, mother and son John. Papa had been a white hunter of repute in his younger days but was now semi-retired and only made occasional *safaris* with friends. The farm was beautifully run and we in the RAF were very lucky to have an open invitation to visit on any Sunday. We would normally take our rifles and shot guns with us, the principle idea being to get a small bag of game for the family kitchen and African staff. This plan worked very well for us in that we learned so much of the expertise from our friends and appreciated that it was not so much sport as a necessity. We discovered that the African air was deceptively clear and what looked like a Thompson's gazelle 200 yards away in fact was nearer double that distance. We would invariably be out all day, ending up with some game bird shooting in the late afternoon. A Sunday on the Percival property was to be well remembered. One day I discussed with Mrs Percival the early days of farming in the early nineteen twenties and no question but that it was good pioneering stuff. When I asked her how she travelled to Nairobi to replenish the household requirements, she replied, "On horseback, James. How else?" Ho hum; seventy miles there and back for the toothpaste and another bush shirt!

There was also a very small and colourful collection of people who although coming under the convenient title of 'settler' in reality were well-placed and well-heeled men and women from home who found that Kenya was their *shangri-la*. The vast majority of settlers were genuine and serious lovers of the outdoor life, the hardworking pathfinders to creating civilisation in what previously was undeveloped paradise; they were productive and loved what they did. I met many of them and very charming they were too. However, as is the way in this world, the small close-knit minority came just to enjoy themselves and – let's be honest – usually to run away from circumstance elsewhere. They found the apparent freedom from European convention and criticism to suit them 'to a tee'. When visiting Nairobi from their properties, people like Lord Erroll and Sir Delves Broughton could often be found staying in the comfortable Muthaiga Country Club, just a short distance out of town. They also frequented the single Nairobi night-spot called The Flamingo – known by all as "The Flaming – O". One naughty but to some extent apposite definition running around the Nairobi clubs and hotels in those days was that 'A Kenya Gentleman is a fellow who lays down his wife for his friends'. The Happy Valley *coterie* even blamed the altitude for their misdemeanours. Altitude my foot! No wonder they were such a jolly lot; they had jam every day, so to speak, and not a care in the world.

Some well-remembered episodes of life in Kenya come to mind. Eric Atkinson was one of the ground engineers who kept the small fleet of commercial, privately owned, and Flying Club aeroplanes in serviceable condition. One late afternoon, whilst putting some aircraft away into a hangar, he came across pilot Kirkam's lion cub. As is the nature of animals, 'Joe' was beginning to grow faster (and bigger) than any of us cared for. Eric's difficulty was that Joe's owner had left the aerodrome so he had no option but to get Joe outside, close the hangar doors, and then later tell him to collect his large 'cat'. But Joe was in no mood to leave. After sundry admonitions, the only course left was to walk up to him, give him a good clip over the ear, and nudge him smartly out into the fading light. Having 'closed the shop', Eric set off for home. On the way he called at Kirk's house and advised him to go back and pick up his bloomin' pet that was last seen close to the hangars. The dapper pilot looked surprised and perhaps a little hurt. He replied, "Eric, that is *not* my lion – it must be a wild one as Joe is in the back yard . . .!!"

Eric must have led a charmed life. Not long after the lion episode he was attending a DH 86A 'Express Air Liner' four-engined aeroplane belonging to Wilson Airways. With all four motors turning over, the pilot beckoned, and our engineer went into the aeroplane and up to the cockpit to find out what the pilot had to say. Having learned what the problem was, Eric left the cockpit, and descended to the apron. He then very properly went underneath the port lower wing where he undid the cowling of the inner (no 2) engine, made some kind of adjustment, and closed the cowling again, locking it securely. I happened to be watching at the time. To my horror and dismay, the next moment I saw him walk forward towards those lethal turning propellors and I closed my eyes as I could not bear to look. Two or three seconds later I looked and there was Eric about six paces in front of the aeroplane. He stopped abruptly in his tracks, turned his head and realising what he had done immediately collapsed to the ground in a dead faint.

Eddie Sladen was a white hunter. He was short, stocky, and blessed with big shoulders. He spoke out of the corner of his mouth because his face had once been mauled by a lion and so his jaw was out of alignment. One afternoon he came into the Flying Club and mentioned that he had seen a pride of about eight lion on his way to the aerodrome. Never having seen a lion in its natural surrounding (Joe, and the one at Juba notwithstanding) I asked him if he would take me back to have a look at them. This he agreed to do and I appreciated his generous reaction as lions to him were his way of life. I climbed into his Ford roadster which was the kind with a soft top as the Americans say. The top however was down. On the way to the site in the bush he briefed me about the characteristics of lions. He said that as it was about sundown the lions had probably made a kill, filled their stomachs, and were relaxing just like everybody else. However, something or somebody might annoy them; like us, for instance. If that should happen, as a precaution he was going to reverse the roadster carefully up to them and approach as close as he dared and we would be ready if necessary for an immediate getaway. Already my pulse rate began to quicken. Eddie said that there are certain clear indications that lions give of displeasure. First of all, they look at you searchingly. Second, they may decide that you are intruding and if so they crouch. Finally, the lion's tail comes slowly forward and lies flat on its back and when the tip of the tail curls over – that is the moment of attack.

When we arrived on the scene, lazing about like great big pussycats in the bush were a male, females, and some cubs. Eddie turned the car around, stopped, and had a look. So far, so good. "Nice pride", said Eddie, with admiration. Slowly he backed, closer and closer. When we were about twenty five yards away, a beautiful lioness stood up, gave us a baleful look with her yellow eyes, and obviously decided that we were intruders. She growled softly and then she got into a crouching posture and that long tail now began to come forward – just like Eddie had said. That was it. He let in the clutch and off we went very briskly. As I looked back over the folded canvas hood I was relieved to see that the lioness had returned to her offspring and I think I saw her smiling. Back at the Flying Club the cold beer never tasted better.

It was my good fortune one day to meet a chap called Rupert Watkins-Pitchford who was on the staff of the Kenya Government as the Senior Public Relations Officer. Apart from being a genial and hospitable chap he was also a keen trout fisherman. I told him about my adventures when fishing for Nile perch in the Sudan (of which the biggest one that I had landed was 150 lbs), and he offered to take me trout fishing. Being a regular Kenya resident Rupert's local knowledge was profound and as he knew all the good rivers to fish and with all the tackle and a safari car available we made a plan to go fishing on the forthcoming Sunday. Rupert's style of trout fishing was to leave Nairobi at 3 AM with his African boy, the food, drink and all the spares stowed away nicely in the safari car. For my part all I had to do was to dress in the gear that he advised me to wear. This amounted to slacks, bush shirt, floppy hat, robust and expendable boots. He picked me up at the mess at the ungodly hour and we headed north towards Mount Kenya. After getting well away from Nairobi, climbing steadily, we began to cross innumerable streams and passed small African villages, a small town called Thika, and then onwards towards Mount Kenya. By now we must have been around 9,000 fet above sea level, possibly more. A little time before we got to 'base camp' the daylight began to show up the African countryside. We were now on the thickly forested slopes of the mountain, heavy with growth of all manner of nature's delights and the track now getting distinctly rougher with pot-holes in the rich-red soil. After pulling off the track at a good spot under tall trees we began to unload the gear. The sun was now getting up higher and I was feeling warmer. The African boy was preparing coffee and eggs and bacon for breakfast. What a splendid way to start a day of trout fishing!

Suitably refreshed after the meal, we set off with our fishing tackle and the boy stayed behind to tidy up and attend to the *safari* car. Rupert had warned me beforehand that trout fishing in Kenya was quite unlike that which for example a few fortunate ones get on the River Test in Hampshire and with the Grosvenor Hotel at Stockbridge to visit, there to have meals and to tell tales of the whopper that got away. Kenya fishing, he told me, was going to be more like an Army assault course and how right he was. We scrambled up and down steep slopes to the *dongas* (river beds), and waded right into the streams to fish as the banks were either too thick with undergrowth or impossible for fly-casting. Now I understood why I had to wear slacks and old boots and tuck my trousers well inside them. The streams were full of leeches! Using wet-fly, (for the *aficionado*, the Coachman is a killer in East Africa,) Rupert and I fished for the whole day. We travelled from one stream to another and I slipped often on the steep banks, thus getting wet and muddy, but who cares? The brown trout were plentiful. They were not much bigger than a pound or so, but excellent sport in those icy streams. We put back practically all the trout that we caught, keeping perhaps half a dozen each to take back to Nairobi. For the fishing log book, in one day we each took the Game Department's maximum quota of fifty trout per rod. How's that for good trout fishing?

The long return journey to Nairobi was pleasant and uneventful, like the outward one. When Rupert dropped me off at the Mess, it was 11 PM and we had been on Safari for twenty hours and had travelled 200 miles in the process. I fell into bed and once again slept soundly. What a fabulous country Kenya is, to be sure.

Apart from routine transport flights over East Africa and of course the occasional test flights when necessary, there were the 'showing the flag' events. One of these in particular is well remembered. Sq Ldr John Whitworth-Jones had been asked to provide RAF participation at an Air Rally organised by the colourful and forthright Brigadier General Arthur Lewin. He farmed hundreds of acres in splendid country high up in the Highlands and he was an avid private pilot using his Miles Hawk two-seater in the way that aircraft should be utilised; regularly he used to take his African cook with him to go shopping for household needs in Nairobi. It was normal to see him going home with items like hams, fresh vegetables, strawberries, soap, tooth-paste, and wine to replenish the cellar.

On the appointed rally day we had prepared a 'maximum effort' of two Valentias and three Gordons. (Supposing a war started, I thought? Most of East African total air power away on a jolly week-end outing!) We took off and got into loose formation appropriate to the two different types of aircraft and climbed steadily in the direction of the General's airstrip at N'joro. The detachment CO was appropriately in the Flight Commander's aeroplane and I tagged along behind. The weather was good with some nice *cumulus* clouds to make the vista a pleasure to see and in due course we arrived overhead at N'joro in a tidy formation. Victor Streatfeild put his Gordons into echelon starboard formation by the usual wing-waggling – no voice radio in those days – and his pilots followed him down to a stream-landing, suitably spaced to suit the small airstrip. Now it was the time for Rudolph Taaffe to bring in his Valentia and I waited my turn. Then it happened – my port engine suddenly decided to quit and there was nothing to it but to lose height with my heavy load of fuel on board for refuelling all the aircraft later on. Fortunately the Valentia was nicely positioned to make a turn cross-wind, and then just scrape in to a satisfactory touch-down on the strip. It is said that a real forced landing comes unexpectedly to a pilot sooner or later and my first and successful one was a singular piece of good luck. After almost coming to a stop, all that I could do was to turn off the air-strip after a fashion onto the long grass and shut down the starboard engine, leaving the strip clear for the CO's Valentia to come in and land. Whilst the fitter began to investigate the engine failure I walked across to the assembly point where the three Gordons and ten light aeroplanes were neatly parked. Truth to tell, I felt quite pleased with myself and Victor (who was an excellent pilot and instructor) gave me a pat on the back.

After Rudolph Taaffe had landed and taxied in to join the other aircraft, the first man out was my esteemed Commander. A finger beckoned me. Ahah, I thought, a nice word of congratulation, perhaps even a mental note to recommend me for the Air Force Cross for flying so skillfully in the face of Providence? But no! Sq Ldr Whitworth-Jones was furious. He demanded an explanation as to why I had had the temerity, the damned nerve, to land before him. My explanation pacified him but even today I suspect that he thought that I was just making a thinly-veiled excuse to protect myself from retribution for a silly act. The engine fault according to my fitter was that another airman had made a nonsense of fitting the split-pin to a bolt in the throttle linkage after an engine change. As a result the split-pin fell out, the bolt worked free and the arm on the carburettor had moved to the 'closed' position. I decided that it was politic not to pursue the matter; under certain circumstance these things sometimes are best forgotten. For myself, I had now been blooded and had made my first (and successful) forced landing on the highest landing ground at 7,200 feet that I had so far experienced.

During the period of detachment of 216 Squadron to Kenya, the Governor of the Crown Colony was Air Chief Marshal Sir Robert Brooke-Popham. He had recently retired from the Royal Air Force after a distinguished career and had been (as has been mentioned earlier) my VIP passenger on the tour of inspection of the Sudan. He was enthusiastic about East Africa and as Governor he was very well liked and respected; so indeed was Lady Brooke-Popham. With the new policy from London under way to proceed with the development of an increased military presence in those parts of Africa under British protection, one item was to create the first-ever RAF airfield in Kenya. Sir Robert wished to have a look at the proposed site. Apart from being a very experienced airman himself from World War One days and post-war service with famous squadrons that he commanded, his deep interest encompassed the whole military planning for East Africa. My Flight Commander Rudolph Taaffe and I were more than happy to accompany him to make the 'Governor's inspection' of the Eastleigh site.

One sunny morning we set off in a convoy of the Governor's car with the two RAF officers leading the way in a Ford *Safari* car. The route took us through an unsightly shanty-town area outside Nairobi where so many Africans eked out a precarious living and soon afterwards we reached the area annotated on our planners' map. It was certainly an improvement on the Wilson Airport location in that many of the essential factors for siting an airfield were good. However Rudolph Taaffe and I had some reservations, not least that it was still a bit too close to high ground. To get the geography and the layout of the new airfield orientated correctly, I remember laying out the Master Plan on the bonnet of Sir Robert's car whilst all three of us checked and made comments like "the hangars will be over there; the single runway will run from those trees to our left to where the ground starts to fall away on the right; this area will be where the domestic accommodation will be constructed" – and so on. It was fascinating to be in at the start of such a big and expensive project. In immediate post war years it was my good friend Dicky Abrahams (the mimic of Heliopolis) who based his Lancaster photographic Squadron Unit there to make a survey of East Africa and thus I could later dispense with Jim Irens' old map of Kenya and wait for some accurate ones based for the very first time upon photographs taken from the air by specialists. No 82 (United Provinces) Photographic Reconnaissance Squadron of Lancasters succeeded in photographing 1,216,000 square miles of East Africa for the Directorate of Colonial Survey. It was a very remarkable and successful undertaking that was never given the acclaim that it merited.

Like all good times, the three months on detachment in Kenya for me had now come to an end. After an interim job of shunting personnel between Khartoum, Cairo and Nairobi, occasioned by 47 Sqdn going to Egypt to collect new Vickers 'Vincents' and the newly formed 223 Sqdn going on to Nairobi with them from Khartoum to replace the 'Gordon' Flight, I flew my Valentia back to Heliopolis. It was nice to be back with my parent unit, but just the same I made a note that if ever a chance came my way to get back to Kenya, I would leap at it.

Before leaving the East African scene, perhaps I could spell out some statistics of aviation interest that will illustrate something of my enthusiasm. In three months, I had taken my aeroplane to twenty-six aerodromes or landing grounds. The highest was N'joro, the private strip in the Kenya Highlands of General Arthur Lewin. It is 7,200 feet above sea level and it is also right on the equator. The most desolate was Wagir which is in the top right hand corner of Kenya close to Ethiopia and Somalia. It is very hot, very dry and featureless. The District Commissioner's headquarters-cum-house looks like nothing so much as a scene from Beau Geste with its dead white walls, its crenellated turrets and the eternal sand. On one occasion when waking at 3 AM after enjoying our amiable host's hospitality – and with a healthy thirst to prove it – to my dismay I found that the tap water was so hot that I could not drink it. Before departure in the morning I was told that I had been elected a life member of the Royal Wagir Yacht Club. However, I have to say that the nearest sailing water is in the Indian Ocean, 300 miles away to the East.

As a pilot I had added one hundred and fifty hours as Captain of aircraft to my log book and the total now stood at almost 700 hours. I was still a Pilot Officer, but hoping for a Flying Officer's thicker stripe before long. It was now 1937, and my pilot's assessment was in the category of 'above the average', and I was twenty-five years old.

Chapter VIII

A Delivery Flight

Before returning to Heliopolis at the end of the excellent detachment to Kenya I met a Frenchman in the Aero Club. He was a tall and amiable fellow; his name was Gabriel Prudhomme, and he told me that he had come to Kenya because he had an interest in a gold mine. Rumour however had it that he had left France under a cloud because had been so indiscreet as to steal his papa's mistress! We got into conversation and I mentioned that I was a pilot in the Royal Air Force on temporary duty in Kenya but expected to return to Egypt in a few days. I envied his good fortune in being able to live in Kenya, a country that I had learned to know and like very much. He fully agreed with my sentiments; he had made many friends in Nairobi and with up-country settlers as well. In every way it was very much to his liking. During our talk about aviation and life in East Africa he suddenly said "I wonder if you would be interested in delivering my aeroplane to me? It is at Cairo Airport." As Almaza was close to Heliopolis it was an attractive proposal worth further investigation and the questions that naturally followed were all about his suggestion. Monsieur Prudhomme's aeroplane was one of the latest types being manufactured in England and it was called a Percival Speed-Six Gull. He had recently purchased it and had flown it to Cairo en route to Nairobi where he stayed for one or two days with friends. It seems that they were so hospitable that the luncheon party on the last day went on for so long that when he eventually departed it was in the late afternoon. By the time that he had reached Aswan, 400 miles to the South, it was getting dark and on touchdown the Gull swung badly with the result that the undercarriage collapsed. He had to abandon the aeroplane, return by train to Cairo, and then fly by Imperial Airways to Nairobi. My French friend told me that the Gull had been taken to Cairo by the Shell Company and was now repaired. The problem was that his business activities prevented him from returning to Cairo so he was looking for a pilot to deliver the Gull for him. As I was going back to Cairo soon and knew the route he thought that I might care to do the job. The idea appealed to me so much that we discussed the proposal in detail. The only difficulty as I saw it was to get leave of absence from 216 Sqdn coupled with how to get back to Heliopolis after the Gull had been delivered. The second obstacle was resolved by Prudhomme who said that he would be glad to pay my airfare for the return journey plus my expenses in transit so the whole trip would cost me nothing. It was such an attractive proposal that I promised that I would do my best to carry it out.

The first move was to seek the blessing of Wing Commander Gardiner. As he was an enthusiastic pilot he thoroughly approved of the plan and said that he would give me leave to do the job. The essential prerequisites of the project were now so favourable that I moved on to the practical aspects which were to visit the Shell Company in Cairo and then go to Almaza and have a look at the new aeroplane. The last item of course was the one that I looked forward to most of all. A visit to the Shell Aviation Department, people housed in handsome offices in Cairo, needed no preliminary explanation from me as they had already heard from Prudhomme and were waiting for my call. All the administration aspects were dealt with and I was issued with a Shell *Carnet de passage* – a document which in effect put me under the umbrella of the famous oil company for virtually anything that I needed on my journey. This remarkable facility ensured that anywhere that a pilot travelled he could depend on help, cooperation, even financial assistance if necessary, from the Shell organisation. The system provided that if a pilot landed at some remote spot – like any of the many landing strips in Africa – he could refuel the aeroplane himself from the stock in the Shell hut and sign for it in the book before taking off again. It must have cost a fortune to organise, both for the RAF and civil aircraft, but without it the probability is that in those days aviation would have been severely handicapped. It should be remembered that as the majority of aeroplanes in the nineteen-thirties had at best a maximum range of some five hundred miles it was necessary to have refuelling stops on most of the routes outside Europe. All too often a day's run would include at least one landing somewhere en route – requirement that the modern air traveller does not experience. Today, in many ways it has taken away a lot of the fascination of travel. The new way to go is to journey, so to speak, from one Hilton hotel to the next. It may be quick, but it is also very boring. I always think that the earlier days of air travel were really interesting because one got the feeling of getting to know so much more of new countries. By contrast, flying non-stop from London to Capetown completely misses out the whole of Africa. What can people know of that huge continent as a result?

After the visit to the Shell people I went to Almaza aerodrome to have a look at the Gull. In the nineteen thirties Almaza was not only the main base for the Royal Egyptian Air Force (equipped with the Hawker 'Audax' with 'Panther' radial air-cooled engines), it was also the civil airport for Cairo.

Almaza was also the location for the Royal Egyptian Aero Club together with all manner of aeroplanes either based there or in transit. Thus it was a well-used aerodrome and as busy an aviation centre as one could find in the whole of the Middle East.

I called on the Aero Club's Chief Flying Instructor and that popular Egyptian took me to the hangar where the Gull was stored and looking somewhat forlorn with a layer of dust covering it. After gazing at its general appearance (which was very handsome) I noted that it had the British registration letters of G-ADEU. I could not resist the thought that I was glad it was not G-ADIEU – that might be pushing my luck somewhat!! The Gull had been repaired by the Aero Club engineers with spare parts flown out from the UK, and it had been left in the hangar awaiting instructions from the owner. After inspection of the Gull, including getting in and having a look around the cockpit, I suggested that it should be given a clean up, the battery re-charged, and then prepared for a test flight on the following day. As planned, I returned to Almaza for that purpose. This time the Gull was looking much more presentable after a good spring clean and it was now outside on the apron and so much easier to walk around and admire its general appearance. The designer-constructor was an Australian called Edgar Percival who had established his business at Gravesend initially and then moved to Luton where 'ADEU' was probably constructed. Earlier variants of the Gull had been fitted with smaller engines but the D.3. – as it was designated – was fitted with the new 200 hp. de Havilland Gipsy Six. As the latest version (of which nineteen only were made) was faster than most RAF fighters of the day it was natural for it to be given the name Speed Six. There is no doubt that Edgar Percival, (a talented designer-pilot who always flew wearing a trilby hat) was ahead of his contemporaries. The Speed Six had a top speed of 180 mph and sold in 1937 for about £1,500. It was a handsome three-seater low-wing monoplane with two streamlined undercarriage legs and the cowled-in-wheels were fitted with brakes. The de Havilland six-cylinder inverted engine was neatly enclosed by a slim cowling and the Fairey Reed metal propeller had a spinner that gave the nose a racy look. The cockpit was entered by a side door, just like a motor car, and the pilot sat slightly to the left-hand side with a handy map shelf alongside on his right. The only minor criticism was that the view ahead with the tail down was adequate but not good and this was to be a situation – as subsequently with the Spitfire – that pilots had to get used to and develop an expertise, especially when taxying. The Gull – an all wooden aeroplane – was fitted with a landing light, cockpit lights, instruments for blind flying, and a self-starter unit for the engine. The general lines were good and nicely balanced, giving the impression of speed and easy handling qualities. Although there were no 'pilot's notes' in those days it did not worry me too much because I was in good flying practise and the essential need-to-know data was straightforward. One missing item that I decided to make provision for was to arrange for a specialised aircraft tool-kit; it was something that I was not to know at the time would be vital during the journey to Nairobi. Even if a private pilot does not know how to use them – or even what needs to be done – a specialised tool kit is highly desirable for others to use.

After another look around the Gull I decided to test the engine. Using the self-starter – a new innovation in my experience – the 'Six' started up with no problems at all despite that it had not been in use for many weeks. It ran very smoothly with a nice deep note and at full throttle it was healthy and showed the normal small drop in rpm on each magneto. It was now late afternoon and I decided that I would return later and make a test flight and practise some landings before starting out on the 3000 mile journey to East Africa. I sent off a message to Luxor advising my passenger-to-be when to expect me. She was a Parisienne friend of Gabriel Prudhomme by name of Suzanne Calmettes who had intended to fly to Kenya by Imperial Airways but the weekly flights were well booked up and rather than wait she was offered a seat in the Gull.

On February 15th, 1937, after two satisfactory test flights I took off in the early morning for Luxor to collect my passenger. The route was all too familiar and as I flew along the 350 mile run with the Nile in sight all the way I was delighted to find that the Gull was making a ground speed of 160 mph. This was almost twice the speed of anything before in my piloting experience, so the contrast was marked. At this speed and with increased range the normal Valentia itinerary should be halved, other things being equal. After landing at Luxor I taxied across the sand and I could see my passenger waiting for me; she was accompanied by a friend called Mario Guichard who had come to see her safely off in the small machine. After the mutual introductions the conversation during refuelling put a certain strain on my school-boy French. However, what better way to get some practice than when one has no choice? The need to communicate soon breaks down language barriers and it is surprising how inhibitions are set aside. The refuelling had now been completed and my passenger's luggage was stowed away safely. We had been on the ground for less than an hour before the Gipsy Six was started up and the Gull was taxied out, placed into wind, and we took off from Luxor for the next stage to Wadi Halfa. This was an uneventful flight, overflying Aswan, where the dam in recent times had been modified to provide the huge Lake Nasser that now stretches all the way upstream for some 200 miles. The landing at Wadi Halfa in the cool afternoon air of winter was accomplished safely and by now I was getting the measure of the tendency of modern low-wing monoplanes like the Gull to swing after touchdown. Wadi Halfa in summer has landing problems of its own because the flat and featureless sandy aerodrome has a heat-shimmer above it that makes a judgement of height difficult to get right. With only a wind sock and the small Shell fuel storage hut by which to give guidance, the safe method was to make a careful 'wheely' touchdown and so 'feel' for the ground.

Although by accepted standards the Nile Hotel was not exactly even in the 'one star' category, it was quiet and peaceful and so nice to look out onto the broad river in the early evening. The river boats that were berthed nearby, collecting or despatching their passengers at the point where the Sudan Railway system terminates, adds to the colourful scene and there was always something of interest going on, not least when one of the Imperial Airways flying boats alighted on the river.

Dinner with the charming Suzanne gave me increased fluency in French and she pleased me by saying that travel in the Gull was much better than she had expected; so the first stage of the journey must have been satisfactory to her and I confess it was good news for me. It is always a worry to find that a person that you have only just met is a poor passenger in a small aeroplane. What does one do under those circumstances, I wondered, especially on a long journey?

In the morning, with only a direct flight to Khartoum to deal with we had breakfast at leisure, collected our overnight luggage and got a lift back to the aerodrome. We took off soon after 10 o'clock and headed across the desert to Atbara, the railway line providing a visual guide as well as a safety factor in case of a forced landing. In later years some new pilots some-how contrived to lose themselves to the extent that the Sudan Government prescribed that small single-engined aeroplanes had to wait until an escort was in transit for the 500 mile journey to Khartoum. Admittedly the route looks daunting from the air with only a vast wilderness of sand to be seen, but keeping the thin line of the railway in sight as far as Atbara and then following the Nile to Khartoum is straight-forward enough.

The Gull was throttled back suitably to give good range and it took us almost four-and-a-half hours to make the non-stop flight to Khartoum; it was the first time that I had been able to fly so far in one hop. At 5,000 feet we encountered a few turbulent patches – the usual problem when flying over the northern Sudan at most times of the year – but Suzanne never turned a hair and after that long flight both of us were glad to get our feet on the ground. Suzanne was taken to the Grand Hotel and I stayed with my RAF friends of No 47 Squadron thereby saving Gabriel Prudhomme undue expense. We ferry pilots are caring people! In the morning, after the beautiful Gull had been serviced by RAF personnel we took off from Khartoum to continue the journey south and once again we were able to leap-frog by overflying the small landing strip at Kosti and press on across the Upper Nile Province towards Malakal, 450 miles away. The Gull was now blessed with a light following wind and we were making a ground speed of 170 mph. All the familiar scenes of the change from desert to green, giving the impression that the 'real Africa' was about to unfold below us was as exciting and interesting as ever. We could see the thorn trees, the clumps of coarse grass, the wisps of smoke rising up from small clusters of grass huts, and a few cattle with attendant owners. Suzanne was now taking much more interest as there was something to see at last and I gave a commentary in my ever-improving French. Everything seemed to be going well and I was by now getting the feeling of being a private owner of a fast aeroplane on an African journey.

Alas! The notion that all was well was soon to be banished; when making one of the periodic checks of the twin magnetos, to my dismay the engine faded. Rapidly I switched on the other one and the engine resumed power again. These happenings certainly do spring nasty surprises on pilots when least expected and cause the heart-beat to falter alarmingly. With the engine now throttled back slightly, a move that was more psychological than technical but it does calm the nerves to some extent, we flew on towards Malakal. Every possible forced landing area was carefully noted as we flew past them and then subsequent ones ahead earmarked in similar fashion. These occasions call for maximum concentration on the job in hand and acute awareness sharpens the reactions. The final twenty minutes flying before we reached Malakal seemed to drag interminably and I was very thankful at last to put the Gull's wheels down onto the small airstrip, taxi to a suitable parking spot, and switch off the engine. A desolate place like Malakal, normally abandoned for days on end until the next aeroplane arrives, is a much better proposition than somewhere in the bush. It was now early afternoon, and I told Suzanne that we could not go on because *un de les deux magnetos et en panne* but I doubted that she understood a word of my technical French! Truth to tell, although I knew the symptoms I was by no means sure that I knew the cure. Circumstances invariably generates untapped reserves so I sat under the wing to think out what I should do and how to set about doing it.

It is a strange feeling to be in a remote place with a technical problem to solve and limited practical experience to fall back on; so I lit a cigarette and tried to work out a plan of action. It was better to try to do something rather than have a miserable time waiting patiently for the next aeroplane to arrive and rescue us, so the amateur aero-engine fitter got down to work. The engine cowlings were undone and a check carried out to see if there was anything obviously wrong like loose wires to the spark-plugs from the unserviceable magneto. Everything appeared to be in order except that the tell-tale set of cool plugs now gave a clue; the fault was probably somewhere in or close to the dud magneto so this narrowed the search. Unfortunately they were positioned on top of the crank-case and so not readily accessible except by the use of steps. This snag was overcome by borrowing Suzanne's stout suitcase, and standing rather precariously on it in the upended position the fixed cowling along the top of the engine was then removed so that I could get a proper sighting of the installation. With such makeshift facilities, to say nothing of inexperience, the process took time to accomplish. Eventually the magnetos were accessible and the wiring from them was checked and found to be secure. The next task was to attempt magneto inspection and that needed another set of the spanners that I had taken the trouble to obtain in Almaza. The first job – and I sincerely hoped the only one! – was to check the contact breakers for the correct gap and in order to do this I needed a helper to turn the propellor whilst I was balancing on the suitcase to see what was happening. Suzanne was much too small in stature to help and anyway it was likely that the sharp edge of the metal propellor blade was a deterrent for feminine hands.

The answer to my prayer for help came from an unexpected source; a very tall African fellow was walking past and he was carrying an old peach tin to get water from the river. He was impeccably dressed in the manner of his *Nuer* tribe, naked but for some beads around his neck and his only other possession was his long spear. To say that these *Nuer*s are well endowed by nature is really an understatement – Suzanne gazed in wonderment if not in admiration. The game now was to wave to my African in friendly fashion and beckon him to us. That accomplished, I somehow persuaded him by sign language and demonstration to turn the propellor in small movements every time I said something that sounded like *poli*, the Swahili for 'slow'. It was not his language but it worked, and we began to work together very well. With the contact-breaker visible after the cover had been removed I could see the cam turning with every movement, so that part was functioning. When the moment came for the cam to open the points, thus enabling high tension current to reach the spark plugs, to my surprise there was a click and a whirring noise and the thing spun round rapidly. Oh dear, what was this? I got down off the suitcase and began the mental process of trying to figure out what was happening. After some reflection I remembered that Gipsy engines had what is called an impulse starter. This is a spring-loaded affair that holds the magneto mechanism back and then suddenly rotates it briskly at the right moment to give it a chance to produce a fat spark for starting up, after which the device disengages for normal operation. It took me some time to appreciate that the only possible way to check the contact breaker points was to turn the engine backwards; sometimes one learns these things from sheer necessity! My African helper and I now began the process all over again with the propellor turning backwards and to my astonishment I discovered that the points did not open at all. No wonder the magneto was not delivering high voltage current to the spark plugs! At least I had traced the cause, and that was more than half-way to the cure. I set the gap at fourteen-thousandths of an inch and hoped that this was somewhere near the correct figure. Whilst the cowlings were still off it was prudent to repeat the inspection of the 'good' magneto. We carried out the same propellor-turning business all over again and by now my *Nuer* friend and I had become an admirable team and we were working at twice the speed. The check of the second set of points revealed an equally disturbing situation. At maximum gap I was appalled to find it was just one-thousandths of an inch and it was obvious that the second magneto could not have worked for much longer. We must have been within a whisker of total engine failure and it was not a happy thought. Sufficient for the moment to re-set the gap and when the job was done I put everything together again and then the two workers sat down side-by-side to enjoy a well-earned cigarette.

I do not know what I would have done without him. It was now late into the afternoon, I was tired and I needed a rest. All this time Suzanne sat quietly under the wing with nothing to do but watch the unusual sight of one Englishman and one naked African working together in great harmony. The only practical way that I could show my appreciation was to give him the packet of cigarettes and he happily went on his way to the river.

The next move should normally have been to try to start the engine and check both magnetos for correct functioning. However, a truck appeared seemingly from nowhere and as the driver indicated that he could take us to a Government rest house nearby I accepted willingly – I had had enough. Suzanne and I took our overnight kit, made the Gull as safe from the elements as possible and left the airstrip. We were surprised to see on arrival a bungalow by the river that presumably was intended for the District Commissioner's use or possibly even for people like ourselves; either way it looked for all the world like the Grand Hotel! The two Sudanese who looked after it made us very welcome, prepared food for dinner, and the tired travellers were given rooms for an overnight stop. It had been a long day and I was very glad that I had remembered to bring some whisky along from my emergency bag. It tasted damned good and I hoped that it would keep the mosquitoes away.

After a good night's sleep we had an early breakfast, Sudan style, and were driven back to the airstrip. The first job was to see if by good fortune the two magnetos were going to function but although naturally a little apprehensive I had a feeling of optimism. I stowed the gear in the Gull, left the stones in front of the wheels in case the aeroplane rolled forward, and using my tie to hold the control column well back, everything was ready for a hand swing of the propellor to avoid draining the battery. With a rag to protect my hand and a propellor blade at a good angle of purchase I gave it a swing and to my astonishment the engine started up immediately. I could not have been more surprised. I got into the cockpit quickly and set the throttle to fast idle for a short time before increasing the engine speed and testing each magneto in turn. All was well; all was very well. Both were working.

It is difficult to describe one's reactions in a situation when a technical job by an amateur under primitive conditions in a remote place proves successful. Without further ado we got ready to go by removing the stones and my patient and even-tempered lady passenger got on board and we taxied out for take off. A second engine test was made on the strip, all was well with the magnetoes and away we went at exactly 7.30 AM I made a third engine check over the airstrip before heading south for 320 miles across the Sud to Juba, the southern-most point of the Sudan. We were now a day late in our itinerary, the Gipsy engine was running well and the African gods must have been pleased because with a good following wind we were really motoring. My log book has an entry that reads with laconic brevity, 'Magneto trouble; remained overnight; ground speed Malakal-Kongor 202 mph!' It should have been written in red ink because it was the first time that I had broken the 200 mile barrier and it was also the first time that I had attempted serious work on an aeroplane engine. The fast run to Juba got us there before 10 o'clock and whilst refuelling I asked Suzanne if she would like to stay for the rest of the day or go on to Kisumu and possibly to Nairobi as well. She smiled sweetly and said that if I was happy to fly on, so was she. It was apparent that both of us wanted to complete the journey as planned and I admired her resolution. She really was a splendid passenger.

We now had only one more stop to make at Kisumu on the northern shore of Lake Victoria before the final flight to Nairobi. As we travelled across Uganda I pointed out Nimule, Lira (where the Valentias refuelled), the area on our right hand side where the White Nile begins after leaving Lake Albert, and the 14,000 ft Mount Elgon to our left. The scenery was now what I call proper Africa and we crossed the equator just before arriving at Kisumu. This pleasant small town is in Kenya, so we were now in the right country and as we flew round the grass aerodrome before landing I saw a small posse of cars making their way to meet us. I recognised the Shell company's car and the agent came forward briskly even before we had time to get out of the aeroplane. "I can refuel you in fifteen minutes", he called out "Will that be alright?" The extra fast service surprised me and I thanked him but added that we would prefer to stop for a rest and a meal in the town hotel; could he give us a lift? The chap looked quite astonished and replied "But what about the record flight to the Cape?" It was a case of mistaken identity; he and the other people assumed that I was a famous airman called Llewellyn who in fact was expected to arrive any day and the confusion arose because he had the same type of aeroplane. I explained that I was only on a delivery fight to Nairobi but I was very flattered to have been taken for one of Britain's ace flyers.

We had lunch with the Shell representative and he took us back to the aerodrome for our final leg of the long journey. The Gipsy Six engine started up right away and after getting airborne we began the fast climb to clear the high ground in the Highlands of Kenya. As we flew along I pointed out to Suzanne all the beautiful sights of the forest areas, the grassy plains, the lakes, the farms, the African villages with their shambas – grass huts – and the smoke from their domestic fires. The panorama was enhanced by beautiful white cumulus clouds which we flew around to maintain visual contact with the high ground. It was good to see Kenya again, and the Gull's speed enabled us to get to Nairobi in ninety minutes, thus making an average speed of 130 mph. Bearing in mind the need to climb up to 9,000 feet this was very satisfactory. As we made a circuit of Wilson airport in some style to suit the occasion we could see a good gathering of people outside the Aero Club and the final landing was one to be pleased about. By now I had become an experienced Speed Six Gull pilot and I wanted the spectators to know it!

The delivery flight in the event was completed on schedule and Gabriel Prudhomme and his party of friends were there in force to meet us. With Gallic enthusiasm he greeted Suzanne and congratulated me on the timing and the safe delivery of his beautiful aeroplane. Whilst a whole lot of animated chatter was going on the travellers were given glasses of champagne and we joined everybody in the celebration. It is a charming custom that I commend in every way! I told Gabriel that I strongly advised no more flying until the engine had been professionally inspected but he insisted on making a short flight. After he landed I made sure that the Gull was pushed into a hangar and asked the Chief Engineer Archie Watkins to immobilise it. The experienced technician took charge and promised to make a thorough inspection right away. What he discovered after stripping down the magnetos was unbelievable – the wiring on the ill-fitting rotating armatures had lost the protective shellac and the copper was burnished bright by rubbing inside the casing; it was impossible to understand how they could have operated in the circumstance. The incorrect contact-breaker settings similarly were a mystery and Archie concluded that the dry Egyptian air had shrunk the Tufnol pads and they could not have been checked since the crash at Aswan. We had been amazingly lucky since all the evidence indicated that complete engine failure should have occurred at any time.

Lunch on the following day at the New Stanley Hotel gave me an opportunity to discuss with Gabriel all the details of the delivery flight, the engine trouble at Malakal that caused the overnight stop at the small rest house, the exciting speed made good across the Sudd, and the long run to Nairobi on the fourth day to make up lost time. The day's flying time Malakal-Nairobi had been just over seven hours and I gave full marks to Suzanne who had been such a good passenger. The total flying in the Gull had been twenty-two hours, including the two test flights at Almaza. The expense account that I showed him produced expressions of complete incredulity – he just could not believe that it was so small. "Surely you must have had more expenses? What about the aperitifs, the wines, the cognacs and perhaps a cigar? The hotel bills alone would have been double!" I assured him that it was not so and anyway the night in Khartoum with the RAF cost nothing. I resisted the temptation of telling

Top: The author test flying Gordon Light's model, 1933

Centre: The author on Wimbledon Common, 1929

Bottom: A meeting of the Society of Model Aeronautical Engineers (SMAE) on Wimbledon Common, 1928 *(Noel Baker)*

Left: Lord Brownlow's garden at Belton Park. The author with the impresario, Gilbert Miller, and Mrs Condé Nast, 1935
Right: A Royal Navy Shark of 820 Sqn at RAF Heliopolis, 1935

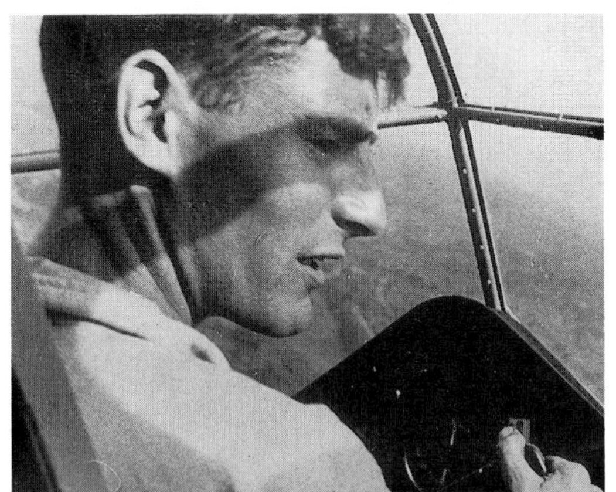

Dick Wrightson flying the DH84 Dragon from Heston, 1934

P/O Campbell-Voulaire and the author outside the Mess at RAF Heliopolis, Cairo, 1935

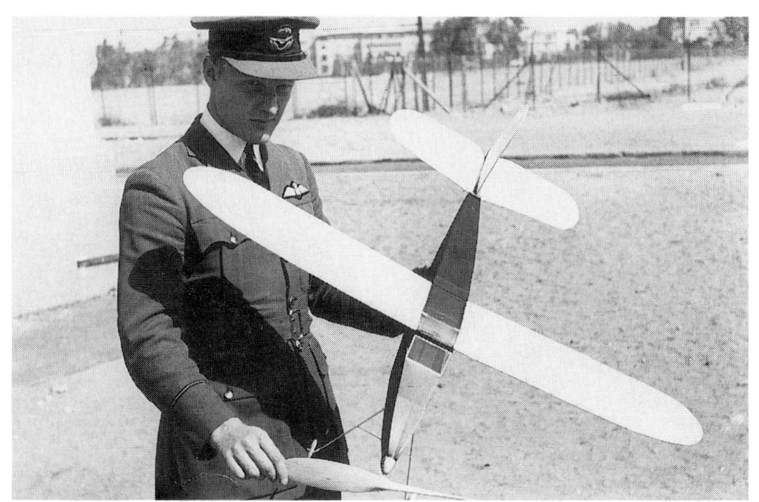

Top: The author continued his model making in Egypt, 1935 *(Grant Lindeman)*
Centre: Canadian pilot 'Moose' Fulton and Philip Mackworth sailing on the Nile, June 1936 *(Grant Lindeman)*
Below: Vickers Valentia of 216 Sqn, 1936 *(Grant Lindeman)*

Anthony Tinne and the author sailing on the Nile, 1936 *(Grant Lindeman)*

Jean Brook drives her golf ball from the top of the Great Pyramid, March 1938

The author's brother, Arthur, tees-up for his wager winning drive, March 1938

AOC Palestine, Air Commodore Arthur Harris on duty

Top: An Army-Air Exercise in the Hebron Hills, 1938. *(l to r)* Bert Harris, W/Cdr. Addison, Capt. Tony Crossley, Brig. Tidbury and Col. Thornton

Centre: The GOC Palestine, Gen. Sir Robert Haining inspects No. 33 Sqn at Lydda. *(l to r)* Capt. Crossley, ADC, F/Lt Cooke, W/Cdr Sanderson, the GOC, Bert Harris and F/Lt Bennett, 1939

Bottom: Air Commodore Arthur Harris inspecting a 33 Sqn Gladiator at Lydda, Palestine, 1939

AOC Palestine, Air Commodore Arthur Harris off duty

Above: Fishing party, Gulf of Aqaba, March 1939. *(l to r)* Col. John Chrystall, Jill Harris, Mrs Chrystall, Clarence Buxton, Lady Haining, Bert Harris

Centre: Bert Harris, now Air Vice-Marshal, with his daughter Jackie, late 1941

Below: Bert Harris relaxing in the Dead Sea, March 1939

No. 233 Sqn Wellesleys in flight over Khartoum, 1940 (formation flying was not practised very much!)

The author as OC No. 47 Sqn at Khartoum, 1940

Emperor Haile Selassie of Ethiopia visiting RAF units at Khartoum, September 1940, with F/Lt Joe Lynch and, with his arm in a sling, F/O Robinson of 47 Sqn

F/O Collis' Wellesley about to take Brig. Sandford and Major Orde Wingate from Ethiopia to Khartoum, 1941 *(R Collis)*

him that compared to his admitted income from his wealthy father of what he called a pittance of £400 per month, my Air Force pay was thirty pounds.

A few happy days were spent in Nairobi before I was due to fly back to Egypt by Imperial Airways from Entebbe and I was lucky to get a lift in Alec Noon's 'Puss Moth' when he was making the mail run. We arrived at Entebbe in good time to see the big Handley Page 'Hengist', registration G-AAXE on the aerodrome and I joined the other passengers for the scheduled flight to Khartoum and beyond. Although I had seen these extraordinary aeroplanes before at Croydon, this was my first opportunity of travelling in one and by chance I happened to know the two pilots. After the majestic take-off which felt like an enormous four-engined Valentia, Captain Paddy Woodhouse and First Officer Johnny Johnson flew across Uganda towards the Sudan. One passenger who I recognised was the Earl of Erroll who two years later was to become the victim of a sensational Kenya murder case in which Sir Delves Broughton was accused of killing him but was acquitted. The sordid affair highlighted to the world the life-style of the 'Happy Valley' set in Kenya and thus became a heaven-sent opportunity for the gossip columns of the media eager for this kind of sensational material. 'Hengist' was now approaching the Sudan and as we settled down in the cabin for morning coffee Captain Woodhouse came aft for the usual Captain's public relations chat with the passengers and for me a big surprise because he invited me to the flight deck. No sooner had I taken up the offer than I was asked if I would care to fly the aeroplane and for the first time in my life I was sitting in the Captain's seat of a HP42 and trying my hand at a 'giant airliner'. Visible from my window were the massive struts connecting the huge wings together with the four sets of wooden propellors driving us along; optimistically I had thoughts of four gold stripes on my sleeve to replace the thin Pilot Officer's ribbon of the RAF. The big aeroplane lumbered along and was very cumbersome to fly compared to the speedy Gull. When checking the instruments I noticed that the air speed recorded seemed to be too low and I concluded that as a little more power was required I eased the four throttle levers gently forward. Captain Woodhouse was standing just behind me drinking his coffee and said "What are you doing, fiddling with the power settings?; leave them as they are". I explained that all I was trying to do was to get what I estimated to be the correct cruising airspeed. "The aeroplane flies just the way it is Pelly, so for heaven's sake leave the dam thing alone". The pride of British civil aviation, flying majestically at four-thousand feet over Africa, was showing an indicated airspeed of seventy-eight miles per hour.

Chapter IX

The Spice of Life

After the East African travels and adventures had ended with that fast run to Nairobi in the 'Gull' I was now back at Heliopolis with the Transport Drivers Union. The next eighteen months were devoted to all manner of fetching-and-carrying in Egypt and sorties across the Suez Canal to Palestine and Transjordan. The destinations and the loads carried were typical of the varied work carried out by 216 Squadron. We were transporting sports teams; Senior Army Officers on reconnaissance into the desert; making inspections of landing grounds; moving personnel on posting; collecting aircraft spares from the RAF Depot at Aboukir; Army-Air exercises in the desert, and we participated in the May 1937 Royal Coronation Day Fly-Past over the Gezirah Sporting Club in Cairo. I had become a Squadron Flying Instructor and had been promoted to Flying Officer; a lieutenant in army language.

Some of the jobs were routine but some certainly were not and such variation in an air transport pilot's work made it all the more interesting. The nature of the task not only entailed travelling far and wide, it also brought with it much more flying than was normally enjoyed by other RAF pilots. In 216 Sqdn it was not unusual to put in 50 hours per month, twice as much flying as in other squadrons.

When Piloting Captain Harold Balfour (later Lord Balfour of Inchrye), His Majesty's Secretary of State for Air on an official tour of the Middle East, one tedious stage from Alexandria to RAF Ramleh (near Tel Aviv) prompted him to ask how much longer it would be before we arrived; he had every reason to complain because the going was slow and bumpy and it seemed even to me to be interminably long. "Sir", I replied, "If you will give us a faster aeroplane we will all be delighted and your discomfort will be reduced accordingly". There is nothing like a captive audience in cases like this but the reality is that nothing much of consequence happens afterwards.

There was the curious affair of the Baron von Sthorer. He was the

German Ambassador in Cairo and an avid desert adventurer who used to participate in the annual car race from the Pyramids at Gizeh to the *oasis* of Bahahariya; It was a popular if mildy hazardous hobby that lasted a few days. On this occasion the *Khamseen* (the forty-day wind so named after the Arabic number) had started earlier than expected but the organisers decided to keep to the timetable and all the competitors pressed on although most of them abandoned the race in the early stages rather than drive across the desert in a bad sandstorm. Not so the intrepid Baron and not surprisingly he was declared missing by the end of the second day. Whilst the worst of the winds were abating and the visibility had improved in consequence, a search was instigated and the Royal Air Force was one of the organisations galvanised into action. Three squadrons and extra aircraft from No 4 FTS were also diverted from their normal training activities to join in the search for one Ambassador and his mechanic. I cannot now but smile when I relate that His Excellency's mechanic was Jewish! After five days of searching, when dozens of aircraft had combed the desert from dawn to dusk, the bold Baron and his assistant were found by a Valentia of 216 Sqdn flown by Flying Officer Dicky Richardson and soon after Squadron Leader Philip Mackworth landed and picked up the two men. I could almost hear him saying "Just the usual 216 Sqdn Service, your Excellency!"

Very shortly afterwards the adjutant received a message to say that the Ambassador was so very grateful for the efficient rescue that he would be pleased to entertain the squadron pilots who had participated. Would they please meet him at Finnish's Restaurant in Cairo? It was a good gesture, but surely there was somewhere better than this small establishment for an Ambassador to chose? Perhaps Shepherds Hotel was more in keeping with his status? The reality proved to be a complete anti-climax because on the appointed day a telephone call from the German Embassy cancelled the dinner 'with regret'. We all wondered just what had caused this *volte face*? A message from Berlin, perhaps?

In September 1937, I was summoned to RAF Headquarters in Cairo to report to the Senior Air Staff Officer, Wg Cdr Lawson, and on arrival he told me that I had an important job to do. It was to make an air reconnaissance from Port Said to Suez and the reason was to select suitable sites for aerodromes to be constructed along the west bank of the Canal. I could make my own arrangements but the whole business was to be regarded as very confidential and he produced a large strip map for my use that was mounted on thick card and covered the area in question. I could use any type of aeroplane and I could land anywhere as I wished if it helped in the task. When I asked him if I really did have a free hand he replied "Yes; if you break the aeroplane – well, that's alright too".

I decided to use the trusty Avro 'Tutor'. It could be put down almost anywhere and to help in the reconnaissance I asked Jim Irens to come with me because if he sat in the back seat – all sixteen stone of him – his weight would help keep the tail down if we ran into any soft patches. We finished the job in three hours flying, annotated all the good spots including four landings for closer inspection, and I returned the long strip of map to the Wing Commander. Before leaving him I said "I thoroughly enjoyed the job, Sir; it's not often that I get some really free-lance flying like that with complete freedom to do as I pleased. As a matter of interest, what is it all in aid of?" He gave me an enigmatic smile. "Pelly, a valuable job of work has been done on instructions from high up". So I was no wiser.

In due course the secret was revealed; all the best sites that Jim Irens and I had marked on the map became war-time aerodromes along the Suez Canal and names like Fayid, Geneifa and Shallufa will be all too familiar to the Forces who were stationed there during the Hitler War. The Planners in London had been making preparations at least two years before World War Two started.

In early 1938, when sanctions were being imposed by Britain on Mussolini in an attempt to cure his ever-increasing ambitions in Ethiopia, Admiral Sir Andrew Cunningham, Commander-in-Chief Mediterranean Fleet made a number of visits to Cairo to see the Ambassador Sir Miles Lampson, later to become Lord Killearn. I had now become one of the senior pilots in 216 Sqdn and the task was to go to RAF Aboukir, pick up the Admiral, fly him to Heliopolis, and later in the day ferry him back to rejoin his flagship in Alexandria harbour. During one of his visits to Cairo a message came to say that he would be late for the return flight because of the unusually long conference. A warning radio message therefore was sent to RAF Aboukir to say that a night landing was probably going to be made. I took off so late from Heliopolis that the sun set soon afterwards and in the moonlight huge cumulus and cumulo-nimbus clouds could now be seen ahead, something that the weather men had not briefed me about. We pressed on; torrential rain and very strong winds were encountered such that the Valentia behaved more like a lifeboat in a heavy sea than anything else. When we got to Aboukir, all that I could see by moonlight was a flooded area with all the palm trees in the plantation nearby bending alarmingly in the wind. Figures in the darkness could now be seen lighting the paraffin-burning Money Flares (used in those days to mark out the 'Tee' of a flarepath) but whoever was in charge clearly did not know the procedure because the flares were being laid in haphazard manner all around the perimeter. However the wind direction and strength was painfully obvious so I motored the aircraft into the correct flight path, flew crazily over the swaying palm trees and landed with a big splash. Fortunately the sand was firm and I taxied in very slowly onto the tarmac where I beckoned to the driver of the C-in-C's car to move closer so the Admiral could get in quickly. Standing in the downpour to bid him farewell I asked him if he needed me for another visit to Cairo so that I could make the necessary arrangements. The Admiral gave me a look of pained surprise, shook his head firmly and said, "Thank you Pelly-Fry; I think I will go by train in future". Thus I lost my favourite client.

Another VIP passenger – and a very charming one – was occasioned by a bit of good fortune. One day Wg Cdr Joe Gardiner asked me if my private pilot's licence was still valid, and the answer was a positive 'yes'. "Well, that's a bit of luck. I have just had a call from the Embassy asking me if I have a pilot who can fly Lady Lampson to Mersa Matruh".

By way of a preamble, in pre-war days the Air Ministry had an inflexible rule that other than women in uniform (like nursing sisters) no other feminine passengers were allowed to fly in RAF aircraft; not even the wife of the British Ambassador! Sir Miles Lampson, our impressive envoy (both in ability and stature as he was well over six feet tall) had occasion to make an official visit to the Western Desert. Lady Lampson was the diminutive daughter of *Signor* Aldo Castellani, the Italian surgeon of international repute, and understandably she wished to accompany her husband. To her great chagrin the C-in-C was obliged to say that this was unfortunately impossible in an RAF aeroplane. Forceful Italian lady that she was, she declared that she would go anyway but in a private aeroplane; and as I was the only Service pilot available with a civil pilots licence I was given the job. I hired a de Havilland Hornet Moth (DH87) from the Aero Club at Almaza; it was a two-seater, side-by-side biplane and powered with the reliable Gipsy Major four-cylinder inverted air-cooled engine.

On the appointed day, having previously ferried the Hornet Moth from Almaza to Heliopolis, the neat private aeroplane was parked alongside the three RAF Vincent aircraft and the Station Commander and his team awaited the arrival of the distinguished passengers. The Ambassadorial Rolls Royce appeared and Sir Miles and Lady Lampson prepared to leave and my passenger got into the Hornet Moth. She turned to me and said, "This is much more civilised than that draughty old thing my husband has to fly in!" Three Vincents took off, the Hornet Moth was airborne immediately after, and the formation set off in a north-westerly direction for Mersa Matruh. The three Vincents with big Pegasus engines rumbled along at about 110 mph and at the same time our neat little Hornet Moth with 130 hp only was keeping up with them without any trouble at all. Whilst His Excellency had to withstand the noise and the slipstream in the rear cockpit of his aeroplane, my charming passenger and I sat in cosy comfort drinking coffee en route and could converse at will. It was a very pleasant run to Mersa Matruh and after an overnight stop in the small hotel alongside the lagoon all four aeroplanes returned to Heliopolis in good order and I flew later to Almaza to return the Hornet Moth. It was another type to record in my log book and another VIP passenger to remember with nostalgia.

On another occasion, when flying back to Heliopolis with a leave party from Khartoum we made a night stop at Aswan. The next day in the cool early morning I saw parked nearby a de Havilland DH 90 'Dragonfly', a four-seater cabin bi-plane powered by a pair of Gipsy Major engines. The pilot was obviously having trouble with getting his engines to start and the sole passenger was watching with some sign of impatience. I walked across and found that he was a Belgian by name of Baron Empain, a singularly rich man who had married a cabaret dancer called Goldie. One of his many houses was a strange and flamboyant mansion in Heliopolis more reminiscent of an Indian temple than a house and it was known as 'The Baron's Folly'. His pilot was getting weary of endlessly swinging propellors by hand and was only too glad of some help. I told him that the Gipsy Major engine in cold weather needed a little trick to get them running and the thing to do was to soak a rag in petrol and place it lightly into the carburettor air intake to give a good rich mixture. Assisted by my crew in no time at all we had both engines ticking over nicely and pilot and passenger were duly impressed and grateful. Just as they were leaving I said to the Baron, "Oh by the way, where are you heading for?" His brief answer was "Cairo", to which I asked "Will you be staying for a few days?" He shook his head. "No", he replied, "I'm only going for a haircut". Cairo was 450 miles away!

In mid-1937 my log book had recorded over 700 hours on a variety of types and a new requirement came about. After eighteen months since the trio of Moose Fulton, Jim Irens and myself had first arrived at Heliopolis we were put to work as flying instructors for the new intake from the Flying Training Schools. Instructors indeed! It was only a short time since being pupils ourselves, the learning curve had now climbed to include the mantle of part-time teachers, and truth to tell we were flattered to be selected for the work – if you can call it work.

Back we went to 'A' Flight – the Training Flight. Back to the dreaded Trader Horn who had been our hawk-eyed Chief Flying Instructor. It was delightful to be accepted by him now as 'one of the chaps' – not a bog-rat. The so-called Instructors Course in reality became a check-out of each other for about five flying hours and we practised the routine, the sequence of training, and the use of the instructor's patter in the air. I expect that any pukka flying instructor who reads this account quite understandably will explode in professional dismay but I have to say that we were given a thorough check-out by Sq Ldr Charles Horn before he declared us fit for the purpose intended. Truth to tell all of us had the feeling that we were now just about as good on twin-engined aeroplanes as he. Included in the programme – believe it or not – we were told to practise circuits and landings wearing gas masks! Whose bright idea that was is now best forgotten but it showed if nothing else that thoughts of war were already in the air. Of the nine pupils, two are remembered in particular. Wallace-Tarry for some obscure reason was known as 'Popham' a tall handsome fellow who later in Bomber Command was shot down and when in Stalag Luft III as a prisoner-of-war was a tunneller during the 'Wooden Horse' exploit; the other was Kirby-Green, he of the dark handsome features and the habit of sporting bright orange pyjamas. Alas! He fell foul of the Gestapo as a prisoner of war in Stalag Luft III when participating in the Great Escape.

The situation in 1938 with economic sanctions persisting (but to no apparent purpose) against Mussolini because of his adventures in Ethiopia, periodic alerts occurred for service personnel because we were geographically close to possible action. This threatened to jeopardise a special sortie that I had planned. A very beautiful girl called Iris Johannessen who I had met in England a few years before and who was now very happily married to a Norwegian shipping executive in Hong Kong was about to travel back by sea from England to her home. The plan was that I would meet her at Port Said, fly her to Cairo, and later the same day take her by road to Suez to rejoin the MV *Jutlandia* after its passage through the Canal. This diversion of visiting Cairo was a regular feature for passengers wishing to do so but invariably they went by train. I managed to get leave of absence and In DH Hornet Moth SU-ABT I took off at 5.30 AM and headed for Port Said. It was a wonderful flight with the sun casting long shadows as it rose slowly above the desert and only one small vessel was seen in the Canal between Ismailia and Port Said.

After landing on the small sand airstrip I got the heartening news from the agent that the *Jutlandia* was due to arrive shortly at Port Said and Mr Samir of the Egyptian Shipping company suggested that he and I fly out to meet the ship to have a look at her. The short flight was nicely timed as the ship was sighted about five miles from Port Said and we circled around her a couple of times and then went back to land on the strip. My Egyptian friend took me to the port where I met Iris, and then he very kindly drove us back to the Hornet Moth. The flight to Cairo included an aerial view of the pyramids with Iris' camera clicking away happily and then we landed at Almaza to return the Hornet to the Aero Club. The rest of the day was fully taken up with sightseeing and included lunch with Freddie and Mollie Milligan at the Gezirah Club. In the evening, John and Joanne Tomes gave us dinner in their apartment in Heliopolis after which John's Ford V8 roadster was provided for the eighty mile run along the desert road to Suez. It was a lovely journey. With the soft-top down, the cool desert air and millions of stars to be seen above, what nicer ending with such a wonderful companion?

We arrived at Suez on time, only to find the port deserted. Some local people were questioned and to our dismay we were told that the ship had already been through the canal and was now well into the Gulf of Suez! Oh dear, what a very nasty situation for poor Iris who had left her baby son on board in the care of the her Chinese *amah*! This was one eventuality that I had not bargained for because she had been assured by the Captain that if she was at Suez by 11 PM that would be early enough. There was a gambling casino at Suez built out into the water rather like a small seaside pier and I suggested that we had some coffee there whilst discussing what on earth to do next. Two very despondent people went into the casino, where to Iris' immense relief she spotted some of her fellow passengers. A little later, when the ship was sighted I helped Iris into the launch and then saw her scramble onto the gangway of the moving ship, clutching a very large 'Ali Baba' laundry basket that she had purchased in the Cairo *bazaar*.

The return trip across the desert was enlivened by picking up three young french girls whose car had broken down. The male driver stayed behind to await rescue but the girls had to get back to their jobs in Cairo. As I had by then been awake for very much longer than I care to admit it was a godsend to have such jolly passengers talking and singing to prevent me falling asleep. We arrived at Heliopolis at dawn and I duly reported for duty at 7 AM after a most enjoyable long week-end but not without its unexpected incidents in the final hours of Sunday night and early Monday.

After two years with 216 Sqdn Joe Gardiner decided that I should become his Adjutant so after such a long spell of flying I was now trapped into doing a ground job. I suppose that one should be flattered to be chosen for this kind of appointment; if nothing else it presupposed that the incumbent could read and write! In my case I realised that my flying activities were temporarily curtailed and I had no choice but to follow the dictates of my Commanding Officer and do the job as best I could. In practise it proved to be an interesting appointment and there was much to learn about the administration and day-to-day running of a squadron. All manner of business had to be attended to and it was like being a mixture of general manager, technical secretary, legal clerk to the court, personnel officer, disciplinary guardian, PRO and general factotum. It was excellent training for the future.

There was also our esteemed Station Commander Raymond Collishaw to cope with – he with many wartime decorations and that very characteristic Canadian way of communicating in his forceful style. Whenever the squadron activities prescribed that a VIP was destined to be flown somewhere it was the Station Commander's perogative to attend the departure. Thus the telephone would ring and I would answer formally "216 Sqdn Adjutant". That well-known voice would say "Ar now, you see, you see, Pelly-Fry; Station Commander here"; as though I needed any guidance – or was it Milligan or Abrahams yet again?!

Raymond Collishaw would then go on to say, "I understand that the Army Commander-in-Chief is due to leave by air today; what time does the General wish to go to Siwa Oasis?" After earlier enquiries like this had come my way, something prompted me on this occasion to reply "Yes Sir,

Sir Robert Gordon-Finlayson will be leaving at 1030 hours. Number two platform, Sir".

"Oh yeah yeah, Pelly-Fry; Number two Platform. Very funny; very funny officer indeed. Thank you". There was no need to tell him that No 2 Platform was 'B' Flight. After all, he was the Station Master.

Chapter X

A Journey Across Europe

In recent months I had been sharing a big American Stutz eight cylinder open touring car with Moose Fulton (which was enormous fun to drive if a bit thirsty on petrol) and I was now contemplating the prospect of getting a motor-car of my own for the first time. Apart from the Stutz, the Squadron pilots between them had some other cars, including George Musson's 1926 Bull-nosed Morris Cowley tourer which answered to the name of 'Health and Strength'. It was everybody's vehicle, thanks to George's generosity, but drivers had to learn how to prevent the gear lever from 'coming away in his hand'! One day in the Cairo winter season four of us decided to absorb some culture and we went to the Cairo Opera House to see Giuseppe Verdi's *Aida*; an appropriate venue because the famous Italian composer had intended its debut to coincide with the opening of the Suez Canal in 1871. Unhappily his dream of making the inaugural presentation at the Temple of Luxor never materialised so it was first produced in Cairo. Perhaps one day an enterprising impressario of the stature of Gilbert Miller will fulfil Verdi's dream? For the four young officers we wore dinner jackets to suit the occasion and we enjoyed the spectacular and very appropriate opera enormously. Afterwards we decided that a visit to the Heliopolis Palace Hotel would complete the evening, particularly so as a Ball had been planned to complement the opera. The four of us left the city and took to the well-known road back to Heliopolis where the RAF aerodrome, the very good sporting club, and the ornate hotel were all conveniently close to each other. What a superb posting RAF Heliopolis was to be sure!

As we approached the hotel, so did the traffic increase. Clearly the Ball was the Mecca for all the top people to be seen attending, so we were in good company. As George Musson drove us along in company with a number of limousines containing a plethora of wealth and beauty, somebody said, "George, for heavens sake do try and park closer this time; it's such a bind to end up streets away". Dear George, he took the request literally. The Hotel boasted a very fine flight of steps leading to a wide terrace at the centre point of which was located a large set of revolving doors. Without further ado George turned into the driveway and then in bottom gear ascended the broad steps in a series of lurches. At the top, and now parked where no vehicle had been before, he said "Sorry chaps, I don't think I can manage to get through the revolving doors!" We had a splendid Ball and enjoyed being partners to the daughters of Cairo and Heliopolis residents whilst carefully observing the formalities of the times.

At about this time I heard tell of an Imperial Airways flying boat captain who was due to be posted to another section of the African routes and he had decided reluctantly to put his 1928 2-litre Lagonda up for sale. I left a message for him in his Cairo office expressing my interest and subsequently we met at the Turf Club to discuss the sale. The sight of the Lagonda arriving at the club was an exciting moment and it was even more so when I was allowed to try her out for myself. Although back home in England this fine example of a British sports car had been rudely described as the 'poor man's Bentley', so far as I was concerned this was the one for me. The only problem was the proposed selling price, something that was beyond my purse, and my only course of action was to say honestly what I could afford and await a decision. As we parted I had depressing visions of cavalry officers queuing up with their cheque books in hand, a contest that I could not possibly have joined. My first try at private ownership of a car seemed destined to fail at the first attempt and I concluded that I was aiming too high. When the owner telephoned me three days later to say that he would accept my offer I could hardly believe my good fortune and that same day I became the proud owner of my first motor car. Best of all, it was a Lagonda and I paid the princely sum of seventy pounds sterling for her. when I returned in triumph to the camp, Group Captain Raymond Collishaw came out to admire it and said "Oh yeah yeah Pelly-Fry – sure looks good, your automobile". It was a big moment in my life. There seems to be something very special about ownership of one's first car and for me it was super to know that it was a Lagonda. The car was used regularly and I was endlessly cleaning it and admiring its design features. Although some people were doubtful about its general use in an Egyptian setting, especially in summer conditions, it performed very well and gave a whole lot of satisfaction. I began to make trips with friends as far afield as Suez and Alexandria when the Lagonda showed that she could cruise effortlessly at sixty-five mph. The acceleration of course did not compare with the 3-litre Bentley with its bigger engine but for me that was of secondary importance.

The chance of a really long trip came about when a letter arrived from my brother Arthur in Colombo to say that he was due for home leave in England and suggested that he broke his journey by visiting me on the way. This was a fortunate proposal because I now hit upon the idea that he and

I might drive across Europe together. I was also due for home leave and the timing was right as I was to be best man at Freddy Milligan's wedding to Mollie Ickringill in London. I arranged for Arthur to stay in the Mess, was myself granted three months home leave and we began to plan the expedition. It was going to be our first visit of consequence to Europe and what better way than to drive from one end of the continent to the other, choosing an interesting route to do so? The idea of using a sports car that some people thought was not very practical was one that neither of us took seriously. We were happy to think that we had a good car that was very well constructed and reliable.

Arthur was duly collected from his ship and we returned to Heliopolis where he was made an honorary member of the Mess, a big change from the life of being a tea broker in Colombo. During his stay we used the Lagonda extensively. We visited the Gezirah Club; we went on picnics in the desert; we dined with friends at the Turf Club; we explored the huge covered Cairo *bazaar* where a guide is essential to find the route back to the exit; and of course we enjoyed the Pimm's party in the Mess garden that was a regular Sunday morning event.

There was also an expedition to climb to the top of the Great Pyramid of Cheops. This was occasioned because at a Mess party Arthur challenged the legend that it was impossible to drive a golf ball from the summit and for the ball to reach the desert floor in free flight; the hitherto accepted theory was that the vast mass of the pyramid meant that the ball would inevitably strike the face before bouncing away down to ground level.

The wager was between Jean Brook and Arthur who, like our late father, was always known as Pelly. The stakes were a bottle of whisky to a box of chocolates; Jean stood to win the chocolates and Arthur the whisky so the odds were about five to one against him. The pyramid party consisted of Bill and Jean Brook, Sq Ldr Denis Barnett and Jean's sister Pamela who married Denis and eventually became an Air Chief Marshal.

The huge pyramid as seen from the base is really formidable. Enormous blocks of stone hewn by hand from the Moquattam Hills nearby are placed one above the other in seeming unending geometric array and rise to some 450 feet at the summit. The tragedy is that, so it was said, a Turk called Saladin following his capture of Egypt thought fit to strip not only the marble from the pyramid faces of Cheops, he also took away the wonderful alabaster from the sister pyramid nearby; and all this was for building mosques in Cairo.

The climbing party, each armed with a golf club and old golf balls, set off on the big ascent and wisely we took a guide to show us the best route up the steep face. Eventually we scrambled up to the summit and once there we saw that the tip had become a flat area about the size of a tennis court. It was quite alarming when looking down from the top as each of the four sides seemed to be almost vertical; it was no place for sufferers from vertigo. The golfers now began to try their hand from the unique 'Tee' and Arthur said that he could not bear to stand near the edge to drive off because he got the very unnerving feeling that when he hit the ball the club also wanted to fly away with him hanging onto it! Standing close to the edge and observing every ball's flight it looked for all the world as though the trajectory became a parabola with the ball curving back into the side of the pyramid face. So perhaps this was reason for the legend?

The solution after the closest observation was that it was purely an optical illusion. After following the flight path to the highest point, the white ball now a speck in the blue sky begins its fall. Just as soon as it reaches the horizon, seemingly curving down and back towards you, nine times out of ten you lose it against the desert background. However, with all eyes staring hard, two or three balls were definitely seen to drop straight down to the desert accompanied by a little puff of sand as it landed. Thus brother Arthur won the wager and all of us had a splendid outing and we returned to Heliopolis. The bottle of White Horse Scotch whisky duly arrived for the winner and it had a neat label attached to the neck with a blue ribbon. The message read; 'Not be to opened until you get to Budapest – and I hope it chokes you!'

On March 10th 1938, with the Lagonda looking smart and well polished after a thorough servicing, we loaded up our personal kit and spares like extra inner tubes for the tyres, spare fuel cans, a first aid kit, and so on. The Grand Tour was about to begin and we set off from the Mess to the sounds of good cheer from our friends. The asphalt road to Alexandria across the desert was a good one and we motored along in style. After an overnight hotel stop we made our way to the docks in the morning to look for a Greek ship called the SS *Atiki*. The first job after meeting the shipping agent was to watch anxiously whilst the Egyptians rolled the Lagonda onto sacks and rope netting, attached the sling to the crane's cable and called to the operator to hoist on deck. It all looked distinctly unstable and the equipment not a little flimsy but all went well and the car landed safely on deck and made secure. At mid-morning, we sailed out of Alexandria and out into the Mediterranean; the sea voyage had now become the second stage of the journey to Athens, our gateway to Europe.

Unfortunately the weather soon decided to banish the image so cunningly portrayed in the brochures of the travel industry. Not for us those glassy blue-green seas, warm sunshine, deck chairs, beautiful damsels and bronzed men about to dive into the inviting pool. Alas! No. A massive depression attacked us within hours of sailing from the North African coast and we were battered by raging winds, a wild sea with seemingly bottomless troughs to the huge waves and with white spumes racing angrily off the crests. I looked anxiously at the poor Lagonda, said a prayer, and the two of us retired to our bunks and stayed there for about twenty four hours. As we were in the aft end of the good ship *Atiki* we endured the unnerving and continuous uneven propellor speed each time the whole of the stern came clean out of the water with every shudder of the hull. I really must tell those Mediterranean holiday travel people that I no longer trust their seductive advertising; for the two brothers, the Med was awful!

After what seemed like an eternity we arrived at Athens and were never more thankful for the calm of the fine harbour and to see the Lagonda still safe on deck. It took a couple of days to recover our composure, have a look the city, check over the Lagonda and get our appetites back in working order once more. On the third day the safari moved off out of Athens and headed North in the direction of Salonica. It was a bright March day, a bit cold, and we made an early start at just after 6 AM. We planned to keep going North through central Greece, pause for a break, and then see where we would get to at about tea-time. The bad news came about ten miles out of Athens because abruptly the asphalt road surface stopped and what Americans call a dirt road began. It got worse as we motored on, the driver swinging the car from one side of the track to the other to miss the pot-holes and for most of the time the Lagonda never got into top gear. Fortunately we carried reserve petrol in a four-gallon container and apart from brief stops to change drivers every two hours and have our picnic lunch we motored on. Road traffic was virtually zero. If this was a sample of motoring in the Balkans, well, take me back to Egypt. Eventually we reached a small town called Lamia situated high up in the hills; it was 120 miles out of Athens and we had motored virtually non-stop for 10 hours, thus our average speed made good was a miserable 12 mph.

Fortunately we met a Greek in Lamia who was preparing to open his new hotel. He had returned recently from America so he spoke Yankee English and was a friendly fellow who gave us a room sparsely equipped with just two beds, two chairs, and a table. He provided a very passable meal for the two tired motorists and we tumbled into our beds soon afterwards and in no time at all were fast asleep. Breakfast in the morning consisted of good coffee, local bread, butter and apricot jam. Our genial host arranged a picnic meal on the basis that it was wise to take something with us in case we failed to find a roadside tavern; his fears were well founded. All that day we climbed up steadily, the winding road getting steeper as we went. Mount Olympus (11,000 ft) could be seen before we descended into the plain to Larissa which was our second stop and we paused at the 5,000 foot high summit of the Catania Pass to top up the radiator, a small over-heating situation because the Lagonda had no fan for cooling purposes. Larissa is the main town in central Greece and so accommodation was good and very welcome.

On the third day out from Athens the road improved on the 100 miles run down the valley to the coast and then came the long coastal run to Salonika. It is a somewhat uninspiring city but it adequately provided creature comforts for the intrepid motorists driving a motor car the like of which had never been seen there before – or since, I'll wager. We had now crossed most of Greece so the next country on the itinerary would be Bulgaria. After Salonika the road heads North East and climbs up into yet more mountains and then descends into the big plain with the river Strimon flowing leisurely into the Aegean Sea; this is Macedonia country where good tobacco grows. Once across the river a left hand turn takes the traveller to the Greek-Bulgarian frontier. The police post that we arrived at nestled up in the hills and consisted of a primitive hut that was manned by some half-a-dozen shiftless characters who were so astonished to see us that all they did was to smile, have their photographs taken, look at the Union Jack painted on the bonnet, and then lift the frontier pole so that we could drive on. Not quite Heathrow Airport standards, shall I say, but considerably easier and quicker for travellers.

We pressed on towards Sofia and estimated that we had about 120 miles to go. The time was around midday, and so we had about six hours of daylight in hand and by now we felt that we had the measure of road travel in the Balkans. Alas, our optimism and luck changed for the worse – we had a puncture, dammit! The spare wheel was fitted and we set off again but for no more than about twenty miles because puncture number two came about. Heavens, that meant all the business of removing the inner tube, replacing it with a new one and then the chore of using a foot pump. This was not at all amusing in the middle of Bulgaria but we got down to the job and then Allah be praised! our luck changed again. Thundering along the road towards us was a vast Mercedes truck. It stopped, two Bulgars descended from the cab and they immediately appreciated our situation. They brought their vehicle closer and finished the job for us by pumping up the new tube with their vehicle on-board pressure system. After lots of smiles and hand shakes to convey thanks to our new friends they motioned us to go ahead of them and I managed to pronounce 'Sofia' in such a way – after some practise – that they knew our aiming point. I suppose it must have been obvious where we wanted to go because there was nowhere else of consequence lying ahead anyway.

When all was ready, the two-vehicle convoy moved off once more in a northerly direction towards the capital of Bulgaria. The road was improving slightly in quality, thank heaven, and traversed some splendid countryside. Although it was mid-March the wintery scene gave it a certain charm with many fields with last year's stubble showing through the snow and with many deciduous trees, conifers, and wooded areas to be seen. There were fruit orchards, the products of which end up inside those distinctive dumpy jars of quite delicious black cherry, morello cherry, black currant, apricot, strawberry, plum and other conserves for which Bulgaria is very well-known. Bulgarian wines are also excellent.

The time was now late afternoon, and the sun was a little above the horizon. The snow lay everywhere; it was pretty to look at but not too comforting for driving over unmade roads. The two vehicles occasionally distanced themselves from each other as the Lagonda took advantage of slightly better road surfaces whenever they materialised. It must have been another ten or fifteen miles further along the route when we heard the unmistakable and disagreeable sound of yet another puncture and now it was not so much curses as expressions of dismay from the brothers. There was no option but to stop, get out the hydraulic jack, hoist up the wheel and await the very welcome sight of our friends. Puncture number three was attended to, the tyre and new inner tube fitted and once again we were able to continue. We had now used the last of the inner tubes carried. Despite the admonition on the label of Jean Brook's bottle of whisky – 'Do not open before Budapest' – it was decided that rules must be broken under conditions of *force majeur*. Brother Arthur removed the cap and offered the bottle to each of our friends to sample. They both took a good swig and each made that mildly explosive sound when the whisky 'reached the parts that other drinks cannot!' Now it was the turn of the hapless Englishmen to sample the product and I confess that by so doing it gave us strength of purpose to press on once more. It was now dark and getting distinctly colder and to add to our problems certain cross-roads and forks began to show up in the headlights. As our knowledge of Bulgarian with its *Cryllic* script on signposts was non-existent, even looking for a short word looking like 'Sofia' was a dangerous way to navigate. We decided to wait for instructions from our friends. They soon understood the difficulty and by sign language told us to switch positions in the convoy and follow them. With each road diversion or intersection they indicated the route by those swinging arms with a red light on the tip flapping up and down on one side of the driver's cab or the other as appropriate. The 'Straight on' signal was both arms waved simultaneously almost like semaphore; it was simple but it worked admirably. To compress a catalogue of unhappiness, we had one more puncture and by now I was too cold and tired to try to diagnose the trouble. Our Bulgarian friends however were just as cooperative as ever; no sooner had they seen our flashing headlights than they stopped and the whole damned business began all over again. By now the whisky had taken effect; and upon the bottle being proffered again with much shaking of heads and circular hand movements around their ears each of them indicated that Scotland's glorious product had proved itself. Taken neat straight from the bottle in the cold night air this was not too surprising really.

Eventually, to our heartfelt relief the lights of Sofia beckoned in the distance as the convoy rumbled on; and on reaching the city our friends signalled to keep following them. At some place more or less in the centre of the city the big Mercedes truck stopped, and all of us got out from our vehicles. The burly Bulgarian driver pointed to a doorway with an illuminated sign above it, indicating that that was where we should go. Clearly it was some kind of a Bulgarian night-spot! We shook hands – with unusual warmth, I might add – and then the Mercedes departed. What excellent and friendly fellows they were. I looked at my watch; it was 2.30 AM and it had been a very long day. Whilst standing on the pavement debating our next move because we had no Bulgarian currency, no native tongue and slightly bemused to say the least, a man emerged from the night club, paused, looked at us, and then said, "Hello!" He took us into the club and bought us double measures of Scotch. It transpired that he was a Jewish tailor and had been working in London which explained why he spoke English. After plying us with more (and such very welcome) drinks he telephoned to a hotel nearby and booked a room for us. The hotel was a large one and had a distinctly 'Russian' look about it. Our big bedroom had double glass windows, wooden shutters, and heavy sombre curtains reaching from the tall ceiling right down to the carpeted floor. The huge beds were provided with curious bolsters and thickly padded bed coverings. All the furniture, not least the huge white wash basin and water jug, was so very different from our normal experience and the contrast was marked. With the Lagonda parked outside in the snow, canvas hood up and side screens in position, the brothers literally climbed up into their beds and slept soundly; it was well into the next day before we surfaced. So this was Sofia! When I drew back those heavy curtains to have a look across the square I saw a handsome church of the kind with an enormous onion-shaped dome.

The immediate requirement after a late breakfast was to get something done about those endless punctures and it was not an easy task for the two foreigners to carry out in a strange Balkan country. However the hotel manager surprised us by saying that there was an Englishman who had a garage business in the city, a most unusual circumstance we thought, and we set off to meet him. Luck seemed to swing from disaster to rescue with every hour that passed. The Englishman was a man called Snowden Hedley and his name is still engraved on my memory fifty years later. He had been a pilot with the Royal Flying Corps in WWI and his squadron had been stationed in Bulgaria to fight the Turks. He had taken a great liking to the country and decided after the war to stay behind and start a garage business. Hedley examined all our wheels and diagnosed that the inner tubes did not match the outer covers and the bad roads were causing the tubes to chafe, thus developing small punctures and slow leaks. All wheels were stripped down, the beadings taped up and then everything re-assembled after the punctures were repaired. Hedley reckoned that his makeshift modification would hold good and his forecast proved correct. When we told him about the Bulgarian chaps and how the Jewish tailor had been so very helpful he said that it was typical of the people. Only the politicians were devious and suspect; they were playing games as usual and were now leaning towards Russia. The tailor had done us proud because Scotch whisky was £10 per bottle (at 1938 prices) over the counter and so what it cost in the night club was anybody's guess.

After a second night in 'Grand Hotel' we prepared to move on once again. The next stop was to be Yugoslavia and as it was country number three on our list we were making steady progress. We gave ourselves two days of resting in Sofia where we continued to enjoy Snowden Hedley's hospitality and we began to hope that the tyre troubles so well dealt with by him were now cured. The Yugoslav countryside to Nis and thence to Belgrade was pleasant enough but lacked the wild mountain scenery that we had seen in the Balkans. Beyond Belgrade we made good time to Szeged, just inside Hungary, so Yugoslavia was but a brief encounter. The attractive Hungarian city is well remembered if only because the restaurant where we dined seemed to have minstrels in the band who were all composed of amateurs. Frequently one of them would walk away to join his friends at a table to enjoy a glass or two of Tokay and he would then be replaced by another fellow to join his musical friends and enchant us further with those dreamy melodies.

The next stop was Budapest. It is a handsome city with the river Duna (Danube) dividing Buda from Pest but we wanted to make up lost time so we did not do real justice to it by our brief visit. The Lagonda was now heading west to Austria and as we approached Vienna a bonus was that with the good road we were now cruising along much faster than our earlier speeds of 30 to 40 mph. The worst part of the road systems were now behind us and we were able to regain sports-car cruising speeds of 60 to 70 mph.

In Vienna both of us were surprised to see a multitude of flags with a device called a *swastika* emblazoned on them; to add to our confused thinking the main streets seemed to be singularly empty both of vehicles and pedestrians. Oh well, it was nothing to do with us and perhaps it was some kind of special occasion? Our immediate thoughts were that we had no Austrian money and as it was a Saturday the wise move was to go to one of the big hotels where at least someone could speak English and help us appropriately. The guide book listed a five-star hotel called the Hotel Imperial so we asked for directions in halting German from a pedestrian. He looked blank, shrugged his shoulders and walked on, so it seemed that my schoolboy German was getting us nowhere. After my fourth attempt, the man looked distinctly surprised and then pointed along the road. Was there something odd about a Lagonda with two Englishmen on board and the Union Jack showing on the bonnet? Eventually we found the Hotel Imperial; it was large and impressive with a crescent shaped drive-in. As the Lagonda swung into the driveway the first thing we saw was a line-up of military silver-grey Mercedes touring cars. All were parked in impeccable herring-bone formation and each one with a helmeted driver in dark uniform sitting impassively at the wheel. They were definitely Germans, so something important must be happening in the hotel.

Being a tidy person I backed in alongside the nearest Mercedes, taking care to get the spacing correct and so not upset the pattern. Turning to my brother who was standing nearby I said, "Just look at those tyres! Boy, I could do with a set as good as those." With that I gave one of them a friendly kick and as I did so Arthur then said, "Ahem; the drivers are getting a bit restive. Let's go inside and cash a cheque". So we ascended the flight of steps and I led the way to the big revolving doors. As I approached they began to move so I entered and I almost collided with a man as he made to leave; He stepped back and then took the next segment. He was wearing a plain light grey overcoat that was so long that it almost touched his shoes and he was sporting a green pork-pie hat. As he passed me the man's heavy jowled face struck a chord for I was sure that I had seen it before somewhere and when I turned to look inside the hotel a quite extraordinary sight greeted my eyes. The big entrance hall had one of those wide twin staircases that sweep up grandly on each side to the first floor and they were crowded to capacity with motionless uniformed men who were holding their right arms stiffly in front of them. Ho, ho! So this must be the Hitler salute – and it looked for all the world as though the whole thing had been stage-managed for our benefit.

At the reception desk I asked the pale-faced manager if he spoke English. He nodded. "Good", said I, "First of all may I ask if the gentleman who has just left the hotel is General Goering, head of the German Air Force?" He nodded again. "What is he doing in Vienna?" This time I got a whispered "Please say no more". Poor chap, he seemed frightened out of his wits and Arthur told me to shut up as I was disturbing the peace with my penetrating voice. After Goering had departed the Germans dispersed quickly and we succeeded in cashing a cheque. We now decided that whatever had been going on in Vienna was best left to the citizens and we returned to the Lagonda. It was now standing in splendid isolation as all the Mercedes cars had departed and we too drove out of the city. We were completely vague about what had been going on in Vienna and this was not surprising as we had been in Balkan countries for many days and thus out-of-touch with the outside world. However at our next stop we heard that Germany had 'invaded' Austria and it was called the *Anschluss* – whatever that meant. When the German word was translated for us (and its meaning was the annexation of one country by another), I began to ponder about what kind of people were the Austrians who had surrendered their sovereignty so easily without even a mild protest, let alone any attempt at resisting. Admittedly the big German army invasion force must have looked quite threatening to anybody who tried to cross their paths but to throw in the sponge without a murmur seemed to me to be extraordinary. I concluded that Austrians were either easy to conquer without so much as a single shot being fired or for some reason best known to themselves they welcomed the German invasion. Certainly the few citizens that were seen on the streets seemed to be more frightened than angry. Not being an Austrian I could not pass judgment on another country's affairs but just the same it was not what I had expected of them. What is the point of being an independent country if the population accept the arrival of a bully-boy without even raising a finger in protest? It was a foretaste of things to come.

We abandoned Vienna after the Goering encounter and motored along a magnificent three-lane highway to which the Lagonda responded like a greyhound. Surely this was what was called an Autobahn? Whatever it was the Lagonda behaved in the way that the designer intended and at long last we were able to motor along joyfully at a spanking seventy mph; This was proper motoring and it had been a long time coming. The excellent three-lane highway was the greatest possible change from our erstwhile battle with dust, snow, potholes, mud and the seemingly endless gear-changing. Now the concrete ribbon stretched away into the distance and on this new wonder of highway construction you no longer had to steer, you just pointed the car straight ahead and relaxed.

After a number of miles of effortless travel with the rev. counter showing a steady 2500 rpm, in the distance we saw what looked like a vast crocodile of large vehicles. This was no problem as it would be easy to overtake with a second or even a third lane available. We motored on in style and it then became clear that we were now passing just about the longest convoy that I had ever seen. What else but the German Army leaving Austria? We were faster by some twenty-five mph so that meant that they were cruising at a speed approaching forty-five mph. Heavens! I always thought that military convoys like those of the British army never exceeded 30 mph. These German vehicles therefore were certainly much faster than I ever expected. Eventually we reached the front end of the Whermacht's mechanical might and expected to leave them behind. However we had not bargained on those leading Mercedes staff cars impeccably spaced at about thirty metres. When closing up on the leader the driver began to increase speed and so did the Lagonda and as it did so I could not resist waving in thinly disguised triumph. The number one Mercedes was now going even faster so nothing to it but to show Goering's men what the Lagonda could do too. When we finally overtook it we were travelling at well over 80 mph – the maximum speed for the old girl. The impassive Germans did not even look but we sensed that they were not amused, particularly so as I am damned sure that they recognised the Lagonda as the same one that had been parked so audaciously alongside them outside the Hotel Imperial. The aftermath of the Austrian *Grand Prix* awaited telling later in London but meanwhile the journey right across Germany to Heidelberg enabled us to see something of the Rhine Valley and sample the delicious wines of the area. From an airman's point of view one interesting observation was that every military aerodrome that we sighted had all the aeroplanes dispersed around the perimeter and not lined up neatly on the apron. This dispersal seemed distinctly unusual to me but of course it was only a matter of months before the reason for it was manifest. The Germans clearly were anticipating a war-like situation even in the spring of 1938.

An interesting insight to the German people who ran the guest houses that we stopped at en route was the obvious apprehension that they had about the political situation. Conversations were guarded; there was a token admission that Hitler was doing a good – if risky – job and there were loud protestations that the English and the Germans should never again get to loggerheads and a deep hope was expressed that Germany must not get tangled up in aggressive European activities. When we said that Austria had been invaded with not a single protest and we had witnessed the event, the matter was embarrassingly shrugged off as 'something that the *Führer* had to do' without their questioning it. Clearly, they sensed what was afoot and were resigned to it but they had grave forebodings just the same. How right they were!

The hotel in Heidelberg was comfortable and well run and it was good to enjoy such efficient management. That afternoon Arthur and I set off on foot to admire the splendid setting on the River Neckar (where the best white wines come from in my judgement), had a good dinner, and turned in at a reasonable hour. We were awakened very early in the morning by bangings on our bedroom door and loud authoritative voices calling out *Politzi*. Neither of us moved but I called out "Come in". With a tramp of heavy boots two black-uniformed men came in and said one word, *Passeport*. No excuses; no explanations; not even token manners. I pointed to the dressing table and said "Help yourself". One man took a good look, compared the photographs in the passports with the owners, and without further ado departed whereupon the two brothers promptly went off to sleep again. At breakfast time we were told that a massive check was being carried out in the city because Hitler was in town. I was not too popular when I suggested to the hotel manager that someone should tell the *Führer* to get better mannered police on the pay-roll. In the city all traffic had stopped and as the streets seethed with people lining what presumably was the route for their hero we had no choice of going anywhere so we just watched the passing scene.

After a while the official convoy arrived, led by two pathfinding cars, and then standing up in the third Mercedes open tourer was the new boss of the German people. We were so close that we could easily see the ashen face, the silly little moustache, the uniform of sorts, and of course the little Ruritanian peaked cap. His right arm kept flapping up and down as though it was a puppet working off a string. So this was Mr Big? In a few fleeting moments he had gone; the shouting stopped, the spectators right arms were lowered, the crowd departed, and so did the brothers. We walked back to our hotel, paid the bill, loaded the car with our overnight kit and set off to follow the Rhine valley for some miles before heading west. It took three leisurely days to cross Holland, Belgium and so into France and then to Calais. That made a total of nine countries in all starting from Athens and we had made the European Grand Tour in a way that perhaps Lord Byron would have been pleased about. Our crossing to Dover was uneventful and the sight of those famous white cliffs looked distinctly welcoming. The Lagonda loved travelling on the correct side of the road once again; and so did I.

A return to Britain from a spell overseas is always a heartening and relaxing affair. Apart from seeing my family and friends and enjoying a change of climate, this is also a period of recovering the old values, cultures, and attitudes that are so important to restore a balanced outlook. Nice simple things return that previously were taken for granted; village life, the postman, the pub, telephones that worked and English newspapers of your choice that could be read on the same day as the date-line. Yes, England looked very good once more.

Although still a bachelor with no proper home to use as a base, I managed to get about happily and go as I pleased but the truth is that one lives in a bit of a vacuum and circumstance forces a defensive screen to be built up to compensate. I now realised that the need for my father to travel to the ends of the earth to earn his living had considerable side-effects on his family. Although modern air travel softens the blow on a time-scale basis – psychologically 'papa is not really far away' – the problem is ever present and does not disappear. In my case I visited friends and I stayed in the Royal Air Force Club in Piccadilly whenever a London requirement arose. In its fashion this is nice enough but not much more than a makeshift arrangement. I began to get the feeling that I was looking forward to getting 'back home to 216 Squadron' before my leave period ended and this was endorsed by the realisation that long bachelor holidays are an expensive way to live on a junior officer's pay. The highlight of the home leave (and the principle reason for it) was to act as best man at the marriage of Freddie and Mollie. So with all the participants now in London, plans were finalised for the wedding. The church was to be St. Mark's in North Audley Street which was handy for everybody and in my case it was only a short walk from the RAF Club.

In the halcyon days of the Royal Air Force before World War Two officers had the opportunity (in common with the other Services) of wearing full dress uniform. This consisted of mess kit overalls – those tight-fitting trousers – and an equally tight-fitting tunic that buttoned right up to the neck. It was not very comfortable but it was exceedingly smart to wear and the ensemble was completed by a swanky close-fitting rounded hat not unlike that of a Hussar's and topped with a fine plume. Finally, the whole vision of sartorial military elegance was made complete by the carrying of a ceremonial sword. It was not often that officers, especially the junior ones, had the luck of owning all this finery so it was the practise to make a visit to that admirable establishment near Covent Garden called Moss Brothers – 'Moss Bros' to us all. Freddie and I duly called on them and in no time at all were kitted out in the style that an RAF officer should be seen when in the role of groom and best man. On the second day of June, 1938 (as recorded in the silver cigarette case that I received for my efforts as best man and one that I have carried with me ever since) Freddie and I walked smartly along the length of North Audley Street to St. Mark's for all of Mayfair to gaze at in wonderment and admiration. The church was filled to capacity with relatives and guests and at the right moment Freddie and I made our entrance, removed our smart headgear and walked towards the altar; soon the beautiful bride appeared and she was escorted by her father to join the groom.

Two memories in particular remain vivid. The first was that the wedding ring was so small that without pockets I could only keep it on the top section of my little finger and I kept touching it with my thumb to reassure myself that it was still there. The second was that in order to produce the ring when called for by the officiating priest, I had to release my sword and as I lowered it to the ground it seemed to go down a long way before coming to rest. Having delivered the ring, I went to retrieve the sword and return to my pew but to my dismay I found that the fishtail end of the scabbard had somehow got enmeshed in the iron grill of the ventilating system. I could not leave the sword behind and I certainly could not remove it from the scabbard and after embarrassing moments that seemed like an eternity I eventually found a way to extricate it. Then it was Freddie's turn. Having now been declared 'man and wife' he also found that he was anchored by his sword as he tried to escort his bride to the vestry so the whole game started for the second time! Neither of us had ever donned full dress uniform before and in retrospect I suppose that it would have been appropriate to have removed our swords before approaching the altar. Unhappily the Air Ministry subsequently abandoned the use of the smart RAF rig for reasons that are as obscure as they seemed unconvincing at the time and I wonder what poor Moss Bros. did with their stock of full dress uniform hire equipment? The dressing-up game for special occasions was now at an end but at least we could tell our children that we had participated in our time, and with a photo to prove it.

Prior to the wedding there was the usual requirement to report to the Air Ministry and establish contact by provision of addresses and telephone numbers. When making my way to the Personnel Department I was delighted to meet my recent CO, Wg Cdr Philip Mackworth, who was now a staff officer somewhere in the corridors of Power and of course he wanted to know all the Heliopolis news and how 216 Sqdn was faring. He asked me how I had travelled home and when I told him that my brother and I had motored across Europe he took me along to see some people who would be interested and the whole tour was related mile by mile. When I reached the Vienna stage and told my lighthearted tale of Goering, those Mercedes cars, and the race with the huge German army convoy along the *Autobahn*, someone suddenly exclaimed "So that was it!" I said "Sir, what was what?" The reply was as unexpected as it was surprising. I was told that they had heard that a large percentage of the convoy had inexplicably broken down between Vienna and the German border and this was a complete mystery to the transport specialists. Now all of a sudden the answer was clear; the two brothers in the Lagonda had forced the pace of the convoy and for reasons of prestige the senior General had instructed his driver to press on, thus forcing all the drivers behind to keep their feet down hard on the throttles in a vain effort to maintain the correct spacing between vehicles. The *Autobahn Grand Prix* had gone on for mile after mile; and as Mae West used to say "Something had to give!" In retrospect, I sometimes wonder if we had not unwittingly begun the destruction of the Wermacht some eighteen months before WWII began in earnest.

One visit that I made during my leave was to drive up to RAF Mildenhall to see my good friend Moose Fulton who was now flying with a Canadian 'Wellington' Squadron and it was a big surprise to see the station so well set-up since my previous visit in October 1934 for the start of the MacRobertson Air Race to Australia. Moose had returned to the UK and was posted to Mildenhall where his twin-engined flying in Egypt was put to good purpose. He was happy to be in England again and loved the Wellington Bomber but added that perhaps one day he would have, as he put it, four motors and a handful of throttles to play with from the cockpit of a Lancaster.

I had an overnight stop in the Mess and we talked at length about Heliopolis. I told him about the journey across Europe and the adventures that took place. I also said that I would be leaving the Lagonda in England as I could not afford to take her back to Egypt. I asked him if he would like to have her and so give the car a good home. Dear Moose, my best friend from Kamloops, British Columbia, was very happy to say yes and we arranged that I would continue to use the Lagonda until I was about to leave for Egypt and then he would take her over. Neither he nor I mentioned the vulgar detail of price; that small matter could be attended to later.

I managed to get a concessionary Forces air ticket (based on fifty percent of the standard fare) to travel by Imperial Airways flying boat from Southampton to Alexandria. It cost me twenty-two pounds. Flying boat travel in those days was a very pleasant and leisurely affair and after the take off from Hythe with lots of green water splashing about and spray covering the windows the 'Solent' became airborne. I always wanted to be a flying boat pilot as to me it seemed to combine the best of both worlds.

The passengers enjoyed a night stop in a comfortable hotel near Marseilles, another equally good one in Agusta, Sicily, and then we made the last run across the Mediterranean to Alexandria. Those pre-war air journeys were so civilised; we may not have flown quickly but at least we had every evening ashore and a comfortable bed to sleep in overnight. Equally good in the case of those excellent Imperial Airways flying boats, you could make your way upstairs to the aft compartment where you could sit in the lounge and have a drink whilst chatting with the other passengers.

The alighting in Alexandria Harbour, followed by the transfer by a launch to the quay ended a wonderful trip. Once ashore, I telephoned to Heliopolis and spoke to the Squadron Adjutant. "Thank heaven you are back early" was the message. "The new Flight Commander of 'B' Flight became ill tragically, and died in the Cairo Military Hospital two days ago. We need you badly." I flew back pronto to Heliopolis. I was now temporarily Officer Commanding 'B' Flight, and although still a Flying Officer Joe Gardiner told me that I would hold the job until a replacement was appointed. Some weeks passed and Joe Gardiner called me into his office. He said that a new Air Ministry Order had just been issued which said that it was now possible for an officer to hold the acting rank of Flight Lieutenant. I was instructed to apply and dutifully wrote out the application which was sent off to the Air Ministry. In due course a letter in typical third-person fashion arrived which said "Please inform this officer that he cannot be an Acting Flight Lieutenant because he is doing a Squadron Leader's job". Joe Gardiner was incensed and said that if the Air Ministry was going to play clever then I must apply to be an Acting Squadron Leader, the rank for the job. At this I blanched visibly, but Joe insisted and so I wrote another application. A second letter arrived from the Air Ministry it said "Please inform this officer that there is no such rank as Acting Squadron Leader". So that clever person in London succeeded in cheating me on both counts and may the miserable perpetrator of it forever rest uneasily in his grave. For the record, the extra cost to the tax-payer of this denied extravaganza would have been a miserable two shillings per day. Dear God!

Chapter XI

The Promised Land

Life at Heliopolis continued to be a satisfying affair. It was enhanced, and the scope considerably widened, because I was now a Flight Commander although still a Flying Officer. I soon began to appreciate the responsibilities of command that previously were confined to being Captain of Aircraft. Now it was all about personnel, serviceability of the five Valentias, spare parts, discipline, and all the other facets of being in charge of a small military unit. It was my job to select which aeroplane and what crew was to be employed in what way and for what purpose. As events were to illustrate in so telling a fashion eighteen months later, I now put my own name down for flying duties rather than be told to do so by someone else. The responsibility of leadership prescribes that you lead; and to this end the privilege of choice must not be abused by selecting for yourself only the less exacting tasks. The formula is self-evident, but its application sometimes requires an iron will.

In September 1938 a major air search was instigated that lasted for five days. A Fairey Gordon was posted missing after it had failed to arrive from its starting point in Egypt to a destination called RAF Ramleh, not far from Tel Aviv and close to what nowadays is called Ben Gurion Airport, Israel. Initially the Gordon had left its home base at Ramleh and had flown direct to Heliopolis. Early on the following Monday morning, after a call at the Flying School at Abu Sueir near the Suez Canal, the pilot had taken off to return to Ramleh. He never arrived. After some initial air sorties made from Canal Zone aerodromes had proved fruitless the search was stepped up to a maximum effort and by the third day there must have been some sixty aircraft engaged in the search. Wing Commander Gardiner was in charge of the operation and to that end he had positioned himself at RAF Ismailia alongside the Suez Canal to be close to the area of search in the Sinai Desert. Each dawn dozens of aircraft set off in pre-planned order to cover every square inch of the search area and all of this was based upon the probabilities of the flight path taken by the Gordon. The massive search continued to be inconclusive and by the end of the fourth day the prospects of success were waning alarmingly. The pilot of the Gordon was Flying Officer Desmond Bell, Personal Assistant to Air Commodore AT Harris, Air Officer commanding RAF Palestine and Transjordan. The sole passenger was a civilian called Scarborough who was on the Headquarters Staff in Jerusalem as Cypher Officer.

As the massive effort to find the Gordon seemed to be a fruitless undertaking I suggested to Wg Cdr Gardiner that another approach to the problem was to delve closely into all the events that took place on the ground prior to the Gordon's ill-fated departure from Heliopolis and then as necessary carry out the same investigation at Abu Sueir, the Gordon's last stopover point before flying into oblivion. I hoped to pick up some clues to work on and I wanted to go through the entire affair with a fine tooth-comb to check precisely what had occurred before the ill-fated flight. The Wing Commander, rather unusually, was not clear that my plan had any substance to it but on the premise that by now everything was worth a try he agreed to let me return to Heliopolis to check up on everybody who had the slightest connection with either the aeroplane or its pilot. All clues were important, and not one single factor however innocent should be disregarded. It was in effect the process of elimination; and apart from the unhappy loss of two men and one aeroplane perhaps the most important issue now was to find out precisely (even to make an inspired guess) about what had happened. Any conclusions reached as to what had caused the incident was vital for learning any lessons and thus profit from them in future. Mysterious accidents, especially aviation ones, are unnerving for later participants and it is therefore essential to track down the causes and by so doing eliminate them.

The long and detailed step-by-step process eventually produced the vital clue. What had happened was that the Communication Flight at Heliopolis had very recently been issued with a small fuel trailer (of some 250 gallons capacity) that was fitted with a Zwicky hand-operated pump. This new piece of equipment was a considerable improvement on the hitherto tedious business of refuelling by four-gallon tins with all the associated rigmarole of petrol funnel, chamois leather, and gauze filter that had been standard practise in the past. What nobody had appreciated was that for certain types of aircraft this new and convenient facility required a new expertise. In the case of the 'Gordon' – as my investigation revealed – the gravity tank in the top wing centre section was connected by a pipe to the main fuel tank located in the fuselage. In the past, the four-gallon tin formula by gravity feed was straightforward. However, once the new pump-operated unit was used, the output from it was in excess of the capacity of the 'Gordon' to accept such a high rate of delivery. The result was that Joe Erk on the top wing saw the petrol overflowing and called to his mate on the ground to stop pumping. It was as simple as that. The refuelling crew, not knowing how much fuel was needed to fill the tank (or tanks) and possibly not technically familiar with the particular type of aircraft anyway, somewhat understandably assumed that they had done what was expected. The filler cap was replaced and the amount of fuel delivered was then recorded in the petrol book.

Mistake number one was that the refuelling airman did not check that he had fully topped up the Gordon's tanks by the simple process of having a look. Mistake number two – the one that really mattered – was that the pilot failed to check how much fuel had in fact been put into his aircraft. Had he done so, he would at once have realised that something was amiss and so investigated the matter. All that he did was to accept verbally that his aircraft had been fully refuelled. In the event he departed from Heliopolis with a lot less fuel than he should have had and he presumably did not operate the rather primitive fuel state system either. All that I had to do was to calculate what the Gordon's reduced range was, make allowance for the visit to Abu Sueir, and then draw an arc on the map from that departure point beyond which it could not fly. The pencil line crossed the curved Mediterranean coastline at a place called Rafa, a location where some pilots were in the habit of flying a little out to sea en route from Egypt to Palestine to shorten the distance to travel. As the time saved was minimal it was a dangerous route to take, particularly so in a single-engined machine. I reported to Wg Cdr Gardiner that in all probability the Gordon had fallen into the sea and the air search was abandoned. Ever since that unhappy episode (when one learns from other people's mistakes) I have always made a point of advising the refuelling party approximately how much fuel they could expect to put into a tank and then carefully checking for myself afterwards. I use the same drill today with my motor car.

Shortly after the loss of the Gordon and the tragic end to Desmond Bell and Mr Scarborough, the Station Adjutant passed a message informing me that I was to report to Air Headquarters on the following day. I was to see the Commander-in-Chief, something that had never come my way before and understandably I wondered what was afoot. Freddie Milligan was now personal assistant to Air Marshal Sir William Mitchell – Ginger Mitch as he was affectionately known – and I telephoned to him to find out the reason for the summons. Freddie of course knew that I was due to present myself to the boss man but was unwilling (or unable) to give me a lead. All that I had to do was to get out my best uniform, make myself look presentable, and then go to Cairo to await whatever was in store for me. When I arrived at Freddie's office in good time for my appointment he intimated that the C-in-C had me in mind for a posting to a new job. There were some thinly veiled pointers about Palestine and like all good PA's Freddie was giving nothing away, but the slim clue that I picked up was that the job was a pretty good one. That at least was encouraging if only because it meant that I was in favour and not the reverse.

So it was that Flying Officer Pelly-Fry found himself in front of the Air Marshal, standing stiffly to attention, and awaited events. Right away the message came across when he said, "I want you to go to Jerusalem and take on the job of personal assistant to Air Commodore Harris. As you know, Flying Officer Bell is missing after his aircraft disappeared and in the absence of positive evidence I have to assume that he was drowned. I want you to replace him as PA to the AOC, and as you have had a good run with 216 Squadron a change of job will be good for you. The Air Commodore is an excellent officer and I feel that you will enjoy working for him". So that was that. I left the C-in-C's office with mixed emotions. I was loath to give up a flying job but at the same time I was flattered to think that I had been chosen for the appointment without so much as any preliminary vetting somewhere down the line beforehand. When I returned to Freddie's office and told him what my visit was all about he had a distinct twinkle in his eye. I sensed that he had connived in the affair and wanted me to become a member of the exclusive Personal Assistant's Club. Although Air Commodore Harris had been in Jerusalem for only a short time, the buzz was that he was making quite an impact – perhaps an understatement – and so I would have to be on my mettle. Anyway, this was to be another job to take-on and as I motored back to Heliopolis to tell Joe Gardiner what had happened – I expect he knew anyway – I had a mild sense of elation that I had been chosen from any number of other equally suitable people. One of the fascinating aspects of Service life is that inevitably a posting comes your way on average every three years and the probability is that it bears no resemblance at all to the previous one. Sometimes you are unlucky in that you are landed with a dud one in which case you have no option but to sweat it out and hope for something better next time. For me, so far in my young life in the RAF I had no complaints at all. I sensed that my lucky star would not let me down.

On November 24th, 1938, I flew up to the very basic landing strip at Kolundia (just outside Jerusalem) for what was to be my last sortie in a Valentia of 216 Squadron. It was a sad moment to watch K-2798, 'U' Uncle, fly away and seemingly abandon me for evermore. The famous squadron had given me three splendid years and in the process had enabled me to put in over one thousand flying hours all over the Middle East and Africa. The circumstance also gave me a degree of self-confidence and assurance that perhaps had been lacking previously. I had become a Captain of aircraft, a VIP pilot, and ended up as a Flight Commander long before my age and seniority prescribed – even if the Air Ministry denied me an acting rank and the miniscule extra pay on an absurd technicality. That apart, the 216 Bus Drivers Union had done me proud, and I will always remember it with great affection. To this day, when the occasion demands that I must wear a dark suit – which thankfully is infrequent – the only tie that I like to wear is invariably that dark blue one in silk bearing the squadron crest of an eagle carrying a bomb. '*Dona ferens*'; we bring gifts.

The Air Commodore's driver took me and my few personal possessions into Jerusalem, a journey that was short but full of interest for the newcomer. My first sighting of the Holy City revealed any number of features, from the rocky terrain in an attractive brown to an unexpected greenness occasioned by more rainfall than I had been used to in Egypt. The setting of the city is distinctly attractive; it was smaller than I had expected and graced with some superb buildings constructed from local stone that has a pale pink-cum-light brown tint. On the skyline could be seen a number of religious places of worship, each one of a different style and each seeming to vie with its neighbour. Although the religious choice for the visitor is almost unlimited I could not but ponder about how civilisation divides itself in its view of what is the correct interpretation of the Almighty. The moslems say 'There is only one God' – but how does one decide which one to believe in? On the happy thought that our souls in due course will end up in Heaven, perhaps one day we will all find out. It will be interesting, to say the least.

Jerusalem has a certain quality in the light that gives unusual clarity and this seems to bathe the area in a heavenly aura that makes one feel that the city is something special. Artists who I met confirmed this impression and said that it was one of the reasons why painters from overseas made a special point of going to Jerusalem to enjoy their work under such beautiful conditions.

We arrived at the King David Hotel, a handsome building that housed the Army and the RAF Headquarters in Palestine. With the two top floors so occupied, (and the RAF having pride of place on the highest one), the views all over Jerusalem are spectacular. One can almost discern the seven hills upon which the city had been established centuries ago. The immediate task for me was to present myself to my new boss and I was shown initially into the office of the Chief of Staff, an appointment in the RAF known as Senior Air Staff Officer – SASO for short. Wing Commander CEV Porter was a very tall man with a military moustache and the bearing and manner of a cavalry officer. 'Wingers' – as I learned later was his nickname – took me next door into the boss's office that was on a corner of the hotel wing and faced North and West. For the first time in my life I was looking with great interest at Air Commodore Arthur Travers Harris. He was sitting behind a large desk and I saw a broad-shouldered man with sandy hair and lots of ribbons on his uniform. He was wearing half-moon spectacles and when he looked unblinkingly at me over the top of them he gave me the slightly unnerving feeling that I was transparent. Wingers introduced me, and I was left to fend for myself.

"Well, Pelly-Fry, welcome to my headquarters as the new PA; I hope you will enjoy the job. I expect that you will find it interesting although a big change from squadron life. How did you get here from Heliopolis?" I replied that I had flown myself up in a Valentia with my personal possessions, such as they were, and this answer seemed to meet with his approval. He then asked me some questions about my time with 216 Squadron, my flying experience, and wanted to know if Sir William Mitchell was in good health. To the latter I could only say that he looked very well on the only occasion that I had spoken to him during what passed for an interview for the new appointment.

The Air Commodore asked me if I had arranged anywhere to stay, a domestic touch that I appreciated, and I replied that I had only just arrived but hoped to find something suitable as a starting point. This new situation of the need for finding accommodation was in complete contrast to my previous RAF life where everything was provided as a matter of course. Now I was expected to hunt around and do the job myself. The prospect, with all its pitfalls for a young bachelor in a new land was something that I did not relish; in a squadron one takes everything for granted but now house hunting by a young Flying Officer was not my idea at all of a happy start. In the event I was invited to stay for a short time with my new boss and this relieved my anxieties considerably.

It was past midday, and after further conversation I was invited to accompany the AOC for lunch with him and his wife. As we drove away from the King David Hotel my new master said "I will have to think of a name to call you. Although your Christian name is James I have decided to call you Pelly." I responded happily; I said that this had been the way with my father in Colombo and my elder brother had inherited it. It had a personalised identity that somehow conveyed acceptance – perhaps even a touch of popularity – that a mundane Christian name could not match.

The official residence that came into view was called Villa Haroun ar Raschid and was a square house standing on open ground with a flight of steps leading up to the entrance. On the flat rooftop was a white flagpole carrying the Royal Air Force ensign; it looked good! There were spectacular vistas, the most prominent one on the gin-clear skyline being the tall bell tower of the Young Mens Christian Association (YMCA) headquarters facing the King David Hotel. Surprisingly, many years later a very old friend Group Captain DJ (Judy) Garland told me that the AOC's villa at one time had been used as a boarding house!

I had the pleasure of meeting Therèse, the Air Commodore's charming and attractive wife and she looked so young that I guessed that she was about the same age as I was. It was an estimate that was close because on her forthcoming birthday we compared ages and she was two years younger than I! Once in the house and looking around in some kind of a daze I could barely take in the dramatic change in my life. I had moved from the routine (if quite acceptable) Mess accommodation that the Air Force provides on an aerodrome to a nice villa that was beautifully appointed by its hostess. Clearly her tastes appealed to me; I liked all that I saw.

Jill (her family name as I was soon to call her) made me very welcome, smiled sweetly, and suggested a gin-and-tonic; the dreaming stopped and I got back onto my feet again. The three of us had lunch together and I was made to feel at home because the conversation centered on my earlier activities as a long-distance transport pilot with 216 Squadron. When I mentioned the magic word Kenya my new boss's eyes lit up. 'East Africa and the Rhodesias in my book are the finest that God made. I would happily go back there, given half-a-chance'. We were now talking the same language and lunch passed all too quickly. It was a splendid start.

Three days of search for somewhere to live with one of the Air Commodore's airmen navigating me around the city proved a fruitless and exasperating exercise. It was difficult even to visualise in my mind's eye just what I was looking for; a house was out of the question, a small flat – if one existed – was marginal and probably too expensive anyway on my pay, and plain digs like I had in London was to be avoided like the plague. Rescue came when Bert Harris suggested that I abandon the search and continue to live at the villa as one of the family. This was music to my ears and I accepted like a drowning man clutching at a raft. Not only did this plan stop the agony of further search, the converse was the prospect of being able to live well and comfortably with no domestic hassle to worry about. Best of all, it was superlative to continue to be with such wonderful people. For the first time I had the feeling of being in a home of my own and it had taken me years to reach that happy situation. Gathering momentum as each day passed was the experience that in the company of a man like Bert Harris a completely new vista opened up because he was so well versed in all manner of subjects outside Service life; he read books avidly and talked in his very stimulating and articulate style. Service life tends to bring varying degrees of limited outlook and perhaps it is the reason why it is so easy to identify military people outside their particular sphere of activity. For me a breath of spring had arrived and my horizon widened very considerably, thanks to one man and his wife. Life now consisted of a lot more than take-off speeds, fuel consumption figures, constant shop-talk, and the superficiality of Mess parties. I was growing up rapidly.

Chapter XII

The Contented PA

With such a good start in the new appointment as a personal assistant, it was a painless transition from squadron life to a completely new environment. The new job, if you can call it that as it was full of interest and variety, was essentially one of being on hand to look after the requirements of one man. It was a compound of assisting him in his tasks as private secretary and being a companion whenever the occasion prescribed. The important part of the job as I saw it was to get to know the Air Commodore's ways of operating and by so doing make his task as smooth as possible. Nothing is more irritating to the top man than bad administration that prevents him from concentrating fully on the requirements of command and keeping his finger on the pulse of events. A good PA can often tell his boss about all manner professional and social straws-in-the-wind that may not necessarily come his way. You become a watch-dog, aware of the passing scene, and in this regard your faculties are sharpened considerably. In a way, you take on the professionalism of a private detective, constantly straining to be well informed and so productive in the appointment.

Apart from Headquarters activities, most of which falls into the secretarial bracket where the PA is a compound of contact man, telephone operator, filter man for visitors both expected and unexpected, and general dogsbody but operating from a position of strength, real or imagined! The other side of the coin is the much more active part of getting about away from base to see physically everything and everybody that makes up the framework of the Commander's sphere of responsibility. In this regard the Armed Forces are particularly active, and there is no doubt at all that it is one of the principle reasons why the military way of conducting affairs is so effective. The boss goes to see and be seen and he thus gets a cohesive and efficient organisation. Perhaps best of all, the human factor is paramount and personnel at all levels get the feeling that they have identities and not just cogs in a wheel. As a comment upon the comparable (and equally essential) requirements of civil life, particularly in the sphere of industry where productivity is the key word, it happens all too often that the system fails lamentably. In recent times I met a man whose job it was to deliver fuel to my household in a huge tanker. A strike – euphemistically called industrial action by the participants when precisely the reverse applies – was in full swing at the time. He and I discussed briefly the cause and in this context I mentioned that it might well not have started had the senior people involved followed the excellent example of the Forces by regular contacts from top to bottom. He agreed, but added "I wish my own company did that. In my fourteen years service I have to tell you that our Managing Director has never been to the Depot – I don't suppose he even knows where it is."

Bert Harris was a singularly good example of an energetic commander who wanted to get about and see for himself what was going on. On these occasions two pairs of eyes have a much better chance of putting the visit to maximum advantage although I soon appreciated that his speed of perception and rapid comprehension was exceptional. He not only rapidly grasped the important issues, together with the implications that they raised, he was swift and forthright in his reactions. I have never known any other man who was so quick to appreciate, so accurate in his judgement, and so swift to take action. Whenever he spoke about the particular visit afterwards he was pungent in comment and completely articulate. It was a joy to listen to him. Equally, his written word, whatever the subject matter, was succinct and had that certain style about it that was masterful.

The domestic scene at Air House was remarkable for its happy and efficient management. Although Buddy – as Jill called him – struck a formidable note when on duty, (something that later on most of his staff in Bomber Command have good cause to remember!,) his home life immediately shed that forbidding mien, the silent stare, and when necessary his explosive and withering comment. Almost as soon as we entered the house after the day's work was over there was the loving Jill to welcome him and the affection was returned in kind so much so that I wanted to vanish like a mirage because I felt that I was intruding. The spell would be broken by a gruff voice saying, "Pelly, let's have a damned good whisky-and-soda". Who would not wish to be in my shoes?

There were so many interesting incidents in the life of following in the footsteps of my master that I confess it is difficult to compress or select suitably into one chapter. It is hoped therefore that some highlights from a plethora of material will give some insight into life as a personal assistant to such a remarkable man. One of the joys of my appointment was that every day was different from the previous one; there was never a dull moment and the unexpected was often round the corner.

On one occasion I was given a document to deliver to an Army officer whose office was on the floor below. I went down the stairs, checked through the security police, and was directed to the right door. In the manner of the Services I knocked once and walked in. Sitting bolt upright behind his desk was a chap holding a Colt '45' – and he was aiming it at me. His name was Captain Orde Wingate. When he saw who it was the revolver was put down within easy reach on his desk and I handed over the document. Wingate looked at me with intensely unblinking eyes, something that I was to encounter frequently under different circumstances later on in the Sudan. After my natural comment about his gun he said, "You never can tell around here; things happen quickly".

Orde Wingate was masterminding some kind of a Special Forces Unit, a job that he was probably very skilled at and the experience put to good purpose later on first in Ethiopia and later when commanding the *Chindits* in Burma during the Japanese war. During his time in Palestine he had developed a lasting admiration for the Jews and he had a special regard for those in one kibbutz who, so I was told, literally saved his life when he became desperately ill during one of his forays into the countryside. A few days after my first encounter with him, one evening at Air House we were having coffee after dinner when we heard a lot of shooting nearby. Bert Harris said, "There must be another skirmish going on; I wonder who is shooting at who this time?" A few minutes later when the firing stopped the front door bell sounded I went to see who it was but in the dark it was difficult to determine if it was friend or foe. I called out, and a voice replied 'Wingate'. He and about five of his Jewish friends came in because they wanted to rest temporarily from further activity. All of them were dressed in dark clothes, black plimsoles, and had blackened faces. All of them were well armed. It transpired that Wingate and his party were chasing up some arabs who were attacking a small Jewish settlement and as soon as they entered the fray the arabs melted away into the night and the shooting stopped. The strange-looking and somewhat sinister posse had some coffee with us, spoke little or not at all, and after Wingate had said his 'thank you' they picked up their weapons and set off on foot as silently as they had come. It was just another night's work.

Wing Commander George Beamish, famous athlete, boxer, and international Irish rugger player was the Senior Operations Officer on the Headquarters staff. George was a huge and charming man, a very well liked and distinguished RAF officer who became an Air Marshal in later years. It was his brother Victor who spotted the German battle-cruiser Scharnhorst escaping down the English Channel when flying in his Spitfire, and nobody believed him at first!

One day in Jerusalem George asked me if I would like a game of squash with him; it happened to be one of my favourite sports but to play against such a formidable opponent made me wince. However I accepted and no prizes offered for guessing who the winner was. After the game, (when George was kind enough to say that I actually made him run some of the time), he offered to take me back to Air House in a newly purchased Ford 'V-8' tourer that he was very pleased about.

No sooner had we got in and the engine started than it was clear to me that this was no Ford 'V-8' but one of the four cylinder 24 h.p. versions such as the Shell Company operated in the Middle East. As we motored along I tentatively said so, whereupon George became quite peeved. "Pelly, I thought you knew a lot about motor cars; you do surprise me". I replied, "Well sir, I do take a keen interest" and left it at that. When we arrived at Air House I dutifully admired George's new purchase and after an glance at its exterior condition I discreetly asked to lift the bonnet to have a look inside. Poor George! He was silent when we gazed down at a four-cylinder engine. Without further ado he climbed in, I thanked him for the game and the lift home and he drove away. As I entered the house I could not resist laughing about the embarrassing affair. Bert Harris must have heard me because he called out "What's so funny, Pelly?" and I told him about George's Ford eight-cylinder car that had half of them missing. "Typical", said Bert, "they send a chap like George at great expense to attend the two-year engineering course at Henlow and what do we get? Someone who cannot tell the difference between a four and an eight cylinder engine running just by listening to it". He added, "Dammit, he probably never even looked under the bonnet!"

One of the AOC's tasks of making his annual inspection of the units under his command took on a new angle for me because I was now on the other side of the fence; I was an observer, rather than the observed, and so could participate with equanimity. It also had the advantage that I was able to travel all over the Command, in itself of the greatest interest if only for the reason that I could look, listen, and learn from an experienced leader what his requirements were, the items that were important to him, and his methods of finding out. It was soon clear that what he expected was competence from his subordinates and their ability to use their equipment to good purpose rather than a special tidy-up prior to his arrival.

No 33 Squadron was visited at Lydd Airport, their Gladiators having flown up very recently from Egypt to assist in the air surveillance necessary because of the ever-growing Arab-Israeli situation. We travelled down by road from Jerusalem accompanied by the usual RAF armoured car escort (in case of ambush from either of the warring parties) and we were met by Squadron Leader Hector MacGregor who was commanding the squadron. The famous unit was still on a somewhat makeshift basis so all that we saw were Gladiators on the apron, the pilots and ground crews, and some aircraft ground equipment. We then moved into the Terminal Building where the squadron had contrived to set up some accommodation for their scanty possessions by using the space belonging to absent air lines. Bert Harris stopped at one booking-in counter, took a cursory look in the back, and said "Anything to do with you, MacGregor?" The squadron commander replied "Yes sir; it's the Motor Transport Section store". The AOC and I then looked closer, and all that we saw was one solitary wheel! That was the sum total of 33 Squadron's motor transport support equipment and all that they had been able to bring with them from Egypt. Not surprisingly I was told to make a note of the matter for immediate action. One spare wheel only or not, No 33 Squadron was putting up a remarkable showing against the arabs hell-bent on killing every Jew they could find. Perhaps the most distinguished fighter pilot was Flying Officer 'Pat' Pattle – later to be shot down into Athens Harbour in his Hurricane when attacking a huge force of German aircraft. On one occasion in Palestine he killed three arabs; They were all found shot vertically through the head when taking cover at the bottom of a well. On another sortie, following a message from our ground forces he flushed out more arabs who were hiding underneath a low road bridge at the bottom of a steep culvert. He was a fantastic pilot who could do things with a Gladiator that seemed like magic. 'Pat' Pattle was a South African in the RAF. When commanding No 33 Squadron, after earlier successes in battle with No 80 Squadron, he continued his brilliant leadership right up to his death on April 20, 1941, when he took on overwhelming Luftwaffe forces over Athens Harbour and was shot down. He was credited with no less than forty enemy aircraft destroyed and almost certainly many more had the records of this turbulent period been fully on record. Thus by definition he became the all-time top scorer fighter pilot in the Royal Air Force during World War Two – something that is not generally known even to this day.

The main base in Palestine, in fact the only one with pretensions to any permanence, was Ramleh; it is situated some ten miles from Tel Aviv. It had a natural if poorly grassed small aerodrome that was roughly egg-shaped and with a maximum length of barely 1,000 yards. The squat hangars, technical buildings, and the domestic areas were neatly laid out and with trees and gardens provided a pleasing appearance which made life agreeable for the personnel. From the point of view of the visiting airman, particularly on his first sortie, Ramleh had an extraordinary natural camouflage and I always found it necessary to follow some good landmarks nearby before I could identify the aerodrome on the run-in. The neat and compact Station was commanded by Wing Commander 'Sandy' Sanderson, a popular and amiable officer who with his wife made an excellent team to produce a happy and efficient RAF overseas base.

Ramleh was the home of No 6 Squadron, a maid-of-all-work unit equipped with Fairey 'Gordons'. Although nominally described as an Army Co-operation Squadron, a lot of extra work was done during the troubles when the luckless British were endlessly trying to stop the factions in question from killing each other – or both killing the Brits for that matter – and a secondary function was to provide aircraft for staff officers such as the AOC and myself. The procedure, other than going by road all the way to Ramleh with all the armed escort requirements, was for two 'Gordons' to fly up to Kolundia outside Jerusalem and there hand over one to the staff pilot and the ferry pilot would return to Ramleh in the back of the other one. The small strip at Kolundia with no more than a windsock in the way of facilities was no place to leave an aeroplane over-night because the baddies would quickly destroy it. Thus a positioning flight by two or three Gordons always had to take place and in winter and early spring there was always the low-cloud factor to contend with.

The other unit at Ramleh was the famed No 2 RAF Armoured Car Company, equipped with vintage Rolls Royces from earlier days and commanded by the tall and outspoken Squadron Leader 'Tiny' Stilwell, a pilot in his day but now enjoying a specialised ground job and wearing the ribbon of the Military Cross on his uniform. Considering the great weight of the armoured Rolls Royces (and of course no four-wheel drive in those days) it was quite remarkable how they coped with Middle East conditions. They invariably escorted RAF convoys and on one trip to Amman rather than ride in the AOC's staff car, I travelled by armoured car. Standing in the back along-side the airman manning a machine gun was an experience that made me realise what tough hombres those men were. For their part they just loved it and would not have changed jobs for all the tea in China. When a new Alvis type designed to replace the trusty Rolls Royces was sent out from Britain for evaluation under overseas conditions they looked disdainfully at it. In the event they were right.

Although some of the officers of the Armoured Car Company were posted direct into it from other branches, often they were pupils from Flying Training Schools where their aptitude as pilots somewhere along the line was inadequate. The RAF retained some of them and those concerned were delighted to have the chance to serve in another branch of the Service. One such was a very remarkable fellow called Flying Officer MP Casano MC – 'Cass' to everybody. Who was a real Lawrence of Arabia type whose name became a by-word right across the Middle East. With his flamboyant desert dress, his spotted red scarf, and his undoubted charisma and fearlessness, he was an operational leader of great fame. During the war in the Western Desert on one occasion he moved his unit unbelievably from Mersa Matruh all the way to RAF Habbaniya in Iraq in six days and it entailed almost continuous desert driving for well over one thousand miles. No wonder the Armoured Car Company had a magnificent *esprit-de-Corps*! It was my great pleasure to come across the legendary desert warrior more than once, the last encounter being at a jolly party in Malta when I was delivering a Mosquito to India.

There was some excitement at Ramleh one day when one of the new Westland 'Lysander' aeroplanes arrived for field trials and test flying by the pilots of No 6 Squadron. The AOC always took a keen practical interest in a new type of aeroplane – I have to say that he was the first Air Commodore in my experience who was a practising pilot – and he went to inspect it and test-fly it. After he had been briefed about cockpit drill and handling procedures, he took off and made a short flight. After landing, (when he seemed to be impressed with its short take off and landing characteristics), I asked Squadron Leader Noel Sinclair the squadron commander, if it was my turn to have a fly around too. 'Sinc' said 'No' firmly; it was much too precious for PA's to go joy-riding about in. As wartime conditions proved, the Lysander was much too vulnerable for front-line daylight operations with Me. 109's waiting to pounce and so it was very successfully diverted to the very specialised job of landing and picking up agents by night from fields in occupied Europe. In that role its remarkable qualities were invaluable and so indeed were the Cassano-type pilots who flew them under such tricky and dangerous circumstance. Not for them the public adulation of being fighter or bomber aces – they relied on stealth and secrecy.

One day in Jerusalem my boss told me that he had a need to go to Haifa to greet the new divisional Army Commander who was arriving by sea. I asked him who it was and he said "It's a chap called Montgomery". Question number two, "Do you know him, sir?" "Yes; we were both at the Camberley Staff College". My third question was brief; "Any good?" "Yes Pelly, he is a very good soldier and he will make a dammed good general. Incidentally he is the first soldier that I have come across who has a proper grasp of the vital role of a tactical air force in land battles. I expect he will be putting it to good purpose before long". When I said that I would lay on a 'Gordon' to fly Bert down to Haifa he gave me what could be called an icy look; "Pelly, I'll dammed well fly myself there, thank you. If you want your own aeroplane – well order two". And so I did. It was just as well because in the event the AOC took Admiral Sir Dudley Pound, C-in-C Mediterranean Fleet, in the back of his Gordon and I tagged along as escort. When making the run in to Haifa, losing height from the Palestine hills and Mount Carmel now in sight, I thought the occasion merited a neat arrival in the style that the pilots of the Red Arrows aerobatic team would have approved of; so I tucked in close on the leader's starboard side and felt quite pleased with my station keeping after three years as a transport pilot. Bert soon noticed that my wing-tip was within spitting range, whereupon his gloved hand emerged and he waved me away to a more respectable distance. I was disappointed; I thought that one Air Commodore and one full Admiral going to meet the new Major General waiting on the apron was reason enough to make a stylish arrival and impress the other two Services. After landing the three senior Commanders met and I kept to a discreet distance before they went away somewhere to have a conference. The new general was a small dapper man with an aquiline nose who spoke crisply with a slightly high pitch in tone. About an hour later the flying party took off again and the two Gordons headed up into the hills back to Kolundia. It had been a good day.

Life in Jerusalem provided all manner of official activities that included Bert Harris and Jill as a matter of routine. In addition we had the informal and more pleasing social events in which to participate such as cocktail and dinner parties, gymkhanas, and amusing diversions like a dog's fancy-dress competition when Jill's dachshund aptly named 'Endless' was kitted out as a flying clown complete with an even longer nose and a pointed hat. Amongst the formal functions the grand reception at Government House to celebrate the King's birthday claimed pride of place for pomp and circumstance and we used to chuckle at the stories of the pecking order that was contested by the many religious groups in the Holy City. It is perhaps indiscreet to 'name names', as they say, but the grape vine told us how one holy eminence insisted on being the last to arrive at Government House, behaving almost like Royalty.

I had arranged to play squash in the late afternoon of the big day in question and after the game was over fate decreed that my return to Air House was delayed unduly. When I eventually got there, to my dismay I found my boss sitting in his official car dressed in Mess kit with Jill and 'Wingers' also in their finery. Oh dear, the p.a. had blundered. With a hasty 'Sorry, sir', I flew to my bedroom and put on my Mess kit in record time before dashing pronto downstairs and into the car. We arrived at Government House just in time to join the queue of all manner of important personalities and their ladies awaiting their turn to be announced by the Master of Ceremonies. It was an impressive scene and of course it was enhanced by the unique nature of the great variety of people that Jerusalem boasted. Once past the grand entrance we made our way to the Reception Room and as we walked the gruff voice of authority turned to me and said, "Pelly, so it's Grecian carpet slippers instead of Wellington boots tonight, eh?" I looked down and to my embarrassment realised that it was true! Thank heaven they were black leather. The next day, 'Wingers' told me that whilst they were waiting impatiently in the car for the junior member to show up, Bert turned to him and in his inimitable style said, "You know, I sometimes wonder if Pelly is my p.a. – or if it's the other way round".

The sad affair of the loss of my predecessor Desmond Bell and his passenger Mr Scarborough on the ill-fated flight now took on a bizarre turn. We received a report from the police at El Arish that the body of a white-skinned man had been found buried in the sandy shore of the Mediterranean coastline; he was naked and a rope was still round the neck of the corpse. I immediately surmised in the light of my investigation at Heliopolis that it might well be Scarborough because he was a good swimmer and Desmond Bell unfortunately was not so. To verify if it was Scarborough, the medical people advised that he had sustained a broken arm and this together with dental records would be evidence enough. The investigating team soon confirmed our fears so now we knew for sure that my reconstruction of events had proved correct. The Gordon had run out of fuel out to sea beyond gliding distance of land and he had swam ashore only to be murdered by the arabs. It was all very nasty indeed. The only saving grace to the tragic affair was that we all learned from someone else's bitter experience that in aviation nothing should be taken for granted. One checks and checks; and then one checks again.

A road journey down to the Gulf of Aqaba was planned for late March in 1939. It is a good time to make such a safari as the Spring rains would be over, the air cool and clean, and best of all it was the time when all of nature's glories could be seen and admired. The outline plan was to travel south across the desert to Aqaba, in those days a small arab settlement, stay for two nights with the Transjordan Frontier Force and then head north to Amman and visit Petra *en route*. The last lap was to leave RAF Amman and head west, cross the Jordan at the top end of the Dead Sea and finally make the long climb from 1000 feet below sea level up to the hills of Jerusalem. The trip was planned to last for ten days and cover a distance of more than 500 miles, almost all of which would be on unmade roads or tracks; allowing for the overnight and longer stops it meant putting in more than 100 miles per day on some stages. I contacted the Transjordan Frontier Force and RAF Amman during the planning stage, in each case saying that we would appreciate advice and such accommodation as was available and the TJFF endorsed the itinerary. However Group Captain Douggie Harries at Amman expressed doubts about our ability to keep to the schedule between Aqaba and Amman. He said that the Spring rains were late and anyway the track from sea level rising up to well above 3000 feet was difficult enough in dry weather. When I told the boss he grunted; "No worse than some of my Rhodesian and East African experiences". The plan was left unchanged.

The party consisted of Bert and Jill Harris, Lady 'Coppy' Haining the delightful wife of General Sir Robert Haining, General Officer Commanding British Forces, the dutiful PA, and the usual Armoured Car escort as far as Aqaba. A two-ton truck would accompany the two cars all the way round the route, thus carrying all the tents, the baggage, spare parts, camping gear, rations, water and the various other items necessary to make us independent. It was like old times in Kenya making a check-list of everything and then assembling it all before departure; it is a job that I get the greatest satisfaction in doing.

The expedition set off in style and we travelled south past Hebron and Beersheba, familiar in Biblical connotation, and then came the desert run into Sinai where we stopped in the late afternoon to set up camp for the night. We were now on the 3000 feet high plateau with an unbroken vastness all around us, a situation that for me has the greatest appeal. In the desert you are master of your own destiny; either you love it or are frightened of it and therefore hate it. I well remember the night stop and sleeping under the limitless stars above. In the morning it was so cold that my blanket was stiff and crackled with ground frost when I arose from my camp bed. After breakfast *al fresco* all the gear was packed up and we set off towards the top of the escarpment at the head of the Gulf. At this point the descent down to sea level is so steep and with many hairpin bends to negotiate that the armoured cars were obliged to turn back whether they wanted to come with us or not. They were not needed in practise as by now we were out of the bad-lands of Palestine and at Aqaba would enter peaceful Transjordan.

The view looking down into the Gulf of Aqaba from the top of the escarpment is breathtaking. Many hundreds of feet below one can see the vivid pale emerald green water in the shallows changing to blue-green water further out from the shore. Beyond, the colour turns to cobalt as the under-water shelving drops rapidly into the depths, in parts over 3000 feet down where light never penetrates and marine life goes about its mysterious ways. The Gulf forms part of the Great Rift, that huge fissure in the Earth's surface that begins in Turkey, traverses the Dead Sea 1100 feet below sea level, moves down to the Gulf of Aqaba, follows the Red Sea and then works its way across central Ethiopia before running on to Lake Rudolf in Kenya. Beyond that it is known as the Rift Valley and ends up close to Mount Kilimanjaro. It is a 3000 mile long geographic masterpiece that even Texas cannot beat.

When we reached Aqaba we were met by Colonel John Chrystall, famed commander of the equally famed Transjordan Frontier Force. I admired this striking man and had I been a soldier his organisation would have been for me. The open-air life, the tents and the clean desert, minimal office work, and a huge parish to operate in without being told what to do all the time. We were given comfortable and attractive huts lined with palm fronds for accommodation. It was now pleasantly warm and the water lapped onto the sandy beach invitingly. In the evening we enjoyed a pleasant and relaxed dinner provided by Mrs Chrystall and sat comfortably afterwards to talk by the light of those good Tilly pressure lamps that come from Belfast. The whole affair comes back to me with nostalgia and it was splendid to be in such excellent company. For the moment the rest of the world and its problems faded into obscurity and I noted that Bert Harris looked as benign as ever I had seen him. Aqaba must have special qualities to soothe the savage breast.

The following morning after a breakfast that we all tucked into with gusto, John Chrystall announced that he had laid on a fishing party for us. For Bert Harris and myself this was an outing close to our hearts and what better way to spend Day Two at Aqaba but to get onto the water? In quick order everything was made ready, the gear and picnic baskets stowed aboard the two local fishing boats (powered rather incongruously by outboard motors to supplement the lateen sails) and the party set off down the Gulf. The aiming point was Faroun Island, a small rocky islet ten miles away close to the Sinai shore and separated from it by an immensely deep channel. The whole of the crest of the island is covered by the ruins of a Crusader castle built by a warrior called Reynald de Châtillon, the Prince of Transjordan during the days of the Crusader Kingdom when English knights set forth to attack the moslem unbelievers. Once again religious prejudice had struck a blow against freedom and man was fighting man with a fervour quite unrelated to reason. The greater part of the remaining walls are 'dry built', thus having neither cement nor mortar to hold the stones together and the workmanship was so excellent that most of the structure was still standing. The castle fell eventually to Saladin, the Kurdish general who as related earlier had stripped the Egyptian pyramids. The remarkable part of the island's capture is that in order to do so boats for the water crossing somehow had to be transported across the desert from Suez, the nearest place where they could have come from. The mind boggles! Why the intrepid but frankly piratical Crusader elected to build his castle on the small Faroun Island at the northern end of the Gulf of Aqaba is uncertain. It could not command the entrance at Ras Muhommed, far to the south, and so the guess is that he used it as a fishing lodge and between times harried the arab camel trains coming up from Saudi Arabia. Although some excellent game fishing can be found in these waters, the fighting barracuda in particular, our luck was out. The only minor success came my way with a few small fish brought up from the deep by hand line. Poor Bert and Clarence Buxton, (the political agent and a distant cousin of mine), both used big-game rods and harness and so looked the part but that was all. In spite of such disappointing fishing it had been a wonderful day on the water and we returned to Aqaba by sailing quietly and peacefully along and admiring the splendid scenes. For the three ladies that was the part of the day's outing that they liked best of all.

On the fourth day the safari set forth again and we headed north for Ma'an, some seventy miles away. The rough track follows the Wadi Ytem, one landmark of which is a cliff-face rising 5000 feet sheer up into the sky. The two cars, one the AOC's carrying Lady Haining and myself and the other Bert's private Ford that he drove with Jill by his side and with the support truck following up behind, began to travel ever upwards into the hills. A wonderful vista now unfolded. The skyline was cut by jagged rocks against a background of white clouds. In the valley on either side of the track could be seen acres and yet more acres of beautiful wild black irises, crocuses, anenomes, and jonquils all growing amongst the grasses and other vegetation in the area. Nature had done her work to perfection, we had arrived at the right seasonal moment, and of course Jill Harris and 'Coppy' Haining were enchanted. We stopped frequently to get out and absorb the sea of colour to the full and I could not resist the thought that in all probability we were the only visitors able to enjoy the splendors in an area the size of Scotland.

The difficult run up to Ma'an was eventually accomplished and we arrived at the TJFF rest house a little tired but contented. We were now just over 2000 feet above the Gulf and in cooler air with even bigger and more majestic cumulus clouds towering above us it was a reminder that the rains were still with us as the Group Captain at Amman had forecast. We got out our overnight kit, unpacked, and after a tidy-up were well cared for again by Frontier Force hospitality. Ma'an's claim to existence was generated in the first place by the old single track railway line that the Turks had laid all the way from Damascus to the Hejaz; the track that Lawrence and his arab tribesmen used to blow up by way of interdiction during World War One. We had an early dinner and all decided to retire soon after. Tomorrow was going to be another long day, but of an entirely different nature.

The plan was to visit Petra, a unique ancient city situated in an almost impossibly remote spot and accessible only by one route along a fissure in the earth's crust. It is so narrow that only an animal or a human can traverse it conveniently in single file and at one place the walls are so close that you can touch both simultaneously with outstretched arms. It was in the city of Petra that people called Natabeans lived many hundreds of years before and their commanding position enabled them to extract tolls from the caravan trains in transit. It was a lucrative Eastern Mafia. Petra has been described in later times as 'the rose-red city almost as old as time'. For the traveller the only way to get to Petra is to drive from Ma'an to Wadi Musa across the scrub and then complete the last ten miles on horseback. So it was that the four riders set off on the final run-in to our target. We may not have looked like a Rotten Row scene in Hyde Park but circumstance changes both the mounts and the attire of the riders.

We threaded our way along the tortuous track with hoof marks faintly to be seen from previous visits, pretty infrequent though they must have been. The walls on either side got closer and closer, so much so that we wondered if we would not have to dismount and walk. They parted a little later to reveal the astonishing sight of the city's Treasury; it was hewn out from the solid stone. Beyond the Treasury the ground opened out into a huge bowl that housed the city where most of the hand-cut stone buildings were in a pitiful state and had a look of lost grandeur. At the time I thought it would need considerable restoration and tidying up before it could become a tourists' attraction but the problems of geography must be such as to deter all but very avid travellers. However it seems that today the ruins are more accessible. After some time looking around and having a picnic lunch we retraced our steps. We all agreed that although Petra was impressive because of its unique setting and background the general consensus was that it had been a lot of effort that did not justify a whole day's hard travel. When thankfully back at the rest house and enjoying our pre-dinner drinks, the ever charming Lady Haining said, "I must say that I am nothing like so stiff and tired after riding to Petra as I had expected". When Bert asked her to elaborate, she said, "Well, I have to admit that I have never ridden a horse before. If I had said so previously I was afraid that you would not allow me to come with you!" For a lady who was easily the oldest member of the expedition her determination not to be left out was a splendid effort.

The cloud build-up and associated rain overnight prescribed that we took the precaution of an early start on the following day. My fears were well founded because all the vehicles began to slide about alarmingly at times with the support truck having the worst of it. As the two Fords were faster we pressed on leaving the heavy vehicle to follow as there seemed no point in slowing down. We were making quite a respectable speed considering the poor conditions when suddenly a Wellesley of No 14 Squadron from Amman arrived low overhead. On the aeroplane's second pass something fell out and landed close to the now stationary cars and I splashed across the muddy ground to retrieve it. It was a message bag and inside was a note from the pilot that read 'Consider route north of your position impassable. Suggest return Ma'an.' I showed it to my boss and his comment was 'I've seen worse; we go on'. This suited my purpose because I not only agreed with him, I was very keen to press on to Amman and keep to the schedule of arriving at 1700 hours.

The rally-type of driving continued non-stop and I admit that sometimes it was pretty hairy. When we eventually arrived at the Guard Room of Royal Air Force Station Amman the clock outside on the verandah showed exactly 1700 hours. The Sergeant on duty saluted and grinned approvingly at the good timing. Even Douggie Harries was impressed but he added that we had been lucky. I had to agree.

The final part of the journey from Amman to Jerusalem was almost a routine affair because it was a regularly-used road of passable quality; the interesting feature is that the traveller starts off at an altitude of some 2,500 feet from Amman and descends down into the Dead Sea valley at over 1,000 feet below sea level before climbing all the way up to the 2,000 foot level of Jerusalem once again. The crossing of the river Jordan with it's emotive connotations was made over the small bridge named after General Allenby (now called the Abdallah bridge) and beyond that the ruins of Jericho can be seen. The Jordan river and Jericho may well have had an important place in Biblical history but to us the river, the old city, and in particular the surrounding area had nothing at all to offer. All is seemingly desolate and nothing grows except miraculously very briefly if it rains; in summer the heat is quite unbearable and it is very surprising that man willingly elected to live there at all. There had been talk of the possibility of connecting the Mediterranean to the Jordan Valley by some engineering feat of canals and tunnels but nothing has happened and the probability is that it never will because the political problems will prohibit such action even if the project was feasible.

The return to Jerusalem enabled us to shed the trappings of long-distance travellers and we now resumed the normal life of the city, a comfortable home in all respects, and of course the commitments that attendant work and duties prescribe. We all thoroughly enjoyed the ten-day experience of seeing superb country and the opportunity of travelling in a way that few others have had the chance to do. Although an airman by choice of profession I had to admit that by far the best way to get experience first-hand is by surface travel.

Chapter XIII

The Secret Visit

The days slipped passed all too quickly – the sign of a contented way of life – but it was not to last because a problem arose in the household. The fact of the matter was that Bert Harris was obviously not well and he seemed to be getting worse. He had now lost his appetite, and for a man like him who loved his food this was very out of character with his normal healthy habits. Previously he used to talk enthusiastically about memorable meals enjoyed at what he called the dirty shirt department of the Café Royal (near Piccadilly Circus) where a Russian dish called *Sashlik Grushenska* – barbecued lamb – was his favourite choice. Prior to this change of lifestyle he used to send me to Cairo to visit the Nile Cold Store where I would purchase items like uncooked English hams, whole sirloins of beef, and saddles of lamb, all of which was flown back in the 'Gordon' and duly delivered to the household. The sorties gave me useful flying practise and a couple of nights away which is always a good thing when one is 'living above the shop' as HRH Prince Philip Duke of Edinburgh describes it. My arrival at Air House was invariably the signal for Bert to go to the kitchen and carry out the job of cooking one of the items himself. His speciality was a whole ham cooked in the Virginia style with brown sugar and cloves – it was delicious! The chance of real and tasty food was most enjoyable in contrast to all the slightly tough and tasteless variety that Jerusalem provided. The fact was that only supplies from Europe (where the grass is greener) were worthwhile and fortunately the Nile Cold Store company in Cairo imported them.

The position had now changed and my boss had lost his interest in food; on a number of occasions all that he was in the mood to have for dinner was a poached egg. At first I thought that it was a temporary affair and I assumed that he had picked up a bug, something that is easy to do in an area where they abound; but after a while I had the feeling that it was something more than that and in my fashion began to think that it was possibly an ulcer. After pondering about it for a few days I plucked up courage and asked him what the trouble was; he confirmed that something was amiss which was causing him to lose his appetite but he did not pursue the conversation and I sensed that he wanted to keep the problem to himself. Jill was obviously as concerned as I, but both of us were somewhat inexperienced in these matters and neither of us was old enough – or brave enough – to tackle Bert successfully with the result that we kept a discreet silence and pretended that it was not important. However I continued to be worried and on another occasion I asked him outright why he had not gone to Ramleh to see the RAF medical people; at least that would be the normal thing to do and it would clear up uncertainties by getting a diagnosis. His reply was that he had no intention at all of doing so but he did not say whether this was because he had no confidence in the RAF medical service or that he did not want to admit to being unwell. Soon after that unproductive effort on my part he made discreet visits to an Armenian doctor in Jerusalem but never said anything about it to me – and possibly not to Jill either for all I knew. The whole affair was now becoming taboo and as I could not see any progress in his health I wondered what options there were of getting something worthwhile done. It was a tricky impasse; I was living in the house so I was well aware of the problem and poor Jill was obviously getting more concerned as the days passed. So what to do? I decided that the only course of action was to take the bull by the horns, as they say, and once again go to the top of the tree to see the Commander-in-Chief in Cairo. On the ploy of having the week-end off – even PA's sometimes like to get away – my request was agreed and I organised a Gordon from Ramleh.

On the 17th of June 1939 I flew down to Heliopolis and immediately contacted Freddie Milligan to find out if I could see Sir William Mitchell for a few moments, ostensibly to make a courtesy call. Freddie said that he could fit me in to the programme on Monday morning and that was good news because I was due back in Jerusalem the following day. In the meantime I trotted round and saw my friends and did the usual rounds of Heliopolis and Cairo; the only nagging thought was that I was now committed to the essential purpose of my visit and hoped that I was not going to make a fool of myself by the clandestine nature of it. It is pretty unusual for a junior officer to walk into his C-in-C's office and tell him that his principal air commander is a sick man and will he please do something about it! However I was certain that this was the only way that anything positive would result and I judged that I was the only one who could spark it off effectively.

At the appointed time Freddie showed me into Sir William's office and I wondered how to begin. Fortunately almost the first thing that he did was to ask about Bert and Jill Harris and how things were going in Jerusalem. It was the cue that I prayed for and without any preamble I said "Sir, I have come specifically to tell you that the Air Commodore is not at all well".

Whilst this startling piece of news was being absorbed I went on to say that my guess was that he had an ulcer; but whatever it was I knew that something was obviously wrong with him because I lived in Air House and so had good reason to know from close observation. Warming to my subject I said that although Jill and I had unsuccessfully tried to help, the longer term issue was that unless something positive happened there was the possibility of the RAF losing a very valuable officer. I then waited for his reaction; I had said my piece.

Sir William was clearly taken aback. He thought for a moment and then said "Why haven't I been told about this before? What have the medical people been doing about it?" I explained that I had suggested to my boss that he saw the RAF doctors in Ramleh but he had turned down this idea out-of-hand without giving reasons; instead he had been seeing a civilian doctor in Jerusalem whose name I did not know because I never met him. I could only surmise that he was anxious to keep the matter to himself for whatever reason but the reality was that he was not getting better – quite the reverse in fact. By now I was feeling so confident that I had done the right thing that I even went so far as to say that the best course of action was for Bert Harris to go back home to England where the specialists would take him in hand and so eliminate all the anxieties that we had. They were heady words from a young officer but I just had to say them. Bert Harris was a special person and although I continued to be a little frightened of him I was very fond of him and could not bear to think that he might fall by the wayside because nobody had made a move. I dared not tell even Jill about my action; if my visit was uncalled for, all the blame could fall on me.

Sir William looked distinctly thoughtful after hearing my speel and all he said was that he was very grateful for my action and thanked me for taking the initiative. Just before leaving his office I said "Sir, I hope that you will keep this matter as confidential as possible; if the Air Commodore hears that I have been telling tales behind his back – well, he will probably shoot me!" The C-in-C was as good as his word; apart from Freddie (who now knew the reason for my call) not another soul that I am aware of knew about the visit and I returned to Jerusalem to await events.

Before the month of June ended a nice surprise came my way; Bert Harris told me that I had been promoted to Flight Lieutenant! When I looked mildly astonished at this unexpected windfall, unexpected because Short Service chaps like myself never thought that it was possible, Bert's typical comment was "Pelly, I could never fathom the strange and devious ways of the Personnel Department; they must have pulled the long straw out of the bag with your name on it!" I noted that he said it with a twinkle in his eye so concluded that he was pleased. I was delighted; I was about to ascend another rung of the ladder and could now add a second stripe to my sleeve. To hell with the extra two-shillings-a-day that I had been cheated out of by the man from the Ministry; now I could collect the extra pay whether he liked it or not. It did however introduce a new factor in that the PA's appointment was in my old rank and in that case it was reasonable to suppose that a posting was in the offing. I asked my boss what to expect and he said that a posting would be good for me and added that after many months of trotting around after him like a labrador following his master it would be a good change to go to a job where I could manage something of my own. So what would I like to do next? Immediately I replied that I would love to get back to flying, and if it were possible nothing was better than to join a squadron in Kenya. This reaction was obviously one that he approved of and he said that he would see what the possibilities were by asking Middle East Headquarters to advise him.

The months of June and July 1939 seemed to be full of incident and events. Soon after my return from Cairo, and learning the good news of my promotion, I was told that I was posted to No 223 Squadron, based in Nairobi. The appointment was to be senior Flight Commander and so second-in-command. This was a job that appealed to me immensely because it was not only a flying job but it would take me back to my favourite Kenya. My lucky star was still shining in my direction. Another bonus was that my new squadron was equipped with the Wellesley light bomber such as 14 Squadron operated from Amman. I was now about to leave the old-fashioned biplane behind and move into monoplanes with retractable landing gear and other modern devices for greater performance. The overall prospect pleased me very much – it all seemed to be a move in the right direction.

The much more important news was that Bert Harris was promoted to Air Vice Marshal; so both the Air Officer Commanding and his Personal Assistant stepped up one rung of the ladder – the same formula but the appropriate rungs were very widely spaced! So he in turn could expect a move and this was revealed to him in a letter from the Chief of Air Staff in London who advised him that this would take place on or about January 1st 1940. His next appointment was not revealed at that stage, and whether this was by design or because it was not yet determined can only be guessed at by the uninformed.

The significant fact is that he did not stay on in Jerusalem for the next five months as was intended but travelled back to England very soon after receiving the letter from the Air Ministry. Perhaps it was wishful thinking on my part, but naturally I could not avoid the conclusion that my visit to Cairo was at least a contributory factor in the matter and may well have been the primary cause. Anyway, I like to think so. What is certain is that Bert and Jill Harris left Jerusalem having completed only half of the normal tour of duty. He arrived back home at a critical time, about one month before the declaration of war against Germany and thus fate had decreed that he was in the right place and the right time to move into Bomber

Command in charge of No 5 Group and subsequently became the Commander-in-Chief.

Just before Bert Harris' affairs were resolved I myself prepared to leave and began to say my 'good-byes' to everybody and finally to Bert and Jill. This was a mixed emotion of being very sad at parting with such a remarkable man and his very charming wife coupled with the thought one has to move on in the Services or get left behind and stagnate. It had been wonderful to have been with them under such agreeable and pleasant conditions; equally it had been a complete education to be alongside a master of his trade who knew precisely how the concept of air power should be pursued relentlessly.

So it was that in late July I departed from Jerusalem in the same way that I had arrived nine months earlier – by air; this time it was in a Gordon bound for Heliopolis. The next stage was to determine the manner of my going to Nairobi. To my surprise, (and I confess a certain degree of pleasure) it was ordained that I was to travel by sea on the ten-day voyage to Mombasa in the SS *Mantola*, a medium-sized vessel operated by the British India Shipping Company. Four young pilots accompanied me, all destined to join No 223 Squadron, and the time passed in good company; not least an attractive and charming young lady called Alice who we adopted. After arrival in Mombasa we airmen took the famous train journey up to Nairobi and for my companions this was an excellent introduction to the sights, sounds, and even the smells of East Africa. As an old hand I was able to initiate them into some *Swahili* – like *Bwana n'degi*; Mister bird-man. I was a happy man because I was back once again in Kenya.

Chapter XIV

Wellesleys Over the Sudan

Most of us who recollect the Vickers Wellesley single-engined military aeroplane will associate it with the remarkable record-making flights that were carried out by the Royal Air Force. On November 5, 1938, three long-range Wellesleys took off from RAF Ismailia, adjoining the Suez Canal, and set off for Australia – destination: Darwin, in the Northern Territories.

Each aircraft carried a crew of three. All were pilots; the second pilots were also navigators, and the third members were signals specialists or aircraft engineers.

The ambitious target was to break the world's record for distance in a straight line non-stop, currently held by Russia with a flight of 6,306 statute miles – 10,146km. For the RAF record attempt each Wellesley carried about four tons of fuel – this represented a 71 per cent overload compared to the standard all-up weight. Each take-off, along the specially prepared sand runway, was uneventful, each aircraft was airborne in the cool air at 0400hr with an average take-off run of 1,200 yards – yes, 1,200 yards!

After encountering unexpected headwinds and a nasty patch of weather over the Bay of Bengal which persisted for over a thousand miles, all three aircraft successfully reached Indonesia. However, No 2 aircraft landed at Koepang, its fuel state being judged insufficient for the safe crossing of the Timor Sea before reaching the Australian coastline. For a brief time, however, it had in fact broken the record. After refuelling, it took off again and headed for Darwin. The other two Wellesleys flew on and, some 48 hours after leaving Egypt, Sqn Ldr Kellett and Flt Lt Combe, with their respective crews, landed at Darwin. Both aircraft had comfortably broken the old record with official flights of 7,158½ miles (that half-mile is intriguing!). Subsequently, the pilots of Nos 1 and 3 aircraft were awarded the Air Force Cross; poor Flt Lt Hogan and the crew of aircraft No 2 (who had showed good airmanship by their precautionary landing at Koepang) got nothing. One wonders how these decisions were arrived at in the Air Ministry. For the two aircraft that reached Darwin non-stop, the fuel remaining in the 17 tanks (a total capacity of about 2,000gal) was, as they say, a bit dodgy; with the dreaded Timor Sea to cross on the final run-in Kellett had 44 gallons, and Combe a mere 17 gallons – a header-tankful!

I visited Ismailia from Heliopolis (Cairo) just before the record attempt. There I was shown round by the incomparable Flt Lt George Musson, second pilot and navigator in No 2 aircraft. Flt Lt Brian Burnett, in No 3 Wellesley, will of course be well-known in modern times as Sir Brian Burnett, Mr Big of Wimbledon tennis.

Spectacular record-breaking flights apart, Barnes Wallis' remarkable geodetic airframe construction – a type of basketwork with a spiral criss-cross motif – was incorporated into the 177 Wellesleys delivered to the Royal Air Force in the late 1930s. It was the end product of the Air Ministry, in its wisdom, stating an Operational Requirement to the aircraft industry, and of the Vickers Company trying to interpret the specification but at the same time doing some intelligent cheating that would in practice produce a better aeroplane – and then allowing the Air Marshals to believe that it was their own concept. Better wine in new bottles!

Initially, five bomber squadrons of Wellesleys were stationed in East Anglia. However, when new aircraft like the Whitley, Hampden, and Wellington (the latter basically a twin-engined Wellesley), came into production, Wellesleys were relegated to overseas work and scattered right across the Middle East Command. Out there, so it was thought, nothing much would happen to them. Overseas squadrons, like kid brothers, always get cast-off clothing. Fine, so long as a shooting war does not start up. Thus the Wellesleys were distributed between 14 Sqn in Amman, 45 Sqn in Helwan, Cairo, 47 Sqn in Khartoum, Sudan, and finally 223 Sqn in Nairobi, Kenya. A spread of some 2,000 miles, north to south. It was like having one "bomber" squadron every 500 miles all the way from London to Cairo to provide air power – and incidentally, no fighter support of any consequence.

The four squadrons in practise fell into the vague category of being "General Purpose" – a euphemism for the pious hope that by some good fortune they would be able to adapt to whatever situation might arise. In retrospect, one has to smile at the optimism of the whole business. For example, 47 Sqn, with some 20 aircraft and 150 personnel, was expected to take care of the entire military aviation requirement in the Sudan, the biggest country in Africa at one million square miles.

By good fortune and competence, and the fact that nothing untoward of a warlike nature had happened since 1922, the squadron carried out its "General Purpose" tasks very well.

The Air Ministry planners certainly made one good move; and it proved to be a winner. In 1938, when the war clouds developing over Europe became alarming, three Wellesley squadrons were earmarked to be formed into a bomber wing based in the Sudan. The fourth squadron, No 45, was to be re-equipped with the new twin-engined light bomber, the Blenheim. The concept was that the Wellesleys would be located in the northern Sudan and would thus be available to tackle Mussolini's forces in Ethiopia in the event that *Il Duce* decided to rattle his sabre. The Wellesley wing would be the air component to attack from the north, and possibly later from the west, one essential task being to keep the Red Sea open for our seaborne supplies to get to Egypt unmolested. This would of course be accomplished in conjunction with such ships of the Royal Navy as were stationed in the Indian Ocean – Red Sea area. The southern part of the possible theatre of war – for practical purposes the then Crown Colony of Kenya – would have to scratch along on local resources and such help as might come up from Southern Africa.

Overall, it was not a healthy picture at all. Geographically, both ground and air forces had a huge area about the size of Europe to encompass. In terms of comparative strengths, we would be very seriously outnumbered on the ground and more evenly balanced in numbers – but not by type of aircraft – in the air. We had the Wellesley and sundry left-overs like the Vincent. The Italians had multi-engined bombers and the effective Fiat CR.42 fighter. So the erstwhile General Purpose Wellesley theme was now looking a bit outdated, considering that we had to expect a shooting war.

Alas! all thoughts of a newly-promoted Flight Lieutenant, with his safari car, his trout rod, his shot gun, and maybe even a beautiful girlfriend (who knows?) faded like a desert mirage. Within a week of arriving in Nairobi came the stunning news that the squadron had to pack up and fly away north to some unseen and unknown spot in the Red Sea hills in the Sudan. It was goodbye to all that Kenya had to offer.

During the brief stay in Nairobi I had been introduced to the Wellesley. Flt Lt Jack Roulston had checked me out from the air-gunner's position, using a make-shift dual control affair, although his view looking ahead was abysmal. Following that adventure I managed to put in 2hr 25min of flying before leading "A" Flight toward Khartoum and beyond "as to the manner born". We all hated the idea of leaving Kenya; equally, we abhorred the prospect of becoming bedouin and making a tent in the desert our home in the months to come. The prospect of war at that time, unpleasant as it was, now began to have a nasty ring of truth about it. This only compounded our discomfiture. It began to look as though we were soon to get the worst of both worlds; a shooting war *and* sand in our shoes.

No 223 Squadron arrived at Summit landing ground, on August 31, 1939, during one of the rare tropical rainstorms that made us think we had seaplanes as we splash-landed.

After 12 hours of flight, in four stages, Sqn, Ldr RT Taaffe had successfully moved his unit some 2,000 miles with only one minor technical fault at Juba, in the southern Sudan. After the final touchdown we all sat in our cockpits and waited for the rain to stop. Even then, problems were manifest. Only three or four tents had been set up by the advance ground party that had come up, over 400 miles by train from Khartoum, the day previously. With a grin and a flash of brilliantly white teeth, our new and impeccably attired Sudanese cook said, "Sorry Sahib – meat is tough". Things, as they say, were not going to be the same any more.

After a makeshift meal – enjoyable for all that – the boy scout business of putting up more tents began, and went on until darkness fell. The following morning we carried on; quite soon, sheer requirement forced us to learn the trade rapidly. Later on, with a number of re-sitings in the light of bitter experience to reduce the blown-sand factor, we became highly professional. Lord Baden Powell would have approved. Beautiful Kenya was now a forgotten paradise.

Settling in

The three squadrons forming No 254 Wing were now in their new locations: 14 Squadron just outside Port Sudan; 47 Squadron at Erkowit, Red Sea Hills; 223 Squadron at Summit, the new landing ground close to the railway halt of the same name that looked so incongruous in the middle of nowhere. At about 2,000ft altitude, it was the highest point on the route to Port Sudan and the alighting point for the Government officials and their families going to the Hill Station at Erkowit, about another 1,000ft higher up. This was the "local leave" station in summer, when Khartoum boasts a shade temperature of almost 50°C. Yes, you could say that Khartoum is quite hot in summer! So up in the Red Sea hills, with a wild landscape that was a blend of black rock, scattered thorn trees, clumps of tough grass, yellow sand, and the occasional "fuzzy-wuzzy" tending his hungry goats, at least it was tolerable by day and pleasantly cool – sometimes too cool – by night.

The squadron layout, where to put the tents and the aeroplanes, became a matter of experiment. As new boys playing boy scouts on the eve of war, we had to compromise between dispersal and accessibility; with the emphasis on the former. No wonder that we all became so fit; with transport limited to three or four trucks, medical and firefighting vehicles and the CO's estate car, we walked to work and back for hundreds of yards every day.

Very rapidly we abandoned the standard form of RAF dress regulations and adapted to local conditions; bush jackets, desert boots, and no topees. The airmen took off their shirts and worked only in shorts. The squadron doctor was the first to admit that going by the old-fashioned book was now a thing of the past.

No 254 Wing Headquarters had by now moved into the hill station –

where else? It was commanded by no less a person than Group Captain SD Macdonald – the famous "Black Mac" – who later became an Air Vice Marshal with important assignments in the UK and NATO Europe. Under his overall direction, the three squadron commanders (Sqn Ldr Selway with 14, Sqn Ldr Elton with 47, Sqn Ldr Taaffe with 223) soon had everything running smoothly under our new and difficult conditions. We had a good aeroplane – as wartime use was soon to prove conclusively – and we got down to the business of air and ground training. The first days of September had arrived. On the third day came the first "Most Immediate" signal that ever we had seen. It said – and the wording is vivid to this day – "War has been declared against Germany only". The war in Europe was on; the deadly game was about to start. But not for us – yet.

We immediately accelerated the flying programme. More bombing practise, air gunnery practise, much longer cross-country flights. A lot more night flying, much more, with our very basic facilities only. The Wellesley seemed to be able to take all this in its stride. The pilots of "A" Flight were definitely getting better and more confident, and overcoming some earlier problems. During my brief time in Nairobi there had been talk of engine troubles (white metal in oil filters), retractable undercarriages that did so at the wrong moment, hydraulic happenings, flexible wings, and other cautiously worded comments. Watching the general flying one got the impression that the pilots were a little nervous of these new fangled modern aeroplanes. The mild anxieties were compounded by the altitude factor, Nairobi being close to the equator and about 5,000ft above sea level. Most take-offs saw the Wellesley clawing its way up in the thin air, propeller in fine pitch and the Pegasus engine bursting its heart out – and no respite until some 2,000ft of altitude was gained. The whole business was carried out in reverse prior to landing, some aircraft making two complete circuits with "everything down and out" in the process. Finally, a very long and cautious approach before a "wheelie" touchdown. It all seemed akin to a Mini driver doing his best with a Ferrari.

Soon I summoned my pilots, and said, "So far as I am concerned, all aeroplanes fly like Tiger Moths. Perhaps a difference of emphasis here and there; but in principle they all work the same way. So let us be relaxed and get the aeroplane to fly nicely, as it wants to. Treat it like you should treat a woman – stroke it, not fight it". The homily worked wonders, I am happy to relate. With the type of long-range flying to come, largely by night and high above the Ethiopian mountains, close affinity with and confidence in the Wellesley became a vital requirement.

Some data and comments about the Wellesley Mk I might be of interest. With a wing span of 74ft 7in it was a big single-engined aeroplane. The wing area was 630ft^2, and it was fitted with split trailing edge flaps – another innovation to fuss about. The machine was powered by the very excellent Bristol Pegasus XX, a nine-cylinder air-cooled radial delivering

835 hp for take-off and 935 hp in level flight at 10,000ft. A hydraulically operated, wide-track, inward-folding, tail-down type of undercarriage was fitted. The bombs (or whatever) were carried in containers slung under each wing, internal stowage not being possible with the geodetic airframe construction. The pilot had control of a Vickers .303 machine gun embedded in the starboard wing (outside the propeller disc) and the observer (who combined the functions of air gunner and radio operator) had our old friend the hand-operated Lewis .303 machine gun so reminiscent of Biggles and caps-on-back-to-front. The generally clean lines of the aircraft was spoiled by a Vokes tropical carburettor air filter that some soulless person decided could just hang down in the fresh air underneath the Townend Ring engine cowling. It must have cost double-figure mph loss of performance. Aerodynamics? What's that?

All sweetness and light

With a maximum speed of 220 mph under optimum conditions, we used to fly the Wellesley at a comfortable and economic 160 mph and a nice sweet-sounding power setting as a result. By now, with much better pilot handling and improved airmanship, the 'Peggy' engines were running like sewing machines. Everybody was happy. Perhaps it is useful to mention that none of us had the benefit of the Pilot's Notes (such an excellent idea) issued later, or any of the specialist pilot training schemes introduced to cope with a very rapidly enlarging Air Force. Pre-war, it was the Flight- and Squadron-Commander's job to train new pilots. Night flying, as can be imagined, tended to be a heart-stopping business for the participants.

Blessed with docile handling characteristics, nice approach and touch-down speeds of 65–70 mph down to 55 mph – comment is superfluous, surely? – perhaps the most impressive element was the Wellesley's payload and flight endurance capability. The geodetic construction, with fabric covering almost everywhere, produced a disposable load well in excess of the empty weight. That is, empty weight 6,245lb; gross weight – officially – 12,500lb. Due to the nature of our operational wartime requirements (to be touched upon later), we found in practice that we were regularly exceeding the official maximum all-up weight by well over 1,500lb. The cry was "If the tyres look a bit flat, well, pump 'em up a bit more and press on"! We operated those splendid aircraft not only with the maximum bomb load of 2,000lb but with all fuel tanks brim-full and sometimes a third crewman and more guns as well. In this condition we could get airborne in about 1,000yd, climb to well over 20,000ft to miss the Abyssinian lumpy bits, and have a flight endurance of up to 15hr – just in case. Cannot be bad! The only problem was a human one – the poor pilot. A fuel flow oddity of uneven tank draining (which was never properly diagnosed but which must have been something to do with the non-return valves in the junction box misbehaving) inevitably introduced a wing-low condition which was surprisingly tiring to the pilot on a long sortie. We worked out a simple 'autopilot' system which entailed the use of the rubber bungees that helped parachutes to open by flipping back the flap coverings. You took three or four with you, and as the 'wing-low' got worse, so you added more 'rubber bands', sliding them along the spectacle control to vary the tension. Simple, but very effective.

Another problem – but this one sinister in its implications – was the nasty habit of the smaller bombs hanging-up over the target and deciding to drop upon touchdown or when taxying. The trouble was essentially one of electrics in desert conditions, particularly so when using those most unpopular things, Small Bomb Containers, fitted with drop-off arms for each compartment. The solution was to do the Pelly-Fry Rope Trick. The game was to get the armourer to lash up each bomb box (hanging under each wing – the geodetic construction denying any internal stowage in the Wellesley) immediately after switching off the engine. When properly secured, the bomb box doors were freed of hydraulic pressure from the cockpit by the drastic measure of flicking the undercarriage lever to 'up' and then quickly 'down'. It sounds alarming, but it worked. With pressure thus released, the bomb doors then drooped by gravity but were arrested by the rope taking up the slack. The resulting gap enabled the armourer to peep inside, although the familiar and potentially lethal metallic rattle was evidence enough, and any 20lb or 40lb bombs found could be removed by hand as the rope was gingerly slackened off – rather like loosening one's tie. Great fun being an armourer, playing with live bombs all set to explode. Unhappily, Blenheim squadrons could not employ the same trick and, alas, there were casualties, usually upon touchdown.

By late 1939, and then moving into 1940 (when we were having increasing anxieties about the news of war in Europe), the daily pattern of our lives was relieved by the occasional Red Sea fishing trips from Port Sudan; a conference at Wing HQ; your turn to do the mail run to Khartoum, 400 miles away; a picnic using the CO's estate car; basic exercise, although we were disgustingly healthy anyway; and of course the horses! Our 'elderly' Adjutant, Bunny Isaac, was a Kenya farmer and champion polo player. He and our equestrian pilot, Flying Officer Witty, contrived to get four polo ponies sent up from Khartoum – thank Heaven for the excellent Sudan Railways. The owners, now enlisted in the Sudan Defence Force, also provided Indian syces to look after them. The officers paid five shillings (25 pence) per month, and the airmen paid nothing. All could ride – or try to – with saddles and so on provided. We were desperately short of building materials, like timber, but some discreet night sorties to the nearest habitation of Sinkat (important only because of the railway), bits of crashed Wellesley – yes, it happens to us all – and straw matting from Port Sudan, enabled us to construct stables for our string of polo ponies. The Group Captain (with that engaging smile and infectious chuckle) now referred to No 223 Cavalry Squadron.

A state of war

The only local 'media' (at that time a word happily yet to be invented) was a broadcast from Asmara. This fellow (whose cockney accent caused us to give him the nickname of Bill Bloggs) would come on the air at 2000hr local time every evening. He would then bore us to tears with eulogies about *Il Duce* and how pleased Italy was to hear of the successes of Hitler's armed forces. We had to guess at the truth of his news; but at least it was something to listen to in the mess tent. As the days went by, Bloggs' eight o'clock broadcast became more and more aggressive. Eventually, it happened. On the night of June 9, 1940, we were told by Bloggs that at midnight – four hours to go! – Italy would be at war against Britain. It would have been appropriate for Mussolini to have called it 'Operation *Bandwagon*'.

In our Mess tent, for some moments that seemed like minutes, silence prevailed. Each of us, understandably, pondered upon the implications of war. Now it was our turn, living like nomads in the sunny Sudan. The quiet was broken by distinctly rude expressions from the articulate chaps about the habits, pedigree, and sex life of all male Italians. I doubt if it made any of us feel the braver; after all, going to war, as I see it, is not funny; particularly not in a remote part of Africa, with slender means, and with nature to fight as well as the human enemy. At least we tried to make ourselves feel braver. Either way, something was now going to happen; something nasty. The nitty-gritty would soon be upon us.

In the event, no-one, not even Mr Bill Bloggs and his friends, had bargained on the speed with which Group Captain 'Black Mac' would react. He was not a seasoned warrior for nothing. The first Operation Order arrived overnight, in home-made code, from 'Black Mac'. It was transmitted with the willing consent of the Sudan Railways management on the open telephone. A good example of Hobson's Choice! The snag was that the code – or rather the message – seemed liable to misinterpretation at the receiving end. So nothing for it but to use the railway telephone system again and put in a call back to Erkowit Hill Station. "Sir," I said, "reference to item 'G' in your message" (which was the instruction about the method of attacking Gura airfield, the main Air Force base in Eritrea, and which cryptically said 'High to low'), "we are not sure of your intention". A pause, during which I was sure that I could hear the ice tinkling in the Group Captain's whisky and soda. "Well Pelly, I'm not sure that I know myself; I had to put in something! Do what you think best. After all, you will be on the spot and so you are the best person to judge". So we worked out a plan that we would climb up to a good height above the target (which was 5,000ft above sea level), somehow identify it visually, and then individually swoop down and bomb the biggest things (like hangars) that we saw. The reader will be correct in deducing that we had no target maps, no approach maps, no photographs, no data whatever about fighter defences or gun positions. All that each pilot had was a map to the scale of one in two million; which is roughly 32 miles per inch. Oh well, better than nowt to go to war with for the very first time; we did not even know what happened when a real 250lb bomb hit the ground. One learns fast in this business.

At 0605hr on the early morning of June 11, 1940, the day after Mussolini had declared war, eight Wellesleys of No 223 Squadron – later christened 'Pelly-Fry's Hell Divers' after a certain raid on the docks at Massawa – took off to locate and attack Gura airfield. I was in the lead aircraft with Leading Aircraftsman Pitt as my crewman. It is difficult to describe one's thoughts and emotions when faced with specific war conditions for the first time. Perhaps fortunately, the need to be professional and concentrate on the job in hand absorbs all one's attention and energy. The worst time comes when all is set, nothing more to be done, and then one is waiting for the clock to tick away until it is time to climb in and get started; the dreaded 'point of no return.' One curious feature of air warfare is that whereas pilots in a Flight, together with their crews – if any – are detailed to fly to war, the Flight Commander (and equally the Squadron Commander) has to put his own name on the list. It is so much easier to be told than to tell oneself. Another curiosity is that Air Forces, unlike other armed forces, adopt a gladiatorial stance – but in an inverted way. The chiefs go off and do the fighting and get killed; the Indians stay behind.

After a stream take-off, we assembled into a loose formation over the landing ground – airmen like to show off – and then set course in a southerly direction over the Red Sea hills, climbing steadily to 10,000ft. It could well have been yet another practice, except that this time the bomb boxes underneath the wings now contained 250lb bombs. They were to be aimed by each pilot, in his own time, and at the specific target of his choice. The only instruction of note was for all aircraft to try to keep together, for all the usual reasons.

The target, according to our very small-scale maps, was about 400 miles away. You left Asmara, capital of Eritrea, just on your port side on a direct route. This was handy for first-time-sighting pilot navigation, but probably a bad thing as it would give warning of our approach and so increase danger of attack before the target was reached. The seven Wellesleys kept station nicely on the lead aircraft, Pitt keeping me informed generally as we flew along. The cloud began to build up a little, but of no consequence. Everything, or so it seemed, was quiet and peaceful. Just the same, all eyes were busy scanning the skies around us; this was no time for musing.

No radio contact with base was expected as we went on our way. We had tried it often before, and usually without success. Just one of those things.

Odd, in a way: the RAF had perfectly competent Signals people who were paid to provide communications essential to us. When radios failed to work they just shrugged their shoulders with mild incredulity showing on their faces. What would have happened if the same attitude had been adopted by the airframe and engine people?

On approaching Asmara (we were now at 12,000ft and seemed to be on track just to the West of the city), we could see black anti-aircraft puffs at eye level, apparently indicating that 47 Squadron was attacking the airfield. Then followed ground level bomb bursts which seemed to be straddling the hangars and other buildings. We still had another 20 minutes' flight time to reach Gura. Time enough, surely, for warnings to be sent to get those CR.42s into the air to receive us? We were now a bit envious of 47 Squadron heading back for home. Well, hardly 'home'; but at least back to your very own tent. Life is comparative.

At last what could only be Gura appeared ahead. Quite a large green aerodrome with hangars and buildings on the near side. The amount of cloud was still favourable and insufficient to upset the plan. At the right moment – which is another way of mentally saying "I think this is it" – a waggle of the wings, a slight pause, bomb doors open, and checked, bomb switches 'on', and then downhill at ever increasing speed towards those hangars. We were now doing what the Group Captain called 'High to low'. Each to his own aiming point now, and the best of luck.

With thumb on the bomb release button, a final check of switches, the Wellesleys swooped down at around 250 mph. When the moment seemed correct, peering over the top of the Townend Ring engine cowling, each of us pressed for 'Release', paused momentarily (when at least we *thought* we could feel that the bombs had gone) selected 'Bomb doors closed', eased back gently on the control column, and then a gentle turn to port to return the way that we had come. So far as Pitt could see, all the other aircraft were following; but it was necessary to throttle well back to let them close up on the leader. As we left the target Pitt said, "Crikey," (or words to that effect), "the hangar seems to have taken off in a great cloud of dust and smoke!" We seemed to have actually hit what we had aimed at; classic beginners' luck.

Hotting up

The return journey, surprisingly, was uneventful. I could only guess that our first attack, so soon after *Il Duce* had declared war, had caught the defences on the wrong foot. Not one puff of anti-aircraft smoke; better still, not a single CR.42 in sight. Four hours and 40 minutes after take-off we landed back at Summit; eager faces greeted us as we stepped out of our cockpits and jumped down onto the sand. The consensus was that it has been a successful sortie. Equally, the 47 Sqn attack on Asmara and the 14 Sqn attack on Massawa seemed successful. Later we heard through the grapevine that 14 Sqn had destroyed 350,000gal of aviation fuel. Yes, the Wellesley wing was in business. The score seemed like forty-love. The air war carried on, week after week; we were learning fast all the time. It was not long before it got tough – CR.42s were now buzzing about like angry hornets. One Italian fighter pilot we favoured with the nickname of 'Pedro – the Spanish Ace', because he was far and away the most aggressive of them all. He should have had a red aeroplane! The daylight sorties, unless essential for Army tactical support, were now becoming too risky, particularly with our limited means and little prospect of getting replacements. After all, was not the East African Campaign of minor importance? – or so we surmised. Thus we now moved into the night bombing game, with single-aircraft sorties, even though the target was the same. We had now exchanged the hazards of attacks by CR.42s in daylight for perhaps the even greater risks of night flying in most difficult circumstances. Alan Moorhead, a distinguished war correspondent, in his book *Mediterranean Front* (very good reading!) writes:

"We watched the Wellesleys take off, great ungainly machines with a single engine and a vast wing spread but with a record of security that was astonishing. For weeks now they [the pilots] had been pushing their solitary engines across some of the most dangerous flying country in the world – country where for hours you could not make a landing and where the natives were unfriendly to the point of murder – and they had been coming back; sometimes collapsing down on the sand with controls shot away and full of holes."

Inevitably, there were losses. Inevitably, very worrying, for all the reasons. Too often, all that we knew – or would ever know – was that an aircraft had failed to return. We rarely found out why, where, or how. Flying in wartime under bush conditions, particularly at height in single engined aircraft and across high mountains, had its own hazards. The problems of pilot navigation and difficult terrain required us to develop a particular kind of expertise and airmanship that, with respect, the modern Service pilot would raise his eyebrows about. Here, in the East African Campaign, the paramount requirement – other than making a successful attack – was survival, with no aids or help whatever to that end except, perhaps, that you included a windsock, a Very pistol, and some gooseneck paraffin flares by night. Some of the operating problems became apparent on my second sortie, a second attack on Gura. The plan was to make an attack on the aerodrome, but this time at last light so that the CR.42s would not be able to cope. If we were lucky with the timing, we could dive down as before then escape into the darkness and make our separate ways back. Unfortunately, on starting up engines, one aircraft had an electrical malfunction with the parachute flare, which promptly ignited on board. The heat generated – a million candlepower – was so great that firefighting equipment could not extinguish it. The whole machine was quickly ablaze and soon the 2,000lb bomb load would explode. After a short pause to assess the situation I decided to go with four aircraft only, despite the fact that the burning Wellesley was close to the starting point for the take-off run. In rapid succession each Wellesley taxied into the corner of the landing ground, opened the throttle, and away; just about the briskest Flight take-off that we had accomplished to date. All four got off safely, but we were now about ten minutes late in departing. With a little increase of power, and hence airspeed, I hoped to make up the loss – at least my slide rule said I would! As we flew across the landing ground in open formation all of us heard the big bang as the bombs exploded, throwing large lumps of aeroplane high up into the sky. We hoped that nobody was injured, and nobody was – one advantage of dispersed aircraft against enemy attack.

Once again we headed south, climbing as we went. The route was now familiar, except that we kept a discreet distance from Asmara and the 'baddies'. As we entered the Eritrea airspace, still climbing, the clouds began to build up as before; still no problem. In the event, although we had made up most of the lost time, it was the onset of darkness that forced the formation to separate – I even tried putting on my navigation lights – and thus each aircraft would have to make a completely individual run. Pitt could not see any results from the rest of the formation, but he thought that our own attempt caused bombs to fall on the airfield; perhaps, as so often happens, merely to make holes in the ground. We turned round and headed back in a northerly direction. The idea was to climb up again, fly a little right of track, and identify the Red Sea coast with the help of a bit of moon. Slowly the cloud thinned out; it would not be long before we were safe back in the Sudan. In truth, nothing was 'safe' in that part of the World!

After being airborne for some 4½hr, gazing at the vastness of the skies, checking instruments, and keeping a knee-pad log of courses, times, airspeeds, heights and so on, suddenly an intense bright light appeared on our starboard quarter, approximately at our altitude. It was almost impossible to judge the range, but as it could well be from one of the Wellesleys – what else – I altered course and aimed at the parachute flare. Whose was it? why was it employed? the only sensible answer was that a pilot had released it for a good purpose; more than likely to see what was below. All that was below, alas, was steep hills, scrub, and wilderness. The flare became extinguished as we raced towards it, making any investigation virtually impossible. However, we noted the time, the compass heading, the estimated location, and then did a series of wide orbits in case anything showed up below. Nothing. No fire, no Very light, no trace of anything. Nothing for it now but to head back for Summit. By now we were flying at 5,000ft – a pleasant change from high mountain work without oxygen, a commodity seemingly unheard of in foreign parts. In this context, I personally often went up well beyond 20,000ft in order to miss the lumpy bits in the dark. Nowadays, I am told it is an offence to fly above 'ten grand' without it!

Pitt and I now seemed to be flying on, and on, and yet on, with nothing by which we could identify our position. In the setting moon, getting too low on the horizon for comfort, nothing was familiar except a hazy impression of coastline. No matter; soon Port Sudan would show up, and then we would know what was what. So we pressed on, but alas! no sign of Port Sudan. It was not long after this that I confessed to Pitt that I was lost. My pride was hurt, but *all* was not lost – yet. Perhaps we had been airborne too long, too high up, and were just plain tired? We had been flying now for six and a half hours, and I wanted to get out. The decision was made to go down to 1,000ft, hunt around for a possible landing spot, put the Wellesley down on its wheels, have a rest, and review the situation after sunrise. The fuel state was still healthy; even so, there seemed no point in swanning about any longer, getting more and more tired. The plan was to keep a cool head, not do anything rash, and survive.

We were now below 1,000ft, and still descending. The low-level night vision had adjusted to looking down at the desert. We could see the usual pattern of light and dark; the gullies and the flat areas between them; the light patches indicating soft sand, the dark ones meaning, as a rule, a firm gravelly surface suitable for touchdown without sinking in. At least we knew our desert by now; this was going to prove whether our bedouin expertise was up to expectations. One feature was that there was not a single tree or bush of any consequence to be seen. Not much rainfall in these parts. The search procedure was to spot a possible area from about 500ft – from the altimeter readings we were now away from high ground – and if it looked promising to throttle back and have a closer look by landing light. Apart from general levels, type of surface, and so on, 'bogeys' like soft spots, holes, little bushes and other hazards had to be checked out. It was a task requiring alertness and patience, qualities in shorter and shorter supply as time went by. However, survival considerations generate their own reserves.

A lonely furrow

After a number of rejects, a patch finally showed up with good promise. We made a couple of passes, and then came down for a really low run, undercarriage lowered and flaps down for good measure. Then fine pitch, landing light on, and a turn in onto the longest run of dark sand. There seemed to be no wind. As we coasted over the selected spot, tail well down, playing the throttle to control the flight path, and airspeed showing about 65 mph, we got lower and lower. Suddenly an unexpected noise came from the back; it lasted for a few seconds until power was applied and we gained height. It could have been only one thing – the tailwheel had been rumbling over the desert with the main wheels and the rest of the aeroplane still airborne! 'Touch and go' with tailwheel only was, I confess, a new experience for me; especially in the small hours of the night somewhere in the Nubian Desert. No matter; with luck the tailwheel might have left a furrow to indicate the condition of the ground. And if I was lucky to make an accurate square circuit by directional gyro, we might get back to the same spot again and see the mark. In the event, that is just what happened. The landing light picked up the furrow – well, really more like a long scratch, which was good news – the power was gently taken off, and my favourite Wellesley touched down at no more than 50 mph and quickly came to stop after a discreet touch of brakes. Pitt jumped out, checked the surface with his torch, and waved me a short distance back to nice firm ground. We had arrived. The Wellesley was in good shape. Then careful cockpit drill, fuel state checked, gentle engine run-down, magnetos off, hydraulic pressure released by a quick flick of the under-carriage lever up and down – a trick of mine that sounds disastrous, but it works – and then utter and complete silence. Pitt and I had been airborne for just over seven hours. First things first, after leaving the cockpit, was to spend the longest penny on record – which was bliss. Second item was to get out the silver cigarette case – a present from Air Commodore Freddie Milligan and his wife Mollie for being best man at their wedding. As I opened the case to offer Pitt a cigarette, to our dismay there was only one there. Dear God! Of all the times for this to happen. . . . Moments later, all was well; I found a brand new pack of Players in my flying overalls. Non-smokers will never know or appreciate just how much our morale rose after that – as Pitt related so vividly at Upper Heyford when we met some time later.

After a sip of coffee from my flask, that superb smoke, and a chat, the rest of the night (with no moon now) was spent each going his own way, for some strange reason. Walking about kept us warm; and during our brief encounters – not too far from the Wellesley in case we lost our way – we both came out with ridiculous pleasantries; rather like friends bumping into each other in Bond Street or the RAF Club. Clearly, the Nubian Desert (or wherever we were) does strange things to people under certain conditions. We waited for sunrise.

Dawn brought the desirable commodities of light to see by and warmth to get the circulation going. First of all we checked out the aeroplane, and then we checked out the rations and, particularly, the drinking water. We might well have to be there for a long time. Then a shared cup of coffee from the Thermos, and one cigarette each. Now came the game of trying to find out roughly where we were. To this end, those small-scale maps were spread out on the tailplane, the flight log inspected, and an attempt made to plot our wanderings from Gura in Eritrea to where we had landed. After a while, allowing for wind effect, looking for the aeroplane that put out the parachute flare, and lastly swanning about to find a landing place, we concluded that we were in the Nubian desert, and an estimated 60 miles

NNW of Port Sudan. In other words, well beyond our aiming point. Overshooting, from previous experience, tends to confuse search organisations; they cannot believe that you were so foolish as to overfly your aiming point. If we had, then we were certainly on our mettle – we just *had* to get airborne. To that end, we carefully walked over the ground, noting what we had to cope with, and assessing the situation. We seemed to have just over 250yd of good going to play with. With a lightly loaded Wellesley, even in nil wind conditions, that would do. The big item now was the dreaded engine start-up. We knew that we had to get it right at the first or second attempt; internal batteries just do not have the muscle to keep turning an engine over for long.

With the greatest care, we carried out the usual procedures. Fuel on; turn the big three-bladed propeller over three times with throttle set at one third open; master switch on, everything electric off. Now the moment of truth – press the starter button, and magnetos on as soon as the engine turns. After about three or four agonising revolutions of the propeller our splendid Pegasus fired and ran smoothly. The utter bliss of that engine noise! I wondered if the men who had assembled that engine would ever know what it meant to two airmen, somewhere out in the deserts of the northern Sudan?

Pitt climbed on board, we strapped ourselves in, and I carried out the pre-flight checks, never more carefully. Then a gentle taxy back to the wheel-mark starting point, and a cautious engine run-up with stick back and brakes on. Now plenty of throttle, release brakes, and very soon full throttle. It was now 0700hr, the sun was warming us up, the much lightened aircraft soon lifted its tail and we were airborne in about 150yd; Tiger Moth stuff! Then wheels up, throttle back, coarse pitch, a final look at our lonely overnight resting place, and so off on a course (from memory) of 150° magnetic. We climbed to 3,000ft (to get a better view), and after twenty minutes the Red Sea appeared hazily on the port bow. So far, so very good. Ten minutes later – Port Sudan. That torrid seaport, so beautifully denigrated by Alan Moorhead in his book, could not have been more inviting to two airmen returning from oblivion. I suppose it is all a matter of comparison.

Soon we had touched down, and 14 Squadron took us in hand. We were refuelled, victualled, rested, and in the early afternoon we were on our way back into the hills once more. The whole sortie had taken eight flying hours, more than half by night. Apart from the usual need to exercise the maximum degree of airmanship in difficult circumstances, the important lesson was that even with simple pilot navigation of the 'bush flying' variety it always pays handsomely to keep a log during each flight; noting courses, times, speeds, landmarks (if any) identified, and any general observations.

Upon return to Summit (where another message had to be sent off cancelling an earlier one requesting replacements for Pitt and Pelly-Fry – shades of Mark Twain!), as we feared, one Wellesley was missing; Pilot Officer Jenkins and his observer had failed to return. The immediate reaction was initially to search the area where the parachute flare was seen and then work outwards from there. We searched for some five days; but alas! nothing was found. That aeroplane must have flown off somewhere else, only to vanish for evermore. The East African war was now only five days old; it made us ponder.

In mid-August I succeeded Wg Cdr John Elton to the command of 47 Squadron. My first command, and what a fine squadron at that. (Of interest, in recent times, is that 47 Squadron equipped with Hercules aircraft have been making spectacular non-stop flights to the Falklands Islands: 26-hour sorties. At least they had four engines and two complete crews, *and* flight refuelling and modern navigational aids). The move from 223 to 47 Sqn for me was simplicity itself; just a few miles down the track to Erkowit. Promotion – I like the word! – brought with it a little wooden house and a Ford Estate car; both commodities that were bliss to have, compared to a Bell tent and feet previously.

Meanwhile the Wellesley war carried on. Sometimes targets chosen by our Wing HQ, sometimes targets requested by the land forces. No 14 Squadron at Port Sudan continued in large measure with Red Sea activities. One problem was pilot fatigue when flying many hours over the hot and steamy 'gateway to Suez', so vital for supplies reaching Egypt. Two squadron-inspired ideas were incorporated. The first was initiated by the discovery that the pilot's seat was hinged and could be dropped down – this purely for inspection and maintenance purposes. The pilots now went out in pairs, exchanging places in mid-air in what seems to have been a pretty unusual and hairy way; no room for error when playing this game! No reports come through of any awkward happenings, so presumably those mixed up in the feats of gymnastics must have been good at it. The second innovation was to convert the Wellesleys into gunships by adding two more Vickers machine guns. The mountings were made up by the ever-useful Sudan Railways people at the Port Sudan terminal; each gun was mounted at the small window half-way down the narrow fuselage, port and starboard, and operated by volunteer aircrew. The area of safe firing of course was limited more or less to shooting on the beam and above the wing. If nothing else it seems to have been a useful deterrent to the CR.42 pilots; not counting of course Pedro the Spanish Ace!

Although, by definition, not a Wellesley episode, one 47 Squadron sortie of note concerns the use of a Vickers Vincent – that overseas workhorse 'General Purpose' aircraft. As the fortunes of war changed, 47 once again found itself back in Khartoum for a short time. Major Orde Wingate, the singularly eccentric soldier in charge of 101 Mission operating in the Ethiopian mountains on a guerilla basis, came to the squadron to ask to be parachuted into the mountains; he wanted to meet up with Brigadier Dan Sandford, the colourful commander. I reluctantly rejected the proposal because of the problems that arose, but respected the spirit of the would-be parachutist. What chance would he have had, descending into mountain country close to the Equator, and with no previous training? However, an alternative plan arose overnight; it was to use one of the Vincents abandoned by 47 Sqn after the Wellesleys arrived. One of my pilots was Flying Officer Collis, an ex-fitter, ex-Vincent pilot, and most competent. The plan was to fit the Vincent with a standard 120gal extra fuel tank slung between the wheels under the fuselage, and to have my own navigator Bavin-Smith (the only navigator we had), Wingate, and an Ethiopian multi-lingual officer, all tucked in behind the pilot. I was told that the Brigadier "knew about flying because he had gone solo at Heston". He would build a strip at about 10,000ft up and all would be well. In the event, almost a fatal situation; the Brigadier was no airstrip maker.

Collis and party set off in the Vincent, refuelled at Roseires en route, and then climbed up into the hills. With a little luck and some excellent airmanship the airstrip was located – although it seems that it looked about the size of a polo ground. Using all his skills Collis landed safely, whereupon the reception party summoned the braves literally to cover the Vincent with foliage. The air party stayed for two nights (this from memory) and meanwhile Collis and Bavin-Smith removed the long-range tank, now getting empty. When they came to inspect the makeshift airstrip they found that the long grass concealed very large stones and hyena holes. Once again the braves were summoned; they cut the grass by hand, picked up the rocks and put them into the holes. For the return flight, the Vincent staggered into the thin air, downwind and downhill, Bristol Jupiter engine flat-out and the wing-tip slots wide open. Once the dreaded take-off was accomplished the return journey was uneventful, with another refuelling stop being made at Roseires, on the Blue Nile. For this excellent feat, and bearing in mind also his Wellesley operational record, Collis was awarded the DFC.

A helping hand

This successful use of the aeroplane opened up new thoughts about the principles of air supply. Wingate became enthusiastic. Could we deliver money, bullets, fuel, food, whisky, even a monocle for the Brigadier? Rapidly we began to learn the tricks; we co-ordinated closely with Wingate about the initial successes and the failures, and the lessons to be learned. The Air Drop became the new game for 47 Squadron in between the bomber operations. It all had the merit that we worked at squadron level without having to wait to be told how to do the job by directives from armchair specialists. It was not long before Orde Wingate was in Burma with his *Chindit* force, using those lessons learned in the East African Campaign.

Another extra-mural activity was the Christmas Eve Rescue, 1940. A Wellesley from Digger Magill's 'B' Flight actually succeeded in radioing a message that engine trouble was about to cause a forced landing following a bombing attack on enemy ground forces. The estimated position was some 80 miles south of Khartoum. After two search aircraft had returned without finding the grounded Wellesley, I elected to make the third sortie. Still no luck. After cruising about for some time and getting nowhere, the only solution seemed to be to land and ask for news. So Sgt Barnes and I co-ordinated, a landing spot was selected, and down we came. The villagers nearby, in answer to my kitchen Arabic, had no news to offer. No 'tiara' had been seen or heard. So back to the Wellesley, get airborne, and try somewhere else. Again no news. At the third touchdown, when taxying along gingerly to get closer to the village (airmen never walk any more than they must), I found to my surprise and amusement that we had a gent riding a camel at our starboard wing-tip. As we moved along in excellent formation – I confess that never before had I experienced a camel-riding wing man – 'Red two' was signalling 'Red Leader' to keep going straight ahead. As he obviously knew something important I waved him on to take the lead and I followed in line astern. He was good, that fellow. He traversed the ground where the going was good, and constantly looked back to check that all was well.

Repatriation

It must have been after some 2,500yd of taxying that we were led to the spot where the missing Wellesley was seen, wheels down, with the crew (Sgts Aldous and Lund) smiling broadly at our unorthodox arrival. They had been singularly well provided for by the friendly villagers; beds, food, water, cooking utensils, the full treatment. Some of the men were still there, attired in their spotless white garments and turbans, smiles revealing gleaming snow-white teeth. Splendid people, the Sudanese. So the search was over. We left the lame Wellesley in the care of the head man and all four of us flew back to Khartoum.

The following morning (which was Christmas Day), we returned to Abd el Magid, a fitter soon rectified the fault, and I made a test flight. All was well, and so I handed over to Sgts Lund and Blofield and we flew back to Khartoum together. It had been an entertaining episode; certainly not one that we would have been allowed to carry out in 'civilised' conditions. The charm of life in remote places is that you make the rules to suit the prevailing circumstances. The Christmas Day ritual of the officers and sergeants serving the midday meal to the lads was definitely enlivened by the successful rescue of the Wellesley and crew. It could not have been better timed.

In the first months of 1941 the British and South African forces, not forgetting the fine Indian Army element, began to close in on Ethiopia – Abyssinia as it was popularly called. By the end of May the campaign was virtually over. It had taken our forces less than a year, starting from scratch, to carry out the job; for practical purposes it was the last six months that mattered and our land forces were able physically to occupy half a million square miles of Emperor Haile Selassie's kingdom. In round figures, 20,000 men had defeated 200,000 of the enemy – and incidentally defeated geography and mother nature as well. By any standards of military endeavour it was a very spectacular performance. All three elements of the fighting forces, naval, military, and air, contributed to success. In the main it was a hard slog by all. Certain highlights animated the newspapers, just to boost morale at home. One such was the brilliant feat of navigation by Wellesleys of 223 Squadron that attacked the airfield at Addis Abbaba. Led by Flt Lt Jack Roulston (who had checked me out on Wellesleys in Nairobi), the attack originated from Aden with a refuelling stop at Perim Island – situated at the entrance to the Red Sea – before making the 400 mile run up into the mountains. They got the full treatment from the weather; cloud, icing up, turbulence, and of course the no-oxygen no-radio formula.

From the Sudan, we had General Sir William Platt directing all forces, with the new No 203 Group of Air Commodore LH Slatter providing the small air element. As with Wingate and 47 Squadron, the integration at all levels was manifest. We were now aware of the problems and capabilities of each other.

Despite our successes, we also had some reverses. It was ever thus. In October 1940 a special element of 47 Squadron moved from Khartoum to a landing ground at Gedaref, about 230 miles south-east of the capital and conveniently on the rail loop coming down from Port Sudan and swinging on to Khartoum itself. The unit, with a very streamlined number of personnel which meant that every man virtually did two jobs – it works very well with the right lads – took along eight Wellesleys and four Vincents of 'D' Flight. The concept was to take a calculated risk and operate closer to our targets, thus saving considerable flying time for aircrew and aeroplanes alike.

It was only a matter of days before our location was spotted late one evening by a Savoia Marchetti SM.79; it proved to be a bird of ill omen indeed. At dawn the following day back came the SM.79; but this time it brought with it six Fiat CR.42s. This was the moment of despair; the moment that Digger Magill and I had feared, but gambled upon not happening. We had underestimated the Italian Air Commander, *Generale* Piatsantini. We heard later that he accompanied the attack in person, thus leading from the front. A good man!

With no ground defences of consequence against air attack – even with an Indian Brigade nearby – and poor communication with a flight of Gladiators stationed on natural ground which gave quite remarkable camouflage, the Italians had a field day. Soon the CR.42s set on fire all our aircraft, the *Generale* no doubt smacking his lips from his good vantage point about 3,000ft above us. It was all over in minutes, and for the first time in memory the sun in that part of the world was eclipsed by dense black smoke rising thousands of feet above us. It was an utterly depressing sight: burning aeroplanes dispersed all around the landing ground. I could have wept.

The only moment of relief came with Black Mac's telegram, which said simply, "Do you want your horse?" I was too preoccupied to reply. So back to Khartoum by train – what else? We had learned our lesson the hard way; I should re-word that in the first person, as the idea had been entirely mine. Quite simply, if you must get closer to the enemy, make damn sure that you can defend yourself properly from air attack.

Siesta surprise

The sad episode did have a compensation. Two mornings later, Captain S. van Schalkwyk (I cannot pronounce it for the reader on paper!) took his three Gladiators off on another sortie, this time when we estimated that the Italians were resting after the *spaghetti* and *Chianti* of their midday meal. The ruse seemed to work splendidly, the three pilots successfully destroying just about the same number of aircraft as we had lost. Poor van Schalkwyk was shot down not long afterwards; he was a splendid fellow.

On one occasion General Platt returned from Cairo to Khartoum after a conference at Headquarters Middle East Command. The Wellesley flew non-stop which made a pleasant change. While greeting our distinguished passenger as he stepped from the aircraft the General said "Thank you" and very kindly invited me to dinner on board his houseboat – what nicer? After dinner, and now happily clutching my brandy, I could not resist recounting the brief conversation between two of my airmen watching the General's arrival on the apron. "Who is the geezer talking to the old man [JP-F]?" said one lad, looking at a very sun-tanned officer in Sudan Defence Uniform. "Dunno", said his chum, "some wog or other, but he speaks bloody good English". After the laughter had eased up a little I was rewarded with another brandy. My kind of General.

Following No 47 squadron's return to Khartoum after more than a year in the desert I had the opportunity of meeting Emperor Haile Selassie of Ethiopia. He and his family had recently arrived in Khartoum from England and as a temporary measure was occupying a Greek merchant's villa until such time as appropriate accommodation elsewhere could be provided. For the moment he could not return to his own country as the Mussolini war was still being fought and at the same time it would have been unwise to locate him too far away – until the outcome was known. I discussed the unusual situation of Ethiopian royalty in our midst with Flt Lt Joe Lynch, Senior RAF Intelligence Officer in Khartoum, and we agreed that the Emperor was not getting anything like the right amount of attention that he merited. Admittedly there was not much that could be done officially in the circumstance but on the basis that an informal contact was better than nothing Joe undertook to become an emissary with the result that he and I were invited to make a call.

My first reaction as we were shown into the Emperor's drawing room was of a good-looking man of very small stature who immediately gave an impression of very considerable dignity and composure. Even under the adverse situation of a monarch-in-exile receiving us in what frankly was an oversize bungalow, His Imperial Majesty welcomed us with elegance and grace such as one expects from a royal personage. With one of his sons in attendance and an interpreter to fill the gaps in hesitant French we were invited to sit each side of him on a wide settee whilst coffee was served. The main topic of conversation of course centered on the East African war and Joe Lynch described the general situation and how the main Allied thrust was progressing from the Sudan with the extremely difficult military task of moving into mountain country against a well-entrenched defender. I contributed some aspects of the war as seen through the eyes of an airman and the Emperor was very interested in the account of Major Orde Wingate's remarkable flight up into the high mountain country near Lake Gondar to meet up with his resistance forces and the resultant air-drop methods that we developed subsequently. One commodity high on the delivery list was money and it was the replica Maria Therese 1780 *Thaler* silver coin originally minted in Southern Germany that was in those days still the only acceptable coin in Ethiopia. The silver mines in Bohemia produced the *Joachimstaler* in the days of the Austro-Hungarian Empire and it was the abbreviation '*Thaler*' that produced the word '*dollar*' subsequently. For the first practise drop Wingate had arranged a supply of thalers packaged in triple bags and we estimated that if the first and second bag burst on impact the outer third one would hold. A Wellesley made the run fifty feet above the sandy aerodrome and we watched as the small object with long white locating streamer hit the ground, whereupon silver coins in abundance flew through the air in every direction. Fortunately they were easy to find and we recovered them all to try again; the second drop, this time with an extra fourth bag was successful. As I still did not know precisely what the special markings on the coins were like, His Majesty asked his son to get one and when produced it was presented to me. The coin now forms the base of a beautiful pin tray specially made up by a silversmith in the Bagdad bazaar. That coin, together with my linen-faced identity 'blood chit' printed in *Amharic* and with the Emperor's personal seal superimposed on it are two souvenirs that I still retain.

The Amharic word '*ras*' means prince and thus the Emperor's basic name was Ras Tafari; hence the modern word *rastafarian* as used by certain West Indian people and others who today are possibly unaware of it's origin. When discussing the Lake Tana area I asked His Majesty if he could describe it to me as I had only seen it from the air and then only by night. His noncommittal answer however was such that I concluded that he had never been there and so it must have been the domain of another Ras. As events were to show later with a Marxist Government in power, any subsequent distinction between one prince and another was academic but long prior to that I had a sense of foreboding; in late 1940 those early schoolboy illusions of enchanting Abyssinian damsels playing on dulcimers, great emperors, and Queens of Sheba had already begun to fade. Although we were not to know it at the time, a mute pointer to the coming demise of a royal lineage as old as history itself was manifest on our final visit to the royal villa. This time the settee had gone and Haile Selassie was seated on what looked like a home-made throne more suited to stage pantomine property than something befitting the Emperor of Ethiopia. In retrospect that comic opera item of faded grandeur must have been the harbinger of ill tidings. However I could at least claim to have contributed to the initial liberation of his Ethiopian Empire even if it was to no purpose at all in the end. Ras Tafari, the Messiah, the man who was destined by his followers to lead them back into the Promised Land was alas overtaken by events – and singularly disastrous events at that.

Chapter XV

The Two Desert Wars

Digger Magill and other members of 47 Squadron came to see me off at Khartoum Railway Station on New Year's Day, 1941. The popular and gallant New Zealander had taken over command and I was on my way to Cairo to see what new job would be found for an unemployed Squadron Leader. The inconsistency about it was that Orde Wingate (with my cautious concurrence I have to say) had earlier asked that I should join his No 101 Special Forces Mission hidden up somewhere in the Ethiopian mountains, but the answer from Cairo to Khartoum was a curt signal from the C-in-C that said 'This officer cannot be spared'. My emotions were a blend of slight relief that Wingate's proposal had been rejected and the happy thought that the RAF seemed to need me for another job. I was not too enthusiastic about any more rough living, particularly so in enemy-held country. After eighteen months of *bedouin* life the prospect of a return to civilisation certainly had its attractions and I decided that a 1000 mile journey by train and Nile steamer would be a nice prelude to reporting to my masters at Air Headquarters in Cairo.

The excellent train service out of Khartoum goes across the wilderness to Atbara and then to my old haunt Wadi Halfa. From there the Nile steamer sets off on its leisurely run downstream towards Abu Simbel where we stopped to have a close look at the huge carved statues on the river bank. At Aswan the passengers disembarked and took the Egyptian State Railways train to Cairo.

In five years I had moved from Heliopolis to Jerusalem, to Nairobi, to the Sudan desert, to a brief stay in Khartoum and now back to the Egyptian scene for the second time. Unhappily my visit to the Postings Officer proved to be a complete anti-climax to my expectations because the fellow told me that there was no available job for me. When I told him that Major Orde Wingate had specifically asked for me to join his 101 Mission, and that the answer with the C-in-C's name on it was 'No', he commented that it was considered a silly idea for Pelly-Fry to go skulking about in the

Ethiopian mountains playing boy scouts with a mad Brigadier. I was given a few days leave whilst he tried to find me a posting and I now knew that I was by no means the valuable officer that I had been led to believe. For the time being though I could enjoy some good living, have a daily bath, wear clean clothes, go to the Turf Club for civilised food, and even make a foray or two into Cairo night life. The city was now bursting at the seams with all manner of military personnel, to say nothing of the host of young women who somehow had appeared on the scene to work on wartime duties in offices, hospitals, and the like. I began to wonder who was out in the Western Desert keeping Mussolini's forces at bay. The man from the Sudan, still wearing a bush jacket – for which I was given a wigging for being improperly dressed incidentally – began to feel overwhelmed by it all.

The short leave now over, I reported back to the Postings Officer and he startled me by saying that I was to join the Intelligence Branch. When I protested and said that I knew absolutely nothing about that kind of work, he said that the reason was that my recent operational experience was needed to produce a new series of target maps for air-crews. Remembering the way that we tried to navigate to targets with those absurd very small-scale maps issued to the Sudan Squadrons I had to agree that there was a whole lot to be done in this regard. For all that I sensed that I was being fobbed off with a job invented for me and there was little that I could do about it; thus for the first time in my life I became that unenviable being, a staff officer. I supposed that it had to happen sometime or other; it would of course be something different and for the time being I could at least live in a civilised way. I could also go around Cairo with that smug feeling that the girls would think I was a hero because I had actually gone to war and been shot at.

One extraordinary chance encounter was to meet my Sofia friend Snowden Hedley at the entrance to Air HQ when he was trying to make an appointment with the Personnel Department. I took him to my office and he told his story. One Saturday morning at his garage in Sofia the Security Police arrived and told him that he had 24 hours to leave Bulgaria. No reason was given; no explanations. He quickly realised the clever timing of the expulsion as the banks were closed for the weekend and so he could only take what cash he had in his office, so all his possessions had to be abandoned. He made his exit south by road, crossed into Greece, and thence by devious ways to Cairo. As he seemed such a useful person with intimate knowledge of the Balkans I introduced him to my boss. For a reason never divulged – possibly because he seemed to be such an odd character who might well be a mole and who could prove otherwise? – he was given a safe job in the RAF Transport Department. At least he knew all about road vehicles. The story now has to jump another five years. When my wife to be Irène was arriving in England by sea from Kenya and I went to meet her, who was at Plymouth Railway Station but Snowden

Hedley? He survived the war and had built up a good business in London where he lived in swanky Knightsbridge. He was obviously one of those entrepreneurs who knew how to fend successfully for themselves. I never did discover the sum total of his unusual Bulgarian activities and I never met him again.

The domestic side of life in Cairo presented me (as with most of us) with the tiresome business of finding somewhere worthwhile to live; and other than Jerusalem (where I was so lucky) for the first time in my RAF experience I had to search for my own accommodation single-handed. The housing officer and his staff were always helpful in this regard, but they could only suggest what they had available and it was quite apparent that all the new arrivals were faced with the typical city scurge of too many people flooding in and chasing too few homes with inflated wartime prices. My old friend Wg Cdr LA 'Jacko' Jackson from Heliopolis days had a comfortable flat close to the Gezirah Club; it could accommodate three bachelors and very fortunately he had room for me. The bachelor-flat formula has the advantage that costs are shared by the inmates and it is also very convivial, given the compatibility of the occupants. At various times the flat was inhabited by good friends like Wg Cdr RN (Bob) Bateson, DSO, DFC, of Blenheim and (later) Mosquito fame and Wg Cdr Al Bowman DFC, the light bomber ace of the Desert Air Force. Alas! poor Al was shot down by one of our own gunners who mistook his Blenheim for a German Ju.88 when flying Gp Capt Christopher Dearlove to inspect an oasis landing ground. The episode was tragic but that's the way it goes; Al Bowman was one of many splendid and forceful leaders that the Royal Air Force could ill-afford to lose. He was head and shoulders above most of us and that description applied to Bob Bateson as well.

My new job in intelligence proved to be a very curious affair if only for the reason that my Air Commodore boss seemed to be caught on the wrong foot as I did not fit the pattern of his normal staff. In practise I was left to make my own arrangements and was able virtually to invent my own terms of reference. This suited my purpose admirably in that I now began to pursue the production of better target maps, made contact with the Photographic Reconnaissance Unit (No 2 PRU) at Heliopolis for the latest pictures and generally go my own way without having to account for my day-to-day activities. However I was well aware that it was essential that I must be productive, and to this end I set about trying to do something worthwhile, but in my own fashion. The key was to think up an idea, pursue it, and develop it relentlessly. Thus it was that one day I presented myself to the new Air Commander-in-Chief; his name was Air Marshal Sir Arthur Tedder. I outlined my plan and to my great satisfaction he liked what I had to say.

The concept was simple enough; in fact I wondered why it had not been developed previously. It was based on what I called watching a tennis match at Wimbledon and the plan was that I would use his Conference Room to display the necessary data about the activities and the potential of the two warring sides; for the purpose, two large identical maps would cover the entire area of opposite walls. Using simple visual symbols on the lines of an ideogram he could go whenever he wished to the 'Operations-Intelligence' Room, sit down in a comfortable chair and like an umpire see at a glance the latest information displayed as seen on either side of the 'tennis net'. Whenever anything special caught his eye a specialist officer could then brief him about what it was, what had happened, and (as called for) what the implications were. It was like a newspaper editor reviewing the latest news and then deciding how he was going to take advantage of the information presented. Apart from giving the current state of play with the hot news displayed on opposite walls, I hoped that a simple but accurate bird's eye picture of the whole theatre of operations would produce three reactions. The first was 'Am I doing the right thing?' The second was 'What is the enemy up to?' Thirdly, 'What should I do next?' As in tennis, one action produces a reaction; if you keep one jump ahead of your opponent, well you ought to win the match. It was an absorbing business setting up that special operations/intelligence room and I was lucky to find a couple of enthusiastic officers who soon got the hang of running it along the lines of a newspaper. The key was to collect hot news, digest it, and then decide on the best way to act.

Apart from the 'News Room' that Sir Arthur Tedder now employed to good advantage, I was able to make my escape from Cairo fairly regularly. It was all part of what I call 'news gathering' in the job of being an intelligence officer. Those sorties made a wonderful break from the artificial life in the city to the fresh air and contacts with the people who were actually doing the fighting; the sharp end of the business. Somehow or other I became Joint Senior RAF Intelligence Officer Western Desert with the Hon Patrick Kinross, a talented and entertaining fellow who ran Intelligence for the Desert Air Force and who later become Lord Kinross. The arrangement was that he ran the day-to-day business whilst I was the free-lance chap feeding back to him all that I gleaned in my desert travels. As I was very mobile with a Ford safari car I could go where I wished and 'come back with the bacon'. I really enjoyed the job of being a desert reporter, and all this activity brought me in touch with the people who were actually doing the fighting.

The Desert Air Force was run by a highly competent team under the direction of the colourful – if Prima-Donna like – New Zealander Air Vice Marshal Arthur Coningham. The new army-air force arrangement was that Montgomery and Coningham literally worked cheek-by-jowl for the closest possible army-air coordination. This integrated liaison (which Bill Brook had fostered at Heliopolis so carefully before the war) was now very much the effective instrument of tactical warfare. The two leaders with their small teams now really began to get results which later formed the pattern of activity during the invasion of Europe. All the tricks were learned in the Western Desert in the first place and the desert was a tacticians paradise even if it was a quartermaster's hell.

In December 1941 I was out on yet another desert sortie looking for likely landing ground locations and at the same time hoping to come across some which the enemy had abandoned during the ebb-and-flow of battle. At one point I was so deep into the southern desert that I estimated that the nearest human being must be at least 100 miles away somewhere along the Mediterranean coast. To my surprise I saw in the distance the tell-tale dust being kicked up by a vehicle; so I stopped, put the safari car 'hull-down' as best I could, and watched through my binoculars. The unidentified vehicle now changed course and made its way in my direction and I had the urgent problem of trying to determine if it was friendly or one belonging to General Rommel's Afrika Corps. It was a big-wheeled armoured reconnaissance vehicle and I thought that it looked friendly. After agonies of suspense it got close enough for me to decide that after all there was no need to bolt like a frightened horse and I reassured myself that if it really became necessary my safari car was faster. When the recce-car stopped two elegant young men emerged and began to walk towards me. I fingered my Colt .45 nervously but I hoped that all was well as all that Wyatt Earp cowboy stuff was for Tombstone, not the Lybian Desert. The first chap smiled and said, "Dear boy; how fraffly nice to see you!" It was that Bond Street accent again! I was told that they too had been on a long reconnaissance deep into the desert and had seen my dust so they came to investigate. We compared notes about what we had seen, where we had been and so forth, and then one of them said "Oh, by the way, old chap, where are you dining tonight?" This took me so much by surprise that all I could do was to grin and mumble that I had some hard tack in my waggon and would get to it later on. "But you do not seem to realise that it's Christmas Eve". He went on, "You cannot possibly dine out here on your own, can you?" That was a good question. "Well now, my dear fella, you must dine with us; Second Battalion Irish Guards and we are located here". With that he made a pencil mark on my map and said that I was expected by nightfall. As the two soldiers climbed into their waggon, one of them said "We must be orf now – see you later".

After traversing the lonely desert and finding nothing of consequence I headed north again and eventually arrived at dusk at the 'spot on the map' where I located two well-camouflaged marquees and sundry small tents nicely dispersed. I entered the marquee which had voices coming from it and inside standing on tribal rugs and dressed in smart uniforms was the colonel and his officers. By contrast I must have looked like a tramp and it was rather embarrassing.

The colonel greeted me with "My dear chap, I heard that you were coming to dine with us; splendid! Care for a sherry?" When my protestations about my appearance had been brushed aside, a while later I followed him and his officers to the adjoining marquee. Believe it or not, inside was a long table covered in white linen plus the regimental silver. So this was the Irish Guards at war on Christmas Eve! I was impressed and when I made a comment about it the colonel said "Dear boy, just because the damned war is on there is no point in being uncomfortable, is there?" Yes sir, they were proper soldiers and I enjoyed a wonderful and quite unexpected evening. It was all so fraffly nice, eh what?

On another occasion I was in the Desert Air Force Operations tent when a lengthy signal arrived from Cairo. It had originated from the Air Ministry addressed to all units and ad nauseum it castigated us all for saying unkind things about the Army. Specifically we were instructed to stop referring to soldiers by a particular nick-name and we were told that it was quite unwarranted and it all had to stop forthwith. The reality even to this day is that good soldiers do not mind their nick-name; quite the reverse in fact as today it is almost a term of endearment. Whilst we digested the message in silence the Naval Commander of 820 Sqdn – the unit that had stayed for a time at Heliopolis in pre-war days – came in and asked us what was afoot. I told him about the massive rocket just received from Air Ministry. "Oh," he said "I too have just got one from the Admiralty; care to see it?" I took his copy, and read it out aloud. It said, with typically naval brevity, 'STOP CALLING PONGOES PONGOES!'

I had been ruminating in recent days about a particular matter which had been causing me some concern. From the nature of my job, a glimmer of information had come my way, the details of which were so very secret that I was almost tempted to forget that I ever knew anything about it at all. The problem was to determine how, if at all, its very considerable benefits could be used in a practical way without compromising the system. Fate ordained one day that Sir Arthur Tedder was making one of his regular visits to the desert and at a good moment I asked if I could speak to him. He nodded. "Sir, not here; can we walk away a little further?" He seemed quite surprised but agreed and soon the C-in-C and I now were out of earshot. I began by choosing my words carefully. Did he by any chance know about a certain special intelligence facility that had recently been introduced? Tedder's reply was almost as devious as the question. Yes, he thought so. Did he make use of this facility or did he just know about it? Again, a non-commital reply. It was just shadow-boxing – neither of us conceding anything at all so there was nothing to it but to show my hand. I said that because the matter was so secret, benefits of a practical nature were being overruled by the current need to keep the whole business completely hidden. This was all very well but what was the point of gleaning intelligence if you could not act and so take advantage of the information gained? I added that of course the paramount need was to maintain the greatest degree of selectivity in use as that was the key to avoiding compromise. When our strange conversation ended the upshot was that an instruction was issued for me to be given access to the facility in the desert by suitable means. It now fell on my shoulders to decide what material should be put to work and what to reject. It was a great responsibility.

The game started and I had agonies of indecision; one false move and the whole business might end abruptly. People began to wonder why I used to visit a certain Ford Estate car parked discreetly nearby and I said that it was a weather forecasting facility. To test out the effectiveness of the new arrangement I decided to visit a Beaufighter squadron not far away, ostensibly just to say 'hello'. After asking what operation was planned for the boys and receiving the answer that they were stood down, I suggested to the CO that a sortie over Bengazi at 1300 hrs might be a way of showing the enemy that we were still in business. "The Eyeties always have a long lunch period, so it will annoy them." The lads were keen to go and the squadron commander decided that he would lay on half-a-dozen Beau's and I went on my way. Some two hours later I returned, pretending to be just passing-by again. The six pilots were back in their Ops. Tent and all were talking like crazy. When I asked them what all the fuss was about, they said joyfully that just as they approached Bengazi at 1300 hrs a stream of twenty-three Ju.52 transport aircraft were orbiting Benina aerodrome with one actually coming in to land. They had shot down eighteen in the circuit – "Huge flaming jobs, too" – and later attacked one on the ground as it taxied in. It was the most fantastic day that they ever had and I could well understand it. As I drove away I wondered if Sir Arthur Tedder had remembered our desert conversation about a month earlier; he never said anything and neither did I. Who else but he and I was to know that all those Ju.52's were full to capacity with fuel urgently needed for Rommel's tanks?

On another occasion during a sortie into the Western Desert – I seemed to be spending more time there than in Cairo – a signal recalled me urgently to Cairo. I got a lift in a 216 Squadron Bristol 'Bombay' and reported at once to my boss Air Commodore Noêl Paynter. He told me that a rebellion started by a politician called Rashid Ali had blown up in Iraq and that the very big RAF Base at Habbaniya near Baghdad was under siege. As only a flying school was based there in addition to Air HQ, Iraq, the training aircraft had been rushed into use by modifying them with makeshift armaments. Paynter said that it was essential that the operational procedures of keeping correct records should be instigated and he wished me to go to Habbaniya immediately to that end. I could not but smile at the staff officer attitude; never mind about winning (or losing) the war – just make sure we put it all down on paper for people to write books about it afterwards.

Armed with all those important forms I set off in a Lockheed 'Loadstar' in company with Group Captain SD MacDonald, (the famous 'Black Mac' of the Wellesley days in the Sudan) and we landed at that most-unloved resort for all airmen, that abomination of desolation called Shaiba, not far from Basra. The least said about Shaiba the better; it really was a dreadfully hot place surrounded by a wilderness. As soon as we got out of the aeroplane Wg Cdr Howard Alloway (the Station Commander, for his sins) told us that all was quiet at Shaiba but Habbaniya was where all the action could be found. After a hot and uncomfortable overnight stop Flt Lt Mavor and I took off in a DC2 (yes, DC two!) registered VD-AOD in Indian Airways livery. It had been requisitioned for RAF service and I remember that it was operated by No 31 Sqdn recently arrived from India. To say that the arrival at Habbaniya was eventful is a complete understatement for no sooner had we disembarked and about to get into a car from Air Headquarters than all hell was let loose. Thunderous explosions seemed to assail us from above and it really was very alarming if only because of its unexpectedness. The immediate reaction was to lie face down on the apron and pray. After the bombing run was over I saw where the trouble was coming from – three sinister black Heinkel 111's in formation were over head at about 5000 feet. As they turned away and were pursued by a lonely Gladiator, so did we try to make our escape from the apron and the hangars before the second bombing run started. We found a gap in the wire fencing at the rear of the hangars and bolted like rabbits into an underground temporary air-raid shelter. The second bombing run now showered us with another very noisy and explosive hand-out from above. The only relief from crouching in the complete darkness of the shelter and wondering what was going on outside was a quavering voice with the unmistakable accent of the Indian sub-continent. "*Sahib*", it said, "I have a very big problem". My answer to the voice was predictable; "So have we all". The voice continued, "*Sahib*, my problem is very important; I have left my bicycle outside and I fear that someone will steal it". Poor fellow, if he attempted to rescue his bike he might get killed but if he stayed in the shelter he might live. He decided to stay.

The excellent and revealing personal account of the Siege of Habbaniya has been described so well by Air Vice Marshal Tony Dudgeon in his book 'The Luck of the Devil' that it stands above all for authenticity. An even more comprehensive and first hand account has since appeared from the author. "The War that Never Was" published by Airlie, gives a brilliant and accurate story of the siege of Habbaniya in May 1941. In my fashion I can corroborate his restrained and gentlemanly comments about some of the senior people who found themselves engulfed in an unexpected situation – frankly they just ground to a confused halt. My worst experience was trying to persuade a certain senior officer that the best way to attack the place whence those Luftwaffe aircraft were coming from was to get some long-range Hurricanes. He had never heard of them! After explaining what a long-range Hurricane could do and assuring him that it was the only fighter aircraft able to reach Mosul (professionally I knew where they were based although he could scarcely believe me) he said that he would ask Cairo for modification plans so that he could get the work done at Hab on some Hurricanes expected to arrive in ten day's time. He wrote out a signal addressed to HQ Middle East and gave it to me to despatch. After leaving his office I read what he had written on the message pad. It was that Pelly-Fry had said that such a thing as a long-range Hurricane existed and if true he wanted the drawings to modify the ones that were expected. He was hedging his bets and so able to pass the buck on to me in case of need.

He never knew, but I re-wrote the signal and it read 'Grateful you despatch three long-range Hurricanes earliest.' Within four days they arrived and my friend Flt Lt Sir Roderick MacRobert delivered one of them. The following day he was briefed by me to attack Luftwaffe aircraft on Mosul aerodrome and – alas! – was shot down after he had destroyed most of them by low-level strafing. I knew how successful his attack had been because I later flew to Mosul and saw the results for myself. For the technically minded the Hurricanes were specially modified at the RAF Maintenance and Repair Depot at Abukir, (Egypt), and consisted essentially of removing four of the eight guns and substituting fuel tanks. As we airmen would say, some senior staff officers at Air Headquarters Iraq had their fingers in – as I'm sure Tony Dudgeon will agree.

MacRobert's successful attack on the German aircraft at Mosul (two hundred miles to the north of Habbaniya) confirmed exactly what my intelligence information had revealed, so in keeping with Western Desert habits I now wished to go and have a look at Mosul for myself. There is always something of value, often of considerable value, to be gained by examining the hardware abandoned by a departed enemy so a bid was made to fly in a suitable aeroplane. This entailed getting the approval of the new AOC, Iraq. Once again, the incredulous response; the unsympathetic attitude; all the difficulties spelled out. How can young officers cope with these unimaginative attitudes except to be bold and press home the strongest arguments? Eventually I was given clearance to go but only after a struggle. On June 6th 1941, Wg Cdr Richard Burberry and I with a crew of five flew to Mosul in a Douglas DC2 with Indian civil registration VT-AOQ. Burberry was the chief pilot of Indian Airways and now Commanded 31 Sqdn. When we arrived overhead the aerodrome seemed to be completely deserted with the exception of four Luftwaffe aircraft dispersed around the perimeter plus eight others destroyed by fire. We orbited at a discreet distance to keep away from small arms fire but as there was not a single sign of activity the game now was to guess if the Germans had departed or if they were lying up and waiting to set upon us after landing; understandably we had our eyes popping out like organ stops. After some minutes we concluded that swanning around was getting us nowhere so we both took a deep breath and Burberry as Captain made the decision to go down and chance our arm. Nothing ventured . . .; he made a discreet touch-down as far away as possible from buildings, trees, and other cover for people armed with guns. Nothing moved, so we taxied slowly in – almost on tip-toe – the engines were switched off, the rear door was opened, and we anxiously looked around. Complete silence. It is much better to see or hear something happening however disagreeable because at least you can then collect your wits and do something; it breaks the tension. Whilst we stood near the DC2 (when inevitably Richard and I reached for our cigarette cases) to my astonishment I spotted two small figures appear seemingly from out of the ground. They were Gurkhas! A young officer then emerged from cover and to us he looked like a guardian angel in uniform. The pulse-rate returned to normal.

The young Lieutenant told us that he and his platoon had only an hour earlier arrived from the south and had made their way direct to the aerodrome. When he saw our aeroplane overhead he was not at all sure if it was friend or foe because the civil registration markings had confused him. In the short time that he had been in the Mosul area he heard that the Germans had departed in trucks that very morning and were travelling west in the direction of Syria. Now I began to get the picture; the dozen or so Me 110s and He 111s had originally flown in from Aleppo and the ground party plus one or two aircraft that were serviceable had departed the way that they came with the cooperation of the Vichy French in Syria. Very interesting.

Promptly we unloaded our camp kit for a night stop and Richard and I then began a tour of inspection. We looked at the aircraft that had been left behind and most of them showed evidence of the Hurricane's attacks but with one special exception. This was a Heinkel He 111; it had one bullet hole near the port engine radiator and one sinister tell-tale hole straight through the fuselage where the rear gunner would normally be located. This was the aircraft taking *Maj* von Blomberg from Berlin to Baghdad; this was the aircraft in which one of Hitler's emmissaries – the Field Marshal's son – had been observing the approach to land when a single shot from a *bedouin* tribesman killed him. The Iraqi reception committee were horrified to find that they had a dead man on their hands. Hitler was so furious when he heard about the affair, for this and other reasons no doubt, that he abandoned his plan to go to the aid of Rashid Ali, the man who intended to kick the British out of Iraq and thus give Germany access to the Persian Gulf.

The Germans in Mosul had been using the old RAF airmens' billets as storerooms and it was intriguing to see that the Luftwaffe's method of setting everything up was so similar to that of the RAF. Except for different equipment (and the nasty smell that everything had because of the synthetic paint used) it could well have been an RAF detachment. One barrack room contained a variety of dopes, lubricants, paints and cleaning liquids. What interested me in particular was a quantity of metal containers, all neatly stacked against a wall with their three carrying-bars and neat filler-caps facing outwards. They looked so practical and well-made that right away I said to Richard that I wanted one for myself and I would use it in my Ford safari car as a reserve fuel supply.

When we eventually left Mosul, having checked all the spare propellors, wheels, radiators, instruments, guns, belting-gear, boxes of ammunition, etc, that any good Air Force has to hump about for efficient operations, one 20-litre container with some kind of hydraulic oil inside was brought back to Habbaniya and a 216 Sqdn Valentia delivered it to Heliopolis. Attached to one of the carrying-bars was a label addressed to Wg Cdr 'Jacko' Jackson. It read 'Why don't you store bashers produce something like this? Give the contents to the Shell Company but please keep the container for me. I found it in Mosul after the Luftwaffe had gone.'

The final excitement was the discovery by one of the Habbaniya pilots of a Messerschmitt BF 110 twin-engined fighter abandoned in the desert some thirty miles south-east of the RAF base. This attracted my interest considerably because one of my jobs was to get to know the Luftwaffe's aircraft and their capabilities. Despite the usual – and predictable – unimaginative response from the Air Officer Commanding RAF, Iraq, – "What on earth do you want to recover a crashed German aeroplane for?" – I succeeded in organising a ground party to go out and bring the Messerschmitt back. We took hoisting gear to lift it up after its belly landing and after lowering the wheels we towed it back in triumph across the desert. The necessary spare parts were fortunately available from Mosul and they were brought by train to Baghdad and thence by road to Hab. The initial inspection by flying out in a Tiger Moth – what else? – was not without its moments because the Me 110 had been set up with a booby-trap by the crew before they abandoned it. Fortunately the cunning device was spotted and I was able to immunise the self-destruct 'bomb' before killing myself when I opened the cockpit canopy. For the amateur this kind of activity quickens the heart-beat alarmingly.

The lads at Habbaniya successfully managed to repair the long-range Fighter, an excellent job under the circumstances, but any thought that I had of being the happy owner of the fast private aeroplane were dashed because I had to leave for Cairo before the job was completed. After a successful test flight by my press-on Canadian friend Sq Ldr Al Bocking, inevitably Operation Band Waggon showed its hand and the Top Brass moved in on the act by decreeing that it was to be used exclusively for comparative trials against RAF aircraft. Al Bocking flew it to Egypt, in RAF livery no doubt, – and later on my Kenya friend Alec Noon set off on a delivery flight to South Africa so that the SAAF could profit by testing out its capabilities. Alas! the Belle of Berlin had to make a wheels-up arrival at

Atbara in the Sudan because of a technical malfunction and that was the end of its useful life. So after all the hassle of recovery from the Iraqi desert and the associated obstacles thrown in my path by my seniors, the whole affair ended miserably.

A week after the Me 110 discovery, I left Habbaniya and flew back to Egypt. I was given the job of leading six Hawker 'Hart' trainers to the Suez Canal Zone, the other pilots being newly-fledged from the flying school. In four hops we travelled 800 miles to Geneifa, one of the new aerodromes that Jim Irens and I had selected when we did the secret reconnaissance in the 'Tutor'. The ferry trip was not without incident. One refuelling stop was Ma'an in Transjordan and as usual I landed first to show the way. One young pilot, poor fellow, had awful problems with the high altitude landing ground and only a windsock for guidance. Three times he flew past me and I watched anxiously as the Hart passed so tail-down that I could see a complete plan-view of it. Sir Sydney Camm of Hawker's would have been delighted with its slow flying capability. On the fourth attempt the pilot found where the ground was, landed safely, and so all was well.

As soon as I returned to Cairo Headquarters I went to Jacko's office to retrieve my German container. He told me that the Top Brass, both Army and Air Force were amazed when they saw it and after a conference it was decided to send it to London. In turn London decided to send it to Washington for mass production. By now the reader will have guessed the outcome; it was the very first fuel container of its kind that the Allies had seen and the Americans copied it in almost identical form. Millions were made, and as it was of German origin it became known as the 'Jerrycan'. It could well have been called a Pellycan after the man who first discovered it. Who would have guessed, even in their wildest moments, that the prototype was found in Mosul – of all unlikely places?

The Iraq experiences had an unusual sequence. Within days of the Hart Trainer delivery flight to Egypt I had a requirement to return to Habbaniya, so I cast around for some means of getting there. A short time previously I had spotted an unusual-looking Wellesley at Heliopolis that was parked out on the sand near the Communication Flight; it was one of the eight special long-range Wellesleys, three of which had flown 7000 miles non-stop from the Suez Canal to Darwin, Australia. The Flight Sergeant in charge said that it was 'special' and he kept an eye on it for the Wing Commander in Headquarters who was overseeing the Takoradi-Khartoum-Cairo reinforcing route for aircraft delivered from the UK. I went to see the officer in question with a proposal that I might borrow it to go to Habbaniya. With its enormous range there was no problem about a 2000 mile out-and-home run and I doubted that this flight had ever been done that way before. The visit to its owner produced the guarded response that it was kept specially for him to cover the long aircraft reinforcing route, but, a little discreet prodding revealed that in fact he had never flown it at-all. Eventually, he agreed to let me use it and I undertook to show him how to fly it upon my return.

The first air test was quite alarming. After turning on the standard fuel tanks and leaving the rest to be sorted out later, the Wellesley in flight was dangerously nose heavy so a rapid return was made to mother earth. It was clear that nobody had air tested it in its present condition and the reason for the bad trim was that all the specialised equipment in the back had been removed, hence the nose heavy condition. I now added ballast plus an airman passenger in the back and that put matters right. The next job was to fathom the complex long-range tankage and this I did by the process of 'following pipe lines' from the wings to the junction box in the fuselage. I then had it fuelled up to 50% of the total 2000 gallons possible and the next day I was on my way to Habbaniya.

The LR Wellesley was a lovely aircraft to fly. She was faster than the standard bomber version that I flew in the Sudan and had an optical fuel-flow indicator and an instrument looking like a distance-run indicator in a car which gave precise fuel consumption. Best of all it had an automatic pilot – 'George' in pilot's language – and all I had to do was to point the aeroplane in the right direction, engage George, and sit back and admire the scenery. In the event, for sundry reasons I landed at Ismailia, Lydda in Palestine, H 4 (a landing ground on the Iraq oil pipeline) and thence flew on to Habbaniya. A problem arose on the last lap as after take-off the landing gear would not retract fully so there was nothing to it but to keep going to Habbaniya. I took her up to 10,000 feet, throttled well back to keep the cylinder-head temperatures normal, and after a slow 2 hrs 35 mins flight landed at Habbaniya. It was not a good omen in a borrowed aeroplane and I sensed that lack of regular flying and maintenance – if any – was the prime cause. Upon arrival at Hab I told the Flight Sergeant about the undercarriage problem – I had used the emergency system to lock the legs down for the landing – and went on to say that I did not require any fuel because I had more than enough on board to get back to Heliopolis. At this both he and the lads nearby were quite incredulous so I explained that the fuel system could give a maximum range of over 7000 miles so would he please check the undercarriage and then put the Wellesley in the hangar. I walked away looking a little smug.

Punishment befalls those with big heads. The following morning I was told that although the undercarriage retraction system had been attended to and a minor repair carried out, one cylinder of the engine had been found to have a burnt-out exhaust valve. Curses! How was I going to solve that one in Iraq because the Wellesley was fitted with a one-off special Bristol engine? To add to my discomfiture the wily Flight Sergeant told me that I was wrong about there being thirteen fuel tanks; he too had counted them – and there were seventeen!!

Rather than admit defeat without some kind of a struggle, I went to the engineering stores to see what, if anything, could be found. The stores Corporal shook his head, "No Sir, nothing at all like that here; we do not keep any Bristol engine spares". I happened to look up at the top shelf in the store and sitting in splendid isolation was a complete cylinder with valves, rocker-box and all the other bits that make up the parts of an air-cooled cylinder unit; at a wild guess it looked more-or-less what I needed. When I pointed to it and asked what it was doing on the top shelf the corporal said, "Gash, sir. It was found by a couple of airmen doing some fitness training out in the desert. They brought it in in case it came in handy, or maybe as a souvenir". I reckoned that it had been stolen by Arabs when they ransacked the BOAC flying boat base on Lake Habbaniya during the rebellion and abandoned it in the desert because they had no use for it. As it was a 'gash' item and therefore not on the RAF stores inventory, I took it away and went back to the hangar. The Flight Sergeant really was startled because he had never experienced this very unusual situation before. He had a look at the object that I had brought to him, thought for some moments, and then said that it had possibilities. However he could do nothing until the Engineer Officer authorised him to go ahead and see if it would fit my engine. Soon his boss arrived and for him the whole crazy business was too much so he declared that nothing could be done and he was not going to be trapped into participating in bad engineering practise. I confess that I then 'pulled rank' and said that it was my aeroplane, my responsibility, and please get on with the job.

My hunch was right – it fitted! The cylinder from a flying boat engine was installed, given a trial run on the ground, and I made a test flight which was perfectly satisfactory. The engineer officer wrote a report on the affair in the aircraft maintenance log called a Form 700 and for emphasis the entire entry was made in red ink. Poor fellow, instinct told him that his head was in danger of being put on the block. If anything nasty happened later, well he was going to blame the idiot who gave him a direct order to fit an engine part that was not only non-RAF equipment – worse still it had been lying out in the desert for weeks. The non-stop return flight to Egypt was uneventful.

Although little was known about it in the Middle East, and even to this day something of a mystery unit like the SAS formed by Colonel David Stirling in Egypt, a very remarkable body of men was gathered together at the beginning of the Mussolini war to form the Long Range Desert Group – the LRDG. It's role primarily was one of reconnaissance and surveillance, but that is only part of the story (General David Lloyd-Owen's excellent book 'Providence their guide' about the LRDG is compulsive reading and he writes with authority because he commanded the force for most of its operational life.) The LRDG used to make unbelievably long-distance forays deep into the desert and then make stealthy approaches by night up to the coastal road which formed the supply-line from Tunis to Bengazi and beyond for General Rommel's Africa Corps. From a cleverly concealed hide, almost like bird watching, two or three LRDG men would lie up for weeks on end watching the passing scene and then pass the data back to base. It required a special kind of man to withstand the rigors and the hazards of this exacting work and the best of the volunteers came from New Zealand and Rhodesia. I had some fleeting contacts with the LRDG and the work that they did and realised that aviation interests understandably were secondary to their main role. For this reason I concluded that air intelligence gathered by them was sketchy at best and sometimes inaccurate. Thus it occurred to me that it might be an idea to form a RAF mini-LRDG that could operate jointly with it and so hang onto the coattails of the professionals. In this way we could benefit from their expertise acquired in the tough reality of operational activity and at the same time use our own know-how to send back valuable aviation information. To get approval for the scheme I made yet another visit to Sir Arthur Tedder. (Heavens! he must have been long suffering). After explaining the concept, he agreed to the idea; better still he told me to get on with it and do what had to be done. It was just what I hoped for. It was now the greatest fun to tell all those concerned that I wanted (a) special vehicles, (b) special equipment, and (c) special personnel. The fuss that arose was very entertaining because not one single piece of paper was issued authorising this, that, and the other – and by whom. Each time a difficult staff wallah queried my requirement, invariably saying that it just could not be done, I would say "Shall I telephone to the C-in-C – or would you prefer to do it yourself?" In quick time I assembled three brand-new Ford trucks fitted with the excellent 'V'-eight engine. (I wondered where George Beamish was by now?) All vehicles had everything above the bonnet line removed to give the minimum profile in the desert and each vehicle had a special mounting to take a Vickers 'K' gun – the latest item of hardware available. Of course all the vehicles had the essential items of water condensers, sand-tracks, shovels, desert tyres, first-aid, drinking water containers, long range fuel tanks and those excellent jerrycans that we now found on desert landing grounds abandoned by the Germans.

For personnel, who better than the talented Flt Lt Derek Rawnsley and enemy aircraft specialists Flying Officers Goldie and Ashe? They were given a free hand to go and pick the rest of the team from volunteers in specialised trades and accept no arguments from anybody about releasing them from their current jobs. It was a quickly-formed unit that set off from Cairo out into the desert to get some tough training for the tasks ahead and I was able to accompany them for the initial trials.

In retrospect, those earlier sorties deep into the North African desert entirely on my own were foolhardy; it would have been so easy for personal or mechanical problems to arise that would have been difficult or impossible to surmount. For some people however there is a fascination about huge desert spaces that has immense appeal; either you love the desert or you loathe it and I fitted the former category. A corollary to this is that the desert soon sorts out the men from the boys. Either the desert subdues you or you master it; there is no middle course, no compromise.

It was therefore no surprise to find that desert warriors were all cast in the same mould. The Desert Air Force headquarters, for example, had such champions as the dynamic Basil Embry (with four DSOs), Peter Wykeham-Barnes and Al Bowman, respectively Wing Commanders directing fighter and bomber squadrons; Bing Cross; Fred Rosier; and at squadron level, that charismatic chap 'Buck' Buchanan who led his Beaufighter boys endlessly and amused (or displeased as appropriate) our male world by accommodating Eve Curie, (journalist daughter of the famous French professor) in his tent. Peter Wykeham-Barnes (who became Air Marshal Sir Peter Wykeham) used to keep a Gladiator alongside his tent as a handy means of getting about. It was a splendid manifestation of independent thought and sensible operating but no doubt it would have been frowned upon and stopped by some rule-book officer in high places had he got to hear of it. Pete allowed me to fly the Gladiator but with the admonition to take care because all the servicing it received was petrol and oil put into appropriate tanks. He reminded me of General Arthur Lewin going shopping to Nairobi in his Miles aircraft.

Just before the third advance into Tripolitania before General Rommel and his Africa Corps forced us to retreat, another airman and I decided to visit Bengazi and for the purpose we travelled in my faithful safari car. After inspecting the city (and noting bomb damage etc) a chance sighting of a small block of apartments revealed a vacant one that we decided to borrow as a base to operate from. The apartment was nicely furnished, in excellent condition, and the erstwhile Italian official had departed.

Soon we were well ensconced and it was good to sleep in a bed and enjoy such simple domestic facilities as running water and the loo. Heaven knows who the previous owner was because in one of the wardrobes were all manner of civil and military uniforms which we guessed made him some kind of a VIP in the city. The desert grape-vine being what it is, we began to have a string of visitors from both Army and Air Force and the food problem was solved by a mixture of what they brought with them coupled with what little could be purchased like eggs, fresh vegetables and Arab bread if you were lucky. I became the chef and the speciality *de la maison* was called 'Bengazi goulash', a hodge-podge consisting of everything that was available.

One pair of RAF chaps to sample the delights of the culinary arts was the CO of a Hurricane squadron and his medical officer. After a good meal I drove them back to Benina aerodrome where the Hurricane was parked. As the Squadron Leader prepared to get into the cockpit I asked him which was his landing-ground of the moment so that I could ferry his doctor back somehow or other. "Don't bother, old boy; doc always flies with me on these jolly outings". It was a two-man Hurricane that taxied out and took off, the doc's job, with his CO sitting on him, was to operate the knobs that the pilot could not reach. Parachutes of course had to be dispensed with; after all, it was a communications aircraft now, was it not?

After some days we vacated the apartment, leaving it as good (or better) than we had found it, and, on our way back towards Egypt with the Africa Corps now snapping at our heels I met up again with Peter Wykeham-Barnes. Cyrenaica was in a turmoil with our land and air forces in retreat and once again the shunting game was taking place across some 750 miles of North Africa where the desert gives tremendous opportunities of swift movement. Being on the winning side in these circumstances is exhilarating; conversely, having to quit is utterly depressing as one gets the unnerving feeling of becoming engulfed by an unstoppable enemy.

The ebb-and-flow of the desert war made me realise what a tough and very nasty affair it was for the soldiers and the infantry in particular. If they were not beset by or attacking the enemy at regular intervals they were certainly plagued by millions of persistent flies. Soldiers had to live continuously in perpetual dust out in the open in the clothes that they stood in; water was so precious that it was just about enough for tea drinking whenever that luxury permitted. In the case of the 'armoured' soldiers, the tank men fared worst of all; their major – and very vital – problem was that the Africa Corps with the highly effective all-purpose 88mm gun could out-gun them in range, accuracy, and effectiveness. One of the saddest sights in my experience on one occasion was to leave the desert track and walk some distance across rough ground to inspect about a dozen of our tanks only to find that every single one had been knocked out with armour-piercing shells fitted with incendiary phosphorous material that left every occupant the colour of burnt cinder exactly where he had been sitting or standing. It was frankly horrific. As I walked slowly and pensively back to my safari car some soldiers nearby watched me in silence. When I regained the track one of them said, "You were bloody lucky, sir; you have just walked right across a minefield."

Peter Wykeham-Barnes and I were now travelling across the hilly area of Cyrenaica called appropriately Gebel el Akhdar – the green hills – and the region was one that Mussolini had planned to return to its historic status of being the granary of the Roman Empire. As events were to show, bad husbandry, bad planning, and (as Bert Harris said) the bloody goats and their Arab owners had descended on the area like locusts. In recent times a number of Mussolini-inspired Italian farming settlements had been set up, and it's fair to say that they were making some progress. However the hapless Italians now had a nasty problem to face for with one army in retreat and another one in pursuit there existed a vacuum between them which the Arabs were quick to exploit. They began to indulge in the age-old business of looting and seizing whatever they could before order by which-ever side was restored. We were joined by Dennis Passadoro who was multi-lingual and invaluable for that reason alone. We stopped near Barce, a pleasant small town in the green hills and it was agreed that the least we could do was to try and protect the Italian farming community from the Arabs as best we could. The war was none of their business and the looters took what they wanted because they were armed with rifles and the farmers were not. We equipped ourselves with Oerlikon machine guns taken from a crashed Me 110 twin-engined fighter of the Luftwaffe and with these cumbersome items of hardware we proceeded to hunt down the baddies who were terrorising the Italian farmers and their families. Each time we spotted an Arab humping his loot, up would go the shooting-irons to waist level, the trigger squeezed, and then a startling demonstration of fire power would ensue; armour-piercing bullets, tracer, incendiaries, the lot. How we kept firing without personal injury I do not know; we never hit anybody – but by thunder we scared the daylights out of them. The Italians were delighted, and later gave their protectors cups of delicious coffee. It had been a good day and it also happened to be New Year's Eve, 1941.

When we returned to the Desert Air Force HQ (which took some finding) I was told that I had to return to Cairo forthwith as I was to be posted back to the UK. Well, well, I thought that they had forgotten me. I had been serving overseas 'East of Suez' for over six years and now it was time to go home. Home? Frankly, for me home was the Middle East. No sooner had I set foot in HQME than I was told that Tedder wanted to see me. "It cannot be true", I cried. "I have just this moment come in from the desert in the clothes that I stand up in". My informant smiled. "Tedder wants to see you – now!" The Commander-in-Chief was puffing away as usual at his pipe and gazed quizzically at one of his scruffy subordinates. "Pelly, I hear that you have been running a private war in Cyrenaica; tell me about it". Now what kind of bush telegraph could have worked so swiftly as that? As there was no point in evasion I came clean and gave him the whole story and the adventure seemed to be quite acceptable to him, I'm glad to say.

Now back in Cairo again I could collect my wits, prepare my few belongings for a return to England, and make arrangements to travel home. My proposal that I go back to UK by sea, taking the long route all round Africa, was accepted by the Movements people. Thus it was that I embarked at Suez in the flagship of the Royal Dutch Merchant Fleet, the *New Amsterdam*. My days in the Middle East were over and I had enjoyed every one of them. It had included a very big variety of jobs in many Middle East and East African areas; I had been given the opportunity of meeting and working for some very remarkable and talented people; I had been lucky to endure and survive the fortunes of war unscathed; best of all perhaps I had learned a whole lot and gained much experience. I now awaited with interest to discover what the goddess of fortune had in store for me.

Chapter XVI

The Return to England

The fine Dutch flagship *New Amsterdam* was awaiting the arrival of its passengers at Suez and after embarking I had time to ponder on the past seven years and the varied jobs that had come my way. For me the Mussolini war and General Rommel's Africa Corps was now a vivid memory. Having been so fortunate as to become some kind of a free-lance intelligence officer during the final period, it naturally gave me access to both ends of the activity; the Headquarters in Cairo with its planners and decision-makers, and the sharp-end where the battles were fought. One day when I was in Sir Arthur Tedder's office in connection with the 'Operations/Intelligence Room' that was now a going concern I looked at the 'enemy' map and said "You know, Sir, I have a strong feeling that the nigger-in-the-woodpile is Crete. We have nothing there of consequence and if we lost it that would give the Germans a very good base from which to operate in the Eastern Med." The C-in-C gazed hard at the map, looked pensive for some moments, and then said "It's one of the German options; however, I am not sure that they would go for it at present. They have plenty on their hands as it is without adding Crete to the list. Unfortunately we do not have any more units to send to the island, so let's see how it goes later on". In the event we managed to send a useful force to Crete, but on May 20th the Germans sent an even bigger one, preceded by a massive parachute drop from Ju.52s. It was not difficult to forecast who won that round, even if it was only after a struggle and the Germans lost 4000 men in the process. It proved to be the last airborne invasion that Germany made in any theatre, so presumably they had learnt the lesson that under certain conditions this form of warfare was too costly. The Allied Forces profited by the experience and improved on the techniques employed, but even so, airborne assault can so easily go wrong – as witness the episode at Arnhem after D-Day.

In January 1942, the *New Amsterdam* sailed from Suez and headed down the Red Sea. I felt that I now knew that torrid area quite well; I had not sailed its entire length of 1,400 miles more than once, I had flown along its western edge almost end-to-end on many occasions, both in peace and war. This time I could gaze at it from the good vantage point of a very well appointed liner. The fine Dutch ship had handsomely been put at the disposal of Britain and we used her essentially as a passenger-transport vessel between Suez and Durban, so giving her a comparatively safe route but a very important one all the same.

By virtue of my now exalted wartime rank of Squadron Leader – who would have thought it possible three years ago? – I was allocated a twin-bedded cabin to myself and the steward removed the spare one which gave the cabin almost a stateroom appearance. After unpacking my travelling kit I went around the ship to get the lay-out. She was beautifully appointed in every way so it was a splendid start to the circuit of Africa.

One discovery was that the erstwhile Wellesley king of No 14 Squadron Wing Commander AD 'Mark' Selway and his charming wife Pat and their two children were passengers. This completely changed the nature of a voyage of comfortable travel to the added benefit of enjoying the company of friends. Mark was one of those rare men who had an incisive mind and a classic style of witty description and penetrating comment. No wonder he became a Commander-in-Chief – more than once – and in retirement was appointed Gentleman Usher of the Black Rod. He quickly appreciated that champagne on board was inexpensive so the three of us shared the pleasure of a bottle every midday. What an excellent cruise custom and how dramatic a change from our many months in the Sudan!

The days passed uneventfully as we sailed on at something like twenty-two knots, soon to round the Horn of Africa and move into the Indian Ocean. By now the rest of the world had receded from thought even though we all had nasty awakenings of reality when the ship's news-gathering system told us what was happening in other places. For the moment, sufficient to enjoy what we had; the harsh realities of war would be thrust upon us later on. The spell was broken on arrival at Durban where there was much activity because passengers had to leave the *New Amsterdam* and transfer to the *Oransay* which was to take us to Capetown and thence on into the Atlantic. This was going to be the nasty bit – the run north to England in waters becoming singularly dangerous because of the German U-boats. It was going to be one of those situations where as passengers we would have absolutely no control of our destinies; you just watched the 20,000 ton ship moving through the cruel sea, said your prayers, and hoped that they would be answered. There is nothing so telling in human frailty as appealing to the *Deity* when potential disaster is present. It may not work, but it soothes.

Once the passengers had embarked on the new ship, many of us in uniform but there was also a large contingent of women and children from Singapore who had escaped the Japanese threat, we sailed out of Durban.

The next port of call was Capetown, about 1,000 miles away and further down the African coast at 'the bottom end' of the huge continent. We arrived in good order and stayed long enough for the specialists to carry out the usual complex activities associated with ocean travel. The new passengers who embarked included Air Chief Marshal Sir Robert and Lady Brooke-Popham. They were going home for good from Singapore during the uncertain situation prevailing out there at the time and my interest lay in the fact that they seemed not to be getting any particular VIP treatment appropriate to their status. So, wearing my Personal Assistant's hat once again I approached Sir Robert and persuaded him – albeit reluctantly – to let me look after their day-to-day needs. If nothing else it was a pleasure to do what little I could and it gave me a purpose on board rather than be just another passenger.

The self-appointed ADC now had routine jobs to do like finding deck-chairs and putting them conveniently on deck. I studiously avoided any conversation about the Far East and Sir Robert's recent role of Governor and C-in-C but kept to subjects like Kenya and the Mussolini war. On the second day at sea all passengers were assembled and given lifeboat drill, allocated lifeboats and mustered into groups alongside the appropriate one; everybody, in theory anyway, knew what to do in case of disaster. I was made captain of my lifeboat and when I checked I discovered that my party consisted of forty women and children and one Flying Officer. Brother! How was this going to work out, on the optimistic assumption that we reached the point of being lowered safely into the sea? The only bonus was that my sole male crewman was also a keen yachtsman, so at least two of us had a head start. With my Services training I decided to work out a contingency plan that should help the situation rather than wait for disaster to be upon us and then improvise. There were two basic elements. The first was to make up what I called a Funk Bag. It consisted of a small canvas carrier bag inside which I kept a torch, an aeroplane compass off a crashed CR 42 Italian fighter, a page torn out of an atlas showing the Atlantic, warm clothing, floppy hat, water bottle, dark glasses, first-aid kit, glucose sweets and bars of chocolate. In addition I hoped to take my well-used Hebron sheepskin coat that had been so useful in the desert. All this equipment was kept readily available in my cabin where I could lay my hands on it even in total darkness. The second precaution was to find out how many escape routes there were from my cabin to the boat deck and these were memorised. I practised using each route (some of which were very circuitous) in the middle of the night and using only my torch for guidance. One of the danger points in any enclosed place is not to know the best and quickest escape route so it's simply a question of using one's imagination and having a keen awareness of anticipating a bad situation. After a number of practise runs at dead of night in the completely darkened ship I became quite good at jumping out of bed, still in semi-dressed clothing, putting on shoes and pullover, grabbing my Funk Bag and sheepskin coat, and going swiftly to the lifeboat. It gave me the confidence to get the vital first part of the exercise buttoned-up as far as possible. The major problem that arose was asking Sir Robert which lifeboat he and Lady Brooke-Popham were allocated to; and his reply that if the ship was torpedoed and began to sink, well, he and his wife would go to the bridge and join the Captain. I had nasty visions of all my plans going wrong with none of the women and children able to get to the allotted lifeboat and so I as a dutiful ADC staying close to my boss what time the waters of the Atlantic started to engulf us.

Where the factor of the lifeboat operation was concerned, (assuming that at least some of us had succeeded in that regard) the important decision in the event of being on our own in a huge ocean was to know the course to sail to the nearest land. We might well be somewhere in mid-Atlantic as we were not in convoy and I noted that we were changing course at irregular intervals, the theory being that at over twenty knots and constantly zig-zagging we were too difficult a target for other than a U-boat pack. The snag in my planning was that the ship's navigation officer said that he was forbidden to reveal the ship's position to passengers. The only way round this impasse was that each midday I guesstimated the position by compass and timing the ship's run and headings over a period of time, plotted it on my map and then told the ship's navigator where I thought we were. He would then make a thinly veiled comment along the lines of, "You could be 100 nautical miles out; maybe we are more to the north west, eh?" Well, that was far better than not knowing anything at all, so each day I had a new, if approximate starting point for the next twenty-four hour plot.

A most unhappy moment on board came with an announcement on the ship's broadcast system that Singapore had fallen to the Japanese. Oh dear, oh dear! All those desperately worried and unhappy wives with their children who could only surmise that the husbands that they had left behind were now certainly in the clutches of the Japanese and faced a bleak future. It seemed a wicked thing to tell us about Singapore; far better surely, to let the passenger know later on in a less dramatic and unkind way? Sir Robert, the man who was recently responsible for the protection and administration of a vital area of the Far East must have been greatly shocked; everything that he had stood for had become a ghastly nightmare.

The days passed and we steamed ever closer to our destination, Liverpool. The Atlantic weather in February was what one expects; cold, windy, and rough seas. The final run up from the Bay of Biscay and then up the St George's Channel was an unnerving period. Liverpool seemed to be so far off and the unfriendly waters in my mind's eye was seething with sinister black shapes waiting for a good moment to strike. To an airman it seemed such a helpless position to be in and there was nothing that one could do about it. Finally, to everybody's considerable relief the *Oransay* arrived safely at Liverpool. Although I had never before set eyes on that city it looked attractive indeed. Disembarkation soon took place and the Brooke-Pophams, the Selways (together with their young family) and I parted company and everybody else dispersed to their various destinations. I took the train to London.

The Royal Air Force Club at 128 Piccadilly became my temporary home whilst I tried to find out what the next job was to be. It had the advantages of convenience, a good place to meet my friends, and a handy operating base for a bachelor. I always enjoyed the club with its friendly atmosphere, helpful staff, and comfortable facilities for its members. Thank goodness for Lord Cowdray who so handsomely gave his fine London house to the Royal Air Force many years ago and for good measure added a very substantial cheque to get the Club set up. The cheque can be seen to this day, suitably framed below the portrait of the Patron.

A call on the Air Ministry was the first item to attend to after arrival in London. This time it was not only the 'booking in' process to record one's new address; much more important was the business of talking to the Personnel officer to determine what the next appointment was to be. The process was usually a friendly discussion of the individual officer's aspirations and preferences coupled with the realities of what was available and, understandably, the unrevealed ideas of the Air Member for Personnel with regard to future promotion prospects. On a wartime basis most of us were primarily concerned with using one's professional talents to the best advantage and promotion was of no particular consequence. Without being unkind to some of my contemporaries it is fair to say that we fell into two basic categories; those who were impelled to get into the fight, if only perhaps to justify personal esteem. The second category were those who (maybe genuinely) thought that their professional services could best be utilised in a less demanding and dangerous way. Although I was just as frightened as anybody else I felt that my duty as a trained pilot was to go on flying for as long as I was fit to do so. If you join a gladiator's club and accept the good things that are associated with peacetime benefits, then equally you should accept the risks attendant to a wartime situation and get into the fray rather than take a ringside seat. Where airmen are concerned, there is the added demanding situation that once you become a Flight Commander or Commanding Officer in a fighting unit you must tell yourself to go to war rather than be told.

After the initial greeting from the Postings Officer (and a chat about how the previous job worked out and a general review of one's current affairs) comes the nitty-gritty of the whole business. "Well now, old chap, what are your ideas for the next posting?" This automatically puts the visitor into an optimistic frame of mind because he thinks, innocently, that he has only to say some magic word like 'Spitfire' than immediately the reply is a joyous "Oh well done! I hoped that that was what you wanted". The reality stops

The ME 110 *(wrk nr 4035)* of the Iraq Air Force that had been abandoned in the desert near Habbaniya, May 1941. The author had hoped to commandeer this for his own use — unfortunately the 'powers-that-be' had other ideas!

A captured Me109 of JG27, December 1941

The Luftwaffe pilot *(centre back)* escorted for interrogation at DAF HQ while the RAF pilot *(centre foreground)* looks pleased with himself. On the left W/Cdr Peter Wykeham-Barnes and W/Cdr Bob Bateson, El Adem, Libya, December 1941

A Tomahawk returns a 'bit bent' from an air collision with an Italian Machi 2000

Boston IIIA, RH-A, BZ214, of 88 Sqn. This aircraft was usually flown by the author when CO of the Squadron

Blickling Hall, Norfolk, home of No. 88 Sqn, 1942–43

Celebrating 'Griff' Griffiths' (seen standing behind the author in the centre) award of the DFC leading the Squadron on a bombing raid of the docks at St Malo on 31st July 1944

A V-M Alan Lees *(right)* talking to the author *(centre)* and S/Ldr Griffiths *(left)* during the Dieppe raid August 1942

Crews of 88 Sqn before a sortie during the Dieppe raid, August 1942

The Philips factory at Eindhoven under attack, 6 December 1942

Part of the main Philips factory severely damaged after the attack

In September 1953 the author, at that time a Group Captain with NATO, visited the Philips factory at Eindhoven and was warmly received by Mr Otten, the Chairman. The hand-written note, on the photograph, ends with the message 'No hard feelings!'

The Royal Family at the end of an impromptu shooting party at Appleton House, January 1944. The photographs were taken by the author who was, at the time, an equerry to HM King George VI

The author *(right)* as Station Commander of RAF Holme-on-Spalding-Moor, Yorkshire

The author *(foreground)* with Air Commodore Hodgson *(centre)* at the presentation of DFCs to Norwegian aircrew members of 76 Sqn

S/Ldr John Crampton, another keen modeller, of 76 Sqn. At 6'6" John must have been the tallest pilot in the RAF

right there. The smiling vanishes, there is a pregnant pause, and the head-shaking begins. "Sorry old chap, not a single job going in that line. However, it so happens that I have in mind an important job which is tailor-made for you; it's to be in charge of administering the new Catering School at Blackpool. It needs someone like you to give the staff and pupils the feeling that an airman is going to tell them how the front-line squadrons need Savoy Hotel service to keep them fit and itch to shoot all the Huns down".

I said firmly "I want to be a night-fighter boy". When this request had been made and my destiny man had recovered his composure, the head-shaking began. "Most difficult, old chap; you see, far too many people are after too few of those jobs. Anyway, it's fearfully specialised and Fighter Command has a list as long as your arm of pilots waiting to get into a squadron. The other big problem is that with your seniority you would be a Flight Commander – maybe even a Squadron Commander before long – and you would then baulk chaps with more night-fighter experience than you; it's not fair to them, is it?" He went on, "Anyway, you have already had one squadron, so nobody can say that you have not done your bit. So what prompts you to want to get into night fighters?" My answer, (which I doubt that he believed) was that as I had frequently been shot at in light bombers it would be nice to do some shooting myself for a change. With well over one thousand hours flying on twins I reckoned that I was just as good as the chaps who were having successes over Southern England stalking those German aeroplanes by night and getting lots of kudos in the process. Unhappily I left the Air Ministry empty-handed. I was given some leave which I really did not want, did not know how to spend, and did not need anyway. Heavens, the trip by sea round Africa was long enough to get rested from the rigors of war. I was asked to return two weeks later when a job by then would be found for me. It was all a bit depressing.

The business now began of thinking of friends I could look up, where I could stay, and what I was going to do. It is inevitably a boring and sometimes dangerous situation as there is a temptation to hang about in London, spend much too much money, and probably indulge to excess. I needed an escape route. So it was that I got myself invited to stay with Bert and Jill Harris. My old boss had been home for just over two years and had seemingly recovered at least in some measure from the *malaise* that he had picked up in Jerusalem; he was now the Commander-in-Chief of Bomber Command.

I called first of all at his Headquarters tucked away in Buckinghamshire woodland and it was wonderful to see him looking so much better than when I left him to go to Kenya. After giving him an outline of what I had been doing overseas he asked what was going to happen to me next. I told him about my abortive visit to the Postings people (apropos becoming a night-fighter boy) and how I was sent away on leave to get rid of me. He seemed to approve of my night-fighter aspirations because he said "Write to Sholto; and tell him that I said so". Well now, that was a boost; an instruction to write to Air Marshal Sir William Sholto Douglas, who was C-in-C Fighter Command. It was the organ-grinder formula again.

During my stay with Bert Harris he spoke of the activities of his Command. In his typical style he said that as the bomber force built up, so was he concentrating on much greater accuracy in delivery and the boffins were working away unceasingly on producing new methods of hitting targets that did not depend on visual sightings. It was essential to achieve maximum results with the minimum of effort because a target missed was a target to return to. This was particularly the case when of all military endeavour the long-range bomber had by far the most difficult job of all. It was a tremendous strain on the crews, the like of which no other fighting force previously had to cope with continuously. What other fighting force had the prospect that in book-maker's language not one crew could expect to complete the thirty missions of an operational tour? No, it was a very nasty, tough, uncomfortable and frightening game to be a bomber airman. As things stood at present his Command was the only means of striking at the heart of Germany. "You know, Pelly, the *Boche* are going to be at the receiving end for a change. If I keep attacking their factories, their military and supply bases for long enough, sooner rather than later their will and capacity to continue will be reduced to such an extent that later on the soldiers and their supporting airmen will be able to kick them all back to Germany; what's left of it, that is. It's going to take time. However, if I can get a bigger bomber force – and God knows I am fighting like a tiger to get one – the job will be done that much sooner". Rarely had I seen him so determined, so completely dedicated, and so utterly convinced about the correctness of his views. I felt that this man had a mission and his Bomber Command people reflected his policies abundantly. His work-load became so intense that he very rarely had time to visit his innumerable air stations – they boasted over 2000 miles of runway between them! – but his charisma and leadership permeated all the way through his command. Yes, a man now called Bomber Harris was in business with a vengeance.

As soon as I returned to the RAF Club, I took some smart club notepaper and dutifully wrote to Sholto Douglas at his Headquarters and explained why I had written to him direct. Within twenty-four hours I was called to the telephone and on the line was a Group Captain from Fighter Command. Ah-ha! swift reaction, and it was encouraging. Would I come and see him? Tomorrow; say in mid-afternoon? So the next day I set off to discover what luck I might have. The Group Captain (who I had not met before) had seen my letter which the C-in-C had passed to him for action. The conversation began with an account of my flying experience, now some 1,500 hours on a variety of types, where I had been, operational experience, and so forth; it was the usual catalogue of personal data.

Then came the inevitable snags; the problems of fitting someone like myself into the system; my seniority, (dammit! I was only a Flying Officer two-and-a-half years ago); and all the waffle that I got to know so well in later years. Then the escape clause was produced. "I think it would be a good idea – routine stuff, old boy – if you had a night vision test. I'll arrange it." So this was the trick? Desert warrior returns to England only to find that sun-and-sand has impaired his vision. I went right away to the medical people where I was put in a completely blacked-out room for thirty minutes and then had to write on ribbed paper what I thought I could see projected on a screen at the other end of the room. After a few seconds sighting of each tantalising and palest of images I wrote in between the ribs what I thought it was. Each 'impression' was a silhouette, and a pretty vague one at that.

When all thirty-two images had been screened in the allotted time the lights went up and an attractive WAAF came in and took my score-sheet away. I sat pensively but I confess that I quite enjoyed the test. Now would be the moment of truth, the answer to all that sun-and-sand in the desert for so long. In a matter of minutes the now wide-eyed girl returned with my 'exam paper'. I smiled. "How did I do?" She exclaimed "Wonderful! You have the same record score as Wing Commander 'Catseyes' Cunningham, the night-fighter ace; thirty-one out of thirty-two right". When I checked, I found that I had fluffed the very last one. "Dammit", I said to the girl, "It looked exactly like a plain cross but I tried to be clever and wrote 'plan view of fighter' instead". But for that silly answer I would have got the whole dammed lot right, 100% score, and you cannot do better than that. I do not mind admitting that I felt pretty smug and next time I saw John I would say that I should have beaten his record score.

Soon after the visit to Fighter Command, and the great satisfaction of my high score (that must have caused chagrin!) came the disappointing news that I could not become a night-fighter boy after all. Let's be honest – it was the old Closed Shop game operating behind the curtain and I went back to Bomber Harris and told him what had happened. I then asked if I could work for him again, perhaps to join one of his squadrons. I had visions of a Lancaster as another four-engined aeroplane to record in my log book to add to the Handley Page 'Hannibal' airliner – ahem!! Bert shook his head, saying what an awful job it was of flying for many hours through the night, often in awful weather and in acute discomfort, and having to do sorties again and again and again. He hinted that for the time being anyway I had done enough with No 223 and 47 Squadron flying Wellesleys on those very long night trips over the Ethiopian mountains. Thus it was that reluctantly I made my way back to the Air Ministry where I had to admit that I had visited Fighter Command unofficially but it had not worked. It was now the turn of the Postings fellow to make a proposal. He said "I think I have it! As you are keen to keep flying, how about 'light bombers'?" It was just up my street with my earlier experience but first of all I should go off and do a Blenheim conversion course at RAF Upwood. When that was over – in my case maybe a fortnight would do – he would post me somewhere to a holding job until a squadron come up for me to command. Well, well! command of a light bomber squadron meant promotion to Wing Commander and I left his office with the feeling that things were falling into place after all. In the event, a temporary staff posting to No 92 Group Headquarters was ordained to start with and the new job was located in a handsome mansion near the small town of Winslow in Buckinghamshire. No 92 Group was part of the Bomber Command training organisation set up for aircrew to fly more advanced aeroplanes like the Handley Page Hampden prior to ending up finally in a front-line heavy bomber unit. Once again I was on the payroll of Bert Harris and I telephoned to him to tell him what had transpired. His brief comment was that he hoped that I was happy with the arrangement and to come and see him from time to time.

No 92 Group was a pleasant headquarters and my new job fortunately was directly connected with the flying training programme and it was good to find such agreeable people to work with. The Senior Air Staff Officer (SASO) was none other than (now) Group Captain 'Trader' Horn of Heliopolis! The days passed and Winslow Hall was handy for getting to London. I enjoyed those few weeks in the Spring of 1942, happy in the thought that I would be moving on to Upwood to get in some flying time in the Blenheim. When making a routine staff visit to RAF Bicester, one of the aerodromes controlled by 92 Group, I encountered 'Jock' Cairns, now a Flt Lt and I was delighted to see him again. THJ Cairns had been a radio man in 216 Squadron and was now a qualified navigator with the DFM ribbon showing on his uniform. Whilst having a drink in the Mess we had a long talk and then suddenly he blurted out "Sir, get me out of here!" Apparently he was fed up with instructing pupils and wanted to team up with me again, something that was just what I hoped he would say. In quick order I arranged for him to accompany me in due course to Upwood as my navigator. Things, as they say, were beginning to look up.

Chapter XVII

The Bostons of 88 Squadron

Before leaving Winslow hall and my colleagues of No 92 Group after my short stay I visited my old friend Moose Fulton at RAF Mildenhall. He was now commanding a Canadian squadron equipped with Wellingtons and this quiet-spoken and capable airman wore the DSO, DFC and AFC ribbons on his uniform. After lunch he took me to the back of the Mess to show me the Lagonda and it was as impeccable as I had seen it four years earlier. Whilst I was admiring the old steed Moose said, "James, it's time you had the old waggon back again". I thought at first that he meant to lend it to me until such time as I obtained a car for myself, but it was not so. What he meant was that he had not really bought it, he had borrowed it. He reminded me that he had only paid a token sum that was enough to help to pay my air fare back to Egypt and had subsequently sent me small-value cheques at irregular intervals; he argued therefore that he was only paying a hire charge. We ended the debate by my agreeing that I would drive away in the Lagonda, keep it for as long as necessary, and we would 'figure out' what happened after that.

Three days later I telephoned to ask him to send the car's registration papers. The Adjutant answered the call and to my utter dismay he told me that Moose had not returned from a Wellington sortie the night before. There was no news whatever about its fate – just the usual dead silence. Stunned into disbelief I went right away to Mildenhall and found the entire Station shrouded in an atmosphere of gloom. Alas! They had lost an exceptional commander and I had lost my best friend. The Squadron Adjutant asked me to keep the Lagonda because no next-of-kin could be traced and his only brother had been killed on Army operations. He added that Moose Fulton would have wished it that way. So the Lagonda returned to my care. In later years I heard that he was declared to be one of Canada's ace pilots and he deserved every national acclaim that his country could give him. War is horrible and unforgiving, as I now realised more and more.

Jock Cairns and I climbed aboard the Lagonda on the 25th May, 1942, and we drove north out of London towards the County of Huntingdonshire where we were to join No 17 Operational Training Unit based at RAF Station Upwood. It was fortunately a pre-war bricks-and-mortar establishment, unlike the many wartime aerodromes that had sprung up like mushrooms all over the country, and it seemed incredible that so many could have been constructed so quickly and so close together. For the next month we were to have the comforts attendant upon a permanent RAF Station rather than endure the rigors of those wartime Nissen huts.

Our arrival at Upwood on the Sunday evening (so as to be 'on parade' on Monday morning) was accomplished after an uneventful and pleasant run along the A1, the Great North Road as it used to be called so much more romantically. The Officers Mess accommodation was a great improvement on RAF Spitalgate in 1935 as this time I was given much more comfortable quarters and unpacked what little kit that I had brought with me. At sunset it was time to go to the Mess bar – a new innovation as on a peacetime basis drinks were served by a steward in the Ante Room – and Jock and I met some of the officers on the staff; someone kindly gave us tankards of good draft beer although officially 'treating' was not allowed. A chap in the party during our conversation asked if I had come to inspect something or other in the morning. "No, I'm not a staff charlie," I replied. "I have come to learn to fly the Blenheim and brought my navigator Jock Cairns along to make sure that I don't get lost". Another voice then said, "Oh, I see sir, just a quick refresher course before taking on a staff job somewhere?" To the second question I replied "No, not so. I'm told by Air Ministry that I am destined to get a squadron in 2 Group, but truth to tell I have only a hazy idea what 2 Group is except it's something to do with light bombers". There followed a pregnant silence in the bar so I said "What's odd about going to 2 Group? Is it real or have I said something stupid?" Still a strange silence and then somebody said "No, it's real alright. The best chap to give you the gen is 'Attie' as he is an old hand from 2 Group and is now a Flight Commander here". The conversation then turned to the usual gossip but I still wondered what all the mystery was about and it was mildly worrying. Maybe 2 Group was some kind of an outfit that did something of no consequence? Perhaps that cosy chat in the Air Ministry was to lure me into some backwater after all? Well, the sooner I found out, the better. It might be possible for us to wriggle out of it on the score that we were not told what was in store, so the first thing to do after booking-in with the Station Adjutant was to meet this fellow 'Attie'.

A fine and sunny morning dawned and after Jock and I registered our arrival at Station HQ we were told that we had been allocated to Sq Ldr LVE Atkinson's Flight. I was to meet him sooner than expected. I entered his office and saw a sandy-haired and slightly paunchy officer with more gongs on his chest than I thought possible for such a young man. After the usual courtesies I told him that Air Ministry had planned to post us to something called 2 Group but had no idea what it was. Attie explained that it was a light bomber force and he had completed two operational tours on Blenheims in 21 Sqdn and then 82 Sqdn and was now put out to grass as instructor. He added that by the time that we got into the light bomber business it ought to be a better prospect as new types of aeroplanes were on their way. I now had a distinct feeling that Jock and I were unwittingly walking into a trap.

After questioning some of the other instructors we found that Attie was quite unique. He had an exceptional operational war record and he had beaten the bookies' odds in a very remarkable way. Many years later when Michael Bowyer's book about 2 Group was being written, the author and I visited Attie at his home in Horsham and cajoled him – the brandy helped! – into telling us something of his exploits. The stories confirmed that his very low-level Blenheim attacks on enemy shipping were legendary and he personally was credited with destroying 100,000 tons of shipping both in the English Channel and later in the Mediterranean; all this by one man flying a Blenheim!! Operating from England, the usual three-aeroplane anti-shipping sorties often resulted in one Blenheim at best returning to Manston on the Kent coast and sometimes all three were shot down. Attie flew these sorties time and time again and I concluded that his guardian angel must have been gold-plated.

At Upwood I began to get the general picture. 2 Group was a specialised collection of some twelve light bomber squadrons that had originally gone to France with the Allied Expeditionary Force, its task being to support the land forces. When they were thrown out of France by the German thrust to the Channel, ending with Dunkirk and that sea evacuation epic, the light bomber squadrons had fought most gallantly but to little avail. What was left of 2 Group was re-formed and became part of Bomber Command again until such time as it could be transferred to the Tactical Air Force prior to D-Day. In the meantime it operated its Blenheim squadrons in the many ways that the need or circumstance prescribed. The role and the variety of tasks developed as the expertise was gained was essentially to harry the enemy in occupied Europe to the maximum extent. That task invariably necessitated the closest co-operation with Fighter Command whose Spitfires would protect the light bomber squadrons and endeavour to sweep a path to the targets and back again. It was a kind of Cinderella Air Force but even so some of its raids into occupied Europe became notable as witness the Amiens Prison attack to release French resistance men about to be shot, the Gestapo Headquarters attack in the Hague and similarly another in Oslo, and the major attack on the big Phillips works at Eindhoven. By definition it was a most specialised and dangerous game which attracted only the dedicated crews.

The 2 Group front-line aircraft from 1942 onwards was a great improvement on previous years but still consisted of a very disparate collection of types – evidence enough that some squadrons had to accept whatever was available. The Mosquito took pride of place with its high speed and remarkable versatility in the many roles of bomber, fighter-bomber, long-range reconnaissance, photographic aircraft, night fighter, and – not least – the Bomber Command 'Master Bomber' pathfinder aircraft. The Boston, (the A 20 in America) designed primarily as a ground-attack light bomber by Douglas Aircraft (and used initially by the French Air Force before France fell to the German occupation) was used by the RAF (and of course the USAF) and put to work extensively over Europe, in North Africa, and against the Japanese in the Far East. The night fighter version was called a 'Havoc' in the RAF.

The North American 'Mitchell' was a good work-horse bomber that could carry a bigger load and fly further than the Boston but it was not such a good 'pilot's aeroplane' in terms of handling and manoeuvrability. Given the advantage of fighter superiority it performed excellently and was well liked by the crews. The fourth bomber type in 2 Group was the Lockheed 'Ventura' and frankly it was a makeshift variation of the Lockheed 'Hudson' of RAF Coastal Command. For daylight operations over Europe however it was a different story and the pilots description of 'Flying Pig' says it all. It should never have been subjected to that kind of operational flying and it says much for the men who flew in them that they pressed on with such determination. Discounting the element of luck which is always a big factor in air warfare, the biggest daylight operation by 2 Group Venturas in a mixed force was the attack on the Phillips Radio and Electrical Works at Eindhoven by almost one hundred aircraft in all and entailed losses in the ratio of 1 percent Mosquito, 4 per cent Bostons and 9 percent Venturas with flak damage five times greater for Venturas than for Bostons. It was a yardstick of the measure of the relative effectiveness of the three types of aeroplane, but it has to be said that the overall wartime losses sustained by 2 Group forces (as recorded in November 1942) was only exceeded in the bad news 'League Table' by the Torpedo bomber statistics. At the time of the Air Ministry survey the percentage chance of survival in any light bomber for second-tour crews was a miserable six and a half percent. By contrast, the fighter boys' chances were three times better but they always seemed to get most of the limelight. Forty years after the Hitler war the only RAF name that has survived is 'Spitfire' (and perhaps 'Hurricane' 'Mosquito' and 'Lancaster' in much less degree) but the Bomber had by far the more hazardous tasks to carry out and under the worst conditions.

My instructor at Upwood was Flt Lt Charles Patterson, DFC. He also had been a 2 Group Blenheim pilot and had completed an operational tour and then a second and a third one later on in Mosquitoes in the role of ace photographic reconnaissance pilot which earned him a very good DSO.

Poor fellow, it fell to his lot to take on a pupil (who the instructors uncharitably called a tired old warrior from the Middle East) and try to turn him into a pilot good enough to fly against the Germans over Europe. Many years later Charles told me that his contemporaries at Upwood were incensed because, as they put it, the bastards at the Air Ministry were sending me to 2 Group to a certain death! Charles' Flight Commander Attie even expressed the pious hope that he might find me unsuitable as a Blenheim pilot, and this would solve the problem in a neat fashion. Charles and I now began to fly in a Blenheim Mk 1 dual-control trainer and I found it to be a nice aeroplane with no bad habits or vices. After three instructional sorties I was sent off on my own to do some circuits-and-landings, general local flying, and the usual aircraft familiarisation business. After that I was promoted to the Blenheim IV, a faster machine although not so nice to handle. Then came something awful called a Bisley. This was supposed to be an improvement on the Blenheim but the pilots disagreed! By way of a diversion from the routine work one very curious entry in my log book was to take some wireless operators on a training flight in an Avro Anson. Heaven knows how, or even why, but I recorded twenty-two landings during a flight lasting one hour fifteen minutes.

Towards the end of the month's flying a message came for me to report to Air Vice Marshal Alan Lees, Air Officer Commanding No 2 Group. So it was true after all! The Headquarters was near Huntingdon and thus convenient to drive there in the Lagonda. When I presented myself to the Air Marshal he told me that he had a Boston Squadron for me. Apart from not knowing at that time what a Boston was, or even what it looked like, my reaction was not so much to say "Thank you, sir" as to ask if I might be considered to command one of his three Mosquito squadrons. The Air Marshal replied smartly that no Mosquito squadron was available for me so I would have to be content and pleased with getting Bostons, the new American light bomber that had recently arrived in his Command. I was so abashed that I did not even ask what kind of aeroplane the Boston was and said "Thank you Sir", saluted, and left his office. All that I knew was that the new job was to command No 88 (Hong Kong) squadron, the name allocated to thank the generous fraternity who had donated funds towards the purchase of aircraft for the RAF. Jock and I learned that a solitary Boston was to be found nearby at RAF Warboys and we arranged to make a visit, have a look at the new hardware, and try it on for size.

The next task, now that I knew that the Boston was a pilot/navigator/radio-air gunner type of light bomber, was to find 'the third man'. I discussed the matter with Attie and he said that an excellent chap called 'Buster' Evans, with one tour already behind him and a DFM was an instructor at Upwood for new air gunners. If he could be persuaded to take on a second tour – well, he was the man for me and right away newly-commissioned Pilot Officer CA Evans and I were in deep conversation in the office adjoining Attie's. It was one of those occasions when each closely sized-up the other as there was a great deal at stake. Was I the right kind of man to pilot him to war? Was he the right kind of man to be in the back of the aeroplane? It took only a couple of minutes before we both said 'Ok', shook hands, and that was that. Getting a crew together is a very exacting business – particularly so in the case of a Squadron Commander's aeroplane. We were expected to be tops, the leaders, the team upon which the major responsibilities lay. Particularly on squadron daylight operations, if we made mistakes well that was very bad news for the rest. Somehow I sensed that this very robust ex-policeman from Devon was just the man for the task. I hoped equally that he approved of me. As events were to prove so conclusively Buster Evans was exceptional; more than once his quite remarkable coolness and complete mastery of his trade saved our lives and that of the other crews flying in formation with us.

On the morning of the 21st June 1942 the three of us climbed into the Lagonda and drove over to Warboys where we began to inspect the Boston. A product of the American Douglas Company, it was a twin-engined machine with a high-wing position and having a distinctly purposeful look the first impressions were most favourable. With its two big fourteen-cylinder Wright 'Cyclone' 1800 hp air-cooled engines enclosed in snug cowlings, a tricycle undercarriage, and a tall single fin and rudder and separate crew positions in a deep fuselage, it was a complete change from anything that we had seen before. So far – so very good. A pilot-instructor showed us around and each of us inspected our respective crew positions. In my case I was shown the trick of climbing up onto the back of the wing (using the right foot first as otherwise you got all-of-a-twist!), walking along the catwalk under the long top hatch and then dropping down into a very comfortable and well laid-out cockpit. It was obvious that no dual-control arrangement was fitted (although later I found a make-shift attachment for the air gunner to use in emergency) so the new boy just had to learn what to do, memorise the emergency actions, and go! After reading and digesting the pilot's notes thoroughly I advised the instructor that I was ready for my first flight. Jock and Buster were peeved because I decided that initially I would go solo; to which I commented that there was no point in all of us getting killed first time out. With my teacher lying flat on his stomach on the cat-walk I learned the trick of getting the big engines started; after which he gave me a friendly pat on my shoulder and climbed down onto the apron, shutting the long cockpit hatch as he left. I was now on my own; so no mistakes please!

The first take-off was exhilarating. With a tricyle landing gear under me for the very first time I realised how much better and easier it was than the old tail-down arrangement. There was no swing on take-off, no need to play with rudder or throttles, just a great big surge of power and straight along the dotted line down the runway like a rocket. The Boston was airborne at about 120 mph. Heavens, that was twice the take-off speed of those Valentias I had left behind in Egypt and the Wellesleys of the Sudan! Once airborne and the wheels tucked up like a bird, the Boston really was the best thing that I had ever flown. It was very fast – more than 300 mph if you wished – manoeuvrable, and a delight to handle. During the one hour flight, including two landings, I was never more impressed. All three of us now went off for another trip and it was equally satisfying. We were now starting off in business as a Boston crew.

After a few days leave the next move was to go to Attlebridge aerodrome in Norfolk, the base of No 88 Squadron, but first of all Jock and Buster went home to their respective families and I made another visit to London. We now knew what kind of aeroplane was in store for us and I had succeeded in flying one for just over two hours. It was not much, but better than arriving at No 88 Squadron as green as an unripe apple. The Upwood course had provided excellent flying training under UK conditions with thirty four hours recorded on Blenheims, including that Bisley, and another six hours instrument flying on the Airspeed 'Oxford' with my mentor the famous 'All-weather Mac', Sq Ldr McIntosh. A peacetime commercial pilot with many thousands of hours in his log book, his flying was a masterpiece of most excellent and smooth professionalism. It really was a joy to watch a pilot such as he handling his aeroplane from the moment of taxying out to the final return to the dispersal point; his fluid style and loving command of his aeroplane was something that I have been trying to emulate ever since. in In other fields of human endeavour like figure skating, trout fishing, motor racing, even the culinary arts, it is a joy to see a maestro at work.

Our short leave now over, Jock and I travelled by road from London in the faithful Lagonda en route to Norwich, capital city of Norfolk in East Anglia, whilst Buster was taking the train at the same time from Devon. Our destination was Attlebridge and we were told that as it was only a few miles to the West of Norwich it should be easy to be directed there. The late afternoon run from London along the A11 road through Essex, Suffolk and then into Norfolk was very agreeable; with the canvas hood down and the sun shining Jock and I enjoyed the fresh air and the late June countryside of 1942. This new venture of ours was going to be another association between erstwhile Leading Aircraftsman Cairns and Pilot Officer Pelly-Fry of the mid-thirties with 216 Squadron at RAF Heliopolis. It was another turn of the wheel but the major difference this time was that a major war was in progress. Had it not been so Jock might have 'signed on' for another stint in the Royal Air Force and possibly getting a Corporal's stripes for his efforts. For me, my six-year Short Service Commission would have ended in early 1941 and by all normal evidence I would have been back to civil life again. Hitler was good for our careers – provided we survived to enjoy it.

It was now getting dark as we motored on and it was about 9.30 pm when we passed through Thetford, about twenty-five to thirty miles from Norwich; time enough to find the correct road out of the city and finally to Attlebridge, the name of a village about six miles from the city. As we neared Norwich (which was understandably blacked-out against wartime intruders) it became very apparent that a German air raid was in the offing. Search lights waved about all over the sky, the anti-aircraft guns were firing noisily, and then we heard the regular and thunderous crump of bombs falling accompanied by bright flashes that lit up the sky above the unfortunate city. With all this activity going on we had no choice but to stop by the roadside and watch from a distance of about three miles. We were lucky because we might well have been in Norwich ourselves and so been trapped in one of the streets. The bombing seemed to go on for about twenty minutes and then at last it stopped, the searchlights were dowsed and the anti-aircraft guns stopped firing. A number of fires that were burning brightly in the night became the aftermath of the first Luftwaffe air raid that I had seen in England and it was not a pretty sight. Jock and I waited for the air raid to stop before we cautiously set off again. We hoped that the 'All Clear' would sound as we approached Norwich but we did not hear it and motored on towards the perimeter of the city. As nobody was seen to ask the way and all signposts had been removed on a wartime basis we eventually arrived somewhere near the city centre where we saw the fire services in action and a number of civilians helping as best they could. I spotted a policeman and asked him how to get to Attlebridge but to our astonishment he did not know! He had never heard of the village let alone the RAF aerodrome which presumably was close by. However, a pedestrian came to our rescue and directed us onto the right road so we set off again; the time was approaching midnight and it was certainly not the most propitious circumstance for arriving. As we neared the five-mile run from the city we wondered how on earth we were going to find a blacked out wartime aerodrome with no prominent buildings by which to identify it but a possible clue was some fires burning not far from the main road. Well, they were worth investigating so we turned off onto a minor road and soon we arrived at a gateway with a wooden hut alongside. An airman emerged and after confirming that it was RAF Attlebridge he directed us to the Officers Mess on the far side of the aerodrome. Smoke and flames could be seen emerging from its roof top and we parked the car and went inside to investigate. Clad in pyjamas and running about with buckets of water were a number of young men putting out fires. A tall, handsome chap (who from his looks and stature could have been Gregory Peck's young brother) gave Jock and myself a bucket of water each and directed us to lend a hand. Dutifully we did so, but fortunately our contribution to the fire brigade effort did not last long as most of the work had been done. It was now well past midnight and as soon as all the fires were dowsed, 'Gregory Peck, Jr.'

came over to me and said "Well done sir! I'm Dicky England of 88 Squadron. Who are you?" I smiled at this unusual and quite unexpected entry into the life of a squadron in the small hours – and acting as an untrained fireman in the process. My answer was brief, "Pelly-Fry; I'm the new squadron commander and this is Jock Cairns, my navigator." Everybody laughed at the bizarre situation of the informal introduction between the new CO and one of the Flight Commanders in striped pyjamas. Some coffee was produced, we had a brief chat with the boys and soon afterwards Jock and I took to our beds. It could not have been a more entertaining start to our entry into the lives of what soon proved to be a magnificent bunch of young men; any unusual and unexpected entry from the wings onto the stage (and the centre of the stage at that) can quickly break down barriers in human relationships. I had a curious and confident feeling that Jock and I had made a flying start straight into the arms of No 88 Squadron.

In the morning the general opinion was that by chance the aerodrome had been showered with incendiaries from some unseen Luftwaffe aeroplane shedding it's load. There was no way in which the target could have been identified because there was nothing to see in total darkness. In the event no damage of consequence had been done to the camp and it was one of those chance happenings when a military establishment had been underneath when incendiaries were disposed of by a Luftwaffe bomb-aimer only too glad to get rid of them.

After breakfast in the hutted Mess, comfortable enough in its way, I began the process of finding out what I had inherited. The midnight fire officer Dicky England now appeared in his normal attire and his battle-dress showed the DFC so he was certainly a warrior. Later on he was decorated with a well-deserved DSO. He introduced me to the other two Flight Commanders; Sq Ldr RD Griffiths DFC and Sq Ldr RS Gunning DFC. As events proved so conclusively these three men were just about the best leaders in their field that one could possibly wish for; all had beaten the odds against the enemy and each one had that certain magic which is so vital in leadership. Each inspired his crews to follow their leader in formation sorties or to carry out single aircraft attacks on specialised targets where their own brands of skills and nerve were brought into maximum play. As is invariably the case, every man was complimentary to his fellows and the result was that they all formed a close-knit team. I could not resist drawing a parallel with the men of the Long Range Desert Group in North Africa.

To complement the picture the entire squadron was delighted with its new aeroplane, the Boston. The pilots loved it and the navigators and gunners equally so. The ground personnel found that this new product from America was a machine that was very satisfying to work on with reliability, accessibility, and robustness in full measure. It even had the special characteristic of being able to keep flying when punctured with holes and lots of important pieces missing. So here we had the ideal blend of the best of hardware for a specific purpose and being put to work by enthusiastic men. There were no afterthought additions or clumsy modifications put in after production and delivery as often happened to British aircraft. One most useful attention to detail so typical of our American cousins was that every two months or so I would get a visit by a Douglas expert and a Wright aero-engine specialist and it was a heartening feeling to know that our interests were being so well attended to. On the rare occasions when I mentioned a small modification that I had incorporated in my own aircraft (this more by way of gilding the lily than serious need) those two Americans would have a look and say "It's good; can we use it?" and after my willing assent each and every idea would be fed back to the manufacturer. Within weeks those minor modifications would be incorporated in the assembly line and replacement Bostons would all show them. How's that for high-speed service? It was typical of the flexibility and open-mindedness of American manufacturing philosophy. As will be related later, the same attitude could not be so easily found in much more important circumstance in British aircraft manufacture.

It is repetitive and perhaps ungracious to produce a catalogue of names, events and situations about 2 Group and No 88 Squadron in particular when the story has been so very thoroughly and ably recorded by Michael Bowyer in his excellent book 2 *Group, RAF*. However, there are some personal experiences to relate that perhaps will interest the reader and thus augment his basically historical account.

Wg Cdr Charles Harris, DFC, who commanded 88 Squadron prior to my arrival was on leave so unfortunately I did not meet him. The Canadian airman had nobly contributed to the operational record of 2 Group not only in the 'dark days' of Blenheims (when at times he limped back when the rest had been shot down) but he had been responsible for the first introduction of the Boston to 88 Squadron. It therefore fell to Dicky England to initiate me into the specialist work that the squadron was employed on in daylight thrusts into occupied Europe. It was a mixture of all manner of operational techniques coupled with the obvious risks attendant upon the nature of the tasks and I confess that the implications made me wince considerably. However there was nothing to it but to get cracking as fast as possible, learn the new trade, take a deep breath and hope that I was acceptable as the new squadron commander. The best boost to my nervous system was the knowledge that 88 Squadron had two ace cards – the men and the aeroplane. Although the Wellesley efforts in the Ethiopian war required a particular breed of specialised flying and attendant hazards, all of which had to be learned from scratch with pilots self-taught, the 2 Group role of operating against a more superior enemy was a very different ball-game.

Apart from the personalities of the three Flight Commanders, the squadron was blessed with key men, each in his fashion essential to the cohesion of the unit. One such was Flt Lt Ross-Williams, the squadron Adjutant. 'Rosebud', as he was affectionately called, was much older than all of us. A warrior from past times he was really as much an uncle to us as the good administrator that he was. He came from some Scottish fastness and to his great credit he never grumbled about being away for months on end from his family. I can still see him in the evenings, enjoying his 'wee drams' in the Mess and acting as a father-confessor and good friend to all of us. Such men in wartime were invaluable.

Another undoubted asset was to have a tall, talented and stylish intelligence officer in the person of Flt Lt Robert E Lee – Jim to us all. All too often the RAF used to employ schoolmasters as intelligence officers, this on the notion that the man and the task were complimentary. Not so in the case of operational squadrons. To me the essence of the requirement was a man who could sell the hazardous work to the aircrews with just the right mixture of informed briefing coupled with a magic touch. Jim had these talents in abundance and with his special style of humour to match. He had the difficult job of maintaining morale when all too often Jim knew damned well what was in store yet his presentation was always such that we felt in good heart before we set off. I used to think that his experience as an advertisement manager in the newspaper world made him an excellent RAF Public Relations officer which of course was what his wartime job was all about. To add to his talents, he was an excellent cartoonist and artist so our intelligence/operations room was never dull and boring.

The other key man was our Station administration officer, Sq Ldr 'Robbie' Robinson. He was a pre-war bank manager and he worked away steadily and methodically to provide the organisational back-up without which no military unit can perform its tasks effectively. These types of men all too often went unhonoured and unsung and Robbie gave us wonderful service even if he had to cheat sometimes in the process.

Jock, Buster and I now got down to business. Apart from essential office work (when 'Rosebud' screened me from undue paper work and administration) the three new boys put in about twenty hours flying training. It included formation flying 'somewhere in the back' to get to know the problems of station-keeping, a lot of low-level flying practise, bombing practise, high and low level cross-country flights to perfect navigation, air-sea rescue sorties into the North Sea looking for survivors from Flying Fortresses, and other useful training experience. We began to be a well-coordinated crew and we got to know each other and each other's style and human traits.

On July 31st, almost one month to the day since joining 88 Sqdn, the three new boys joined the club by participating in a daylight attack on the docks at St. Malo. Led by 'Griff' Griffiths and with a refuelling stop en route at Exeter, twelve Bostons set off across what to me seemed an awful lot of English Channel with one hundred Spitfires in attendance; eight fighter squadrons. For our baptism of fire the leader allocated us to a position at the back of the formation and after a swift take-off in succession the twelve Bostons flew at low-level to Bolt Head on the southernmost point of Devon where we joined up with the close-escort Fighter wing and then the armada scooted at wave-top height at 280 mph towards France. When thirty miles from the enemy coast Griffiths gave the wing-waggle sign, all engines were adjusted to a battle climb at full throttle, the close escort Spitfires edged away to avoid the flak, and up we went fast to 8,000 feet before our attack. Then came the run-in with bombs released on command from the leader and a turn away from the target and a fast run back to Exeter. My job of formation station-keeping precluded any sight-seeing and the most difficult moments come when the leader makes a turn and this made me realise once again that to lead successfully first of all you have to learn by flying in the back of the formation. For our first operational sortie we were lucky where enemy opposition was concerned because nothing harrowing occurred. On return to Exeter to refuel the three of us were happy to think that we had reached the first rung of the ladder. Nineteen days later the ill-fated Dieppe Raid came about.

The Dieppe operation entailed a move from Attlebridge to Ford aerodrome on the south coast in order to get closer to the action. The story of this affair has been well documented but amongst all the intense activity one lighthearted tale is worth mentioning. After I had been supervising the numerous details of parking dispersed Bostons, fuel arrangements, tent-age, communications and supplies, I made my way to the squadron's aircrew accommodation. It was a girls school from which the pupils had been evacuated in wartime to a safer place and our temporary home for two or three nights was a short distance from the aerodrome. As soon as I arrived my curiosity was aroused by house bells ringing insistently so I said to the first young pilot that I encountered, "What the devil is going on?" He smiled and said "Have a look at the notice board, sir." Neatly printed was an instruction that read 'Should you require a mistress during the night ring the bell.'

As the days passed, the new boys promoted ourselves, step-by-step to the point when we felt confident to take the lead; the pole position as the Grand Prix drivers say. With every new outing to occupied Europe there was always a new experience and it was the learning curve all over again. Apart from attacking the enemy in a number of ways and places which made the 2 Group type of work so extraordinarily varied, the most important diversion from operations was the visit to the Fighter Leaders School at RAF Charmy Down, Bath. The start of this affair (which was inspired by Fighter Command) was to give a talk to the pilots on the course about our work and after the lecture it was obvious that what was needed was to simulate operations in the air with a bomber force, a fighter escort force, and an equally strong pretend force of 'baddies' in their Messerschmitts. This idea was enthusiastically received and the bosses of Fighter and Bomber HQ gave it the green light. For the first trial run I took three Bostons to Charmy Down, and subsequently I used to take the whole squadron. Those practise 'raids' using the Bristol Channel as the sea crossing and the 'enemy' aeroplanes painted with red rudders and propellor bosses proved to be vital for future tactics. The fighter boys said that a manoeuvre they called a 'corkscrew' was the most effective way to avoid being shot down by enemy aircraft. So we learned the trick of how to corkscrew in loose formation and the Spitfire pilots said that if the manoeuvre was precisely timed its effect was dramatic. This was where Buster Evans came into his own; his remarkable sense of timing was extraordinary and he knew the precise moment to broadcast that magic word 'CORKSCREW'. His cool running commentary 'for real' was ample warning; "Six bandits; 1500 yards; seven o'clock; closing; stand-by". I tilted my tin-hat back, waited for that one word and when it came cavorted about the sky in a controlled way. Within seconds those little red beads of tracer ammo were whistling past the window followed by six up-side down Luftwaffe fighters diving away ahead of me. All too often the whole damned business would start again and if it had not been such a lethal business it would have been a fine spectacle. The man we admired was Buster as his was the responsibility to tell us what to do and exactly when to do it. On one memorable occasion during a Ramrod high-level operation against Courtrai aerodrome, thin cloud and misty conditions caused a temporary loss of the Spitfire escort. According to the navigators log we endured thirty-two minutes of almost continuous attacks by FW 190s. Buster kept his cool running commentary going continuously and we all ducked each time he said 'Corkscrew'. After each attack Buster told me that ten Bostons were still following behind after one for some reason had left the formation only to be shot down as a result. Finally we recrossed the Channel and on landing at Manston to refuel I jumped out of my machine and hastily went to each of my aircraft to assess the damage. To my delight (and equally to my astonishment), not a single Boston was damaged – the Germans had not even scratched the paint!

One interesting development that came out of this close liaison with the Spitfire boys was a request from Fighter Command to slow down when going to and returning from targets, especially at low level. Well, well, this was a change from the earlier days when Spitfires were at a tactical disadvantage staggering along slowly behind the Blenheims. Smiling broadly, I asked our protectors what speed suited them best and the answer was that 240 mph was fine for manoeuvrability, station-keeping, and fuel consumption. For us it was worthwhile to lose forty mph of cruising speed in order to give the Spits their best operating conditions.

The other Spitfire problem was the difficulty of joining up with the Bostons (at the usual height of no more than 200 feet to keep below enemy radar cover) because poor timing caused a lot of tactical problems and undue fuel consumption. We solved this by telling Fighter Command that the Bostons would make the planned rendezvous on the correct heading and at the precise time – give or take fifteen seconds. With a whole squadron of twelve Bostons starting from East Anglia this kind of accuracy was the navigator's responsibility and Jock Cairns never missed a trick. It was exhilarating to lead a bunch of light bombers low across southern England in loose formation and not one of them an inch higher than the leader. As we neared the rendezvous with the Spitfires they would appear as if by magic and looking for all the world like radio-controlled model aeroplanes. The dash over the wavetops then took place and the fighter wing leader (who could have been, say, Wing Commanders Duncan Smith, Jamie Rankin, or Brian Kingcombe) closing up and giving me naughty finger-signs. Sometimes, as in the nature of carefree fighter-boys returning to England's shores after one of those massive operations, I would hear the 'click' of a VHF radio transmitter button being pushed and the wing leader would call "Hi-di-hi"; in unison a host of Spitfire pilots voices would answer "Pelly-Fry"!

Although the association with those jolly fighter boys of the Charmy Down School had taught us the vital element of tactics, I began to realise that so far as the current fighter policy was concerned all too often the use of the light bomber force was not so much to attack targets but to provide the necessary bait to force the Luftwaffe to come up and fight. Fighter Command appreciated that a Wing sweep by Spitfires into France often produced no reaction at all from the Germans. However, include just one light bomber into the operation and vive la difference! I decided that I would not mention or discuss this thought to my crews. It was sufficient only to know that we were contributing materially to wearing down the enemy during the pre-invasion period and we were giving the fighter pilots ample practise to gain that magic situation called air superiority without which no war (in whichever form) had the slightest chance of being won. The third dimension in warfare had come to stay – and you ignored it at your peril.

In late September 1942 2 Group HQ decided that 88 Squadron was to be moved to an aerodrome called Oulton, situated to the north of Norwich, and our base at Attlebridge with it's long runway was to be taken over by the Americans. When I went to inspect Oulton I was surprised to find that it was a grass landing ground of fields normally used for cattle and it was damned small, the corner-to-corner maximum run being 1,400 yards. When I thought about it I began to realise that perhaps we had been cosseted too much and as the Boston was designed to work from makeshift strips what was wrong with a small grass aerodrome? The answer was that we had better improve our airmanship, and the sooner the better.

When I investigated the domestic accommodation, that was quite a different affair. It was a stately home owned by the Marquess of Lothian called Blickling Hall and my first sighting of it was spectacular. I gazed in admiration at a very handsome mansion first constructed in 1628 with a moat around it and boasted a long driveway flanked by the biggest yew hedges that I have ever seen. Immediately to the back of the 'most desirable residence' was a lovely bow-shaped lake about five hundred yards long and probably full of fish. In total it was a property amounting to some 6000 acres. Well, well, what a splendid prospect! I immediately telephoned to Group Headquarters and said that although the aerodrome was marginal for Bostons 88 Squadron would manage the best way that we could, and in real-estate language contracts were exchanged. Yes sir, we had a bargain!

I returned to Oulton for further air tests to check out our new landing ground and the flying was not too easy at first because I had been spoiled by the Attlebridge runway; we would have to become proper pilots all over again. Thus it was that 88 Squadron moved to a small grass aerodrome but blessed with five-star hotel accommodation and everybody was delighted. The nice little town of Aylsham nearby was an added bonus and better still was the discovery that a fine tavern called the Buckinghamshire Arms was barely a minute's walk away, its name derived from the Earl of Buckingham who had lived at Blickling Hall way back in King Henry VIII's days. I decided that what was said to be Anne Boleyn's childhood nursery room was very suitable for the squadron commander if only for the reason that it was very spacious and it looked out onto the big lake; it possessed a fireplace that was so big you could stand up in it. As my boys said soon after we arrived, the Baron Fry of Blickling was now installed as the new owner.

We had a wonderful time at Blickling and the only unreal situation was the tremendous contrast between our war efforts and the utter tranquility of returning thankfully to our lovely home. Jock and I often used to get out a boat and go fishing for pike, as in fact did many other lads. For other diversions Jim Lee told me that his fellow intelligence officer at RAF Swanton Morley (our parent unit) was none other than Richard Murdoch and it was not too difficult to get Richard to lure his fellow actors and actresses like Arthur Askey, (who referred to me as stomach-cadbury!) to come up from London to participate in some of the parties. One in particular was held on New Year's Eve, 1942. Jim Lee and Flt Lt Frank Coxall, DFC, were the master organisers and after the party was over we all agreed that it was the best one of all, the only snag being that we had to go back to the war so soon afterwards. There were other pleasant diversions from operational activities apart from the regular and highly valuable visits to Charmy Down to play war-games with the Spitfire boys, usually ending up with my Boston carrying the picnic hampers whilst being escorted to Portreath in Cornwall by thirty-six Spits for a bucket-and-spade schoolboy frolic on the sand. Other squadron trips were made for Army-Air exercises, one of which was to Shobdon in Herefordshire where we stayed at Shobdon Hall. We seemed to move from one stately home to another. One evening at Shobdon our popular Army liaison officer Captain Leo Cole had his kilt removed by the irrepressible Dicky Gunning who with other conspirators draped it round a handsome chandelier hanging from the ceiling in the ballroom. It was all good clean fun and a necessary escape from reality.

Alas! it was not all parties; grim reality was always round the corner. Dicky England had been promoted and became the squadron commander of the famous 107 Squadron and his place in 88 Sqdn was taken by an old friend called Sq Ldr 'Ace' Hawkins from Canada. On the sixteenth of August, 1943, thirty seven Boston from three squadrons led by Dicky England set off to attack at low level the big steel works at Denain in France. Due to weather conditions a postponement of the operations from morning to afternoon brought unforeseen disaster because no-one anticipated that a combination of flying home into the eye of the late afternoon sun and innumerable summer insects splattered on windscreens would force the pilots to leave the ground-level flying to ascend to a safer height, low though that was anyway. The Bostons were now flying at a tactical disadvantage and 88 Squadron lost four aircraft, two of them were being flown by Gunning and Hawkins. Dicky was caught by light flak, set on fire, and all three crew bailed out much too low for comfort after which they were made prisoners. Ace and his crew were killed, so I lost two valued Flight Commanders and their crews in one day. That was the measure of it; the hazards of light bomber operations over occupied Europe in daylight.

The days passed, the gallant squadrons of 2 Group continued to attack the enemy continuously and it was now midsummer. The pleasant life at Blickling Hall was destined to come to an end and the reason was that the planners had decided to move all the light bomber squadrons from their East Anglia aerodromes to new locations in southern England where they would be better placed to support the planned invasion of Europe. Although this was inevitable we accepted it as part of grand strategy and meanwhile we would just wait and see what happened next. I must place on record the wonderful support that we received from Group Captain Denis Barnett, our parent unit Station Commander at Swanton Morley. He was one of the party that had climbed the great pyramid in Egypt. Denis could not have been more helpful in every way and particularly so in the operational sphere when he was our spokesman in cases where I felt obliged to contest some of the orders and the details contained therein.

One such situation arose when we were ready to go on a run-of-the-mill circus operation. In the middle of the morning to my surprise, (and I confess to my irritation), a new order changed the whole affair by proclaiming that we were now to attack at low-level the German-occupied aerodrome at St. Omer. All the preliminary preparation work, the briefing, and not least the bomb-load now had to be changed. To me and my crews it sounded like a very dangerous and unnecessary switch of target because attacking Luftwaffe bases in daylight was really asking for trouble. I decided to telephone to my Station Commander to ask what had occasioned the change; he told me that the new instruction had been sent without his knowledge but he readily agreed to investigate. Soon afterwards he called back and said that the change of target had been inspired not by 2 Group Headquarters or even Bomber Command – but had originated from London. His enquiries through his contacts told him that it had all started because a Luftwaffe fighter-bomber had dropped its load over Canterbury and the single bomb had exploded not far from the cathedral. This had so incensed the Archbishop that he telephoned the Prime Minister's office and in the process had suggested that a suitable response in a proper British manner should be conducted by an attack on a legitimate target and not on a cathedral city. With the factors of time and availability taken into consideration it fell to our lot to be the instrument of carrying out the job. The Group Captain had fully agreed with my views and had tried without success to cancel the operation but he had been beaten by superior weight from the top. I doubted that Bomber Harris had been involved in what to him would have been of minor import; it was certainly not minor to me and the seventeen other lads who had to accompany me on what we reckoned to be an ill-advised and unduly dangerous mission.

The whole plan therefore was changed, and in the afternoon six Bostons set off from Oulton. We flew low across the green pastures of Suffolk, Essex, crossed the Thames Estuary and the hop-fields of Kent to the south coast and then pressed on across the Channel in open formation. Ahead lay France and after a noisy crossing of the enemy coast – the usual hot reception – we flew on for some forty miles inland towards St. Omer. The opposition now knew full well that we were coming and our discomfort was enhanced by the realisation that the expected Spitfire close escort as we skimmed the tree-tops was nowhere to be seen. Meanwhile the hostile reception was as nasty as ever but we were committed by now to keep going towards the target.

The time was around 1.30 pm and optimistically I hoped that our lunch-time visitation might prove to be a tactical advantage. It was not so. The six Bostons climbed to 800 feet for the run-in and all hell broke loose from the defenders. Unfortunately low cloud obscured the target so I decided to make a second run, something which in retrospect was a stupid thing to do but at times one loses a sense of discretion under stress.

The formation was now down to five aircraft, one Boston being shot down on the first run in. The second attempt was much better and after a good sighting of the hangars and accurate hits registered we turned away, dropped down to ground level again and began the hectic dash for the coast. Four of my Bostons were still in close crocodile formation behind me – by thunder! those boys were good pilots – and as we sighted the flat sand dunes with the sea beyond I spotted a large Germany Army bus travelling towards Dunkerque along the coastal road. It so happened that it was nicely placed to receive the attentions of my four Browning guns mounted in the nose and more in a sense of tension than anger I pressed the button on the control column and a whole stream of hot lead engulfed it. It was the first time that I had actually fired my guns at an enemy target and curiously I was more upset than pleased that I had done so because the bus and its occupants were causing me no trouble – it just happened to be there. I was releasing pent-up emotion because of an ill-conceived operation that had cost the lives of three men.

The Spitfire escort had now joined us but in the event we were not needing their help and so we recrossed the Channel, flew on over the Thames Estuary and East Anglia and so back to our base. The sortie had taken less than two hours and for our efforts I reckoned that I was lucky to have lost only one Boston in six – all the odds were that it should have been nearer half the attacking force. After seeing my aircraft down safely, holes and all, I went to the telephone and told Denis Barnett what had happened. Although under normal circumstance I am an even-tempered person, on this occasion I was so angry that I suggested that he pass a message along the line to the Archbishop to inform His Grace that we had carried out the job and perhaps he might care to accompany us next time to check that justice was not only done but seen to be done.

In an American publication called 'A.20 Bostons at war' by William N. Hess about war-time exploits, a chapter appears from the pen of Jim Mansell, one of my air gunners who participated in the attack on the aerodrome at St. Omer. He writes: 'There was a hole in the side of Wing Commander Pelly-Fry's machine big enough to see Buster Evans through it. He was trying to put a fire out with his gloves, caused by ammunition exploding. When he looked up and saw me he grinned and gave me a thumbs-up sign. Buster was a real operational type. Later on we arrived back at base, somewhat battered but still intact with the five remaining Bostons coming into the circuit together. After de-briefing I sat in a chair with a cup of coffee, utterly relaxed. This is one of the things about operational flying that I remember most vividly; the feeling of relaxation so complete that I felt I could sit there for ever'.

Another episode was one of those chance affairs that can happen in one's life. Felix Vigne was an RAF intelligence officer who was stationed at RAF Swanton Morley. He was a charming fellow who in normal times was with Cockburn's, the port wine shippers; thus his family name was very apposite! Felix had a nice easy style and an equable personality so it was no surprise that he was posted to be the liaison man with the new American B.26 'Marauder' bomber base at Horam in Suffolk. It was a good choice and with his particular talents the Americans got a good man.

In early 1943, when he had been with the Americans, for some weeks, Felix telephoned to me and suggested that I might like to pay a visit, meet his new friends and have a look around the new American Air Base. I welcomed the idea; it would be a nice diversion and a chance to meet airmen who had come all the way from the United States to make their contribution to the fight against Hitler's Germany. With my earlier contacts I was sufficiently impressed with their vigour and enterprise to know that a visit to a United States Air Force unit was bound to be a rewarding and pleasant affair. I told Felix that it would be my pleasure to make a visit; it was only a quick hop in a Boston and it might amuse my American friends to see me arrive in one of Mr Douglas' excellent products.

The next day the squadron was free to carry out training and my crew and I put in some high-level bombing practise on the range and afterwards we flew on to meet Uncle Sam. With only thirty-five miles to travel it was a boys' run at 280 mph to get there and in minutes I was talking to a chap in the control tower with a Texas accent who gave me the 'all clear' to come in and make a landing. I duly acknowledged the message and The touchdown was accompanied by the technique of holding the nosewheel off the runway by use of the elevator control for as long as possible. It is the obvious way to operate a tricycle equipped machine because one gets an air-brake effect with the tail almost touching the ground and it saves undue wear on the front wheel. Another trick on the Boston was to open the engine cooling gills after touch down; the extra drag is quite noticeable. After showing the Americans that we too could fly the Boston as well as they, I taxied to the end of the runway where a jeep met us and led the Boston round the perimeter track to the appointed parking spot. I could now see a small posse of colonels awaiting us; Felix Vigne was in the party and he introduced us to the reception committee who were very friendly and made us feel like welcome guests. We went to a nearby building for 'cawfee and a Chesterfield' and the conversation naturally centered upon aviation matters and the air war in particular. Many questions were asked about 88 Squadron's operational activities. When the coffee drinking was over, one of the colonels said "Okay – let's go" and he led us out to an adjoining building which I surmised was their Group Operations Room and the start-point of what Felix had called 'having a look around'. The large room in fact was crammed full of aircrew sitting on benches and the men were wearing a type of jockey cap with the peaks turned up. The scene certainly surprised me and my immediate move was to turn to my host and say "I think we are interrupting something or other – perhaps we should leave?"

"No sir", was his reply, "They are waiting for you to give them a talk". We went outside, if only to collect my wits, and I explained that I had not come prepared for such an event. However I would be happy to say something off-the-cuff but before doing so it would be wise to find out what the expected subject was and if the answer was 'missions' then I needed to know where to begin and not to say things that they already knew. My natural question therefore was "Have the boys started operating with their B.26 'Marauders'?" The answer was "Yes, the group carried out its first mission three days ago". Well that was a starting point and my next question was "How did they get on?" An undue quiet followed until one of the colonels said very slowly "I guess we don't know". I commented "Surely they told you all about it after they got back?" The quiet became more pronounced and I had the uneasy feeling that something was distinctly wrong. With obvious emotion a voice said softly "Commander, they just didn't come back". Jesus Christ, I muttered to myself, what a really dreadful thing to happen – and particularly so on the group's first mission. It was a stunning admission for them to make and the dramatic disclosure frankly left me so appalled and shocked that for some moments I stood speechless in the roadway. The tragedy was certainly not the happiest moment for a visitor from another Air Force to face an audience but all the same the requirement was there and so after asking for brief details of the ill-fated operation I wondered if all those very unhappy boys were in the mood to listen.

The attacking force consisted of fourteen Marauders with a complement of five aircrew per aeroplane and had set off to make what was described as a low-level daylight attack on a big air base in Holland occupied by Luftwaffe. From memory it was Ijmuiden but this is of no consequence now. The Group Operations Room had a large scale model of the target which had been constructed in great detail and specific aiming points were alloted to each Marauder. Even before the aircraft took off it was an optimistic plan on that score alone and it remained to be seen what other evidence of inexperience would show. I did my best with the assembled aircrew and I seemed to hold their attention for about half-an-hour by describing the organisation and activities of the light bomber RAF Group of which No 88 Squadron was part. I explained how the different types of aircraft were used, the reasons why, and emphasised that as tactics in air warfare were constantly changing it was essential for survival to keep abreast of new situations and try to be one jump ahead of the enemy all the time. The difficult bit was to explain the problems, the risk, the luck factor, and the acceptance of losses as 'just one of those things'. In the main we hoped to be clever and lucky but every now and again things went wrong and in that case disaster struck but there was no option but to accept it and go back and fight again. The more expertise you picked up the greater the chances of survival; where luck was concerned, well that was a bonus. After twenty minutes I sensed that those young men, thousands of miles from home were beginning to relax a little now that they had been given some reassurance from a man who told them what the whole business was all about, warts and all. A few lighthearted stories enlivened the audience and this helped to animate proceedings nicely.

After the talk I rejoined the colonels and said that the most important issue was to do our damndest to find out what had gone wrong; it was the only way to gain vital experience and profit from it. Before leaving in the late afternoon I was able to have a word with Felix if only to chide him for luring me into a trap of presenting me with such a difficult situation at short notice. He said that the colonels had asked him to get someone with experience who could give the talk but the victim was not to know beforehand! The most important aftermath of the visit was the news that a sole survivor had been spotted in his one-man inflatable dinghy and that a Search and Rescue boat had brought him back; he was in Norwich Hospital and was making a fair recovery after his ordeal in the inhospitable North Sea. That chap was damned lucky as a man in a small dinghy is a singularly difficult thing to spot in a large expanse of water.

As soon as I returned to Attlebridge I decided to go to Norwich immediately and locate the American airman and find out everything that he could tell me about the ill-fated operation. Such account as he could give me was the only hope of piecing together even fragments of evidence and the requirement was most urgent because the Americans simply had no clues at all. It was very bad news to take on the enemy for the first time and endure a 100% loss by their top team. I now made it my business to find out what went wrong. The sole survivor was the only hope to that end. The young American was in bed when I introduced myself to him and I explained that I had visited his Bomber Group the day before when his officers had told me of the disaster. Understandably he was very frightened and it took a little time to calm him down. It was interesting to note reactions to his first overseas assignment to England and Suffolk in particular, it pleased him because it was nicer than he had expected. His aircrew job of being an air gunner in the tail of a Marauder seemed to satisfy him well enough and he liked the adventure of being sent across the Atlantic to make his contribution to the Allied war effort. We were now on the same wavelength and talking like old friends.

The difficult part of the visit now had to be dealt with; his story of what exactly had happened. I started from the very beginning and my questions were chosen to include the training, the number of practise flights carried out, the briefing, the emergency procedures, and the fighter escort provided. To my astonishment the last question produced the answer that he had not been told about a fighter escort; this explained why RAF Fighter Command knew nothing about the mission and presumably neither did the American equivalent! The picture now began to show and the questions asked in a specific sequence reminded me of the same requirement in Egypt when we were trying to solve the mystery of Desmond Bell's disappearance in the Fairey 'Gordon'.

The answers produced all manner of disturbing replies, one of which was that after crossing the Suffolk coast the Marauders were flying – as he put it – 'real low', around 500 feet above the sea. Heavens, the German radar would have picked them up almost as soon as they set off! The more I delved into the affair the more I realised that the whole operation was doomed to failure, a classic example of inexperience and overconfidence. The whole chapter of misfortune became painfully clear and can be summarised as follows:

a. No fighter cover was asked for and so none was provided,
b. The so-called low level crossing of the sea was carried out at a minimum of 500 feet, so radar early warning was inevitable,
c. The landfall on closing the Dutch coast had an error of up to ten miles. This was corrected by the whole formation turning to port and keeping out to sea until the landmark was located. When they crossed the coast the defences had a field day and shot down part of the formation.
d. The rest staggered on towards the target and were attacked by fighters – type not identified. This caused the formation to attempt to regain the coast after more Marauders had been shot down and to the air gunner's knowledge the target was not reached.
e. The surviving Marauders were now straggling badly and the fighters picked them off one by one. The Dutch coast was recrossed with a very depleted force and all but one Marauder fell into the sea because they were unable to fly on one engine.
f. The air gunner's aeroplane somehow struggled along on one engine and the crew jetissoned everything possible to keep flying. Eventually it also fell into the sea and he was lucky to get out and use his dinghy; his companions were drowned.
g. After a miserable night he was spotted by sheer chance and rescued; he was the only survivor out of seventy.

There were so many lessons to be learned that I contacted Felix and told him what I knew about the whole sorry business. I included my personal view that the B.26 was most unsuitable for operations at low-level because it was not manoeuvrable enough and could not fly satisfactorily on one engine. Later on a new wing of increased span was fitted which improved it's performance. Quite apart from the unsuitability of the Marauder for the job, the whole affair was thoroughly mis-managed by people who should have been sensible enough to find out beforehand what this very specialised form of air warfare was all about. The poignant finale was that the commanding general of the Group was there to see his men off and waited until there was no chance of even one aeroplane returning. Sorrowfully he made his way back to his Headquarters with a pocket-full of medals that could not be bestowed upon anyone.

It is difficult when writing an account of No 2 Group and 88 Squadron in particular to mention all the personalities further down the pecking order than the prominent people. In the case of the aircrew the reality is that each man could well have a paragraph or two unto himself if only for the reason that he was an exceptionally brave volunteer with a life expectancy of no more than one in four. I have therefore picked out random examples of such men and I hope that those who have not been included will forgive the lapse.

The first character to mention must be an Irishman called Paddy Kinsella from (as I remember) County Cork and so in every sense a volunteer. This tall and curly-haired air gunner with a happy disposition and unmistakable brogue reported one day to me on posting; he had already completed two operational tours on Wellingtons and had been awarded a Distinguished Flying Medal. He had been shot down twice and on each occasion he had been rescued from the sea after sitting overnight in that uncomfortable device called a 'K' Type dinghy; it was like using a motor car inner-tube in a swimming pool, the difference being that one was for fun and the other was a tenuous means to avoid drowning.

Sergeant Kinsella had volunteered to return to operational flying for a third tour, thus stretching the betting odds of survival almost to zero, and with this in my mind I had to ask him if he really was serious in wishing to join 88 Squadron. "Yes", he said, "You see, sorr, it's a great life and I like to be wit the boys". He was my man and I arranged for him to report to the Squadron Gunnery Officer for allocation to one of the crews. As he left my office he gave me some kind of salute, smiled broadly, and departed. I think that I became his friend because I enabled him to carry on doing what he really seemed to enjoy.

It is rare to spit successfully into the face of providence continuously unless you are uniquely lucky and brave like Basil Embry, Attie Atkinson, Derek Roe, Charles Patterson or Hughie Edwards VC, all of whom succeeded in beating the odds in light bomber operations to a remarkable extent. In Paddy Kinsella's case I had a sense of foreboding because as an air gunner he was not wholly in control of his destiny. One afternoon my worst fears were realised because he was shot down for the third time on the same operation that we lost Dicky Gunning and Ace Hawkins and their crews. Three weeks after the Denain raid the telephone in my office buzzed and when I picked up the instrument an unmistakably Irish voice said "It's Paddy, sorr – and I'm sorry I'm late". Heavenly days, Kinsella reappears once again! The man must surely be indestructible. "Paddy, for God's sake, where the devil are you?" He told me that he was at Fleet Railway Station about three miles away and was telephoning from a public call box; I told him to stay just where he was and I would collect him personally. As I got into my Hillman car I called out to everybody within earshot "Paddy's back!" and off I went to retrieve our wandering boy to a big chorus of approval. Paddy was standing alongside the telephone kiosk when I arrived and was wearing a travel-stained battle dress. He grinned broadly as I shook his hand with undue warmth. I asked him whose uniform he had borrowed after his return to England. "It's my own, sorr," was the unexpected reply; "I've been wearing it every day from the moment I left you". This was surprise number one because how he managed to travel about in occupied Europe advertising himself as an RAF airman without being arrested mystified me. He then proceeded to give me a condensed account of his wanderings, and I listened with ever growing astonishment as his tale unfolded; it was enough to make my hair stand on end. As I drove up to the squadron offices practically everybody had turned out to greet our Paddy and his reception was more than somewhat, as Mark Twain would say. Yes, he was back with his chums again and I remembered his comment when first we met; 'It's a great life, sorr!' It was now late afternoon and someone presented him with a large tankard of ale, the spontaneous start of a celebration party outdoors that went on until after sunset. For the next two hours and more the war had stopped for 88 Squadron and Paddy never saw the bottom of his pewter tankard because it was continuously topped up by willing hands. Eventually our hero succumbed to the hospitality and he was carried away to sleep soundly in the bed that awaited him.

Paddy's incredible story was repeated next day in more detail whilst Rosebud and I listened attentively. He told us that the sortie across the Channel with Spitfires in attendance was made successfully and the big Denain steel works attacked as planned. After turning away from the target Paddy's aeroplane was set on fire by light flak and began to fly erratically. Failing to get a response from either his pilot or navigator, with great presence of mind he remembered his emergency control column which he grabbed and pushed into the socket on the floor of his cockpit. This gave him a measure of control; he could not see where he was going but at least he could keep the machine level and prevent a crash. Both engines then lost power and the Boston began to descend quickly. When he got close to the ground Paddy eased the stick back, the Boston levelled off at what must have been about 200 mph, and the burning machine skated over the crops with a few hefty bumps and finally stopped on its belly. When he jumped out his crew were both slumped in their cockpits and with the Boston now a raging inferno he had no option but to run for cover. Some German soldiers arrived on the scene but left almost at once because they assumed that there could not have been any survivors. Paddy laid up until nightfall and began to review his predicament. He was feeling physically sound after his remarkably lucky escape and decided to travel by night across country towards the coast and steal a small boat that he could use for a crossing back to England; the optimism of the fellow! After three days of trudging along in the dark and scrounging from lonely farms – animal food is better than none – he began to realise that foolishly he had been heading south instead of north; he was no boy scout. The tiresome discovery made him conclude that walking, particularly in the opposite direction to that intended, was for soldiers and not for airmen. He decided therefore to use a railway track that he came across and followed it until a station was reached where he could continue his travels in greater comfort. A new problem arose which was how to ask for a ticket in his non-existent French and this was solved by saying 'Paris' at the booking office window and hoping that it would work. In the event it did and in order to pay the fare he handed over his RAF escape wallet to the clerk who extracted the required Francs from amongst the aids for shot-down airmen; like razor blades, saws, fish hooks, mirror, nylon filament, miniature compass, linen map, and sundry foreign currencies. All his escape and evasion training counted for nothing after all.

Armed now with a ticket to Paris Paddy sat on a bench and waited patiently for the train. I asked him about the other passengers and if he had made any attempt to change his appearance such as wearing his battle-dress inside out. He said that the platform was crowded with German soldiers and sure and begorrah he was still properly in uniform, sergeant's stripes, gunner's badge and his DFM ribbon as well! "Surely", I protested, "The Germans must have identified you as an RAF man? If not, what on earth were they doing?" His reply was that they were just staring hard at him. "What did you do about that, Paddy?" He grinned and and in his charming accent he said "Well sorr, I just stared back at them – the stupid bastards!" The luck of the Irish was holding good; very good indeed. On the train journey he pretended to sleep soundly to avoid being spoken to and no doubt he needed a rest from his exertions in any case. Eventually the train pulled up at a Paris station and our hero began to walk along the nearby streets and longed to have something to eat. Whilst gazing into a small shop (a charcuterie from the description) and wondering how to buy some sliced ham in sign-language and without a food coupon, from the recess adjoining the shop came the unmistakable and familiar 'Psstt' which is understood in any language. Paddy turned and saw a man beckoning to him who looked friendly. By sign language his new friend indicated to follow him and in Indian file the pair walked slowly along the pavement to a small house where his guide rang a door bell and a young woman appeared and let them enter. Fortunately she spoke some English and she told Paddy that she was a member of the French Resistance with the particular task of helping escaping aircrew to get back to England. Paddy was hidden away safely and cared for admirably until there was a safe moment later on for the organisation to take him by train all the way to the South of France and across the Pyrenees into Spain and thence to Gibraltar. The last part of the journey home was a flight to England and somehow or other he slipped through the screening process on arrival and took a train to Fleet where he telephoned to his commanding officer and apologised for being away for so long.

It was a remarkable story and of course it was well laced with anecdote and blarney. It could only have succeeded because Paddy – with respect – was not exactly brilliant; he had little imagination and thus had no fear because that human trait generates from an awareness of danger. In terms of escape and evasion this amiable fellow had made all the basic mistakes but his Irish luck enabled him to get away with it, probably without even realising it.

The final and bizarre tit-bit of the adventure only came out thirty years later when Buster Evans told me that Paddy's hide-up in Paris was with a young lady who was pursuing what is described as the oldest profession in the world – she was a prostitute! In retrospect his creature comforts – ahem – might well have tempted him to delay his departure; but that would have clashed with his axiom 'I do like to be wit the boys – it's a great life!' I certainly hope that the well-deserved DFC added to his DFM was something for him to take back to his native land after the war and in due course proudly show to his wife and children. Paddy Kinsella was my kind of man.

Two other unusual personalities who came into the life of 88 Squadron was occasioned by a chance visitation that later produced spectacular results. It was one of those tricks of fortune that was as unexpected as it was rewarding in terms of the sheer professionalism of the participants. My excellent Adjutant 'Rosebud' Ross-Williams told me that two visitors had come to see me; their names were Skeets Kelly and Charles Peace and they were movie camera men in the newly formed RAF Film Unit at Pinewood Studios. They wanted to know if they could be attached to the Squadron to do some filming, the idea being to produce propaganda material for showing on the cinema screens in Britain. It was a way of showing something of the end-product of thousands of working hours put into the manufacture of military aircraft by demonstrating them in action even if in our case they were American. The idea appealed to me very much and my interest was heightened because photography was one of my hobbies.

The visitors seemed to be unusually pleased with my enthusiastic response and it transpired that I was the first commanding officer to show any interest at all; all the others had turned down their proposals on the score that they were much too busy to waste time on the trivia of film making. The three of us now got down to the business of how to set about doing the job and I said that I would arrange for them to fly on training sorties and so get some action shots in addition to filming the day-to-day ground activities. Although the suggestion was gratefully accepted I began to sense that there was more to it than that; and then the penny dropped. "Do you two fellows by any chance want to come with us on operations?" In unison two voices replied "Yes please!". Aha! Now we were talking turkey and the conversation became positively animated. I outlined the various ways that a light bomber force (and Bostons in particular) went to war and as nearly all our missions were carried out in daylight the two fellows were delighted to realise that what we did suited their purpose admirably.

The upshot of the visit was that in order to put the plan onto a practical basis I arranged for the two new members of the squadron to do a crash course in air gunnery so that they could become useful members of the crew whenever a crisis arose. They agreed enthusiastically because by so doing they could become proper members of the squadron and not just film people shooting only with a camera. The two happy chaps left right away to attend the course and returned soon after disguised as air gunners with the brevet showing on their battle dress tunics. Pilot Officers Skeets Kelly and 'Charlie' Peace – named so by the boys after the infamous murderer – had come back to go to war with us and needless to say their election to the club was greeted with the approval that it merited. In addition to our primary role we were about to become No 88 Squadron Film Unit – and who was then to know how the concept and its dramatic development would blossom? There were of course some problems to face, the principle one being that the regular gunner's station had to be given up to a camera man where he had a good field of vision except dead ahead and the former had to man the difficult and awkward ventral gun that pointed down and backwards through the aperture normally used for access to the rear cockpit. The USAF called it the Tunnel gun but we rarely carried a second gunner on circus operations because the field of fire from the ventral position was abysmal and frankly it was not worth the risk of carrying another man to little effect. When Skeets or Charlie came with us, as they invariably did, the two men in the back (gunner and camera man) would swop places to suit the circumstance and it worked very well.

As the days passed so did Skeets and Charlie apply their undoubted talents and enthusiasm to excellent purpose. They organised a fixed forward-facing camera for the navigator/bomb aimer to use and operational planning even reached the stage when both of them were so demanding in their requirements that at one briefing I could not resist saying "Listen, you two; who is running this bloody war, you or I?" They were very popular with all of us and rarely before had I met such dedicated and totally professional men in their own field. The fact that the whole business of light bomber operations was dangerous – if I may make an understatement – seemed to be of no consequence so long as they got good pictures.

Skeets Kelly, a very tall and lanky fellow, quickly took to his new job with enthusiasm and he had a special eye for aerial pictures that really were products of the artist. In post-war years he was the chief camera-man during the making of the 'The Battle of Britain' movie and shot most of the spectacular air-to-air scenes of Hurricanes and Spitfires battling against Messerschmitt 109s and the other Luftwaffe aircraft. Alas! he was killed during a shooting sequence when his helicopter collided with another one 'on location'. Arguably he was the best aerial camera man of them all.

Charlie Peace was quite a different character. With a spare frame and penetrating eyes he seemed to live mostly on his nervous energy. He had absolutely no time at all for the restrictions of Service discipline – or any other discipline for that matter – and he smoked cigarettes incessantly. I asked him soon after we moved to Blickling Hall why he never appeared for breakfast, in his crisp style and a distinctly scratchy voice he said that he had it in his bedroom. "Lucky chap" I commented, "Pretty WAAF bringing you eggs and bacon in bed?" He grinned. "No – just a cup of tea and a packet of cigarettes!" Heavens, what a way to begin the day, but he conceded that he had cut his cigarette intake back – now it was ONLY 140 per day! He was so uninhibited that when I asked Charlie if perchance he was married he produced a dog-eared photo of a very pretty naked and shapely girl who was lying full length in her bath.

Charlie Peace moved on, not surprisingly, to bigger and better things. He began to fly in Lancasters and made such a confounded nuisance of himself in his specific demands that eventually Bomber Harris said "For God's sake give the man his own private Lanc; he gets excellent pictures so he's worth it". With his own photographic Lancaster and special crew he ranged far and wide following the main stream of the attack and used to terrify his pilot by ordering, for example, a return to Berlin from as much as 100 miles away on the return trip because the fires were burning brighter than before! Charlie's singleness of purpose as a professional camera-man, even when "the flak was so thick you could walk on it", was breathtaking.

Of the regulars in the squadron, one was Flt Lt AH 'Rufus' Riseley, a curly-haired pilot with a delightful quiet personality and the owner of an equally nice rough-haired Sealyham dog. Rufus was also one of the unlucky ones who was shot down on the Denain attack and belly-landed his Boston in a field with both of his crew wounded. After getting help from farmers to look after them he promptly set off on his own to escape from being taken prisoner. He experienced a number of hair-raising incidents before getting in touch with the Resistance Movement and volunteered to disguise himself as a labourer on one of the sites where the V1 'Flying Bombs' were to be launched across the English Channel. At the time our information about these sites and their purpose was somewhat sketchy and so it was a heaven-sent opportunity that Rufus was on hand to learn what he could of the new weapon that Hitler had put so much store upon. The information that he gained proved to be quite invaluable and the material was transmitted back by the time-honoured process of carrier pigeon. After Rufus had completed his secret work his French underground friends smuggled him aboard a fishing boat that made a rendezvous with 'a suitable vessel' that brought him back to England and he returned briefly to the squadron, collected his dog and his other possessions, and was told that for obvious reasons his wartime flying was over. The DSO awarded to him for his excellent exploits was proof enough of the measure of his hazardous work.

Another personality (and I confess a sentimental choice) was the irrepressible Flt Lt 'Jock' Campbell, DFC, who before the war was the crooner in Joe Loss' famous dance band. A tall and well-built fellow with something of a craggy countenance and a Scottish accent that was a joy to hear, he was a volunteer for RAF aircrew service and proved to be a natural and excellent pilot. He loved the Boston and I was so taken by his abilities that I nominated him to fly as my 'No 2' on many occasions, thus the man to take over from me in the event that I was shot down. His formation flying and station-keeping was flawless; he was always precisely in the same position on my starboard side from start to finish and never deviated by as much as an inch. On the ground (as with so many young wartime pilots) sometimes he misbehaved and put a foot just that little bit too far over the chalk line. There was never anything of malice or bad manners, it was just the exuberance of a young man and who shall blame them under the strain of war? On one particular occasion, when we were developing new tactics associated with army-air support, the squadron had moved to Northumberland and on the third day Jock proceeded to make a silly ass of himself in a Newcastle theatre, much to the displeasure of the Manager and everybody else. I now had to deal out justice to the offender and the punishment that came his way – of all humiliations – was to be sent back to Norfolk by train. This hurt his pride no end but he took it in his stride and afterwards we continued to remain good friends. I can still hear him singing so beautifully songs like Irving Berlin's 'Blue Skies' (incidentally the 88 Squadron signature tune with the lyrics suitably amended!) and he was the classic example of the Cromwellian 'Russet-coated captain who knows what he does and loves what he knows'.

Dear Jock, he was shot down not long afterwards; that kind of man does not come along more than once in a lifetime. He was indeed one of the many gallant gentlemen of No 2 Group, Bomber Command.

Chapter XVIII

Operation Oyster

A postscript to the previous chapter, one that I should include if only because it is close to my heart, concerns 'Operation Oyster', the biggest and most complex mass air attack ever mounted by 2 Group RAF on December 6th 1942. It was against the very big Phillips radio and valve factory complex at Eindhoven in Holland. Almost one hundred light bombers of very different characteristics and flying performance participated in the lunch-time low level daylight raid on a memorable Sunday morning. The force was drawn from three squadrons of Douglas Bostons, three squadrons of Lockheed Venturas, and two squadrons of de Havilland Mosquitoes. Fighter support consisted of two squadrons of Spitfires and one of Typhoons with one squadron of Mustangs on a diversionary sweep. In all, both on the ground and in the air, many thousands of people must inevitably have been embroiled both by the Allies and the German enemy; something that is not always appreciated where air warfare is concerned.

The big operation was occasioned by the urgent need to deny to the Germans the products of Phillips, the largest factory of it's kind in Europe, and one that was providing the enemy with one third of his requirements for electronic products. The problem of mounting a suitable and effective attack by air – how else? – was that the target was surrounded by the city itself; and by definition extreme accuracy of weapons delivery was paramount. After consultation with the Dutch Government in exile about the risk factor to Dutch people on one hand and the strategic requirement on the other, no easy problem to solve, the options were examined carefully. It was concluded that a high-level attack by night by RAF Bomber Command or a daylight one by the US 8th Air Force had to be ruled out; precise bombing of the target alone was almost an impossible dream. There was only one acceptable answer, and that was to employ light bombers on a hazardous mission in daylight and at low level with each aircraft literally launching it's load directly onto the factory roof-tops – and through walls and windows in many cases. It was a tough decision to arrive at but it was the only one; so often high risks justify a vital wartime requirement.

It was now up to 2 Group, the light bomber force; and to this end a considerable amount of thought and planning had to be exercised by the Headquarters staff, most of whom knew their business from personal experience and thus were by no means armchair specialists only. After a number of options had been thrashed out, only to be discarded for one reason or another, (the major problem being the need to co-ordinate the different characteristics of, initially, four types of aeroplane and finally three only because the North American B.25 Mitchell had only recently been introduced into 2 Group), the next stage was to try out the whole business with a series of smaller formations by type of aircraft and progressively building up to a full 'Balbo' attacking a simulated target under realistic terrain conditions. Using the big area of East Anglia, as flat as Holland and fortunately where the light bombers were based anyway, and the Wash (where King John is said to have lost the crown jewels in bad weather) as the sea-crossing factor, the most used target was the big power station at St. Neots, fifteen miles due west of Cambridge. The eight squadrons were required to get airborne from their respective aerodromes, form into roughly line astern formation, and then follow a route at tree-top level in such a way that each squadron arrived in correct sequence over a rendezvous point before the whole fleet set off in a very big crocodile (like Red Indians on the warpath) to the 'enemy' coast and then divert by type of aircraft into dog-legs that, god willing, would bring them all back again, still in the correct sequence, on the approach to the target.

It was a concentrating business during the many practises, and the mistakes made by so many aircraft flying low for perhaps two hours at a time were monitored at key points and in particular at the point of attack on the power station. We were at first too high, too spread out, wrongly positioned on the run-up, or (worst sin of all) the precise timing was at fault. Visual and photographic evidence, plus yet more practises, was designed to ensure that – human frailty apart – Operation Oyster would 'for real' become a copperplate perfect affair. Even at the late stage in preparations the target was only known by a few; this for security reasons.

After weeks of intensive effort, (when we were all getting a bit overtrained and the strain was showing) we were ready to put the show on the road. As we were to fly along the route as though we were riding on the top of a double-decker bus the simile is quite apt! Remembering the immortal signal to his fleet by Lord Nelson just before Trafalgar, each aircrew member was ready to do his duty. It was a daunting prospect; and now close to the action the worst part of all was to endure the agony of the lull before the storm. Each of us made an assessment of the risks attendant upon the affair, success or failure notwithstanding. Taking a round figure of one hundred aeroplanes participating I made a mental forecast of losses at least twenty-five percent; that was twenty five aeroplanes and with an average of more than three men in each the arithmetic was painfully simple.

In the final days our anxieties were compounded by the weather factor which in December in Western Europe is usually more bad than good. We needed good clear air low down; and we needed a cloud base not much lower than 1,500 feet at Eindhoven for aircraft to zoom up high enough to avoid bomb blast (and a rapid descent to ground level again) and fighter cover airspace upon withdrawal to the Dutch coast where we hoped to use that invaluable umbrella yet again. Three or four times all preparations were made, even to the point of crew briefing and about to go out to our aircraft, and then the very disheartening telephone call on the scrambler would come through to say 'not today; stand by for tomorrow'. As I had been nominated to lead the Boston squadrons (which in turn were to be followed by the swift Mosquitoes and then the Venturas at the back of the long crocodile) effectively I was at the sharp end of the fleet. With this in mind I decided as the leader to call Group Captain Denis Barnett at Swanton Morley (where the other two participating Boston squadrons were based) to ask that he used his influence to cancel, at least temporarily, the operation rather than put it off on a day-by-day basis. That would at least give us all a decent night's sleep or two and ease the strain; I doubted that otherwise we could have endured the tension much longer. Happily this proposal was agreed by our Headquarters (and probably by Bomber and Fighter Command too) and I summoned my own boys to tell them. As it was then mid-week I made a forecast that, as so often happened before, Sunday was going to be the Big Day. And so it proved to be.

On Sunday morning the weather did not look too promising with low cloud and light rain over our bases at Feltwell, Swanton Morley, and Oulton. However the weather men (and probably an air reconnaissance) gave a positive report and so the final briefing at each base took place. Soon afterwards all the crews, as usual armed with all the impendimenta of the trade, made their respective ways to their aircraft. At the final count there were thirty-six Bostons, forty-seven Venturas, and ten Mosquitoes, one of the latter flown by Flt Lt Charles Patterson DSO, DFC, who was at the back of the fleet and armed additionally with cameras to photograph the results. Up front, who else but the intrepid cameramen Skeets Kelly and Charlie Peace in 88 Sqdn Bostons? In quick order, all aircraft got airborne on time, the big Ventura fleet doing particularly well to do so at Feltwell, and then began all over again the business of assembling in correct order before the join-up in that massive crocodile for the familiar crossing of the Suffolk coast at Southwold. (Heavens, so often that small but identifiable seaside spot used to appear on operation orders; so often was it the last bit of England that many crews gazed at, never to return). To complete the overall picture that morning, a big force of eighty four Flying Fortresses of the American 8th Air Force with Spitfire escort was laid on to attack the Lille locomotive works in France, thus providing a valuable diversion at the time that the light bombers were due to make their low level entry into Holland. As Eindhoven was beyond the radius of action of Spitfires the light bombers had to make their way unescorted to Eindhoven, in itself only fifty miles from the heavily defended German industrial area in the Ruhr valley. The best that we could expect was to find four squadrons of fighters covering our exit at the Dutch coast; it was better than nothing, but one has to say that by then those who had reached that far on the way home were mostly out of the wood anyway.

The fleet now settled down nicely for the run across the North Sea at just above wave height. The visibility was satisfactory, the cloud base around 500 feet and lifting slightly, Buster Evans in the gunner's position keeping me in the picture of what he could see of the aircraft behind and master navigator Jock Cairns in his streamlined perspex-covered nose position checking me out for accurate flying and giving me corrections for compass headings when necessary. It was absolutely vital that we made a very accurate landfall between the Dutch islands of Schwuoen and Walcheren, then to keep hull down up the thirty miles long Scheldt estuary before flying between Bergen op Zoom and Woensdrecht, this giving us the best run in before pressing on inland. The problem here was that at zero height the Dutch coastline is no better than a thin line on the horizon and you just had to get it right from the start; flying as we were on the approach at 250 mph there was no room for error – we had to be right on the dotted line.

By a combination of concentrated effort and – let's face it – a degree of luck, we were spot on (as navigators like to say) and we swept dead-centre up the estuary. So far, so very good. Now the bigger problems began. Streaking along in ships-of-the-line fashion the first hazard was not the enemy – it was mother nature. Big flocks of water birds understandably took fright and got airborne at our approach, many more than we had anticipated, and in fact it was later found that of those aircraft that got back no less than twenty three were damaged, some seriously, by bird strikes. Wild duck penetrated cockpits with blood, feathers and carcases everywhere. Others penetrated wings and even bent fuel pipes and other precious items. No sooner had we passed the mudflats than we aroused a hornets's nest of German FW 190 fighters from nearby Woensdrecht aerodrome; we could actually see them taking off and curving round to meet us. Not only that, all the aerodrome defences opened up furiously, the Venturas in particular getting the brunt of cannon and machine-gun fire as they lumbered past with little scope to manoeuvre. Well-named as 'flying pigs' were they called by their crews. At this stage there were inevitably casualties; some pilots managed to keep going despite being hit by flak and fighters whilst some others (like one Ventura with a Canadian pilot who lost five feet of outer wing) had no option but to turn back. However the bulk of the force pressed on and after the initial noisy reception at the coastline it was nice to get to open fields and head for the turning point at Oostmalle.

By now we seemed to be getting the measure of it and Buster reported that as far as he could see behind us a whole lot of Bostons were still in full cry and nicely spaced but still in company with each other. This was the essence of the plan, to fly in a prearranged open style like geese but each pilot had room to manoeuvre to suit the immediate circumstance. All being well, Wing Commander RH Young, AFC, and his forty seven Venturas – I did not know then that he had already lost three of them, one being flown by Wg Cdr Seavill of No 487 Sqn – would be thundering along close behind the Bostons. And then, having caught up with the main body of the fleet, would be the fast, manoeuvrable, and very beautiful Mosquitoes led by the outstanding light bomber ace Wing Commander Hughie Edwards, VC, DFC, whose feats in Blenheims were legendary. By a happy circumstance his navigator Flt Lt "Tubby" Cairns DFC was the brother of Jock Cairns, sitting as usual in the nose of my Boston; fraternal admiration and professional rivalry seemed to be kept well apart and today was going to be no exception after the dust had barely settled.

We left Dutch territory on the run to Oostmalle and for a while we were over Belgium although I have to say this was of no consequence at the time; the map-reading by Jock was what really mattered. To me, the terrain ahead looked dreadfully empty of landmarks, the small Belgian town of Turnhout to our left excepted, and soon the major and vital railway line approach to Eindhoven loomed very large indeed in my thoughts. Miss this cue, and all the trouble, effort, and skills of so many crews would end in abysmal failure. I had in fact made a slight change to the flight plan, (which of course everybody knew about beforehand), and that was to add one more dog-leg about ten miles short of our target. A small railway line heads north to Eindhoven and the idea was to sidle up to it – but not cross it as this would give us dreadful tactical problems – and then with the railway still on our starboard side the final accurate run in would be ensured. Success depended upon seeing the railway in sufficient time to begin the gentle turn and so avoid the pitfall of the long crocodile getting into a pendulum swing from which it would be very difficult to recover.

As the seconds ticked away and the ground rushed past underneath in a blur of fields, minor roads, streams, and farm buildings, we were getting ever closer to the target and Zero-hour; 12.30 precisely. We were now only about eight miles away from Eindhoven; and at 250 mph that meant two minutes to go. Jock and I with our hearts pounding stared ahead; no railway! if we were late in spotting it, and so no option but to cross it, then the whole dammed business would collapse within spitting distance of the target. And then it happened. I saw a thin plume of white smoke, ahead and slightly to left of our track. It could only be a providential locomotive, very nicely placed to give me the message to begin the turn. I said to Jock 'Moving loco with smoke at 10 o'clock; turning left'. He confirmed the sighting (which was a great relief, I have to say) and as we turned we began to fly alongside the single-track line, now comfortably on our right-hand side. That fellow who was driving, (or perhaps it was his mate refueling the boiler) will never know the vital contribution that he made to our cause; a cause that it is fair to say had hung by the proverbial thread a few moments before. Now all was well. All was very well indeed. The job was in the bag.

The Armada was now correctly positioned for the final run up, and with Jock Campbell still chasing my tail I gave a wing waggle to give him the signal for the 'Bomb doors open' where-upon the rest of the Bostons successively zoomed up to 800 feet, the reason being that apart from Jock and I who had eleven-second delay 500 lb bombs, the rest carried instantaneous fuses. Jock was now acting as bomb aimer, and as the main building in the factory lay dead ahead broadside-on – the specific planned target for 88 Squadron – all I had to do was to aim the Boston at it, lift up to clear the flat roof, and leave the rest to Jock. Almost at once he called 'Bombs gone' and as I moved the bomb door lever to 'close' I could see the two anti-aircraft gun positions on the roof blazing away furiously. One of them must have hit us because the Boston had barely reached the target when without warning it shuddered violently and then began to slow – roll to starboard. It was only when the wings were almost vertical that I was able to begin recovery, but it was necessary to employ maximum correction and the response was painfully slow. As we staggered away from the big building, the Boston not behaving at all well, I could not but smile briefly when we passed over a game of football in progress – some of the players beginning to run very briskly off the pitch to take what cover was available. This fleeting cameo illustrated as nothing else could do that our arrival had been a complete surprise to them; but not, unfortunately, to the vigilant German gunners who must have had the advantage of the excellent view from the roof-top. They must have been shooting DOWN at us!

The new problem, now that I had succeeded in getting the aeroplane the right-way up, was that I could not make the planned turn onto a westerly heading to begin the dash back to the coast. The best that I could persuade the Boston to do was to inch it's way to the left very slowly, painfully slowly. The next thing I saw after about sixty miles of difficult flying was the big dock area of Rotterdam with all the cranes sticking up like tall fingers. This was certainly no place to be in broad daylight, as earlier Blenheim crews had discovered to their cost. In the meantime the other Boston pilots were still following and probably wondering why I had wandered so much off track. I called them on my radio to tell them to press on as I had problems, and one after the other they overtook me with their superior speed.

The reason for lack of effective flying control now became obvious. A large piece of the top skin of the starboard wing at the thickest part was sticking up vertically, and to add to the evidence the fabric on the starboard aileron – the one I needed most – was shredding itself into little pieces in the slipstream. To pile on the bad news further, the starboard engine began to rattle and bang alarmingly and had to be throttled well back before it quietened down satisfactorily. So now I had an almost uncontrollable aeroplane and with the engine I needed most to keep straight almost out of action. Thank god the Boston was such a remarkably tough machine that could fly on one engine – and in this case the wrong one at that! We struggled on; but not without more hazards to come. Buster calmly announced that we were being chased by two FW 190 fighters; they were 600 yards astern, at 7 o'clock as we say, and closing. When I heard the single word 'Corkscrew', all that I could do was to bob up and down (as on a scenic railway at Disneyland) and wait for the cannon shells to arrive. It seemed to work quite well during the attacks, thanks to Buster's uncanny sense of timing, and now at last out to sea the two German pilots for some reason gave up the hunt. The reality in retrospect was that they were not up to the job and failed to use proper tactics. A single aeroplane is a sitting duck for two fighters if they had employed the 'scissors trick', each one in turn attacking from slightly different angles in rapid succession. Who am I to complain?

We were now heading back across the inhospitable North Sea at a more respectable height of 1000 feet. We were still flying but dear old England seemed a long way away. Jock gave me a flight time at our reduced speed to reach the Suffolk coast – any old bit of friendly coast would do nicely, thank you, – and the minutes ticked away very slowly indeed. A measure of my concern was that I kept asking him for a new ETA and of course I kept getting the answers that I did not want, so disheartening were they. To pile on the agony of suspense, the port engine now decided to play up and kept fading. I played the throttle gently as we lost height and each time when a ditching seemed imminent it picked up and we slowly got back to around 600 feet. It was a nasty cat-and-mouse game and I suppose that I was too preoccupied to say my prayers as it is said that people do when oblivion is imminent. At long last, the glorious vision of a coastline showed up and after that we seemed to speed up beautifully to the point when I could at least glide down onto the beach. We were back; but we were not down. No matter; the worst was over and I assessed the situation to decide what was the next course of action.

It did not take long to conclude that Blickling Hall had a singular attraction; and assuming that the 'good' engine remained good (now that I had nursed it so gently), well, I might as well make a belly landing on my own grass with no wheels or flaps (and one aileron only) as anywhere else. Jock and Buster declined to abandon ship by parachute and so the three of us gingerly flew out of Suffolk airspace into Norfolk and soon the heartening sight of Oulton aerodrome came into view. It looked so very attractive, I have to say.

I called the control tower and said that the Boston was flying on one engine after a fashion and that I had no hydraulics for undercarriage and flaps, the aircraft was badly damaged, and I would have to make a fast belly landing to maintain adequate control. Fire and ambulance services were put on instant readiness. I was given immediate clearance to land – if land was the correct word – and without further ado the Boston was brought in over the threshold fence at something approaching 190 mph, levelled off, and after throttling back, switching off magnetoes and fuel, made a bumpy arrival and slid across the damp grass. I jetissoned the long pilot's canopy and after freeing the harness and my flying helmet jumped onto the ground. Buster was just as quick to escape but we had to lend Jock a hand as he seemed a bit winded; after all, he got the worst of the bump when the Boston flipped onto it's belly. As all this was happening the fire truck arrived and stood by but mercifully there was no fire.

The three of us gazed at the tired old Boston, full of holes and with bent propellors and important bits missing, and for the first time in my recollection in the abrupt silence I heard Buster mutter "Dicey do; very dicey do indeed!" We then elected to leave 'G' – George, the remarkable Boston that had done us so proud, to the salvage people. As I had cause to realise later, it was not the only one that I had to exchange for a new one after tangling with the enemy. We walked back to the Operations Room to stretch our legs and were met by Denis Barnett who had waited to 'count us back again'. 'G' George was of course the last to return – not forgetting Sgt Tyler in the veteran Z.2211 who landed (or arrived) in a field near Lowestoft – and we joined the other crews being debriefed by Jim Lee in his own inimitable style. It was a happy band of warriors who chatted away incessantly whilst they drank coffee, smoked the odd cigarette with satisfaction, and exchanged tales of excitement and adventure. Operation Oyster was over; it was now time to count the cost. An early casualty, but not serious thank God, was that I decided (after delicious bacon and eggs and then some pike fishing on the lake in the afternoon) to arrange for Jock to have a check-out after the bumpy emergency alighting; x-ray pictures showed a fractured vertebrae and he was put into a plaster-of-Paris jacket. So he was off flying, but not for long; he was that kind of fellow and it must have been difficult and uncomfortable.

With a mixture of excellent flight planning, superb flying by the pilots, accurate navigation, and of course the luck factor, losses were less than expected. We lost nine Venturas, four Bostons, and one Mosquito. Although the personnel losses were slightly misleading statistically in terms of type of aircraft, (Venturas easily predominated), the overall answer and the one that mattered in terms of aircrews was fifteen percent. That in itself was an unexpected bonus. All those practises; all those post-mortems to iron out the mistakes; all the anxieties and irritations of a series of postponements; all were worthwhile after all. The attack on the Phillips works was exactly timed (as a chance photograph of the Eindhoven Town Hall clock proved!) and it was all over literally in a very few minutes. It was precisely the job that the light bomber boys always said that they could do – swift and very accurate low level attacks in daylight. It might be expensive – it usually was – but the results were spectacular. We were masters of the art, and we proved it.

Soon after the Eindhoven Raid, as it became known, Wg Cdr Bob Young, AFC, the Ventura leader, Wg Cdr Hughie Edwards, VC, DFC, the Mosquito leader, and I with thirty five Bostons behind me were awarded the Distinguished Service Order. Flt Lt Jock Cairns and Flt Lt Buster Evans, together with six other aircrew officers were awarded the Distinguished Flying Cross. Two NCO aircrew were awarded the Distinguished Flying Medal; perhaps the most merited of gongs as often these splendid men do not get the recognition that they deserve. That made thirteen decorations all told; the total must come high in the record book in the aftermath of one single but highly effective air operation in World War Two.

Eleven years later there was a completely unexpected and happy sequel. During my appointment on the staff of US Army General A1. Greuenther, NATO Supreme Commander Europe, (his Headquarters at the time was near Versailles) I was making my way by road on an official tour from Bergen, Norway, and back to Paris via Oslo and other points of NATO interest. One of the calls was made on the Royal Netherlands Air Force at Eindhoven.

After business had been dealt with, the Colonel in command kindly took me to the officers mess where I was made welcome and initiated into the custom of taking a tot of *Bols* gin – or two – before lunch. It was quite a painless affair for me, I must relate! During the conversations with my Dutch friends – I have a great affinity with them – I was asked casually if I had ever been to Eindhoven before. Now the secret had to come out. With a grin I admitted that on a well-remembered Sunday morning in December 1942 I had visited the Phillips factory with ill intent in a Boston; and I had been followed by a swift succession of light bombers almost one hundred in all. This admission startled my listeners, raising in the process many chuckles of approval, and at once my host said something in Dutch to one of his officers who then left the Ante Room. Soon he returned, more words were spoken, and then with a broad grin the Colonel announced that Mr Otten, the Chairman of Phillips, had invited me to call on him.

Now fortified with yet another Bols to give me flying speed I said my grateful thanks for the hospitality and set off in the smart silver Allard Tourer for the factory. This was the car (with a big Ford V8 eight cylinder engine) that I was ferrying to Paris from Bergen. It was on loan from the beautiful Iris and her Norwegian husband Reidar Johannessen on leave from Hong Kong and staying in their superb home alongside a fjord. It took a few minutes only to reach the city and the Phillips works was self evident due to it's size and location. As with my first approach to Buckingham Palace in the Lagonda, (as will be related later) the organisation had been alerted and an impressively tall uniformed commissionaire beckoned me to the Grand Entrance. The Allard was parked in regal isolation and I was escorted into the main hall and taken by lift up to the top floor where I was ushered into Mr Otten's handsome office. A stocky, impressive man left his desk and with a broad smile and outstretched hand greeted me warmly. Grinning nervously, the visitor said "How do you do, Sir; I have come to apologise in person for knocking down your factory!". This brought a chuckle from the chairman who said "Do not worry, my friend; as you can see, I have a much better one now".

It was a wonderful start; and now with three of his fellow directors also in the office I was asked to tell the tale of our adventures and misadventures. We then moved on to what had happened 'at the receiving end' at my prompting; some remarkable accounts followed.

Such was the speed and unexpectedness of the initial attack, one director was actually out in the roadway about to go home for lunch. He immediately lay down where he was in the gutter and had to endure the agony of a worm's eye view as each aeroplane in seemingly endless succession flew over the top. The noise and general mayhem was very frightening (perhaps quite an understatement from one so close to the action) and there was nothing that he could do about taking over during the few minutes of the attack. The bombs exploded, the incendiaries from the Venturas (as I explained they were) rained down and caused many fires, and red flashes with billowing black smoke erupted when inflammable materials were hit.

He sadly recounted that one aeroplane flew straight into the factory, (possibly because thick smoke impaired the pilot's vision), and of course the crew were killed. One remarkable sight was to see bomb blast dislodge a gun emplacement from the roof-top and the whole structure like a huge bird's nest descended to street level still upright and with guns still firing. I could not but admire the dedication and bravery of the German crew at the point of immediate extinction. Another director related that later on (when unexploded bombs had been dealt with and fires had been put out) it was discovered that a single bomb had fallen down a lift shaft before exploding and it had lifted up all the floors so much so that the whole building had to be knocked down and then rebuilt.

After exchanging all these personal experiences, and now with some coffee and a small Dutch cigar to hand, I tentatively asked about civilian losses; something that we had tried so hard to avoid or at least keep to an absolute minimum. To my surprise, (and indeed to my great satisfaction),

Mr Otten said that as the attack took place at lunch-time and in particular on a Sunday the factory area had a minimum of people on duty. That, coupled with the precision of the attack resulted in a total of twenty-five deaths. There were of course other casualties, but considering that there were 30,000 people on the payroll the very low figures were far less that I had dared hope.

The conversation now moved on to current affairs and I spoke of my most interesting appointment (and the problems) associated with the defence of Western Europe against a probable enemy by so many and diverse peoples. Language problems alone caused confusion and complication; but all of us were utterly dedicated to making it work. I mentioned that the Allard was not fitted with the yellow headlights that France prefers (and if not fitted often causes French truck drivers to show their displeasure on the road) and Mr Otten at once gave the matter his attention. Within twenty minutes a box of yellow bulbs appeared on his desk and upon asking I was told that they had been made specially for me! Such high speed service; and when I said that later on I would fit a pair onto the Allard my very charming host said "Don't worry; the job has been done for you!"

It was the strangest feeling to re-visit the rebuilt factory that I had last seen many years before under such different circumstances, and I thoroughly enjoyed the experience. I expressed my thanks for the warm reception and the fascinating accounts given to me and then made a move to leave. Mr Otten, boss of the Phillips Empire at Eindhoven and elsewhere, shook my hand warmly with his final comment; "Good bye Wing Commander – no hard feelings!" Those three words said it all.

Chapter XIX

A Royal Appointment

In the summer of 1943, after 88 Squadron had left Oulton – and Blickling Hall, – we spent a short time based at Swanton Morley before moving south to our new home at Hartford Bridge, situated near Camberley in Hampshire and later re-named Blackbushe. This was to be our new operating base – the springboard that would take the light bomber squadrons (and of course the fighters and fighter bombers) across the Channel to Europe after D-Day. The French 342 Lorraine Boston Squadron, ably commanded by Colonel Henri de Rancourt, shared Hartford Bridge with us.

Although aerodrome facilities at Hartford Bridge were good, we were once more back to Nissen hut lifestyle but if coming events were to prove successful any domestic setback was acceptable. All the evidence suggested that the Allied Air effort, not least the massive American support, was at last beginning to turn the tide. Something good was in the air.

The 2 Group operational activities were now inspired and galvanised into considerably greater effort by one man. His name was Air Vice Marshal Basil Embry; and with seven decorations for valour probably the finest fighting airman that the Royal Air Force has ever had. His dynamic style and thrust was completely infectious. He was a man who led from the front, latterly in a Mosquito, and with a million *Deutschmarks* ransom on his head, dead or alive, because of his spectacular escape from the Germans after being shot down for the second time in a Blenheim. He now flew in the guise of Sq Ldr Smith. We were all delighted to have such a magnificent boss and not least myself because I had worked for him in the Desert Air Force. Headquarters 2 Group soon buzzed like a hornets' nest with every staff officer hand-picked by Basil, every one with operational records and a fistful of decorations. Business was distinctly brisk!

It was now Autumn. One morning, my telephone rang and it was Basil Embry on the line. "Pelly, I propose to put your name forward to do a special job with the King. Bomber, Fighter and Coastal Commands are putting up one name each to submit to the Chief of Air Staff. How about it?" When I had recovered my breath I replied that it would indeed be the greatest honour. Basil then said "OK, wait and see". I replaced the telephone and was so amazed that I could do no more than ponder over this extraordinary prospect; the short conversation had so unbalanced me that I forgot to ask Basil if he knew what the job entailed. So it really was 'wait and see'.

Some days after the first call I got a second one. This time it was from the Air Ministry and I was told to report for interview with Air Chief Marshal Sir Charles Portal, the Chief of Air Staff. On the appointed day I travelled to London and arrived at the corridors of air-power to visit the office where the boss of the Royal Air Force was directing all his airmen. His private secretary was a charming man called Group Captain Sir Louis Greig; he was a tennis player of repute, was well known in Palace circles and was now Portal's private secretary. He took me into Sir Charles' room and left me to my fate. The CAS started off by asking about 2 Group activities, and this enabled me to talk easily upon a subject close to my heart. Sir Charles then asked me how I viewed a possible appointment with the King and I replied by saying how honoured I would be if it came my way. After what was supposed to have been an interview but in practise was painless because Sir Charles was such a charming man I made my way to the door after saying my 'thank you'. I then paused; I had forgotten – as with Basil Embry – to ask what the job was all about. "Sir, can you please tell me what the lucky man, whoever he may be, has to do?" Sir Charles smiled. "You know, Pelly-Fry, I haven't the slightest idea. Only the King seems to know!"

I returned to Hartford Bridge and felt elated to have gone that far in the selection process. For a few days nothing happened, but as Basil had wisely said, 'Wait and see'. Well, if nowt else I was on a short list and that was rewarding enough.

Stage three now came along. The telephone rang and the startled RAF operator said breathlessly, "It's Buckingham Palace, Sir!!". Heavenly days, what now? I gave my name and a voice said "Good morning; when would you be free to come to London?" My first reaction was to wonder who it was on the other end of the line. The second was the thought that if it really was someone from Buckingham Palace then I should be told when to go rather than be asked. The conversation developed into a curious issue of whose prerogative it was to nominate a day and time and the voice said that as I was busy on war activities it was for me to say when it would be convenient. Eventually I took the initiative and named a day, which was agreed. Wearing my best Herbert Chappell uniform and new hat from Bates of Jermyn Street, the Lagonda was gleaming like a star as I set off for my appointment. The immediate problem on my way to London was to find out who it was I had to ask for and for that matter which entrance to take at the Palace gates. No matter, everything ought to resolve itself on arrival and as the appointed hour was 2.30 pm I was going to make damned sure that I was in plenty of time even if I had to lie-up nearby in a side street.

The Lagonda now approached the Palace and I noticed that the Royal Standard was flying. As I drove round the statue of Queen Victoria I was so unsure of what to do next that I made a second circuit round it and this time a tall policeman beckoned to me to the right-hand entrance as you face the Palace. I slowed down and then stopped alongside him. He saluted and said "Good afternoon, Wing Commander Pelly-Fry". It was my first intimation of the remarkable system that operates so discreetly and efficiently at the Palace. As directed by my policeman friend I drove in and parked at the appointed spot. It was a surprisingly good start but it was nothing like as surprising as what was to follow. At the entrance called the Privy Purse door a footman showed me to a room that had some chairs and a table with newspapers on it but by now any inclination to glance at the London Times was minimal. The time was 2.30 pm and I was nicely in time for my appointment.

The man who came in was dressed in the uniform of a colonel. We shook hands and from his voice and measured style of speech I recognised it as that of the man who had telephoned to me at Hartford Bridge. However, I still did not know who he was – perhaps I was supposed to know? The conversation was brief and a little superficial and after asking about Bomber Command and how we were getting on he surprised me by asking if I had a dinner jacket! I could not resist saying "Yes; actually I have two of them." At this point he got up and took me along a corridor to an office where I was introduced to Sir Alan Lascelles, the King's Private Secretary. Now at last I had a name and that was heartening. Sir Alan made some cursory remarks, I commented as best I could, and then I was led out of his office to go further down the long corridor and naturally I began to wonder what next was afoot. At the next stop, after my guide had tapped once on the door, he opened it and showed me in. In a beautifully appointed room and standing near the fireplace was the King of England. The Colonel said "Wing Commander Pelly-Fry, Sir", stepped back and left the room. I was now alone with His Majesty King George VI.

After shaking my hand as I stepped forward the King said "I am told that you were in Africa". Well, it was a good start to talking freely and after my pulse rate had slowed up sufficiently it was easy to recover my composure. The conversation for me was on safe ground and after a few minutes I said that as he had visited the Western Desert himself he probably had a good idea of what it was all about. He nodded but went on to say that his visit had been spoiled because he had the very unfortunate luck to be inflicted with a tummy upset; this was not only very tiresome it was also very embarrassing. This admission of such a very personal matter was made so naturally that the human aspect of my audience with the King overtook the formal affair that it should properly have been. At my cry of dismay the King looked puzzled; surely nearly everybody in North Africa, he said, was afflicted at some time or other with the malady? I replied that it was certainly not so; it depended on various precautions, not least one's day-to-day eating habits and being careful in particular never to touch food items like lettuce and certain fruits such as melons. They were usually fed by dirty water and it was invariably the water that conditioned the European's health where 'gyppy tummy' upsets were concerned. I was now asked what perhaps was a natural question; what was it in particular that I did do to keep healthy or was it just luck? I reacted quite naturally. "Sir, my way of dealing successfully with the matter is to have a good tot of whisky every evening. It seems to keep the microbes away quite apart from the enjoyment of the habit." Oh dear, my immediate thought now was that my comment should have been left unsaid but fortunately the King smiled and said, "I will remember next time I make a visit".

At the right moment the King ended the audience and told me that Sir Piers Legh would get in touch with me. Now that I knew his name I realised that he was the Master of the Household. After leaving the King's room a footman took me to Sir Piers Legh's office and to my surprise he asked me when I could be released from commanding my squadron and I replied that there was no problem as I had almost finished my tour and the chances were that a replacement had already been earmarked. As I left the palace, my policeman friend guided me into the traffic stream with a smile and another smart salute.

A few days later there was yet another telephone call; Sir Piers Legh wanted to know when I would be free to take up my new appointment! This very informal way of telling me that I had been given the job seemed to be in such complete contrast to the elevated nature of it. I still only had a vague idea of what it was all about. Perhaps the chain of communication in Royal style was quite different from that of normal activity? Anyway, I gave a provisional date to him and said that I would first have to pass the news via Basil Embry to Bomber Command and the Air Ministry. In the event the date was confirmed and I never discovered whether I had advised the RAF or it was that they were a little slow to tell me. I suspect the former if only for the reason that Palace administration seems to make its own rules.

The first task was to hand over command to Wg Cdr Ian Spencer, DFC; he was already an old hand and so the process with such a receptive and enthusiastic personality was all too easy. Ian brought his own crew with him and Jock Cairns and Buster Evans were later posted to other jobs; as both of them had now completed two operational tours it was timely that they had a rest. This ended a partnership with two men whose support had been magnificent.

On the twenty seventh day of October 1943, Group Captain WLM

Macdonald, Station Commander at RAF Hartford Bridge signed RAF form 1651 authorising me to make an official journey to Buckingham Palace. The vehicle was Lagonda, registration GV 6799, and the distance was given as thirty-five miles. That document is still in my scrap book. This time I knew how to enter by the correct gateway at Buckingham Palace; I had come to stay for an indeterminate time but for how long would be revealed later. The footman at the Privy Purse door directed me to drive across the forecourt and thence to the vehicle storage area where I was told that the Crown Equerry responsible for stabling had provided a place for the Lagonda. The poor man's Bentley had beaten it's rich cousin to it for top treatment.

It is a curious sensation to make one's first entry into the realms of Royal society. One is tempted initially to go about on tiptoe or better still to try and become invisible for the first few days to get accustomed to the grandeur and learn the routine prescribed in a Palace. Commoners, I surmised, had to know the upstairs-downstairs procedures and thus not cause eyebrows to be raised. The reality is that it was all considerably nicer, easier, and much less complex than one anticipates with such anxiety. There are of course a number of niceties of behaviour and protocol without which a Royal establishment would lapse into the realms of mediocrity and thus fail in its standards and purpose. Initially all that one needs is a good teacher and in this regard I was singularly lucky. Captain Sir Harold Campbell, DSO, RN, was such a man. He was one of the long-standing equerries who knew the appointment to perfection and had the Services way of presenting the refinements of procedure in a practical and straightforward manner. As I remember it was he who told me that I was now designated as an Extra Air Equerry and my function would be to make up the third member of the team. Sir Harold explained that on a wartime basis he and Sir Piers Legh were on the equerry strength (and on occasion Colonel Dermot Kavanah, Crown Equerry) and thus the duty had been on a fortnightly basis. My arrival, which appeared to be solely at the King's initiative, would now split the time-scale three ways; a fortnight on and four weeks away but at my suggestion in practise I was on duty for most of the time.

It is not the writer's purpose to devote a chapter of details about the day-to-day affairs in the Royal Establishment; it would not only be uncalled for it would be an intrusion. However, it seems not unreasonable to recall some interesting cameos of personal experience that will give some insight into the participation by a temporary courtier.

Palaces by definition are singularly big. What may appear from the outside to be a handsome structure with a long pedigree of Royal occupancy is about as far as most of us see. We are concerned only with its symbol and perhaps its use on special occasions like a wedding when the Royal Family appear at a good vantage point from which the public can see the Monarch and his (or her) family. I suppose that it is fair to say that on these occasions the apparent element of spontaneity is more imagined than real. The crowds assemble in front of the palace, the message goes inside to the effect that the monarch's presence, together with that of his or her family, would be welcomed with enthusiasm and it is not long before Royalty appear on the balcony. How many people in the happy crowd below pause to think that they are contributing to the magic success of the British Royal tradition? Or even consider that the Royal Family may have to forego their afternoon tea?

At first sight the inside of Buckingham Palace seems to be beyond comprehension and contains a seemingly endless array of wonderful pictures and other specialised collections. It is a plethora of 600 rooms connected by handsome corridors and they in turn lead off to yet more rooms the nature of which is not divulged because no door reveals any distinguishing mark. If one is ignorant of the layout, open a door at your peril. The only sensible way of knowing one's way about is to tackle the problem in small bites. As you progress, so do your horizons get wider. For all that, if the reader wants a real challenge let he or she try a Royal residence called Windsor Castle. It is vast.

On my second day I was presented to Her Majesty the Queen – today the enchanting Queen Mother as the whole world now knows her. Once again I was very conscious of that certain style, that magic, that ease of communication between the Monarchy and those lucky enough to be near at hand. It is almost impossible to describe just what happens; you are not so much spoken to as spoken with. If you begin with butterflies flapping wildly in your tummy, be sure that within seconds they have departed because 'Queen Mum' (if I may be so bold) has given you the distinct feeling that only you and she are in the room and she longs to know about your orchid growing or your collection of South American Folk songs.

If it is seemingly easy for Royalty to set you at ease and so enable you to talk freely without the expected heart-attack beforehand, perhaps the most difficult Royal skill of all is the subtle art of disengagement. I have seen people still in a state of euphoria after the Queen Mother has moved on and still oblivious of her going. As everybody knows, saying 'Hello' is so much easier than saying 'Goodbye'. The Royal Family have the fine art of moving on to the next person in line worked out to perfection. It seems so effortless.

The equerry's routine proved to be similar in a number of ways to that of a personal assistant and this made the learning curve much easier to follow. You are on duty for the same reasons but on a loftier plane. Instead of escorting a person or a brigadier into the boss's office, it was now a bishop or a Field Marshal. Sometimes the system can go pleasingly awry. On one occasion a tall man walked into the equerry's office – seemingly the focal point for everybody – who was wearing a long blue raincoat and had a naval cap tucked under his left arm. Before I had time to identify the visitor a hand was extended and he said "Good morning, I'm the King of Norway. Do you think that I could see the King?" My reply, once I had recovered my breath, was to say that a visit from one king to another should present no problems at all. King Haakon (who was quite charming and so very easy to converse with), was escorted promptly to my master's room. Such was his pleasing way of conducting his own life that King Haakon was embarrassed to find me waiting to escort him upon his departure to the Privy Purse Door, saying that it was quite unnecessary.

On another occasion a good-looking young man walked in, as indeed had King Haakon, and equally quite unannounced. By now I was beginning to develop my intuitive powers to the maximum extent possible. One of the prerequisites of a Royal equerry's job was to know who was who but again it was the same fraction of a second that was available for my speed of perception. The new equerry smiled happily and prayed for inspiration. My handsome visitor then said quite simply "I'm Philip". Desperately wanting a clue, I said "James Pelly-Fry". At least I had a surname – which apparently was more than he had. It took agonising moments before I deduced who my visitor was and I was helped because he gave me the clue of an earlier telephone call that even the new equerry could assimilate. It was Prince Philip.

One morning the telephone rang and when I answered the familiar voice of the King said "Shall we go for a walk in the garden?" Within minutes two men were strolling around the large and pleasant garden of Buckingham Palace and there was not a single soul in sight except a gardener. We were two men enjoying the early winter scene and the conversation ranged far and wide from shotguns to trout fishing; to big game in Kenya to life in the desert; and even a reference to the de Havilland 'Mosquito' that was beginning to show its paces over Europe. Then came the guessing game. It might be a good moment to say that one of a courtier's required talents is to be a mind-reader. A comment will come your way, worse still a question, the nature of which you are required to know about. If you are lucky and are armed with the basic startpoint, you can then go ahead and either comment, embellish or perhaps even criticise the subject of the originator's thought-process.

In this particular instance the comment was quite simple if ambiguous. It was, "I wish he wouldn't wear that silly hat". For me the problem was threefold – who was he, what kind of hat, and what was silly about it? We walked on, and I began to extemporise. Soon I reached the point when I had to come out into the open and make a constructive observation. If my guess was a good one, I was about to dare to speak about a man destined to become a Field Marshal who invariably wore a beret. With caution, which is another way of saying hedging my bet, I damned the victim with faint praise by saying, "Oh well Sir, it's that desert war success and now trying to maintain what he thinks is the right image." As no comment came from his Majesty I went on to say that I could pass a suitable message. As soon as the pleasant walk was over and I was back in my office I picked up the telephone and asked the operator to contact a particular senior man in the War Office. With a degree of discretion prescribed by the circumstance I explained what my telephone call was about and the point was taken. Within a few days a General called Bernard Montgomery was summoned to the Palace to be congratulated upon his successes in North Africa. When I met the distinguished soldier on his arrival it did not escape my notice that he was wearing a brand-new peaked cap, complete with red band.

There was a story running round the London Clubs at that time of an alleged visit by Sir Winston Churchill to the Palace. After the PM had given his report the King expressed satisfaction and asked if Churchill had anything more to add. "Yes, your Majesty, but I hesitate to tell you". Upon being pressed, he said the problem was Montgomery and the King replied "Surely not? – he is our best general". "That is true, sir; my fear is that Monty is after my job". The King smiled with evident relief and commented "Thank god for that – I thought he was after mine!"

The start of one particular journey by train was not without its awkward moments for the air equerry. As it was to be my first introduction to travel in a Royal train I learned that one of the tasks was to approach a certain Mr Simpson at Kings Cross station before we embarked and thank him for his personal services as a courier on the journey; it was the practise to show appreciation in a practical and discreet form by presenting the minor official with a small token in the form of a crisp one pound note. When the Royal party arrived at the station we walked the short distance to the platform – No 1 in this case, not my favourite No 2! – and the small reception party of railway and other officials was there to do justice to the occasion. In addition to the Station Master in all his finery one man in a smart London suit seemed to fit the description of the man I was looking for and at a good moment I asked if he was Mr Simpson. "No," he replied, "unfortunately Mr Simpson has 'flu and so cannot be here." On the assumption that he was standing in and anxious to fulfill my commission I produced the note and began to say my piece as I pressed it into his hand. The recipient however looked so astonished that I rapidly amended my spiel by saying that I would be grateful if he would pass it on to the appropriate recipient. Fortunately we soon entered the special train – consisting of one immaculate locomotive and two coaches and we pulled out of Kings Cross to head north for Bedfordshire. Later in the day I said casually to one of my Palace contemporaries "Oh by the way, who was the tall fellow in the reception party at Kings Cross?" The answer was "Oh, he is the General Manager of the railway; nice chap too". My indiscretion was never revealed.

Another guessing game arose one day and was just as unclear to me as the previous one about 'that silly hat'. The question was "Shall I give it to him when we get there?" Oh dear! Give what, to whom, and where? Out of context, this kind of question without any preamble again requires a high degree of inspired guessing. One ploy is to skirt around the question with vaguely-worded comment, thus establishing whether you are somewhere near the mark or not. Once again, intuition saved the day. It was in fact all about giving – awarding is the better word – the Distinguished Flying Cross to Group Captain Edward Fielden when the King and Queen were visiting RAF Station, Tempsford from whence all the special flying into occupied France with agents was taking place. So I said "Splendid idea, Sir! I will bring one with me when we go next Wednesday." I made a call to the Air Ministry. "I want a DFC sent round to my office in the Palace, please." There was a stony silence and then the voice at the other end said "Who says; and who is it for?" This was my big moment, "The King says so; and it is for Group Captain Fielden". No prizes for guessing that the small package arrived pronto! I telephoned 'Mouse' Fielden at Tempsford and told him what was afoot and at his suggestion the agreed venue was the Ante-room of the Officers Mess. Just before the presentation I produced the gong and it was pinned onto Fielden's tunic.

'Mouse' Fielden's DFC prompts me to enlarge upon the subject of decorations and medals. The King possessed an amazing collection dating from the distant past and was a manifestation of His Majesty's deep interest. He had a keen eye and always noticed what ribbons a person in uniform was showing on his or her breast. He noticed that I was wearing the ribbon of the 'Aircrew Europe' medal but not the 'Africa Star' and naturally asked that as I had been participating in the Desert War why was I not wearing the campaign ribbon? My reply (which I thoroughly enjoyed giving) was that the Air Ministry in its wisdom had recently decreed that if anyone was entitled to both medals he could have one or the other, but not both. I had made the choice of the 'Air Crew Europe' medal because it was by definition specifically for the Royal Air Force. However, I said that I was upset (as were all of us in similar circumstance) because we felt cheated of our just entitlement by what seemed to be a ridiculous ruling. The East African and Western Desert campaigns had been a particularly rough business for all the fighting men and furthermore all of us had to fight 'out of sight and out of mind' and live like desert rats. The joys of a bath, a proper bed, reasonable food, adulation in the local pub, newspaper accounts and so forth were not for the desert men. The King seemed a bit upset by my comments but nothing more was said at the time. The affair had a happy ending for literally within days the earlier decision was cancelled and now both ribbons could be worn if applicable. I would have loved to have seen the red faces of the Committee members who had made the silly ruling and now had to change their tune in quick order.

After Royal investitures the procedure is that the Monarch retires behind the big doors and the recipients of decorations and their families leave whilst the military band plays suitable music. On one occasion when I was still holding the sword with which the Monarch had 'dubbed' two men with knighthoods, he turned to me and asked what ribbon a particular officer had been wearing; it looked not unlike a DFC but the stripes were sloping the other way. Fortunately I had spotted it and I happened to know the answer; it was the Greek Distinguished Flying Cross and it had been awarded to an RAF pilot for his operational flying during the Greek Campaign. The King was pleased to learn about this ribbon and whilst on the subject I could not resist telling him that my contemporaries said that the DFC was given for flying in the face of the enemy and the Air Force Cross for flying in the face of providence!

A final anecdote about decorations must be told and the scene goes back to 1938 at RAF Northolt. In those days there was a wooden hut by the hangars that was occupied by a chap called the Duty Pilot. His function was to record all aircraft movements, notify the destination of an aeroplane's departure by telephone or radio and give visual help to a pilot arriving in the circuit by firing off green or red Very lights to indicate landing clearance or otherwise. It was basic pre-war 'Air Traffic Control' business and it worked surprisingly well.

On a certain day our young Duty Pilot saw a strange single-seater appear, make a circuit, and land. After it had taxied in across the grass and stopped a mature pilot got out. His speech, his strange uniform and the insignia on his parasol monoplane made no sense at all to the Duty Pilot. However, the visitor repeated the word 'London' often enough with lots of handsigns to give the basic message to our young fighter pilot. He got out his old Morris car, put his visitor on board and took him to the Underground Station where he bought him a ticket to Piccadilly – where else? – and sent him on his way. Later that day his friend arrived back by taxi, got into his aeroplane and flew away to an unknown destination.

In due course, the Station Commander at Northolt received a package from the Air Ministry and inside was the handsome decoration of the Order of St. Stanislav, Second Class. The covering letter informed the Station Commander that it had been sent by the Polish Air Force Chief-of-Staff and was to be awarded to the young officer who had been so helpful in taking the General to the railway station and later on seeing him off safely on his way back to Poland. The letter went on to say that as foreign decorations were not admissible for RAF officers the Station Commander will please inform the recipient that under no circumstance will he wear the Order at any time. Inevitably the young man cheated occasionally. After a dining-in night when the party was in full swing his chums would say "Joe, go and get your Polish gong for god's sake and wear it". Our hero would leave the Ante-Room and return soon after with the impressive Order dangling from the wide ribbon around his neck. Honour was satisfied.

Although wartime conditions necessarily curtailed a host of Palace functions there was the occasional opportunity to relax and set aside the cares of war. One such was a dance held at Windsor Castle and whether or not it was because an airman equerry had arrived on the scene that influenced the guest list I cannot recollect. What I do know is that I was asked if I would provide about a dozen RAF chaps to the party and they should of course as applicable bring their wives with them. It had all the hallmarks of being a jolly evening and understandably the idea was to invite young people so that the two Princesses could meet them. I telephoned the Air Ministry and told one of my contacts what was afoot and suggested that the invitations go to pilots from Fighter, Bomber, and Coastal Command. A list was made up and when sent to the palace some of the names were very familiar.

On the appointed evening the two hundred or so guests began to arrive. The party was soon in full swing and temporarily we all forgot the war and the airmen soon caught the eye of the other guests because it was clear from all the decorations on their tunics that they had been, shall I say, quite busy in recent times. A colonel who was on duty at the Castle came up to me and said "Very decorated young airmen here this evening, eh what?" I smiled approvingly. "Nothing special, colonel; just picked at random, you know!" How could I resist a boost for the Brylcream Boys?! The following morning the Queen (Queen Mother today) said how much she liked the party and had enjoyed meeting the flying boys and dancing with a lot of them. One chap in particular she found to be very entertaining and she recounted one gem in the conversation. "You know Ma'am, this is the best party of all; absolutely super. I could do it three times in a row except of course it would mean three hangovers too, wouldn't it?"

One talented and interesting personality who stayed at Windsor Castle for a specific purpose was the artist Gerald Kelly who became the President of the Royal Academy. He had been commissioned to paint the Royal portraits and many visitors were taken to his studio to see the portraits which by now were nearing completion. With the King and Queen dressed in full regalia with orders and decorations, the paintings certainly were impressive and I and everybody else greatly admired Gerald's undoubted skill. However, from the discreet comments made by one or two of my fellow courtiers I surmised that they thought that the artist was employing what is now called Parkinson's Law – tailoring the work-load to suit the desired time scale, and in this case it was possibly the duration of the war.

Christmas was approaching and it was of course pantomime time too. The Royal family were enthusiastic about the Thespian arts so it was no surprise to find that 'Dick Wittington', complete with a six feet three inches guards officer in the key role, was ordained. When the pantomime was put on in the temporary theatre it was packed with Windsor Castle staff and in the manner of a director's licence there were of course some supporting cameos to enliven the scene. In one of them the players were two charming young ladies – no prizes for guessing who – and a man dressed up in a smock and floppy hat. The script went something like this:

1st young lady: "Who is that gentleman over there?"
2nd young lady: "I'm not sure; shall we ask him?"
1st young lady: "Excuse me, sir, may I ask who you are?"
Man with floppy hat: "I'm Kerald Jelly; I'm an artist".
2nd young lady: "Oh, it must be you who is painting the portraits."
Man with floppy hat: "Yes, they are coming along quite well now I'm pleased to say".
1st young lady: "How long have you been working on the paintings so far?"
Man with floppy hat: "Well, I'm not sure; of course it does take time so I forgot when I started".
1st young lady: "Do be careful Mr Jelly; otherwise you may forget when to finish!"
Curtain

Much laughter. I guessed that the younger of the two young ladies wrote the script. She was certainly good at it.

As so often is the case with sisters, the two young princesses were different where their personalities were concerned. Her Royal Highness Princess Elizabeth possessed for a young girl a certain depth of character and an awareness of her future responsibilities even though at that stage it would have been impossible to forecast what lay ahead and the manner of it's happening. I could not resist the feeling that some intuitive process was already grooming her to the realisation that sooner rather than later she must develop a serious intent that would match the requirement of immense responsibility. Just the same we saw so often the winning smile, the sense of fun, and always a deep interest in what was going on around her. If I may be so bold as to make further comment, she impressed me by the way that she comported herself by behaving with measured dignity and composure, something that was unusual in such a young girl.

By contrast, Her Royal Highness the Princess Margaret was quick-witted, mildly extrovert, and so perceptive of other people's foibles and eccentricities that she perhaps took undue advantage of them by pointed comment. It could have been the instinctive reaction of a younger sister making her mark and so ensuring that she was not unnoticed. The amusing skit in the pantomime had her imprint upon it and she was clearly inspired by the notion that it was time that someone drew attention to Gerald Kelly's unduly long stay at Windsor Castle. The clever part was that the skit was unexpected and produced an audience response of much laughter but the barb was delivered just the same; with a good sense of timing the impact was at its greatest. I would be loath to be the victim of such exposure as it does cut one down to size.

The Christmas period brought us back to London and one morning a telephone call came to the equerry's office from the Admiralty. The caller told me that a secret package was on its way and when it arrived would I please open it when the nature of the contents would be self-evident. This was an intriguing one and I waited impatiently for its arrival. I did not have to wait long as the courier only had to travel from one end of the Mall to the other.

Upon opening the small parcel I found inside two lovely circular-shaped trinket boxes (if that is the correct description) nestling inside. Each one was made of ebony and each had a neat silver inlay on the side with the engraving 'HMS *Duke of York*, Christmas 1942'. Recessed into each lid was a polished sixpence with the Monarch's head showing uppermost and the two boxes looked quite beautiful with the craftsman's art at its best. The note that accompanied them told me (as though I had not guessed) that they were Christmas presents for the two princesses from Admiral Sir Bruce Fraser. Would I please package them up separately and see that they were discreetly added to the other presents at the foot of their Christmas tree? I was so intrigued about it all that I got in touch with Sir Harold Campbell to try and find the background to the idea so cleverly thought up by the Royal Navy. The story goes back to the previous year when His Majesty was having Christmas dinner with the Fleet in the Firth of Forth in Scotland. This was an occasion that the King would enjoy and it goes without saying that the Royal Navy were at their best when entertaining their top Admiral. Harold's account of the evening was a masterpiece of lucid description and understandably he too loved the evening with his naval friends.

There came a moment during the dinner of the fine British tradition of the entry of the Christmas pudding burning with blue flame and a heady aroma of brandy. It always pays the diner to hold back on earlier courses sufficiently to enjoy that first delicious tasting! The Naval dinner was no exception to custom and portions of the delectable dish were now served. The King suddenly declared that his pudding had a hidden sixpence in it. Almost a mouthful or two later he was smiling broadly when he produced a second one. This brought forth cries of congratulation from those closest to him and the Commander-in-Chief, Admiral Sir Bruce Fraser suggested that His Majesty might care to hand the two coins over on the premise that Royalty never carry money about with them. There was now some amusing cross-talk accompanied by chuckles and laughter. In the event the two sixpences remained on the plate and the Christmas dinner proceeded to its finish in naval style with the Royal toast made with all officers seated in the traditional way.

Now that I knew the background story I knew how to set about my commission. Those well-practised sailors were operating with their usual panache and it now fell to a "crab" to complete the job. (For the uninitiated, crabs in naval language are RAF pilots). Thus it was that an airman held the last card, the final link in a well-contrived and clever operation. After admiring the two quite charming presents created by the ship's artificers, the job now was to pack them separately in boxes with pretty wrapping paper and Christmas embellishments. I then realised that there was a serious flaw in the plan – there was no indication about who the donor was. Sir Bruce Fraser had gone off to the other end of the world to become C-in-C British Pacific Fleet, and so the crab had to become a forger. The Admiral's handwriting upon investigation was very small and to do the job I obtained some plain cards, practised his style a few times and then wrote the forgeries. Each one said "To HRH Princess Elizabeth (or Princess Margaret), with best wishes for Christmas and the New Year, from Uncle Bruce". The parcels were then passed 'upstairs' for placing on the tree at the dead of night. The crab had completed the assignment.

On the morning of Christmas Day I had a chance encounter with the two young princesses and we exchanged the usual 'Happy Christmas' greetings. I asked them if they had looked at any of the presents that Father Christmas had left for them at the foot of their tree. Almost in unison they said enthusiastically, "Uncle Bruce has given each of us a lovely ebony trinket box with 'HMS *Duke of York*' on the side and a sixpence set into the lid. It's a lovely present!" I grinned enigmatically, "Heavens! How very nice! I would love to see them sometime". Uncle Bruce's Christmas presents had arrived safely, but the secret means of completion was mine.

The 1943 Boxing Day dinner which I was privileged to attend took place at Buckingham Palace. There were about sixteen of us seated around an oval table, and in addition to the Royal family the rest included the Private Secretary, the Lady-in-Waiting, the Colonel of the Palace Guard, the Master of the Household and the Crown Equerry. It was a family affair and it was easy for everybody to be relaxed as we were all part of the household.

The dinner party had reached the last course – no sixpences in my Christmas pudding I have to say – when a footman came in and spoke to Sir Alan Lascelles. He left the table, explaining that he had to take a telephone call. He returned after a short time and spoke quietly to the King who nodded with appreciation. 'Tommy' Lascelles then said in his impassive way, "I have just been told by the Admiralty that the German cruiser *Scharnhorst* has been sunk". The news, coming as it did during dinner seemed to be so dramatic that for some moments there was a distinct hush but quickly the implications of this startling news became manifest when everybody started to talk excitedly. At the time I do not remember any of us knowing the circumstance of the sinking; it was sufficient to know that it had happened. The dinner had now reached the stage when, to use the appropriate expression, the ladies withdrew from the table leaving the King to gather his male guests around him. With coffee now served the conversation soon developed around the main topic whilst I sipped an excellent brandy from a goblet. To suit the occasion and enhance the obvious reaction that the news of the Scharnhorst's demise had produced, two or three of the male guests elected to enliven the evening with what they considered to be lighthearted after-dinner anecdotes. To my way of thinking every one was pretty inept and lacked the timing and pungency that any funny story should have to make the desired impact on the listener. We laughed dutifully as each one was delivered and I wished so much that one of my raconteur friends was there to do proper justice to the occasion. In particular I had in mind the very amusing Jim Lee who was always in demand with 88 Squadron and who had innumerable funny stories gleaned during his days in London and the world of journalism. Upon an impulse, my mind ranged over his repertoire and choosing one that had the merit of brevity I decided that it was the air equerry's turn. Taking a deep breath – and another sip of brandy to give me flying speed – I asked the King if he had heard about the Welshman who was visiting London for the first time. "Aha, a Welshman in London – what happened to him?" I was committed; and so the story began.

A Welshman came to London one day and as he was a countryman his friends suggested that he would enjoy some of the lovely open spaces like Richmond, Kensington Gardens and Hyde Park. On the first morning, he left his small hotel and when a bus stopped nearby he called out to the conductor – 'Is this bus for Richmond?' The friendly conductor readily identified the distinctive accent and replying in similar style said 'No man – for Kew'. At this the visitor took umbrage and called back 'For Kew too – I was only asking!' Even before I sat back to await the reaction the King broke out in hearty laughter; so did everybody else. The air equerry had won the prize, for which I thank Jim Lee who inspired it.

The following day was the Sabbath and I accompanied the Royal family to attend the service in the impressive and beautiful St. George's Chapel at Windsor Castle, the home of the Order of the Garter founded by King Edward III in the 14th century. After the service the short walk back to the castle brought us to the spot where the lady-in-waiting, Lady Delia Peel and I stopped to see the King and his family on their way to their royal apartments before we took another route to our own. At this point however the King paused and I remember him leaning against the wall of the wide corridor, tapping his leg with a leather-covered fieldmarshal's baton and a smile of contemplation on his face. After some moments the Queen said "Come on, Bertie, what are we waiting for?" At this the King looked at me and said "It was Richmond – not Kew – wasn't it?" I grinned back with a mixture of assent and slight embarrassment and everybody looked quizzically at both of us. After a good chuckle my master laughed out loud and said "They don't understand, do they?" The Royal family moved on, still bemused over the little scene between the Monarch and his air equerry. Such episodes as this made the Boxing Day Royal dinner party the evening before even more memorable.

It was during another walk in the Palace garden with the King that the subject of the Bomber Command offensive was discussed at some length. It was occasioned by the news of one of the big attacks on Germany. The King was interested in much more than the bare statement of fact and so I was able to elaborate about the intentions, the personalities, the aircraft, and not least the remarkable crews whose chances of survival were no better than odds of five-to-one against. Because of the need to elaborate in this matter I began to get the distinct impression that the Royal Air Force, unlike the Army and particularly the Navy, was not very well versed in the expertise of public relations. The new Air element in warfare that was rapidly becoming the key to success seemed to have at least one weakness; there was a certain shyness, even reluctance, on the part of the airmen to organise themselves to best effect. The Royal Navy has the subtle art of self-promotion to the n'th degree and the sailors never miss an opportunity to inject the media with the subtleties of naval life and endeavour, be it the Royal Marines in the Falklands, submariners in their nuclear peace-keeping duties, a filmed rescue by helicopter, or a Royal personage on board a ship.

It was with this in mind that I went to see Group Captain Sir Louis Greig. Amongst the pointers to the less-obvious weaknesses of the Junior Service's image – discounting the brief glory of the Battle of Britain – I said that it was surely high time that we also had our own 'Uncle Bruce' to maintain personal contact with the Palace. In my temporary new job I could not but fail to notice that Christian names of sailors and soldiers were used quite naturally but nobody ever seemed to say Bert, Charles or Arthur; it was usually Harris, Portal or Tedder.

With this subtle differential apparent to me, and in the absence of any plans afoot for the Monarch to make a visit to Bomber Command, I made some discreet overtures – a walk in the garden sometimes works wonders. Louis Greig agreed with my sentiments and he also had noticed that airmen were thought of as eccentric people not well known enough in high places to have Christian names. It was a nice surprise therefore when the Palace telephone operator told me that Air Marshal Sir Arthur Harris was on the line. "Pelly" he said, "What's all this I hear that the King wants to visit Bomber Command?" When I replied that it was true, he said "This looks like your doing; what on earth is he coming for? We are damned busy". The short conversation (as usual) ended by Bert Harris saying that I had better go and see him so I arranged for a Palace car and set off for High Wycombe. The visit placed me in the extraordinary situation of advising the C-in-C about how the planning, timing, and conduct of the whole affair should be carried out. Dear Bert, he took it all like the proverbial lamb! I arranged to be there myself which seemed to please him although on the day I was not on equerry duty. That preliminary visit confirmed my view that senior RAF men had still to learn the finesse of developing a personal image.

On a certain Monday afternoon at 3 o'clock precisely the Rolls Royce bearing the Monarch's Standard drove silently through the main gates of Bomber Command Headquarters and was followed by a second car with the Lady-in-Waiting and Equerry. 'Bomber' Harris was there at the Headquarters entrance to greet his Royal visitors and as Their Majesties were travelling after the weekend from Windsor to London the small detour to HQ Bomber Command was a conveniently planned arrangement. The ninety-minute tour worked out admirably and ran like clockwork. His Majesty was completely absorbed in all that he saw and the Queen as usual demonstrated her immense charm and that special style of communicating with people. The last item on the programme was a film show of bomber attacks – cameramen Skeets Kelly and Charlie Peace of course! – whilst Jill and her senior ladies provided tea in the semi-darkness of the cinema to give some privacy. The Royal party then left for London and I stayed behind to note reactions. Everybody was now relaxed – not least Bert Harris – and in his direct way he declared the visit to be a success. Then he added "Now let's get back to the bloody war".

The visit to Bomber command was only the starting point of the plan to further the cause. A visit like this one was of value only if it was pursued thereafter in a policy of continuity and what I called the 'Uncle Bruce' formula. Prior to the Royal visit on that sunny January afternoon I made a point of suggesting to Bert Harris that the King would be very interested to see what he called 'The Blue Book'. This was a very large leather-bound affair that was kept in his office and it contained photographs of ninety targets in Germany that were judged to be of major importance for Bomber Command aircraft to attack. Each photographic mosaic had a thin tracing paper overlay showing the extent to which the target area had been destroyed and the appropriate information was kept up-to-date by trained staff. For easy reference the Blue Book was always available and it developed along the lines of a pictorial progress chart. Just as I had hoped, on my return to duty the King said how impressed he was with the visit and the inspection of the Blue Book and its contents fascinated him. This was my cue; I suggested that he might like to have a Blue Book of his own and thus keep abreast of the bomber effort that was at last showing positive results with new navigation and bombing expertise. The idea was welcomed and the next stage of the scheme was now activated. I telephoned to Bert Harris and told him that the King would like a copy of the 'Blue

Book'. The gruff voice at the other end said, "Well, there are only three of them. Winston has one, Roosevelt has one, and I have one." I broke the silence by saying, "Sir, when Master wants one – well he gets one, I imagine!" 'Bomber' Harris was not as a rule a man to be told what to do; certainly not by a Wing Commander. However this time he relented.

Stage three was that a handsome Blue Book with the Royal Cypher embossed on the leather cover was produced but the essence of the scheme was that no less a person than Harris' Deputy C-in-C, Air Marshal Sir Robert Saundby would deliver the Blue Book to the King in person and he would continue to visit at regular intervals to keep it up-to-date. In this way an Air Marshal would have a regular entrée to the Palace and it would be a subtle way of ensuring that at least one facet of Royal Air Force activity was going to be given the personal treatment it deserved. With any luck at all we might even have at least one senior airman blessed, believe it or not, with a Christian name!

Perhaps the most pleasant experience of all in my time with the Royal family took place at the end of January 1944. I have the fondest memories of a week-end in Norfolk and it was all the more rewarding because I was not on duty and so I was in the happy situation of being a guest.

During the wartime years it was considered prudent not to use Sandringham House as a Royal residence. It was situated close to the Norfolk coast and a large mansion such as that might well receive the attentions of a Luftwaffe pilot who might attack it as an 'opportunity target'. An earlier bomb that struck the covered swimming pool at Buckingham Palace during the London blitz was warning enough.

The alternative accommodation for the Royal family, who understandably loved Norfolk because of many associations, was Appleton House. It was used by Norway's Royal family in normal circumstance and as I remember it stood within the grounds of the Sandringham estate.

On a certain Friday afternoon I set off by train from Liverpool Street Station, London, for Norfolk. As I waited for the train to pull out I ruminated on an earlier sighting when I flew low over it on a cold January evening in the old Avro 504 biplane with neon lights glowing under the wings. This time, sitting much more comfortably in the 1st class carriage, the train moved off punctually and headed north. The route goes via Cambridge, Ely, and thence to King's Lynn and terminates at Hunstanton – the local pronunciation being 'Hunston'. About six miles short of King's Lynn there is a delightful and beautifully kept little station called Wolferton and is the alighting point for Sandringham. The train by now was divested of most of its passengers and only two of us got out at Wolferton. The covered entrance of the small booking hall was decorated with lovely baskets of flowers and the Station Master greeting me was decked out in the full panoply of his status; he had come to welcome the weekend guest. A chauffeur-driven car awaited and the short journey brought me to

Appleton House. It was by royal standards a comparatively small and comfortable Victorian-style mansion with a pillared portico at the entrance. A footman took me to my rooms where a valet advised me of the sartorial details for the weekend and I also had to learn the small points of behaviour appropriate to a guest in strange surroundings, the layout of the main rooms, and the weekend programme. Once again Sir Harold Campbell was there to initiate me and I do not know what a chap like myself would have done without him. One thing was very apparent and it was that being such a small house compared to the Palace or the Castle it might be difficult to cope with chance Royal encounters. My appreciation was well founded. The time seemed to slip away all too quickly and with people like the entertaining and talented Sir Eric Melville, (private secretary), Lady Lloyd, (Lady in Waiting), Lord Rupert Nevill, Captain Roger Hall, and Harold Campbell, it was a weekend party par excellence. Apart from delightful luncheons and dinners, all the activities naturally were of an outdoor nature and we were lucky to have good weather in this regard. A Monarch's shooting party is the epitome of well-planned sporting activity and the King was not only an enthusiast he was also an excellent shot and in my experience I doubt that he missed more than one bird in twenty; whenever he did so I could hear him chiding himself for the error. As the shoot was on a wartime basis the day's bag of around one hundred brace of birds was a valuable addition to the larder and so it combined usefulness and pleasure.

On the Sunday morning, after attending church, the luncheon party was animated and by chance someone spotted some cock pheasants strutting about on the lawn almost as though they owned the place. This brought a reminder that as it was the last day of January when pheasant shooting ends it was the last chance to add to the bag before the guns were put away until the next winter season. The temptation was strong and so the King proposed an impromptu afternoon shoot. There would be two guns only; himself and Harold, and the rest of us would carry out the functions of gamekeepers, beaters, second gun and cartridge carriers. The idea was enthusiastically greeted by everybody and the 'mini shoot' would be held nearby, thus eliminating the need for shooting-brakes and drivers.

We now armed ourselves with walking sticks (we were the beaters), the two guns carried their own gear and away we went into the nearby fields and copses ably supervised by the Chief Gun. Splendid stuff! It was a bright mid-afternoon and the exercise kept everybody warm and in fine fettle. The Royal plan of operation seemed to be putting up a reasonable number of birds although of course it was an adhoc affair and no doubt we failed to flush out the majority of them. No matter, it was great fun to do and it augmented the wartime rationing system that the Royal family complied with like all other citizens of the realm.

During one beat I entered a small copse to flush out any birds that might have been lying up and out of sight. It had a length of netting about knee-high that stretched from one side of the copse to the other and was intended to prevent the birds from running; if they wanted to make their escape to freedom then they had to fly out and chance their luck. Inside the copse was a wily old cock bird who was much too smart to get airborne and all that he did was to chase up and down furiously to avoid the ill intentions of the beater. I now was faced with a dilemma; if I abandoned him, well he would win the contest and he would strut off jauntily knowing (as they do) that he was safe until next winter. On the other hand I convinced myself that wartime food restrictions prescribed that I should not abandon the chase lightly and so my case was as good, or better, than his. The beater now pursued the quarry. When I emerged like a furtive poacher with his swag on what should have been the hidden side of the copse vis-a-vis the two guns, watching me with interest and curiosity was the Number One gun. The conversation went something like this:

No 1 gun: "Hmm – did I get that bird?"
Beater: "No sir!"
No 1 gun: "Well, did Harold get it?"
Beater: "No sir!"
No 1 gun: "Well, who the devil did then?"
Beater: "I'm afraid I did, Sir. . . . I hit it on the head with my stick. I thought that with the war on. . . ."

My master gave me what might be called a distinctly old-fashioned look. Agonising moments passed and then he gave a Gallic shrug of the shoulders, raised his eyes to Heaven as though in supplication, and we moved on to the next copse.

On the way back to London after such a wonderful weekend I began to ruminate about my exalted circumstance and how long it would last. The situation, viewed dispassionately, was that I had been fantastically lucky to have been selected as a temporary equerry. Factor number two was that nobody seemed to know 'how temporary was temporary', as it was completely in the King's command. From remarks made by members of the household it seemed that everybody thought that, as in olden times, the Monarch had decided to show appreciation of his army by selecting a warrior to be his Aide; someone who had earned a rest from the toils of the war. I was often told, "I do hope that the change is doing you good; I'm sure you needed a rest". The reality was that although I appreciated a break, by no means did I feel worn out, excessively frightened, (though heaven knows most of us were scared!) or in need of a desk job. The truth was that I was beginning to feel something of a fraud. I had that certain feeling that gracious living with top people, lovely tho' it was, might well lull me into a state of complacency and a wish to continue a life of comfort and easy living. It would get me into the dangerous position that so long as I followed in the footsteps of the King I was nicely placed because only one man could remove me and he showed no signs of doing so. When I asked Sir Louis Greig what the score was, his answer was "Nobody has the slightest idea!"

The tricky impasse, reduced to its simplest form, had two options; do something – or do nothing. I chose the former. The man to approach was obviously Sir Alan Lascelles and I went to see him and gave him my thoughts on the matter. I explained that whilst I was completely satisfied with my lot – who would not be? – I felt that my 'rest period' should end. My view was that I should get back to work before I got entrenched as basically I was a professional airman. I said that I was very embarrassed at having to raise the matter and I might be talking out of turn. However I had to take the initiative if only to find out what the situation was as then I would know how I stood. Sir Alan was very understanding and he admitted frankly that nothing at all had been said and no decision made. He was complimentary about how quickly I had settled into an unusual job that normally took time and experience to learn and I concluded that I had not failed Sir Charles Portal in his choice. Sir Alan undertook to bring the matter up in the right way and at the right moment.

A day or so later he gave me the answer. The King understood my predicament and he approved of my move to seek a decision; This made me much happier as I had not after all done the wrong thing. The situation was now resolved. He advised the Air Ministry accordingly and it worked out conveniently because Bomber Harris was able to give me one of his operational airfields to command and that was an exciting prospect. For my replacement the Navy provided Commander John Grant, and he was in turn followed by Group Captain Peter Townsend.

On my last day at the Palace I presented myself to their Majesties, sad at heart now that the the reality had struck home, and I made my farewell. I then said goodbye to my Palace associates, put my kit into the Lagonda, and drove out of the gates. My policeman friend happened to be on duty again and he proved to be both my first and my last close contact with the remarkable world of Royal lifestyle. It had been a fascinating experience and one that remains treasured and vivid to this day.

Although it may seem mundane, I must place on record that everything that I dreamed of about the Royal family was abundantly confirmed in every way. Britain and the Commonwealth cannot fully know just how very fortunate we all are to have such a wonderful Monarchy because it is only when one has the unique opportunity of close observation and participation that the impact is so telling. Quite apart from the fact that we have such a close-knit and very human Royal family, their absolute deep interest and concern in every facet of British life is manifest. One insight was occasioned after their Majesties had returned from a visit to see Queen

Mary who was staying at Badminton, the home of the Duke of Beaufort. I greeted their Majesties at Buckingham Palace immediately upon their return and it was natural to ask if they had enjoyed the weekend in the lovely house situated in the Cotswolds. His Majesty said "It was pleasant – but the house was dreadfully cold!" True to form Queen Mary was playing her part of enduring the winter cold like every other citizen and accepted no favours where fuel rationing was concerned.

Although nominally apparent in their everyday activities which one sees through the television and newspapers, we tend to take royalty very much for granted. It would be quite an education if all of us were given, say, ten days of continuous participation in palace life just to see what the job – I use the word deliberately – entails. It is in truth a continuous and unrelenting day-after-day formal appearance on the world's stage. It is all done so pleasingly and effortlessly; it looks so very easy to do, but we forget that royalty are not allowed the privilege of having off-days.

As a nation Britain and the Commonwealth could not be more fortunate than to have such a wonderful Monarchy. Long may it be so.

Chapter XX

Halifaxes at War

It is always something of an emotional affair to make the transition from the realms of fantasy back to reality. The heavenly days in Tahiti, that jewel of the Pacific set in an endless sea of turquoise with the seven thousand foot mountain producing lovely waterfalls, is a case in point. Whilst the dream lasts the rest of the world and its troubles are forgotten and one floats on a cloud until the truth returns. It was so for the ex-air equerry returning to ground level again; I now had to re-adjust to getting back into the groove and it was exacerbated because the fact was that a major war was still with us and as a professional airman I was part of it. I was about to rejoin the military organisation which had started from the beginning by taking the war hundreds of miles into Hitler's Germany. For the participants it was a fearful responsibility, and it was also a gruelling task. It was called RAF Bomber Command.

The Air Ministry confirmed that a job as Station Commander of a Halifax bomber aerodrome in Yorkshire would be my new appointment in a few weeks time. In the meantime I was free to take some leave or alternatively fill the gap to some purpose; I chose the latter, as what I wanted to do was to get back into flying practise. To that end I found myself at RAF Hixon in Staffordshire doing a refresher flying course on Wellingtons; after four sorties with my instructor he was disposed to let me fly solo in that splendid aeroplane. I was now experiencing the second of Barnes Wallis' geodetic-constructed designs and after the Wellesley it was just like its younger brother and possessed the same basic good habits. It even had the same curious way of flexing its structure when moving on the ground. It was like old times in the Sudan, the difference being that I no longer lived like a desert nomad but enjoyed green grass and a roof over my head. During the two weeks at Hixon I put in over twenty-five hours in the air, some of it by night. After some wrist-slapping by my teacher to iron out those bad habits that we all get into – like motorcar driving except that motorists have no obligation to be retested – I cajoled the maintenance wing engineers into giving me a lot of test flying and ferry jobs to do. I thoroughly enjoyed it all and it was a very good way of getting back into the swing of things. I am still grateful to those Hixon chaps who made the return to reality so painless and so useful to my well-being. Life in the palace was becoming a nostalgic memory – like Tahiti.

The second stage, now that I had been reintroduced into the circuit, so to speak, was to try and widen my education by getting to know the type of aeroplanes that I would find in my new appointment. I have always had a conviction that people in military command of anything should be – indeed must be – not only familiar with the equipment used by his men, he should be seen to use it. This applies in particular to an air force. The morale of a flying unit is enhanced if the aircrew see 'the old man' putting in flying time like they do. It gives them the feeling that the boss knows what it is all about. – The converse of course is self evident. Bomber Harris had made it a rule that he would not accept any officer to command one of his aerodromes unless he had previously completed an operational tour. It must also be put on record that because he was losing so many of his Station Commanders (who were pressing on as before) he forbad any of them to fly on operations. Their job, he said, was not to fight – at least not for the time being – but to be the hotel keeper and so give his squadrons a good base to operate from. I only wish in later times that more senior men in civil life would be seen to take a closer interest in the job that their workforce carries out. Even the simple act of going around to see-and-be-seen makes a huge difference. People like to be identified, not just a name on the payroll.

With these thoughts in mind I arranged to go to one of the Halifax Heavy Bomber Conversion Units and try my hand (as dear Moose Fulton had hoped to do) with four throttles. Apart from the brief experience in the HP 42 'Hengist' somewhere south of Khartoum with Captain Woodhouse watching my every move, this was to be the full treatment.

On the fifteenth of April, 1944, I arrived at RAF Rufforth, one of the Heavy Bomber training aerodromes and based near the cathedral city of York. The first step was to present my compliments to Group Captain David Young, DSO, DFC, AFC, the Station Commander. Here was a Bomber Command warrior in the top bracket and he was now having a breather by using he experience to provide the platform from which the new crews went through the final training before being posted to a squadron. It was a critical stage, and he knew it. He exuded confidence; he flew the Halifaxes regularly; and it was noticed.

My initiation into the mysteries of four-engined bombers began within an hour of my arrival and my instructor was Squadron Leader Bill Kofoed. With two crew men in the back of the monster, my log book records the first sortie of 2hrs 35mins of circuits and landings plus general flying. No half measure with these chaps, I thought; any training sortie of less than two hours was for boys – not men. In four days I had completed over ten hours on Halifaxes and I began to get the hang of it all reasonably well – or so I thought – and had even reached the stage of flying safely on two out of four engines. On the evening of the fourth day, Bill Kofoed told me that it was time to go night flying. Well, well; such progress! At 21.15 hrs we took off down the runway with all the little lights making the aerodrome look like some kind of a sea of orderly glow worms as we climbed away. I was now getting the correct perspective as the Halifax was doing what it was intended to do, fly by night. After cruising about over Yorkshire, the ground now showing very little illumination under wartime conditions, my Captain told me to go back to Rufforth, join the circuit, call the control tower, identify the Halifax by its call-sign and ask permission to land. That done, the usual instructions were sent back to us, plus details of any cross-wind on the runway which was very important to a Halifax because of one of its habits of a swing after touchdown. After the initial clearance was given we went through all the standard cockpit drill and checks. When clearance to land was given from the tower, the final checks were made; flaps down, fine pitch for propellors, another look for 'two greens' for the undercarriage, rich mixture, and then down the glide path, over the threshold, and finally I made a passable landing. I was getting better.

Bill Kofoed then directed me to taxy around the perimeter track, – the guiding lights marking the verges, – and stop at the prescribed place to 'put everything back' like flaps 'up', normal engine settings, check engine temperatures, another check of fuel state, and so on. As soon as I had stopped the Halifax and waited for further orders, without a word to me the Squadron Leader undid his parachute and seat harness, unplugged the radio socket from his helmet, and left the cockpit. He was followed out of the aeroplane by the rest of the crew. Not to worry, I thought; perhaps there was some technical drill of a torch-illuminated inspection of something or other. It seemed to me to be routine night flying procedure at the conversion unit so I sat there waiting for the next stage of the sortie. After a minute's wait, the Rolls Royce 'Merlin' engines in the Mk III Halifax growling away happily with such a distinct note, I happened to look down on the port (Captains) side and saw in the shadows the figure of someone waving his arms about furiously. I waved back – though truth to tell I had no idea what was afoot. The shadowy figure now made distinct arm movements that could only mean one thing – I was being told, to put it bluntly, to push off and get on with another take-off!

This was Operation Deep-End; that clever fellow had trapped me into going solo without so much as a chance to chicken out. Oh well, nothing to it. I gently pushed open the four throttles, moved forward along the taxi track, stopped at the 'Hold' spot, got the clearance from the tower (when I'm sure I could detect a chuckle in the controller's voice), moved onto the runway, and off into the very dark blue yonder in the great big bomber.

This time I was by myself and it was an exhilarating feeling. At eight hundred feet I eased the four throttles back, and then after completing the technical requirements sat back and reviewed the situation. It is fair to say that not often does a pilot find himself winging his way through the night sky in a four-engined bomber with nobody else on board. After the initial flow of adrenalin had slowed up – I began to enjoy this new and quite unexpected experience and decided to get my money's worth and leave the circuit. It all now seemed rather a splendid thing; I was in sole charge of one of His Majesty's most expensive aeroplanes.

Twenty minutes later I returned to the circuit. I called the tower, received the affirmative answer that I hoped for, did what I had to do inside the cockpit with knobs, levers, and switches, got the final 'clear to land' message, and made the best landing of them all. As I taxied back to dispsersal I had that smug feeling that I had passed the test. I could now go to my new job looking for all the world like a proper Group Captain qualified to fly Halifax bombers, day or night.

After flying the Halifax at RAF Rufforth, I was free to have some days off before I was to report to headquarters No 4 Group. Part of the time was a weekend spent with Bert and Jill Harris at their charming official residence called Springfield, situated a few minutes away from Bomber Command Headquarters and so within easy commuting distance. The house was big enough to accommodate the procession of guests that seemed to flow through in almost uninterrupted manner.

The Commander-in-Chief now seemed to be so much better in health, and I was stating the obvious when I told him that it would please his aircrews no end if he could spare a day on one of his air stations. His reply was that he would be delighted to do this. "The trouble, Pelly, is that if I leave my office for even half-a-day, when I get back the chances are that I will find that I have lost some of my squadrons to some other damned outfit that thinks it needs them more than I do. As it is, I am only just beginning to get the bomber force I need to carry out the job properly."

That evening after dinner the telephone buzzed by his armchair in the drawing room. When he picked it up and began to talk it was obvious that he was speaking to a very senior person. The one-sided conversation (to me) was all about his great reluctance to part with six Lancaster squadrons and he gave very cogent reasons, saying "Sir" every now and again. I sensed that he was holding his ground and when the conversation ended, he said "Good night, Sir" and hung up. He then looked at me and said, "That was Winston". With feigned casualness I said "What does he want?" The reply was "The damned sailors are at it again and through the back door this time. They are trying to get the PM to bully me. No luck though – as you heard." Now I appreciated just what he meant about never leaving his Headquarters except for a special need to go to the Air Ministry.

One night when he was speeding home from London in his Bentley along Western Avenue two police motorcycles raced past him and flagged him down. The conversation was something like this:

Police: "Good evening, Sir. I have stopped you because you are travelling much too fast. You might kill someone."
Harris: "I am on important business. Now that you mention it, it's my business to kill people; Germans".
Police: "Are you Air Marshal Harris, Sir?"
Harris nodded.
Police: "That's different sir! Sorry I stopped you. Please follow us".

The two motorcycles now set off at an exceedingly brisk pace, so much so that my hero could barely keep up. After telling the story, Bert Harris said with a grin, "It was the quickest trip I ever made; they must have liked me."

My weekend was splendid; it was just like being back again at the Villa Haroun AR Rashid in Jerusalem. One new acquisition in the house delighted him; a very large and handsome pewter dish with a high rounded cover and handle all fashioned in attractive style that he had picked up second-hand somewhere on his travels. As it was in poor condition he had asked Alfred Rose & Son, (the Gainsborough firm that was making Frazer Nash powered gun turrets) if it could be refurbished; a beautiful job resulted. "Typical of those chaps; ultra prompt and efficient service, as with their gun turrets". He then said "Lift up the lid and have a look". I did so, and sitting on the big oval dish was a very realistic baron of beef made of plaster of Paris. Dear Bert, he was tickled pink.

A nice surprise was to discover that Air Marshal Sir Robert Saundby Deputy C-in-C was staying regularly at Springfield. He was Harris' old friend from pre-war squadron days overseas and was a keen and expert fly-fisherman. He was so good in fact that during my stay he went off to catch a particular trout that had cunningly beaten him and other fishermen each season and so grew bigger and bigger. That evening he returned in triumph – he had hooked the biggest one. For the benefit of the reader who is an angler, what he did was to cast horizontally because the prey cunningly lived under a low overhanging tree and it was impossible therefore to cast a fly normally. Saundby cast so as to engage a leaf on a lower branch. He then pulled very gently so that the lure slowly tore through the leaf thus allowing the Greenwell's Glory to fall lightly onto the water just like the real thing. Success! The old rascal took it and the game was on. We were shown the five-pounder with its jaws curved like a nut-cracker, the sign of an old fish, and Jill said "Please don't ask me to cook it – its ugly and is probably tough too".

When my short leave was over I presented myself to Air Vice Marshal CR Carr, Air Officer Commanding No 4 Group. He was my new boss and one of his aerodromes was called RAF Holme-on-Spalding-Moor. This was to be my new appointment as the new Station Master and I smiled when I thought back to Raymond Collishaw and that 'Number two Platform' nonsense. Now it was my turn. No 4 Group Headquarters was based near the cathedral city of York, thus well located to control the dozen or so aerodromes within the 4 Group area. One encouraging thought was that the Senior Air Staff Officer at the Headquarters was Air Commodore Bill Brook and as usual he was working away like a beaver at his new appointment. We looked back on the Heliopolis days and laughed about that Pyramid climbing episode.

The important journey in my life now was to go to RAF Holme-on-Spalding-Moor. Travelling from York I motored along in the Lagonda taking the road towards Hull. About half way to the seaport there is as good an English semi-wilderness as one can find situated to the north of the river Humber. It is just a large flat plain that looks featureless and seems devoid of human habitation except Holme village, some hamlets, and the small town of Market Weighton. The area is drained by irrigation ditches and boasts a small river with the appropriate name of Foulness. This was where the RAF Works directorate thought fit to build a bomber base, the chief merit being that it was on level ground. It was certainly a very big change from the Royal Residence in London that had been my previous home, the very big house that subsequently my young son Jonathan one day jerked a casual thumb at when passing and told his hostess and other young friends that it used to be 'Daddy's old digs'!

The new digs, together with the rest of the 1500 acre site, comprised the home and work place of 3000 men and 500 women. It was of course a war-time constructed base and it's fair to say that it fulfilled admirably the purpose for which it was intended. Some RAF people were lucky to be housed in pre-war brick built buildings but on the other hand some unfortunates had to endure the rigors of wartime Nissen and Secco huts in addition to other prefabricated structures.

As I drove through the entrance gates of RAF Holme-on-Spalding-Moor, my emotions were a mixture of curiosity and a certain shyness at having to look the part of the new man-in-charge wearing 'scrambled-eggs' on his new Bates peaked cap; somehow it did not, in my mind's eye, match the thirty-two-year old face underneath. However, everybody – myself included – would darn well have to get used to it.

I made my way to Station Headquarters and met my predecessor, Air Commodore Hodgson. He had been promoted to become one of the new 'Base Commanders', the idea being to appoint an air commodore in charge of three adjacent bomber aerodromes on the notion that better control and coordination would result. I am very much against unnecessary links in a chain and I was never in favour of the idea; it frankly looked like what was called 'Empire building' or job creation. In my case, the personnel appointments people were so unimaginative as to leave the old CO physically still 'on the set' with the new man having the feeling that he was continually being watched. This in fact is what happened; frequently he used to ask why I did something or other in a different way and what was wrong with the old method? This awkward situation was exacerbated I have to say frankly because he was noticeably older than myself. Furthermore, with the greatest respect, it was very clear that he was a bit out-of-date in his attitudes and to cap it all he was no longer a practising pilot. I bewailed my departure from 2 Group with Basil Embry leading from the front. Here, at first sighting, I began to have qualms about my new appointment. Thank heaven the commanding officer of No 76 Squadron, the bomber unit based on Holme-on-Spalding-Moor, allayed my fears. He was a robust and colourful personality richly endowed with gongs and a flowing moustache; his name was Wing Commander Hank Iveson, DSO, DFC, and like David Young at Rufforth he was a legendary figure in Bomber Command. With a good Yorkshire background, he was direct, competent, and friendly. He well knew the bomber business and with such with a man as he I felt much happier. Hank Iveson continues to leave his imprint on the Royal Air Force. His son – inevitably also called 'Hank' – was the Squadron Commander 'Harrier' pilot of the famous No 1 Squadron who returned to fight again in the Falklands war after being so unfortunate as to allow himself to be shot down by an Argentine gunner. Oh well – just the luck of the business!

The meeting with such a man distinguished for his wartime exploits was a pointer to the way that Hitler unwittingly was doing the Royal Air Force a very good turn in a way that he could never have forecast and it most certainly produced dividends. The outbreak of WWII brought the inevitable rapid expansion of the armed forces and naturally those like myself who were pre-war regulars were lifted up on an accelerating crest of promotion. One of the direct results of this was that a large number of middle-rank officers who were still in touch with practical operational flying moved up to fill the tip of the promotion pyramid and this inevitably brought a breath of fresh air – and fresh ideas – into the higher echelons of power. The pre-war convention that staff officers were almost a breed unto themselves and only occasionally to be seen on special occasions began to change very much for the better, thank goodness. Whereas in the past the majority of the people of Air Commodore rank and above rarely got into a cockpit to practise what they told pilots to do (and had they done so would have discovered for themselves what goes on at the sharp end and the merit or otherwise of the equipment provided for the job) now at last the office chairs were being filled with younger men who spoke with personal experience and conviction.

The new look produced a new generation of air marshals with practical experience and dynamism; men in my experience like Paddy Bandon, Basil

Embry, Gus Walker, Fred Rosier, Bing Cross, the charismatic Atcherley brothers, Hughie Edwards, Peter Wykeham-Barnes, and Sam Elworthy, all beat the odds and survived to inject fresh blood into the RAF. At last the new leaders were practising fliers who directed, rather than directors who were not. The process even produced the healthy situation when, for example, Basil Embry as an Air Chief Marshal continued to fly and woe betide anybody on his staff who did not make regular entries of modern aircraft in his pilot's log book. The process was even more significant because new military aeroplanes had become much more complex – and considerably more expensive in the process – so that the new generation of Air Marshals not only changed the whole system, they did so with considerably more to cope with than their predecessors who frankly had the simplest of aeroplanes to fly and even then fought shy of doing so.

A full description of Holme-on-Spalding-Moor would take too long to relate as it was effectively a small town in size and the Station was big enough to house the three thousand five hundred personnel whose appointments were roughly split into four parts. First of all there was No 76 Squadron, complete with its aircrew, ground crew, hangars, and administrative offices. Secondly there was a maintenance and repair organisation catering for the three aerodromes in the locality. Thirdly there was a Fighter Affiliation Squadron with Spitfires and Hurricanes, the job being to 'play bomber-versus-enemy fighter' for the bomber crews, and these aeroplanes were good news for me. Finally there was the Administration organisation providing accommodation, catering, and technical facilities like the Control Tower, a parachute section, fire services, intelligence, operations and many others.

It was the Station Commander's job to provide the platform from which a war machine of this size could operate efficiently. With my policy of allowing senior men in each unit (and very particularly the Squadron Commander) free to get on with everything as they saw fit, I became a co-ordinator rather than an interfering boss. I always liked the navy way of saying 'I propose to' as opposed to 'May I have permission to'; it gives each man in charge of his part of the organisation a sense of independent responsibility. With the right people in the jobs it works like a charm and if there is a dud somewhere, sooner rather than later he is found out and away he goes.

As the days went by, apart from the necessary office work suitable to a small town, I spent a good part of my time regularly 'going around the shop'. This was not to adopt the suspicious attitude of looking for trouble; far from it. It was designed to do my best to see that we were all working as a team under the best possible conditions. One facet that I was particularly keen to give top priority to was the airmens' catering organisation. The airmens cook-house by definition was big, very big, and soon after arriving I walked into the establishment at about midday. The staff seemed mildly astonished and I told the Officer in charge to muster as many of them as possible; I was now facing a lot of cooks and kitchen hands and nearly all of them were girls plus a few older women. I told them that any notion that they may have had about doing an unimportant job was just not true. I went on: "Now listen girls, I can tell you that if you stop cooking – or even cook badly – well, the danger is that the boys may stop flying, the aeroplanes don't get looked after properly, and our part in the war suffers. Your job is vital, I promise you. Try and cook just like your mother cooks for you at home and the lads will love you forever!" The smiles and giggles that came my way were wonderful, particularly from one little honey that I could have made off with pronto! Dammit, I wished for a moment that I had been a corporal in the airmens cookhouse.

The Station was geared to a twenty-four hour working day with the darkness period taking operational priority. The more I observed the whole cycle of squadron activity from crew briefing, right through to take off, return, and de-briefing, the more I realised what a very long, tough, uncomfortable, and damned dangerous business it was. There always seemed to be something singularly lethal and nasty about night bomber ops. Worst of all was the fact that each loss – and god knows it happened time and time again – was not just one chap in a Spitfire or three in a Boston; this time it was seven young men per bomber. For the public's benefit, Bomber Command's operations in the daily papers was a necessary and routine press hand-out. The message only gets home if you are on the balcony of the control tower and thus close to the action. At 22.00 hrs. for example, 76 Squadron might despatch twenty three Halifaxes and the crews included young men from Norway, Poland, Australia, New Zealand and Canada. All being well, and no snags, they all disappear into the night. The sortie is expected to take, say, five hours. After the departures, if there is nothing else for me to do I leave the tower and go elsewhere. Sometimes there is time and opportunity to go to bed; sometimes – especially if a problem develops – you stay and make yourself available to do whatever is required.

After about four to five hours there is an expectation to hear by radio from some of the aircraft recrossing our coastline. The control tower now begins to count them in and the clock goes on ticking away. Then there's news from the first, the second and so on. By 0300 hrs. we have recorded maybe nineteen out of twenty three Halifaxes. By 0600 hrs we reckon that unless they have landed away, that's our lot. Finally there is one more accounted for – down safely at Woodbridge, the long-runway emergency bolt-hole in Suffolk. By dawn three Halifaxes are not accounted for. They are certainly down somewhere in Europe or in the sea. Well, that's twenty-one young airmen missing, and there is nothing that we can do about it. Three or four days later the whole dreadful business happens all over again and it has been going on for four years at countless bomber stations all over Yorkshire, Lincolnshire and East Anglia. There are no emotional scenes, no tears; at least not in public anyway. Just a bit of silence and a soft-spoken sympathetic comment; that's all. Tomorrow is yet another day.

With hindsight one or two facets of the whole night bomber offensive became clear – particularly in the light of post-war publications where so often the armchair author has deemed it his prerogative to denigrate it to some degree. The first thought that I had was the realisation that for all practical purposes Bomber Command consisted of hundreds of one-aeroplane Air Forces. As each one took off and flew away into the night it became in fact a seven-man bomber free to go as it pleased and in no way could anybody effectively control its destiny. All the greater credit therefore to the crews, all of them keeping to a pre-planned sortie if at all possible. No other military organisation before has ever tried to operate continuously in anything like the same way or in such numbers. By contrast, day-flying aircraft can be said to be at least visually controlled, certainly when flying together as a squadron.

The second thought was that every single wartime aircrew without exception was a volunteer. Why they opted to go flying by night over hostile Germany still mystifies me. More remarkable still is that the great majority were all basically civilians and they had to learn skills in a few months that, for example, I took ten years to acquire. On top of that those new skills were very much more complex than mine had been.

Now comes the post-war nonsense that 'Bomber Command never hit the target' so it was all a waste of time and effort. In this context I would like to draw the reader's attention to making a fair guess about the countless bullets, shells, mortars, rockets, torpedoes and heaven knows what else that soldiers and sailors have loosed off in war to no purpose whatever. It seems that they are allowed a huge 'miss factor' but airmen must never fail in this regard. To pursue the subject and dissect even the RAF itself, how many thousands of rounds per fighter pilot were used up for each German shot down? The reality is that military people of all the services are human; they all do their best with their weapons but for a variety of reasons they miss the target a lot of the time. Airmen are no exception to the age-old rule, so let the critics please be more balanced in their judgements.

To support the constant flying by the Halifaxes and the fighter affiliation aircraft, the commanding officer's job was not unlike that of a farmer or property owner. It was necessary to get around the estate regularly to see if all was well. Soon after my arrival, in order to find out what I had inherited I took the Station Works Officer around with me. It should be explained that 76 Squadron's Halifaxes had moved to Holme a few months earlier, replacing Lancasters that had left for another base. The main runway was of course the chief focus of my attention. One of the weaknesses of an aerodrome – airfield is the word used in modern times – is that an unserviceable runway means no flying; just like that.

After getting clearance from the tower we began at the eastern boundary and motored slowly and steadily to the other end, a distance from memory of 2,300 yards. Driving down a fifty yard wide runway makes you appreciate how big and expensive they are. Lay all the Bomber Command runways end-to-end and you would have a six-lane motorway stretching from London to Cairo! When we got to the end of the runway and were facing the overshoot area that gives a small safety factor during landing runs I could see beyond some kind of a dark line running across and my companion told me that it was one of the principal drainage ditches of the flat plain. Although it was a hundred yards or more beyond the aerodrome boundary I was curious enough to have a look. When we got there the ditch proved to be all of fifteen feet wide and it was half full of slow-moving water. As I gazed in astonishment at it my first reaction was that it was a number one 'black spot' as we say today. Turning to my Clerk of Works I asked him if he knew of any aeroplanes that had overrun, for any reason, and ended up in the ditch. "Yes", he replied, "A total of seventeen Lancasters returning from operations with no brakes or flaps". Dear God! Every one of them had been a write off. The works man said that it had been reported each time to his HQ but nothing was done because the ditch was not Works Directorate property!

The time had come to act immediately and abandon all that letter-writing or telephoning business. With the support of Wing Commander Wally Herbert, Senior Engineer Officer, a team of his men rolled a dozen or so of those very big concrete rings into the ditch, joined them up together and then shovelled in a vast amount of hard core before levelling up with gravel and earth on top. When finished it looked a nice professional job and we tested it with a fire tender (which one day or night might well have to cross over in earnest) and that was that.

A few days later I received a telephone call from the Superintendent of Works Directorate embracing the whole of Eastern England from Yorkshire to East Anglia. He was of equivalent rank to Air Vice Marshal and he was angry. "On whose authority", the pompous voice said, "did you have some work done by your airmen on the irrigation ditch beyond the end of the main runway?" Aha, so the grape-vine was faster than letter-writing Good! "Sir", I replied, "I have to tell you that this matter had to be dealt with immediately. Many letters have been sent to your department in the past, but to no avail, and the result of your criminal inactivity is that the C-in-C has quite needlessly lost seventeen Lancasters." The idiot man continued to vent his displeasure, saying that he would report me to Bomber Command. This was too much and I interrupted him. "May I ask, sir, on whose side you are – Harris or Hitler?" There was no reply. In later years I told Bert Harris about it and he commented that had he known at the time he would have sacked the bloody man personally. The aftermath of the decision to cover over the ditch produced a justification literally within days. A Halifax with no brakes or flaps landed safely, ran off the runway, crossed over 'our bridge', and stopped in the field beyond.

In mid-August 'Hank' Iveson was posted to a rest job with 1669 Heavy Conversion Unit and his place as CO No 76 Squadron was taken by Wing Commander RK Cassels, AFC. Another newcomer was Squadron Leader John Crampton, AFC. Both had previously been on flying training duties and now they had joined the heavy bomber business. A third stalwart was Squadron Leader Max Freeman and the fourth member of the 'top four' was Squadron Leader RG West from Canada. It is very satisfying to record that Ralph Cassels, John Crampton and I are still in touch with each other, particularly so John as he and I have an abiding interest of many years standing with radio-controlled model aircraft. Our long association started in the control tower at Holme-on-Spalding-Moor. The new officer commanding 'B' Flight had arrived to witness a squadron take-off and Ralph Cassels introduced the extremely tall officer to me.

Soon after John had arrived at Holme I got wind that he had brought a powered model aeroplane with him and when I saw him again I asked him if the information was true. Poor fellow, not knowing that I was also an aero-modeller, he began to apologise for bringing it onto the station. When he confirmed that it was serviceable, I suggested that he went to get it from his quarters and fly it that afternoon. There seemed a marked silence from the lads, then somebody said "Sir, what about the war?" My reply was brief; "Damn the war, let's have some fun for a change. The war has stopped for one hour". The party then moved into the middle of the aerodrome, John got the model set up with engine running sweetly and it took off from the grass in style.

Four memorable happenings at Holme are worth recording. Three of them did not cause any loss of personnel; the fourth one was tragic. During a 76 Squadron take-off on yet another attack on the Third Reich, (which happened to be in daylight), a Halifax loaded with sixteen 1000 lb bombs began to swing violently when well down the runway. The pilot Warrant Officer Holmes attempted to correct, only to get into more trouble. We then saw the Halifax lift a wing, swing yet more violently and then collapse in a thunderous heap right in front of the tower. As it did so the fire and rescue services promptly swung into action but as my Lagonda was readily available I got there first just as the big bomber began to burn. I counted six aircrew escaping out of the wreck and waited for the seventh man. As he did not show there was no option but to get in and look for him and I found the young air-gunner rummaging around inside in a dazed fashion. I shouted at him to get our pronto; he nodded and said "I've lost me glove, sir!" We now had to disperse the rest of the Halifaxes on the perimeter track waiting for take-off as they were much too close to the burning wreck and it proved more difficult to do than I had imagined. Whilst this was being done I returned to the tower and using the 'Tannoy' public address system told hundreds of spectators to disperse well away from the aerodrome and damn quick too. All the windows in the tower were opened fully and I took cover, not knowing quite what to do next. The reality was that nothing could be done and as the lads manning the fire engines could no longer cope they withdrew to a safe distance just before the first and biggest of the explosions took place. By a strange trick of blast effect I found myself in total darkness and when I recovered my composure I found that the blast had opened the external door of a broom cupboard, sucked me inside, and the door had then blown shut again. The Station Commander emerged looking startled, dishevelled and covered in dust. That unfortunate Halifax continued to burn for hours with bombs exploding intermittently and eventually there was a hole in the runway big enough to accommodate a London bus. It was not our day.

On another occasion, one night a telephone call came to the tower from one of the dispersal points and the Flight Sergeant said that a Polish captain of aircraft had refused to join the others taxying out for take-off. As neither Ralph Cassels or any of his Flight Commanders were readily available (they were probably flying), I drove round to the far side of the aerodrome to the dispersal point. In the dark I identified the Captain if only by his limited English. "What's the problem?" I asked him. He said he was not going to Germany because one of his 1000 lb bombs had fallen out of the bomb bay. "Well then, that's only one out of sixteen", I told him. "Sir," that splendid Pole said, "When I go to Germany I take every bomb; every bloody bomb". I was able to pacify him by organising a rush job by the armourers who replaced the bomb and then told the gallant Pole that as he would be late on the flight plan he would have to make up time by speeding up as best he could. He thanked me, shook my hand warmly, and away he went. What a fine fellow he was. He got back to fly another day and he thanked me all over again.

The third episode happened not over Germany but right in front of us as we observed the return of the squadron from yet another raid over enemy territory. Sometime in the small hours the Air Traffic Control Officer was recording the return of aircraft by placing small discs on a blackboard, each disc showing the identity letter of the particular Halifax. How I hated that board; nearly every time after an operation one or more discs were absent; it was the devil's harbinger of bad news. After a number of Halifaxes had booked in and then landed, the voice of Sq Ldr RG West, RCAF, came through the speaker. Good! 'A' Apple had come back. He was given 'Turn number two to land' whereupon he started the upwind leg before going all the way round for his final circuit and landing. From the balcony I watched his red port light go past followed by the white tail light. The white light now began to descend steadily and it continued to do so all the way from

800 feet, down and down. I shouted to the control officer, Flt Lt Joseph, that a crash was imminent. Then somewhere beyond the aerodrome there was a huge flash followed by that awful noise of rending metal. After giving some instructions I sped off in the direction of the fire, realising that the chances of rescue were virtually nil but I had to go. I found a route across the fields but the Halifax was burning even more furiously so nothing could be done. Those boys were too low to bail out so all of them had perished and I stood there silently on the verge of tears. This was the first fatal Halifax crash that I had witnessed and with a grand-stand view the impact on my emotions was profound. Poor fellows, they had returned all the way back from Germany only to be killed within moments of landing. Whilst I stood watching I noticed that the propellor of the port inner engine was missing and perhaps that was a clue to the cause of the crash.

Early in the morning after two hours sleep I took off in the 'Oxford' to look for the missing propellor. No luck at all. So I returned and handed over to another pilot to continue the search as I was probably not at my best and a fresh pair of eyes might be better. The prop was found about a mile away and was brought in. I then returned by car to the smouldering wreck on the off chance that I might find another clue to the mystery of the accident and by some extraordinary luck I found the Flight Engineer's log that had escaped the fire. The final entry on the crumpled sheet was a cryptic 'Feather port inner'. I contacted the RAF Accident Investigation Branch and asked for one of their specialists to come up to Holme to make an official report on the crash. This was particularly important because unexplained crashes, especially if nothing unusual pointed to the cause, were bad for the morale of the other pilots. A civilian arrived and Wally Herbert met him off the train at York but when the man discovered that the Halifax had been on an operational sortie he declared that it was outside his terms of reference. He refused to listen to reason so we put him on the train back to London and it fell to Wally and I to do the job ourselves. Thanks to that excellent engineer officer we traced the cause of the crash. It started initially by flak and a small leak in an oil pipe which began to empty the tank which explained why the flight engineer's log showed that the engine was slowly losing oil pressure and increasing the oil temperature. The constant-speed Hamilton propellor unit has a high pressure oil pump that delivers 400 p.s.i. to operate the system. All was well after a fashion until the feathering button was pressed. If that was done, rather than deliver high-pressure oil the reverse happened and the propellor blades would move quickly into fine pitch. With so little oil available and the engine now overspeeding, the reduction gear system seized up and it caused the prop to fly off and it killed the captain; at low altitude the crew had no choice but to wait for the inevitable crash. It was a quite dreadful and horrifying affair to contemplate.

Now that Wally and I had diagnosed the sequence of events leading to the crash we sat down and wrote our report. The essence of the last paragraph was that we had been obliged to do all the work ourselves and we recommended that in future all that was wanted was for each Constant Speed Unit (CSU) to have its own separate oil pressure gauge; this would tell the captain whether it was safe to feather the propellor or alternatively leave well alone. The reply that came back from Bomber Command said that the case had been put to Air Ministry and the answer was 'Regret no action possible'; the reason given was that the proposed modification could not be introduced because it would affect Halifax production! I was sorry in a way that 76 Squadron (and other Halifax squadrons) were not equipped with American aeroplanes because as with the Bostons nothing was too much trouble for American manufacturers who got cracking right away and carried out soundly-based modifications without debating the issues.

The fourth episode was a very curious affair. After a daylight attack on Walcheren Island (on the Dutch coast) that housed German coastal defences the returning Halifaxes were joining the aerodrome circuit prior to landing and I was puzzled to see a protruberance that was sticking out of the fuselage of Halifax MP-K flown by Flight Sergeant Whittaker. A sighting with binoculars confirmed that there really was quite a large 'thing' attached to the port side just ahead of the tail plane and the controller called the Captain to ask what it was. The reply came back "I think we must have had a collision with another aircraft and a bit of the other machine must have stuck in our fuselage". The Captain said that the Halifax was flying well enough but the controls to the elevators were rather stiff. I advised him to climb to a safe height, lower the landing gear and flaps, and see if the Halifax was controllable; sometimes there is a world of difference between a 'clean' aeroplane and one in the landing configuration after a technical problem arises. In the event all was well and K-King came down and landed safely. As she taxied in it was the oddest sight to see a very large piece of what undoubtedly was a Lancaster wing embedded in the Halifax; it had broken off clean like snapping a carrot. It took three or four lads to remove the thing because it was so big and it had forced its way between the tubular elevator controls that Handley Page aircraft used. Everybody looked at it, grinned, and that was that. It was another lucky escape.

When I returned to my office I was anxious to find out what had happened to the Lancaster and with the help of the Operation Order I began to telephone to all bomber stations whose squadrons were engaged in the Walcheren attack. To begin with no luck at all, but after perhaps the fifth try of repeating my question to the Station Commander (from memory) at RAF Coningsby, my opposite number expressed great surprise; "How the devil did you know?" The answer to his question was easy; "I've got the missing bit, old boy! It was stuck in the fuselage of one of the

76 Squadron Halifaxes." I added, "I would post it back to you but it's too damned big."

As the weeks passed 76 Squadron pressed on and the intensity increased as the night bomber forces were given more and more work to do. The effect was made much more telling because we were now using greatly improved navigation and target identification aids and more and more heavy bombers in concentrated effort were swamping the defences. Equally, the American Eighth Air Force was also operating with massive daylight formations, so the two bomber fleets now operated in effect a twenty-four hour delivery service. A thought now occurred to me that we were reaching the stage when with a high degree of air superiority Bomber Command might also operate in daylight. With that in mind I suggested to Ralph Cassels that it would be wise to train his pilots to fly by day in company with each other rather than continue with the old 'one aeroplane' bomber system. (The navigators never looked outside; they drew their curtains because they said it was too frightening to look!) My suggestion was accepted and his pilots (who liked the idea) practised flying in loose formation, thus getting good cross-cover fire for the gunners, and the lead aircraft did the master navigating. Air Vice Marshal Carr must have heard what was happening because he summoned me to his office and gave me one helluva big rocket. He ended by saying that if this heresy continued he would sack me because Bomber Command would never operate in daylight. Once again I sensed the old failing in some senior men of possessing no imagination and therefore no flexibility. He completely refused to listen to my reasoned argument, so that was that. Within a few weeks the news filtered through from Bomber Command that we had to be prepared to operate in daylight, but still using the 'one aeroplane' method of getting to targets. Navigators I presumed would therefore continue to keep their curtains drawn. It was doing the right thing but in quite the wrong way. Not one word of apology from my AOC and frankly I did not expect it or want it, but he knew that I was right. When I saw later on for myself how the daylight operations to the night formula worked out in practise it was abundantly clear how wrong the new system was. The highly decorated Air Commodore Gus Walker (later to become an Air Chief Marshal) had now become the SASO at 4 Group and I sensed that he agreed with my views. Air Commodore Tommy Thomson, DSO, DFC, was now the Base Commander and that was also very good news as he and I saw eye-to-eye.

Bomber Command's new twenty-four-hour-service was now in full spate and the operations could now be timed to suit whatever the requirement prescribed. A number of short trips to French targets came the way of 76 Squadron – "just a quick boy's run" the lads used to say, "almost a shame to take the money!" – and it was clear that we were getting close to D-Day, the Allied assault on occupied Europe. After one night attack on the French railway system some of the lynx-eyed aircrew spotted lots of small moving objects in the English Channel as the Halifaxes made their way back to Yorkshire and at the debriefing we did not know what was afoot; perhaps the Royal Navy was on some kind of an operation? By the time that the last Halifax was safely back I went to my two-room bungalow, asked the operator to call me at 07.45 hrs. and fell into bed. The time was 0530 hrs.

Promptly on time the telephone rang and woke me up. It was another day. I made myself a cup of coffee and switched on the BBC radio to listen to the eight o'clock news. It was June the sixth 1944. Immediately after the time pips the announcer said "This-is-BBC London. This-is – D-Day". I cannot begin to describe my utter excitement, and coupled to that I clearly remember calling out "Christ! I bloody well wasn't told either!" Here was I in command of a bomber station that was actually participating at the time that the first lot of Commandos had set foot on the beaches and I knew nothing about it at all. My second reaction was that the security factor was well and truly in force and there was really no need for me to have known anyway. It was better that way. So I dressed quickly and set off to have breakfast and talked animatedly with Ralph Cassels, 'The Colonel' Pop Bligh (the squadron Intelligence officer who was such a splendid old warrior to give the boys the will to win), and many others. The huge allied forces had now got going and we could support them in our fashion to the hilt. The entire station was electrified with the good news. It was, at long last, the beginning of the end as Winston Churchill said.

Operation Orders and their execution flowed in quick succession and as so many of the sorties were of short duration a quick turn-round of aircraft was making us a Tactical Air Force playing the 'cab-rank' game. The new requirement of constant daytime operations in addition to night ops. necessitated a reshuffle of the day-to-day programme. A twenty-four hour shift system was instituted and the station took on the mantle of the Joe Lyons Corner House Restaurant in Oxford Street; 'we never closed'. Stout-hearted people like Sq Ldr 'Timber' Wood on the engineering side, Sq Ldr Frank Jones and Flt Lt Ted Ingram in Station Headquarters, and of course the ever willing catering girls seemed to take everything in their stride. I continued to be impressed with the way that so many facets of essential work in all the many buildings, huts, hangars, and out in the open seemed to work so smoothly and harmoniously. One factor that made the accelerated work-load that much easier – particularly so for the outdoor men doing miracles of engineering work sometimes in appalling weather – was that it was now summer-time. It was warmer, dryer, and we had a long daylight day that made the workload much smoother and more effective. The skylarks sang joyously as they hovered in the clear blue sky above and we pressed on in unison.

The daylight operations interested me most of all because it was my scene and as an old hand on Wellesleys and Bostons I was keen to see how the night bomber formula – the 'one aeroplane' game – was working out. It was now possible to get a daylight sighting of the theoretical 'bomber stream' designed to keep the force together and concentrate attacks in the minimum time. Admittedly the Pathfinder force was now putting down flares en route and at targets but this did not necessarily produce the 'swarm of bees' formula that Bomber Command had devised. Interestingly enough Bomber Harris had told me that the night collision-risk factor had been worked out by his boffin's at one in ten thousand – which he found acceptable – and the closer knit his force was in time and air space the fewer the chances were of being shot down. He agreed with me that by night, with the earlier navigation aids (that were a bit sketchy to say the least), an accurate swarm flown by captains and navigators with wartime air experience only was not at all easy. In 1944 things were very different and I decided to see for myself despite the Harris Rule that Station Commanders were forbidden to fly on operations. I was lucky because Ralph Cassels became a conspirator; a 'wink-and-a-nod' and off I would go more than once on a clandestine expedition. There were two side-effects to this activity. The first was that each time that I gave Ralph the nod (timing it as I thought to a nicety), by some magic bush-telegraph it was quite apparent that within minutes an entire Station was in on the deal too. The smiling salutes were proof enough – especially from my wonderful WAAFs. I felt like John Wayne. The second was that once committed I was frightened out of my wits; it was the old business again of telling oneself to go. Apart from wanting to see for myself, one very redeeming feature was that the decision to participate seemed to electrify so many people, particularly the aircrew. I had joined the club and I was now a proper chap. I told John Crampton's crew that I only went along with them to provide the chocolate bars and glucose sweets, so I paid my fare and they approved.

The truth inevitably showed once we got into the bomber stream. I almost hesitate to say so but the 'swarm of bees' formula now seen clearly in daylight but using the night bomber navigation 'one aeroplane' plan was abysmal. On one very long sortie to Beyrouth with John Crampton in RG 613, MP – 'Q' Queenie, somewhere over Central Germany as far as the eye could see there were Lancasters and Halifaxes spread out so very far apart that some aircraft to port and starboards were almost out of sight. They were just dots on the horizon and no doubt each navigator was probably saying "Spot on, skipper!" Well, a helluva lot of heavy bombers were nowhere near where they were supposed to be. As I said to John "Thank God 76 is flying in company; enemy fighters would make a meal of all those aircraft out on the flanks". It would have been a massacre, but the virtual absence of the Luftwaffe that day made survival possible for dozens of heavy bombers. Even the flak, 'walk-on' stuff that it was, seemed to be missing us, I'm glad to say.

By contrast, when *en route* to our target we had an excellent and all-too-close view of a contra-flow massive Armada of Flying Fortresses above us returning to their bases in East Anglia. The American Eighth Air Force in all its impressive grandeur was flying in excellent formation, stepped up in layers, and by so doing were a formidable opponent to take on by the Luftwaffe had they been in the air to attack the Fortresses. I commented to John that this was the only way to fly heavy bombers in daylight over enemy territory, and he and his crew saw the evidence in a dramatic form. All the same it has to be said that the Americans suffered heavy losses in earlier months until the famed P.5 Mustang long-range fighters with Rolls Royce 'Merlin' engines were available to escort the Fortresses over Europe. Air warfare is a constant battle to keep ahead of the opposition and new tactics have to be introduced again and again.

The days passed. Ralph Cassels and John Crampton were awarded DFCs. Ralph went off to Staff College and was succeeded by Wg Cdr 'Chick' Whyte, DFC. By the autumn the new plan of reducing the bomber force included 76 Squadron exchanging their Halifaxes for the famous Dakota. Our SASO, the irrepressible and highly decorated one-armed Gus Walker was as energetic as ever. All along he had been the spearhead of organising bomber operations, using his experience and that certain charisma to encourage us all; now he was just as enthusiastic about the new air transport business.

Now that I belonged to Transport Command I was summoned one day to the headquarters at Bushey Park and I was told that they needed me to go to Australia to command the only Royal Air Force Station in that continent. It was of course a Dakota base and the prospect pleased. Whilst discussing the posting with the Air Marshal I asked him where in Australia RAF Station Camden was. He looked at me quite blandly and said "You know, Pelly, I haven't the faintest idea; ask when you get there!" My next question was "Is there anything in particular, Sir, that I should know about the posting?" Once again, that bland smile. "Just one thing, dear boy. Please remember that in Australia a bison is not, as you might suppose, a wild animal."

Before the Dakotas arrived Ralph Cassels took me and six others on a conducted tour in daylight of the Ruhr Valley in Halifax VI – RG 584. It was one of many flights that Bomber Command had allowed squadrons to carry out (in addition to the great food-dropping operations for the starving Dutch people) so that we could see for ourselves what had happened to one of the principle industrial regions of Germany.

The sight that we could see from a hitherto lethal height of around four thousand feet was simply staggering. Almost the entire length and breadth of the area seemed to consist of heaps of rubble and it was as close to complete devastation as one could imagine. Now at last we could see the extent that over four years of hammering had inflicted upon virtually every man-made structure that Hitler's Third Reich had relied upon for the Nazi prosecution of the war. Admittedly there were thousands of bomb craters in adjoining open country but that was the price of human failings. Just like the soldiers and sailors, airmen were not infallible men. They had plenty of misses, but by thunder they had one helluva lot of hits! The bomber force, consisting mainly of all those civilian wartime volunteers with so little time in which to get experience had not done so badly at all. All those young clerks, students, farm hands, office boys, apprentices, perhaps even budding churchmen, all had done a magnificent job. The proof was there to see.

As we made our way back to Yorkshire it was a very strange and unreal sensation to realise that for the first time in years we were not being set upon by nasty little aeroplanes with black crosses on them; and for that matter no longer was there all that stuff called flak bursting everywhere. It seemed almost too good to be true and it certainly made a very nice change. On the way home we flew low over Rotterdam and saw that a lot of the city and most of the dock area had been similarly devastated. This time, however it was the Luftwaffe's attentions that had caused it; air warfare cuts both ways.

Perhaps the most telling comment about the post-war debate on the effectiveness of the heavy bomber offensive arose one day when Bomber Harris was approached by one of those gentlemen of the press forever seeking controversial issues so dear to their hearts. In answer to the inevitable "What do you think now, Air Marshal?" The reply was as brief as one would expect, "Don't ask me – ask the Germans."

Chapter XX

A Long Way to Go

The travel requirement to go to Australia included some investigation into the possibility of getting there on a do-it-yourself formula. Any journey, and particularly a long one, usually entails some research into the best way of travelling under the most agreeable conditions. For me, cost was not a factor; it was a posting prescribed by the Royal Air Force to get an airman from one job to another and the manner of going was normally influenced by the stature of the individual. Even so, very senior personnel do not necessarily get five-star treatment. Bomber Harris used to chuckle over the Air Ministry-cum-Treasury edict that he and his aircraft purchasing commission team could not cross the Atlantic by first class sea passage even though they were going to buy American aircraft with orders worth many millions of dollars. It was only when he suggested that the eminent industrialist Sir James Weir, a team member, would be happy to pay his own way and accept a suitable retainer that the message got across. How much, the Treasury asked, would Sir James accept? His answer was "Well, he might be persuaded to consider, say, a fee of £250 per day". The team travelled 1st Class.

In my case I wanted to be able to go under my own steam to Australia and the 'steam' was a wish to fly a Mosquito as far along the route as possible. I had heard of the large numbers of delivery flights that Ferry Command had been carrying out to overseas Commands, and for my particular purpose it was No 44 Group that organised them to the Middle East, India, and beyond. I telephoned to the Group Headquarters and I spoke to the Senior Air Staff officer who by good fortune seemed to know me; so that was a useful start. The bad news was that he said that the Group had a rule not to take on free-lance men like myself because experience had shown that we were not trained for the job and too often did not deliver aircraft at the right time or even to the right place. It took some persuading on my part to convince him that I was a good guy. I also reminded him of Douglas Bader's dictum that 'rules are made to be obeyed by the stupid but interpreted by the intelligent'. Furthermore, was it not true that Group Captain John Cunningham was about to ferry a Mosquito to India? He agreed to my proposal. Having now got assent in principle, the next job to do was to plan the operation. I managed to track down Jock Cairns (my navigator from the Boston days) who was now doing a job as Air Traffic Controller at RAF Hendon. He agreed to come with me – in fact he was delighted. I then had to arrange to get him released for the trip on the ploy that it was good experience in his new trade and I telephoned again to 44 Group and told my SASO friend that I was crewed up with a very experienced navigator who had two tours of wartime flying to his credit. The first step was to go to RAF Middleton-St. George in Northumberland to become familiar with Mosquitoes; after that we would collect a new Mosquito Mk VI and carry out the standard test flying for fuel consumption, general handling, radio equipment, etc before the delivery flight. I have to admit that the whole ferry business was much more thorough and well-planned than I expected. Like other branches of the Royal Air Force, Ferry Command was an efficient organisation.

In July 1945 Jock and I arrived at RAF Middleton-St George. It was a nice pre-war Station and was an Operational Conversion Unit. There were a number of Beaufighters with 'Merlin' engines on the airfield and it would have been nice to add one of those to the list of types in my log book; but it was not to be. In the event we were sent to RAF Croft, a nearby satellite aerodrome to Middleton, there to be initiated into the expertise of flying Mosquitoes. Although I had made one or two trips in them previously, the twelve-hour flying course proved to be invaluable. There was no question in my mind but that it was a superb aeroplane to fly but it did have some naughty habits on take-off and landing. My 2 Group Mossie pilot friends like Sq Ldr Charles Patterson disagreed; they said that I was maligning the best aircraft in the world. For all that, as my young instructor said at Croft "Please remember, Sir, that you have not stopped flying a Mosquito until you are walking away from it". After the flying at Croft the next move was to the airfield near Melton Mowbray where those wonderful Saxby pork pies come from. This was the location where the crews were introduced to the particular Mosquito that had to be delivered on time, in one piece, and to the appointed destination. It was a hive of activity. We booked-in, our temporary accommodation was organised, and we were fed into the system. We were now part of the Ferry Pilots' Union.

When Jock and I went to have a look at the particular Mosquito that was allocated to us we saw a beautiful Mk-VI Fighter-Bomber version that had been constructed by Standard Motors at Coventry and in its peacetime silver colour it really looked magnificent. Fancy!, a private Mosquito to test-fly for ten hours in order to satisfy ourselves that it was fit for flying away on a long trip to India. Apart from the attractive silver colour, externally the obvious change from the trainer version was the sight of those paddle-bladed propellors designed to absorb the increased power of the later type Rolls Royce 'Merlin' engines. Jock and I climbed into the Mossie and tried it out for size. It fitted beautifully.

The first attempt at take-off I have to confess was quite alarming. A dreaded swing to Port developed in the early stages causing the aircraft to leave the runway and take to the grass. It was not a good start. As I was about to call the tower and tell them what must have been pretty obvious, the Wing Commander Flying (who fortunately was there) told me to try again but this time to open the throttles slowly until I got effective rudder control. The second attempt, this time with a double check on the power being used, told me all. Compared to the Mk-III Trainer we were getting considerably more power in the early stages of throttle movement. With the Mk-VI you only had to open the taps a small amount before Plus 10 lb supercharger boost (full power was an impressive 24 lb.) showed on the dials. This time we made a smooth and straight run 'down the dotted line' and away we went. It was one of those small points of pilotage so essential to know about between one breed of Mosquito and another and I was sorry that this had not been explained to me beforehand. The Mosquito Squadron pilots of course used the trick of opening up the port engine first and then 'following up' with the starboard throttle to balance the reverse swing tendency. However, this was a refinement of pilotage that needs practise after you are well familiar with the type. Upon touchdown there was also a tendency to swing but this was not so much the wrong application of power as the simple fact that the Mosquito has insufficient vertical fin and rudder area to keep it straight on the runway at (say) less than fifty knots. Thus you have to watch like a hawk and correct a swing immediately any whisper of one develops. Although I am very fond of the many de Havilland types that I have flown, I think that most of the 'tail down' varieties suffer from lack of rudder response below take-off speed. Many pilots I believe will agree with this and there must be some validity in it because even de Havillands themselves have been obliged occasionally to increase the size of the rudder or fin area in the light of test flying. The DH 86B is a case in point when additional fins were added outboard of the tailplane. Today the tricycle landing gear of course makes everything so nice and easy but it took a long time before this excellent idea was introduced.

Another problem with the Mosquito was the slow movement of the landing gear during retraction. For an unknown reason the designers used a direct operating hydraulic system rather than a reservoir called an accumulator and this meant that the gear had to be 'pumped up' as opposed to being rapidly operated. This meant that it took much longer for the wheels to retract during the critical period just after lift-off when the pilot had to wait for the airspeed to build up to the safe single-engine speed of 160 mph. The quicker you achieved this speed the better; below it, especially with a full load, it was very difficult to climb away safely if one engine failed. In a twin-engined aeroplane, reducing the 'vulnerability period' to the absolute minimum makes for peace of mind.

After some five hours of local flying to get familiar with our beautiful machine and check out all the points of detail like the flying trim, engine harmonisation, instrument validity, radio effectiveness, and so on, we set off on a three-and-a-half hour fuel consumption check. This was a simulated delivery flight and we headed up to beautiful Scotland and back for the purpose. It was splendid to speed along at 20,000 feet with counties being crossed rapidly as never before. In its natural element there was no doubt at all that the Mosquito was truly a top class gentleman's carriage. The side-by-side seating, so companionable compared to the separateness of the Boston, gave us that certain Rolls Royce feeling. Not surprisingly, the Mosquito became the most favourite of all the aircraft types that I had flown, by now numbering over sixty.

On one non-flying day at Melton Mowbray the specialists gave the aeroplane a thorough inspection. Jock and I prepared all the navigation gear and collected a set of maps for the 6,000 mile journey, completed the administration work prior to departure, and spent the rest of the day relaxing. We were now well organised to go on our aerial safari in the morning. The first leg was to be the usual one of a positioning flight to RAF Station, St Mawgan in Cornwall which was the Despatching Unit from England to the Mediterranean and beyond. One final job was to get clearance to make a diversionary flight beyond Cairo to Lydda aerodrome, (near Tel Aviv,) to see Buster Evans, our Boston air-gunner/radio operator who was now doing a ground job in the Equipment Branch – a 'stores basher' as they were called.

At 11.40 hrs on the 20th September 1945, Mosquito TE 599 took off from the main runway at St Mawgan and headed out across the English Channel. Destination, the French Air Force Base at Istres, Marseilles. We were on our way. The Mosquito climbed up effortlessly to 20,000 feet, levelled off at cruising altitude, and then on reduced power settings for flying-for-range we headed south across France. To begin with there was quite a lot of layered stratus cloud on our route making visual navigation out of the question. However, when over half-way as predicted by the weather men it cleared steadily and soon we were enjoying good visibility ahead of us. After about two-and-a-half hours the blue Mediterranean could be seen (and very nice, too!) and eventually we descended, called the Control Tower for clearance and landed safely on French soil. The flight had taken 3 hrs 10 mins.

After parking as directed by a French airman we both got out pronto because each of had that special urge to spend a penny! A quick look around soon identified the small 'pissoire' – such an inelegant word – and we hurried towards it but once inside Jock was faced with a major problem.

Without delving into the delicacies of the matter, Jock's small stature was such that the porcelain device attached to the wall was too high up for him. He gave me a despairing look. Oh well, nothing to it but to lift him physically off the ground to a height appropriate to the occasion. I couldn't resist saying, "You know, Jock, this business of the Captain caring for his crew first is all very well, but this is stretching leadership more than somewhat!" Thank goodness he speeded up his business before disaster struck his skipper.

After a good night and enjoying the excellent French cuisine we set off again, this time heading for Malta. I was reminded of my old friend 'Attie', the gallant pilot who sank so many enemy ships from his Blenheim of 82 Sqdn when operating from the George Cross island. The three-hour flight was pleasant, now flying high over the sunlit sea, but only spoiled by a message from the Tower at Luka aerodrome to advise us that the main runway was out-of-action due to repair work; thus I would have to land on the very short one. Dammit, it would happen to the new boy on Mosquitoes! When we arrived overhead the runway in use looked singularly short. However, needs must and I succeeded in making a passable landing and stopped within the distance available.

Jock and I had never been to Malta before so it was something new to have a look at. My first impression was that the small island was quite barren, very rocky with innumerable gullies, and to me not particularly attractive. Pick it up and put it somewhere else less geographically valuable and who would care about it? For all that it had a certain charm associated with its early history of the Knights of Saint John, the Crusaders, and the happenings of hundreds of years ago. We were taken that evening by one of our hosts to a Services club and there I came across Tom Fazan from Heliopolis days, a staunch member of the late-night male voice choir in the Mess. Also there was the charismatic 'Cass' Casano of RAF Armoured Cars fame. We had a splendid evening and it was like old times.

Surprisingly, bearing in mind the party of the evening before, Jock and I were airborne at 06.45 hrs and I recollect that essentially it was because of an operational need to take off in cool air on the short runway. After taxying out I put the tailwheel amongst the stones, took a deep breath, and then accelerated down the short runway as fast as my skills permitted. This time there was no swing whilst playing the throttles as best I could and we lifted off with literally a tennis-court length to spare. Once airborne, the agony of waiting for the wheels to tuck inside the nacelles and then the nerve-wracking period of getting to safety speed was evident. Ahead and just below us we could see the nasty island features of rocks, gullies, stone walls and not a single flat place to attempt any kind of a landing. We both breathed again once we were safely airborne and climbing away with lots of speed in hand. So that was Malta.

The run to Cairo West airport took us along the length of the Eastern

Mediterranean and the area which not long ago had seen some bloody battles on land, sea, and air. It was familiar country and from our good vantage point the bird's eye view was nostalgic; I wondered if I would ever again traverse the huge expanse of the North African desert with its many associations. It was nothing if not an excellent area for men to fight each other, consisting as it does of vast open spaces where only the participants would be there to joust with each other.

Our arrival at Cairo's main airport was enlivened by the attentions of a little Egyptian whose job it was to cleanse each aeroplane of noxious foreign microbes by the liberal use of a Flit gun. I always thought that the Land of the Pharaohs bred the nasty little things, rather than imported them. Jock and I were instructed to remain in the Mosquito (which was tiresome as the flight had lasted over three hours from Malta), and our Egyptian friend searched in vain for the door that would give him access when we would then be sprayed with insecticide. Poor fellow, he never discovered the small access hatch on the lower starboard side. Very frustrated he came round to my small clear-vision panel which was open to allow cooling air into the cockpit, said something in Arabic and flitted in my direction but to no purpose. Honour was satisfied; he had done his best.

Jock and I spent two nights at RAF Heliopolis, and our next leg of the journey was to fly to Lydda. This was a route that I could do almost blindfold but the big difference was that we would now travel more than three times faster than before and we sped across the Sinai Desert so quickly that it seemed almost like crossing a very large sandy version of the Isle of Wight. As we taxied in towards the terminal building, to our great pleasure we saw the robust frame of Buster Evans, the best air gunner in the business where Bostons were concerned. It was the happiest of reunions but it was all too short as our itinerary prescribed that we fly away immediately after the refuelling.

The final leg of the day was from Lydda to RAF Habbaniya near Baghdad. This time the route via Amman and the oil pipeline to Rutbah and beyond (a distance of over 500 miles) took just two hours and the speed continued to make me elated. It seemed incredible that only a few years before we were grinding our way at only 5000 feet through all the desert air turbulence at a spanking ninety miles per hour in those tubby Valentias. As we sped along I ruminated about the dramatic change in aeroplane design and performance that had happened in less than ten years. I could not resist making a guess about what would have happened had not Hitler jerked our masters into the realisation that an air force cannot be expected year after year to manage with outdated aeroplanes. More telling still was the fact that the brilliant de Havilland concept was a private venture and only just wriggled into acceptance because of the foresight of Air Marshal Sir Wilfred Freeman who cajoled the Air Staff into giving the Mosquito a chance to show its worth. Once again the Good

Lord and Divine Providence had sided with the good, the noble and the god-fearing. Once again Britain kept to the tradition that she loses every battle but the last one.

One night at Habbaniya was quite enough and so we set off in the early morning for Bahrein and thence along the steamy Persian Gulf and so eventually to Karachi. This city today is the important sea port of Pakistan but at first sighting it did not appeal to us one little bit. The airport building was hot, smelly, fly-infested, scruffy, and seething with humanity. The administration was so bold as to ask us for our certificates of innoculation against all manner of tropical diseases. Jock and I were well endowed with all the paper work and the innoculations to suit but I could not resist commenting to the official that the Indian sub-continent exported the microbes rather than getting them from England. I was so disenchanted with everything and everybody that I turned to Jock and said: "So far as I am concerned this is a bit of the far-flung Empire that can be flung away for ever"; Jock whispered that my remarks were not too well received. Oh well, it was time that somebody spoke out.

What proved to be the final leg of our delivery flight took us to a place plumb in the middle of India and it was called Allahabad. It was not my idea of a holiday resort; it was awful. The worst blow was the discovery that beautiful Mosquitoes were being flown in from England in regular sequence only to be left to rot in the hot and humid climate. Seemingly, the delivery tap had not been turned off and someone at home had not noticed that the Far East war had come to an end. The wretched RAF Senior Engineer Officer now had Mosquitoes parked facing each other along the entire length of the secondary runway. What a way to end his war – burdened with the fastest propellor aeroplanes in the world that were no longer wanted. Before long, all those wooden wonders would be scrapped as they were never intended by de Havillands to be operated in tropical climates. It was tried, so I heard, but after some of them had shed tailplanes and other vital bits the idea was abandoned but in the process nobody ever seems to be sacked for making what was patently a bad and avoidable decision. The only redeeming end-product of our enjoyable delivery flight from England to India in that superb Mosquito was to learn from Jock that we had averaged a speed in excess of 300 mph, end-to-end. Sir Geoffrey de Havilland would have been gratified. By good fortune Jock and I were able to 'thumb a ride' in a Beechcraft 'Expeditor' to Colombo. It carried amongst others a senior WRNS officer on her way to Calcutta and we were very grateful to make our escape from Allahabad so quickly. From Calcutta, another of my very unfavourite places, we flew on to Colombo and I was back once more where I used to live as a child some twenty-five years earlier. By a coincidence we were given accommodation in the Galle Face Hotel and this was precisely the place where as a child I had stayed for a last night before traveling by sea to England with my mother.

For the two ex-Mosquito aviators Colombo was a nice break from the daily routine of travel and the next four days were spent relaxing and chasing up essential arrangements of onward travel for one of us and a return flight back to England for the other. Jock and I were lucky as both of us were placed on a priority list and it was with many regrets that we now had to part company. It had been remarkably nice to get together again and renew an association with flying going back for ten years. Aircraftsman Cairns and Pilot Officer Pelly-Fry had improved their respective ranks to Flight Lieutenant and Group Captain; we certainly could not complain about that.

RAF Skymaster KL 977 awaited its passengers at Ratmalana Aerodrome, a few miles out of Colombo. At the appointed time we climbed aboard, and the four big American air-cooled engines started up with a puff of oily exhaust smoke typical of radial engines. In some ways I was sorry to leave Ceylon – since renamed Sri Lanka. However the priority was to get to Australia and on arrival at Sydney I had to ask someone the silly question of where a place called Camden was located. It is not often that one goes half way round the world to seek a destination known only by name, but it does make for added interest! The long flight across the seemingly endless sea of the Indian Ocean took almost nine hours before we arrived at the Cocos Islands. They amount in practise to what looks like a submerged volcano some five miles across and with the rim partially exposed above water level. The area of coral and sand is attractively sprinkled with coconut trees and with big breakers thundering continuously it was reminiscent of Captain Bligh RN and his famous HMS 'Bounty' exploration. This very remote little bit of real estate was administered by Australia, the Clunie-Ross family owners notwithstanding, and its principle asset was that it was the stepping stone to the Western edge of Australia with each hop a distance of 1,600 miles. Although I was accustomed to big areas and African scale of measuring I was beginning to feel that everything ahead had a thousand-mile tag as a yardstick and anything less in that part of the world (as I learned later) was dismissed as 'down the road'. After three hours on the wild and remote Atoll, passing the time in the palm-fronded structure that passed for a lounge and restaurant, we boarded the Skymaster again and took off into the night. It was 10.30 pm local time and we had another flight of almost identical duration to the previous one before us. Australia – here we come! Eventually the western coastline slowly merged with our route, with Carnarvon, Shark Bay (charming!) and Geraldton somewhere below. It was now three o'clock in the morning I for one was quite content to keep my eyes closed and assume that the Captain and crew knew that the Skymaster was pointing in the right direction. Aussieland would keep until daylight prompted me to get my first-sighting of the big continent.

At early breakfast-time the reliable Douglas Skymaster was told by the

Captain to put its wheels down, and with flaps, propellors and engines equally spoken to we alighted on the runway at Perth. It had been a long business getting to Australia and I was naturally excited even though I was yet another pommie-bastard about to have his leg pulled because I talked as though I had a hot potato in my mouth. Everyone disembarked and I thanked the skipper and his crew for a painless journey. We were accommodated overnight prior to facing the last lap of the journey to Sydney. As with the characters in the very charming 'Teddy bears picnic' song of my younger days, I was soon going to be 'in for a big surprise'.

Skymaster KL 985 – a change of horses – took off from Perth at 19.45 hrs local time and headed in an easterly direction. There was nothing to see from the passenger's window because we were traversing the six hundred miles of a chunk of desert called the Nullabor Plain. At some 10,000 ft altitude the reliable engines droned away with that dark-brown hum so typical of American aero-engines and it was all very reassuring and sleep-making. Every now and again I would open my eyes and look out hoping to see some lights, but in that part of the world any lights of consequence only show every few hours.

After the seventh hour I invited myself to the flight deck and asked how much longer it was going to take to get to Sydney. The navigator grinned and said that the flight plan from Perth had been calculated at nine-and-a-half hours but of course we also had to add on two hours to account for the change of time zones. "Yes" he said, "you could say that Australia is kind-of-big". I was yet another new-boy whose ideas of the size of overseas places is conditioned by his school atlas. England occupies one page – and so does Australia. By contrast, an Australian atlas has lots of Aussieland in the front pages and the British Isles has to make do with one page in the back; it all depends on the viewpoint.

After what seemed an eternity – it is so often the way if you have nothing to do but sit and wait – we arrived at Mascot Airport. Today it is called Kingsford Smith after the remarkable Australian aviator who did so much to bring aviation to the world's attention. It was well into the morning by the time we descended onto the apron, sniffed the clean Sydney air, and awaited our kit from the cargo hold. Now at last I had reached my known destination. The next move might well prove to be interesting!

I did not have long to wait. A smart Flight Lieutenant tracked me down, introduced himself, and told me that he had a Dakota ready to whisk me away to RAF Camden. I now had to come clean and admit that I had not the slightest idea where Camden was, and for that matter RAF Transport Command did not know either. We both laughed, and my guide revealed that Camden was in fact only forty miles away on the highway route to Canberra. Now that I knew it was so close a thought came into my head and I proceeded to explore the possibility of road travel for a change.

The officer who is in charge of a Royal Air Force Transport Command outpost is (or was) called a Staging Post Commander. His function is to attend to all the ground organisation associated with RAF aeroplanes passing through or terminating at an overseas base that belongs to another country. Apart from his task of ensuring a smooth arrival-and-departure system, there is a touch of ambassadorial skill needed to keep on good terms with the host country; the incumbant has to be all things to all people and the job is not as simple or easy as it might appear.

I was fortunate to find that the Staging Post commander at Mascot was Squadron Leader Tony Bartley of Battle of Britain fame; and so he was another kind of 'Number two Platform' greeter-and-despatcher rather than the intrepid fighter pilot that was much more his forte. Poor fellow, he had to abandon the cockpit and become an airline manager. He invited me to his office for a coffee and it became clear that his heart was thousands of miles away because on his desk was a framed photograph of Deborah Kerr. Wedding bells were planned just as soon as he could get back home to claim his bride.

With the immediate requirement of the final forty-mile run to Camden I told Tony that I would much prefer to go by road. Although it might seem ungracious to turn down an easy Dakota flight, literally door-to-door, frankly I wanted to spend about an hour going by road so that I could get the feel of things and get a gradual introduction to the sights and sounds of Australia. Tony saw my point and he offered to provide his staff car and a driver. I felt embarrassed to tell my Dakota pilot about this and it must have seemed disheartening for him to return to Camden empty-handed without his new Station Commander. However, he appreciated my feelings in the matter and the Dakota flew away without me. I was now able to have my first sighting of Sydney from the ground.

The run was fascinating and after so many years have elapsed I still have certain impressions of it. I suppose most of us have a picture in one's mind of what to expect to see upon arrival at a completely new country. Egypt may mean Pyramids and people in nightshirts with inverted flower pots on their heads. Texas means a tall hombre with a cowboy hat walking through those flip-open louvred doors to the saloon. A Pacific island means smiling dusky maidens with garlands of frangipani and a white hibiscus in her hair. For me, Australia would be inhabited by rangy horsemen wearing wide-brimmed felt hats, rolling cigarettes with one hand and a boomerang-carrying Aborigine helping him to round up skinny cattle. Well, the teddy bear's picnic theme had started. My driver gave me a treat by going first of all into the centre of Sydney, a small detour but most enjoyable. I was able to see the handsome buildings, although the narrow streets must have been a relic of earlier days. The famous bridge affectionately known as the 'coathanger' was splendid and it looked handsome and well-matched to the scene; a tribute to Messrs Dorman Long, the constructors. The harbour is spectacular – no other word will suffice. It looked like God's gift to man so

The author and Bobby Snowden attempting to repair the Stinson after its forced landing in Libya, 1946

The author and the Stinson Reliant prior to the flight to Nairobi, 1946

The author *(seated second left)* together with Air Commodore 'Sandy' Heard and other members of the RAF Selection Board, Weyhill near Andover, 1951

The author and his wife, Irène, about to start their journey to Paris in a 1931 Morris Minor called 'Thumper', Appleshaw, Hampshire, 1952

Group Capt Peter Townsend, Teheran, November 1956

The author and Irène and the DH104 Devon used by them during their travels in Iran, 1958

The author at the controls of the Devon *(Peter Needham)*

Cdr Peter Needham and Irène Pelly-Fry

Peter Needham, Irène, author, Charles Agar and a young Jonathan Pelly-Fry, Teheran, 1958

Col Khatami *(left)* and Gen Giulanshah *(second left)* the C-in-C of the Imperial Iranian Air Force

Left to right Peggy Maclean, wife of Col John Maclean the Military Attaché, Irène Pelly-Fry and Air Commodore Fred Rosier (later ACM Sir Frederick Rosier, C-in-C of Fighter Command 1966–68), Teheran 1958 *(Peter Needham)*

The 'Contented Airman' grounded

'Pelly' and Irène in their delicatessen *Epicure of Chichester*, 1966

Like the author, John Crampton still 'mucking about' with models but this one is put to good commercial use taking aerial photographs, Fivehead, Somerset 1982

'Pelly' and son Jonathan carry out last minute checks on the flying scale-replica of the Boston IIIA in 88 Sqn markings. RN Air Station Merryfield, 1984

43 years after last seeing her the author's old 4 litre Bentley was brought to Fivehead by the current owner, Brian Porter of Capetown. Still looking as impeccable as ever! June 1987

that he could wrap a fine city around it. No wonder the Australian flying boys in Bomber Command were so proud of it. An interesting point about a number of the houses that I saw was that many of them had charming wrought-iron work on their balconies shipped from England in the sailing ships as ballast. Once away from the inner city the route passes through suburbs with familiar names like Liverpool and my guide also quoted others like Canterbury, Hyde Park, Regent's Park, Bexley and Enfield. Those early settlers brought nostalgia with them and so perpetuated names from twelve thousand miles away. Not surprisingly most of the houses were built to suit the Sydney climate and in the main they were single storey ones with a covered verandah all round. They must have been inspired by the military cantonement bungalows in India that were constructed by the Royal Engineers about a century earlier.

Although in 1945 the Australian population was not much more than five million people, I was surprised to learn that Sydney claimed about one sixth of them, most of the balance being located in Melbourne, Perth, Adelaide and Brisbane. Australia in the middle is almost devoid of human beings. Surprise number two therefore was that the legend of men on horseback was not altogether true; Just as in other parts of the western world the majority of Aussies wear collars-and-ties and commute to work in the ordinary way.

The run to Camden took us through pleasing country-side with big open areas, a fair sprinkling of trees including the indigenous eucalyptus (with hundreds of varieties) and in the Australian October spring-time everything was about as green as one would hope. The area surrounding Camden seemed to be devoted to farming, with cattle and dairy products predominating. I had been absorbing everything with great interest and it had a certain look about it that was quite unlike anything that I had experienced before. My first impressions were more favourable than those in my mind's eye and I was very glad to have had the opportunity of making the last forty-miles of my long journey by road.

A brief sighting was made of the small town of Camden. It amounted to one main street and then we turned off the highway to the aerodrome. It was journey's end, and including stops it had taken twenty days. The new Station Commander of RAF Camden had arrived at last.

Chapter XXII

The Big Country

After the run from Sydney to Camden I took a look at the aerodrome and the contrast with RAF Holme-on-Spalding-Moor was marked. Bomber Harris' airfields had been designed to operate four-engined bombers; here the requirement was to fly Dakotas from an improvised runway set in what Australians call a paddock. It had the charming atmosphere of a private airstrip in a rural setting of farmland. Rabbits nibbled at the grass close to the boundary, and to me many new types of birds flew overhead. The two hangars used for maintenance were close to the administrative and domestic sites and this contrasted with my previous bomber station in that everything here was conveniently within walking distance and aircraft dispersal was a thing of the past. As I looked around and took in the scene, two thoughts came into my mind; one was that this new job was going to be a big change from the pressures of wartime activity and so almost a holiday. The second was the realisation that I was commanding what in all probability was the only Royal Air Force Station in the Southern Hemisphere. Although of no consequence because it was a statistic that even RAF Transport Command ignored – like Camden's location 'somewhere in Australia!' – to me it assumed the status of being the Number One RAF station south of the Equator and it was worth travelling 13,000 miles to my new posting for that reason alone. To add to the romantic picture of exclusiveness I discovered that the property was owned by one of Australia's oldest families called Edward Macarthur-Onslow; his ancestor had arrived many decades earlier and had become the Governor of New South Wales. His farming interests led to the introduction of Merino sheep to improve the quality of the wool for export back to Britain. Ted and Winifred continued the farming tradition and in recent years had added aviation to their activities by setting up a flying school, something that was a wise choice in a country ideally suited to the use of the aeroplane. With the advent of war the Australian government took over the school and when the air transport requirement arose later on Camden was given a runway and the Dakotas moved in. This in turn increased the accommodation requirement, one result of this being that the Macarthur-Onslow homestead was turned into the officers mess and extra hutted buildings were put up for the rest of the RAF personnel. Ted and his family now lived in a charming house nearby and they took me to their hearts and into their lives and so gave me my first insight into the Australian way of life. It could not have been a nicer introduction to the new job and paved the way for getting to know much more of the country and it's hospitable people than I had dared to hope.

The military air transport requirement in that part of the world was still paramount after the end of the Far East war and so the RAF had set up No 300 Wing with headquarters in Melbourne to control three Dakota units. One was No 243 Squadron at Camden commanded by Wing Commander MacLean, DSO, DFC, AFC, RAAF and the other two differed only in the sense that they were what are called 'lodger units' on Royal Australian Air Force aerodromes. Typical of Australian geography, they were hundreds of miles apart from each other; the second unit for some unexplained reason was designated No 1315 (T) Flight based at Brisbane in Queensland, commanded by Wg Cdr Reg Bailey DSO, DFC,; the third was No 238 Squadron based at Adelaide in South Australia, commanded by Wg Cdr Harry Burton, DSO. A strange coincidence is that the second and third units were initiated at Merryfield, the Naval Air Station just three miles away from the author's home in Somerset. Led by Reg Bailey, the ex-Bomber Command crews travelled to Montreal to pick up their Dakotas, thirty in all, – and then flew them right across the Pacific to Australia. In due course those splendid Dakotas flew back to England when the air transport requirement in the area was superceded by civil airlines; a feat that in the annals of transport aviation must be something of a unique record. The boss of 300 Wing was Air Commodore 'Tubby' Earle (who later became an Air Marshal) with a compact HQ staff in Melbourne and so the whole of his Command was a tidy affair even if it was spread out over an area bigger than Europe. Where Camden was concerned the prime requirement was to provide a weekly air service from Sydney to Hong Kong and in large measure this was for the benefit of the Royal Navy's British Pacific Fleet (BPF) whose Headquarters was in Sydney. Strange to say, all this basic information was given to me only on arrival at Camden by Jock MacLean who had been temporarily in Command of the Station before my arrival; and so only now did I have the picture of what-was-where and who-was-who in the RAF Transport Command structure 'down under'. As a personality Jock was exceptional and we struck up an excellent working relationship together. Typical of so many Australians he was a very amiable character; a lean and sunburned fellow with a long jawbone structure that gave him a purposeful look. It was said that practically all his wartime flying had been on Dakotas during the

Far East war when he had carried out all manner of dangerous and difficult sorties like air supply to Wingate's Chindits and 'flying over the hump' into China. With over 2000 hours of operational flying on Dakotas I concluded that he was probably the most experienced pilot of all in that specialised business. It was very appropriate that an Australian such as he should command the squadron and (probably by design) he had a big proportion of Aussies amongst his aircrew and ground personnel. For me I was delighted to have such a good lot of men on the station. Provided that the pommie from England fitted into the pattern I had reason to hope that the six months tour was going to be straight-forward and relaxing. It proved to be both in good measure.

A priority requirement for me now was to go to Melbourne and call on my new boss 'Tubby' Earle, and I arranged to do this within days of arriving at Camden. He was kind enough to provide transport for a small tour of the city and unlike Sydney it reminded me of an English country town with an air of respectability and a whiff of being pleased with itself. It was not in keeping with my preconceived notion of a city pressing on in the American style and even the climate was surprising as it was cool with occasional rain. As if to dispel the illusion further, Melbourne was the capital of the State of Victoria and in that sense it was well named. The Air Commodore's driver threaded his way through the traffic (including the tramways and the unusual but sensible priority system at some intersections) and I was taken back to Essenden aerodrome to make the return flight to Camden. The 400 mile flight gave me another chance to see the fruit-growing areas and the farmlands of the southern part of Victoria and New South Wales including another sighting of Canberra, the Federal Capital. In 1945 it was still being developed and I learned that apart from government buildings and homes for people engaged in administration and foreign representation there was a whole lot still to be done to make it a city with all the amenities that the visitor expects. Fortunately this was no problem for me as my contacts were not at political level and I had no particular desire to go there as a tourist.

The next job was not so much a duty journey as a courtesy visit to the Royal Navy, our customers where the route to Hong Kong was concerned. The RAF had posted Group Captain Reggie Gaskell to British Pacific Headquarters for liaison duties and he arranged for me to call on the Commander-in-Chief. It was then that I realised that the admiral was none other than 'Uncle Bruce' whose Christmas presents I had secretly delivered to the princesses two years earlier.

On the day of the appointment I set off in the Humber staff car along the Hume Highway for my second visit to Sydney, this time armed with a street map so that I could navigate my way to the Naval Headquarters. Fortunately it was located in a house overlooking the magnificent harbour and the White Ensign together with the Admiral's personal flag made identification easy. The Flag Lieutenant was awaiting me and within minutes I was shown into Sir Bruce Fraser's spacious office to meet the famous man for the first time. He was a broad-shouldered stocky fellow with a weather-beaten face and to me looked every inch the experienced sailor. I explained that apart from making a courtesy call I wanted to enquire if he was satisfied with the air transport facilities that Camden had been providing. His answer was that as far as he knew it was working out very well but I sensed that it was something that he would have taken greater interest in had it been otherwise. As there was not much more to say, I was about to take my leave when upon an impulse I paused momentarily and said, "Sir, I have a confession to make; I have to tell you that on Christmas Eve two years ago I forged your handwriting on two small cards and signed each one 'Uncle Bruce'. I hope you will understand why." At first he looked puzzled but almost immediately afterwards he knew exactly what I was talking about by saying "Of course! the presents for the two princesses; I clean forgot to enclose the cards. Well done!; and thank you very much for standing in for me." As I left his office I concluded that my visit had been of value in more senses than one. The Admiral now knew who was running his private airline and he also knew that the same man had done him a good turn in an unexpected way.

The visit was of considerable benefit to me because I was later invited to official parties given by the Admiral, in his flagship and this was a golden opportunity to meet many prominent members of Sydney society, something that would not have happened otherwise. In this way I met many charming Australians and it was the start of attending a series of cocktail and dinner parties, yachting trips, and week-ends in Australian homes. The job of running the Station at Camden therefore was considerably enhanced because I now had the opportunity of widening my horizon by getting to know so many people outside my immediate sphere of interest. This is an important matter, because only in this way can one form reasoned judgement on affairs in other people's countries. Sometimes the contrast is startling. At one party I met a man who told me that he owned a property 'up North' as he put it. I asked him how many acres he had for his sheep and cattle and he said "I don't know about acres but in my language it's five hundred square miles". Obviously, in Australia everything is big – but then it is a very big country. Another very charming new friend was Marie Livingston, the niece of the famous brothers of big-time yachting, and she had the deserved reputation of being the best and certainly the nicest hostess in Sydney. Her husband had a big property in New South Wales but her interests were such that she preferred the sophistication of Sydney to farming and spent most of her time living in a wonderful apartment overlooking the harbour. It was the meeting place for people from all over the world and every time I visited the apartment it was filled with talented, influential, and entertaining folk. It was an excellent insight into the way of life of prominent people and I considered myself to have been exceptionally lucky to meet them; and it all began with those forged Christmas cards inscribed 'with love from Uncle Bruce'!

The visit to Admiral Sir Bruce Fraser, coupled to the activity connected with the squadron's weekly trips to Hong Kong gave me the urge to go on one of the flights myself – not that I had to convince myself unduly about the idea! The operations carried out by the Dakota boys strictly speaking were of no direct concern of mine but nevertheless it was always my principle to have personal experience of anything to do with the conditions and problems – if any – that arise. The fact that I had never been to Hong Kong before was of course a happy coincidence – ahem! – and when Jock MacLean put me down as supplementary crew on a flight just before Christmas I waited impatiently for the departure day. This was going to be the big one; the five thousand mile flight to Hong Kong and then all the way back again. The interest was heightened because it was barely four months since the Crown Colony had been liberated from Japanese occupation and from accounts given by the Dakota crews it was still far from being anything like a going concern. Accommodation was makeshift, food was rationed, and there was a great deal to be done by the men returning to put Hong Kong on it's feet again.

On December 15th 1945 Dakota Mk IV registration KN 342 took off from Camden with Warrant Officer Nunn as captain and a crew of three plus myself as spare pilot. The route followed the standard refuelling stop at Cloncurry and then to Darwin for the night stopover. We had now crossed Australia from bottom to top and in the morning a new crew took over consisting of Flying Officer Miller and his boys; I carried on with them. Day two brought us to a tropical island called Morotai for refuelling and there I found a very large Irishman (inevitably called Paddy) who a little earlier had received twenty-eight days in the cooler from me for a major misdemeanor and had been banished from Camden afterwards. He stood there in the briefest of shorts and nothing else; for a moment I feared that he would give appropriate vent to his displeasure because I had ordained his punishment. Not so! With a grin and a slap on the back that almost broke my collarbone he greeted me like his brother and said that he was blissfully happy in his island paradise. He even showed his appreciation by giving me a large basket of tropical fruit. "Begorra sir! it's moity foine it is to see you – the good Lord be praised". The next hop took us towards the equator across a sea dotted with islands of every size and eventually we arrived at the big Phillipines USAF base called Leyte for the second night stop. Leyte was awful; it was hot, humid, and water lay everywhere on the crushed coral camp area. We were met by the RAF Staging Post Commander who had been sent to Leyte by his masters without any support equipment at all. However he was a resourceful fellow and with the bargaining asset of a bottle of Scotch whisky he had set himself up admirably with a tent with floorboards, a fridge, a radio, a good camp bed and a jeep. That evening he took us to an open-air movie which was well attended by the Americans and everybody sat on sawn-off coconut tree-trunks; every time an interval occurred (and there were many) there was an admonitory pointing finger on the screen telling us all that we had veneral disease and for gawd's sake go and see the doc. Charming! It was blissful to get airborne in the morning after that overnight experience and I could not but admire all those Americans who had successfully fought the Far East war under such dreadful conditions.

Our luck changed for the worse when we were in the middle of the China Sea and heading for Hong Kong because a radio message told us to return to Leyte because of adverse weather conditions; after six hours in the air we were back at Leyte, dammit. The tiresome business was compounded by minor magneto trouble that had to be attended to before we could leave for a second attempt to get to Hong Kong. I explained the situation to a technical Top Sergeant who said, "Ar gee Captain, don't play about with your motor; take a new one from the store". The lads borrowed the tackle for an engine change and they put our perfectly good engine (that only needed a small electric cable replacement) back into the crate. That done, I went to see my friend with a thank-you bottle of Scotch and when I told him about the old engine he said "You need not have bothered sir, because I am going to toss it into the sea tomorrow". I did not know that Americans were so rich that (in the late forties) a $30,000 aero engine with only a minor fault was disposable.

The second attempt to get into Kai Tak aerodrome at Hong Kong was distinctly hairy because the low cloud was still hanging about and we made the circuit with our starboard wing tip much too close to the hills for comfort. It was certainly a dramatic entry to a place that I had long wanted to visit, and after we landed safely the Staging Post Commander took us to the Peninsular Hotel. Before we left the Dakota, the navigator commented that we were damned lucky because had we been unable to land the only alternative would have been to fly on into Red China. I was now beginning to appreciate some of the problems that the Dakota boys had to face on the Hong Kong run and it made me realise that it was by no means a routine affair; this one was for the specialists. Transport flying in those days certainly had it's hazards and the aircrews were doing a splendid job in my judgement.

My room in the hotel was positively monastic; it was furnished with a bed, a small table, and a chair. This was my first close intimation that the Colony was still struggling to get back to normality and for those who had managed to return to resume government administration and business once more it must have been a very difficult period. Transport (except for the short ferry service from Hong Kong Island to Kowloon) was non-existent although in a way it was not really necessary because there was nowhere to go and nothing to buy. In the morning I took a walk from the ferry to the Hong Kong Bank on the off chance that I would get news of Reidar Johannessen, the Norwegian shipping executive who was likely to be back on the island getting urgent supplies delivered. The bank was the meeting place for everybody and I wanted to locate him if only for the reason that the airline carrier bag that I was humping could be handed over to him. The big banking hall as I entered had the look of a market place with clusters of people everywhere, and as a start I approached three men dressed in rough travelling clothes. It was a lucky choice because they were directors of the bank and knew that Reidar Johannessen was staying with a Persian shipowner called Hadji Namazee. Somehow or other a message was passed and Johannessen arrived, whereupon I told him that the bag and it's contents were for him. To his great surprise he now had ten bottles of White Horse whisky, thus giving him the biggest individual stock of anybody in Hong Kong. I explained that two missing bottles had been necessarily used up in Leyte; one by the crew and myself out of consolation for our enforced second night in that dreadful place and the other in exchange for an expensive aero engine. Reidar was very concerned to see what had happened to his house on the top of the Peak and I was able to borrow the Staging Post Commander's jeep, there being no other way of getting there other than on foot. The house is called 'Sky High' and it was in a dreadful state; it was no more than a shell as the Chinese – not the Japanese – had completely stripped it including the parquet floors, the copper pipes, the doors and the window frames. It was another reminder of the aftermath of the ravages of the war in Hong Kong; in three years the Colony had lost a big part of what had taken decades to set up. For the moment, the image that Noel Coward had created in his famous song 'Mad dogs and Englishman' (where in Hong Kong they strike a gong and fire off a noonday gun) had departed. However, such is the resilience and powers of recovery of both administration and business interests that everybody was now in overdrive and in later months they had returned the Colony back to something approaching normality. It was a remarkable achievement when one considers that Hong Kong is thousands of miles from the western world and Red China literally on the doorstep was unable or unwilling to assist. The war-time problems even for the Japanese had not been easy and they had the greatest difficulty in maintaining an adequate administration and at the same time trying to cope with Chinese vandalism. It was depressing to see such a beautiful island in such a bad state; however my purpose was to see how the Dakota operations were getting on and in that regard all was as well as I could expect.

The bad weather persisted and it delayed our departure for three days. Under normal peacetime circumstance this would have been welcomed but in this instance we had no choice but to stay in the sparsely provided hotel and apart from another meeting with Reidar and going for walks I had nothing to do but wait. The enforced delay affected my programme because I was anxious to get back to Camden to participate in the Christmas Day custom in the Services of the officers acting as waiters to the troops at their festive midday dinner, something that was enjoyed by everybody. The only way to make up the lost time was to press on after eventually leaving Hong Kong and instead of making night stops I joined successive Dakotas positioned along the route. There were some dodgy moments. On the six-hour Darwin to Cloncurry leg a massive thunderstorm with plenty of thick cloud and lightning flashes lay in our path and we failed to make radio contact with the RAAF. Fortunately the navigator's dead reckoning prevented a forced landing due to running out of fuel and it was only when we got overhead at Cloncurry that the airfield lights came on and the tower answered our call. When I jumped down onto the apron, very thankful to arrive after the nasty business was over, I was greeted by a six-foot Australian wearing brief shorts and sandals. I commented that we might have killed ourselves but for our own efforts and his laconic reply was "You poms have forgotten it's Christmas; it's holiday time here, sport!" Eventually Camden was reached on Christmas Eve and I was both happy and tired; I had made the 5,000 mile trip back in under three days and the total airborne time was thirty-three hours of which half was by night.

The Christmas Day happenings were a success but as soon as duties permitted I retired to my bed with a singularly nasty ailment that the doctor diagnosed as dengue fever. The microbes in that damned place Leyte had left their mark and for six days I was left to sweat it out. Time seemed to stop and I dozed fitfully waiting for the fever to abate so that I could get up and become human again; it was now New Year's Eve and as I pondered my ill-fortune the unusual sound of a horse's hooves inside the Macarthur homestead could be heard; was this the fever or was it real? I got out of bed to investigate and in the hall was Squadron Leader Charles Warren sitting on his horse; he was holding a pewter tankard of beer and he grinned nervously at his pyjama-clad commanding officer. The reason for the equine display was that he was challenged to do it, the wager being a tankard of beer, and so he put on his riding kit before saddling up his horse in the paddock and somehow persuaded his horse to go through the front door. It was all good clean fun and when I was offered a Hogmanay drink I cast discretion to the winds and accepted a good tot of Scotch whisky with plenty of iced water. Surprisingly it tasted so good that another followed and the process was repeated until midnight brought us all into the New Year. It was now 1946 and I spent the first hours of it in a deep sleep; the whisky had obviously done me good even if I felt distinctly brittle in the morning!

After my Hong Kong trip a remarkable episode occurred on another scheduled flight about a fortnight later. The Dakota had taken off on the return journey from Kai Tak aerodrome and began to climb up through heavy cloud to get to cruising height. Whilst still in cloud one of the engines lost power; and as if this was not bad enough the second one followed suit. It was thought at the time that it was fuel starvation (possibly due to an air lock in the pipe-line from the big extra fuel tank in the fuselage) but as neither engine would restart the captain was left with nothing more than a big glider. The Dakota inevitably descended and by the grace of God the radio operator's SOS was picked up in Hong Kong and an estimated position given. At around five hundred feet the aircraft broke cloud and below was an ugly China Sea being churned up by gale force winds with white foam spewing off the crests. It must have looked very nasty indeed.

With considerable skill the skipper ditched parallel to the crests, the inflatable dinghies were released from the port wing and the crew and the few passengers except one scrambled into them. Poor fellow, he hesitated before jumping into the water and by then the dinghies began to drift down-wind. To compound the troubles a huge wave caused the aircraft to porpoise and on the downward beat the tailwheel pushed one of the dinghies completely under water. It was a very nasty and frightening situation and to add to their misery it was beginning to get dark. By any reckoning they were in a hopeless situation; all that they could do was to pray. All was not lost however; they had not reckoned on the presence in Hong Kong harbour of one of His Majesty's destroyers. The Royal Navy acted with it's usual efficiency and in no time at all put to sea at speed and headed for the estimated position of the survivors. When the destroyer arrived on station the sky was as black as night but by good fortune her sweeping searchlight picked up the orange dinghies and the handful of survivors were rescued. It had been a fantastic job executed under the worst of conditions and 'Uncle Bruce's' sailors had good cause to be pleased with themselves. A very nice aftermath to the story is that when attending the Service of Thanksgiving at Westminster Abbey for Bomber Harris thirty-nine years later, a chap came up to me and said "Do you remember me? I was a member of the crew of the Dakota that fell into the China Sea".

The year 1946 brought with it the realisation that I was half way through the six month's tour that Transport Command had prescribed and I began to have a gnawing fear about the outcome of my bid for a permanent commission in the Royal Air Force. The grapevine told me of contemporaries who had already been accepted and as the names were published so did my morale falter because I was not one of the lucky ones. The matter was made to appear worse because I could not have been further away from London and I began to sense that I was going to be one of the rejects. The harbinger of ill-tidings arrived one day by letter and it told me that I was not chosen; it was a bitter blow but now at least I knew and I walked back to my rooms in great dejection. I remember sitting at my desk to muse over it and on re-reading the letter I realised that it was not a one-off personal letter but one of many rolled off a duplicating machine. To add to the insult, after a lot of waffle about what a splendid officer I was and how well I had served the RAF, especially in war, etc, etc, the Air Member for Personnel could do no better than put a rubber stamp facsimile of his signature at the bottom. For the senior man in charge of people (and their behaviour) I expected better manners of the Air Marshal.

So there it was; I was no longer wanted and as it was painfully clear and made in such a disagreeable and off-hand manner I made immediate plans to leave. I was now in the same bracket as thousands of war-time airmen awaiting demobilisation and if the RAF no longer wanted me I had no cause to postpone my departure to suit the Air Ministry's purpose; two can play that game. I handed over command to Jock MacLean with whom I had enjoyed such an excellent service relationship, said good-bye to Tubby Earle (who was also upset about my shabby treatment) and booked a passage home by sea. On the 27th of February 1946 I sailed out of Sydney harbour in the SS *Orion*, and that was the end of a happy first association with Australia and it's hospitable people. The big country that I had seen so much of slowly receded into the distance.

Chapter XXIII

A Place Called Civvy Street

After an uneventful six weeks voyage by sea half way around the world, England showed up again. One gets a sense of isolation on long voyages which gets worse the longer it lasts. However, boring or not, it was nice to be able to relax and not constantly look anxiously at the ocean for the unnerving tell-tale evidence of the approach of a long black object called a torpedo. It is far better to be bored than frightened.

The mundane business of day-to-day activities connected with disentangling myself from the Royal Air Force – and the not so mundane prospect of being crossed off the pay-roll when my accumulated leave ended – was enlivened by renewed contacts and activities with my friends. Wing Commander Robert Bowes and I used a de Havilland Moth Minor of the RAF Flying Club to go to Denmark for a rally organised by the Royal Danish Aero Club. Flying to Europe in the attractive two-seat low-wing monoplane, registered G-AFNZ was just like old times before the war. The Danes could not have been more hospitable and they remembered all too well the Mosquito attack on the Gestapo Headquarters in Copenhagen and other brilliant sorties by my friends in 2 Group. When I admitted to having been something of a Mosquito pilot myself, I happily basked in the sunshine of reflected glory because they thought that I had participated. Any disclaimer was not believed so I just relaxed and enjoyed it; it increased one's stature no end.

I stayed with good friends like Lt Cdr Dick Bainbridge, his sister Kiddo and Lt Tony Bentley-Buckle, all of whom attacked my loot of tinned ham and other goodies from Australia with gusto what time we were working on Bentleys at the Speed Services Garage near Camberley. During that spell spent very happily in Dick's garage something very interesting in the way of a job came along. In far away Kenya Alec Noon and Stan Pearce had set up an air charter business and they had in mind buying three ex-lease-lend Stinson 'Reliant' monoplanes based in Britain which were being converted from navigation trainers for the Royal Navy back to civil purposes. The proposal was that I act as agent, negotiate a sale through the American Embassy and then deliver one of them out to Kenya and join them as a pilot. All this had a great deal to attract me. It was a flying job, it had possibilities, and it would take me back to my favourite country where I would begin a new life with old friends. What could be better?

First of all I had to get a commercial flying licence (as without one I was not professionally qualified) and fortunately I found an old friend who also wanted to get a 'B' licence, as it was called. Wing Commander Peter Simmons, DFC, had been a Mosquito pilot of distinction in 2 Group and like me had returned to civil life; we both had the same ambition and to that end we went to school. He and I shared his partially bombed-out flat near Regent's Park in London. It was not particularly comfortable with the rain and the cold air entering at will through the holes in the roof but it worked after a fashion. The flying requirement fortunately was acceptable to the civil aviation authorities with the production of our log books but the written exams had to be taken. We booked ourselves into a specialist air navigation school and went off each day like good pupils; I could not but ruminate about a couple of wartime pilots now having to knuckle down to the realities of civil life. When the big day arrived to take the first of the exams, both of us were so nervous that we could barely write our names on the examination paper. Thankfully when it was all over and all six exam papers dealt with, I scraped through somehow or other and Peter had to re-take one of them.

When the first of the Stinsons was almost ready to fly I went to Prestwick to get acquainted. The Scottish Aviation Company had everything in hand and I was cared for very well by the friendly staff. The 'Reliant' was the same type of aeroplane as I had travelled in before the war with Gilbert Miller and it was appropriate to find myself flying the type that I had recommended to him during that posh lunch at the Savoy Grill in 1933. Prestwick is blessed with an excellent aerodrome which by some quirk of nature seems to have a good-weather factor unbeaten anywhere else in Britain; when not test flying or in the hangar with the engineers I spent some time wandering around the airport. On one occasion I was entering the Terminal Building for coffee and saw a man at the cloak room counter who was asking for his hat. The attendant in a broad Scottish accent requested his cloak room ticket; to which the man shrugged his shoulders, looked mildly surprised, and said that he did not have one. At this our Scottish friend said in no uncertain terms that no ticket meant no hat. As the man walked away empty-handed, I stepped in and addressed the attendant. "Perhaps you do not know who the gentleman is who asked for his hat?" The attendant, now on his mettle and resenting my intrusion into a affair of no concern to me said "I'm sorry, the rule is 'no ticket' – 'no hat'; and that is that". I tried again. The attendant repeated his statement, adding that he did not know – or even care – who the man was. "I think you ought to know who he is" I persisted. "The gentleman in question is His Grace the Duke of Hamilton and he happens to own Prestwick airport" Our Scottish friend could never have moved faster and the hat was delivered pronto.

The plan to fly out to Kenya included taking two other men with me. One was Bobby Snowden, an experienced aircraft engineer who was about to join the Noon and Pearce Company and the other was Peter Dolleymore of the Shell Aviation Company. Peter had a requirement to visit East Africa and his organisation agreed to the suggestion that having a look at the Shell refuelling facilities for short-haul machines on our route was not to be missed. So after saying goodbye to the helpful Scottish Aviation people Peter and I took off from Prestwick and made our way to Eastleigh Airport, Southampton, where we were joined by Bobby Snowden. On May 3rd, 1947 the three of us set off on the start of the long haul to Nairobi. This time it was going to be very different from the Mosquito delivery flight to India less than a year earlier; it was now to be made at about one third of the speed and with four times the number of landings on the way; however it makes for variety and interest and all of us looked forward to whatever lay ahead. It was a nice prospect provided that nothing untoward was in store. Air travel, as we were soon to find out, can spring unexpected surprises.

After leaving Eastleigh, the handsome Stinson Reliant G-AIYW set off across the Channel. I confess that I am always a little apprehensive about sea crossings in single-engined aeroplanes. Admittedly any number of pilots do so quite happily and all those fighter-boys during the war, both RAF and Luftwaffe, were called upon to do so; the Fleet Air Arm people of course as a matter of routine. Perhaps they got so used to it that it did not worry them as they were much too preoccupied with air warfare and they had the advantage in the main of flying solo and having parachutes, the latter commodity particularly vital because ditching in those WWII fighter aircraft was usually a ticket to eternity. Spitfires in particular had the habits of a porpoise; one touch on the water and the instant dive was a foregone conclusion. Today, where a sea crossing in small civil aircraft is concerned, there seems to be complete faith in the engine because they very rarely fail. Just the same, my sense of imagination affects my nervous system badly and it makes my normally acute hearing listen out for the minutest malfunction. In the event we reached gliding distance to the welcome French coast and after that my sense of wellbeing returned to normal.

Two-and-a-half hours from take-off we arrived at a nice little grass aerodrome near Paris called Toussus Le Noble which is a mecca for light aeroplanes as was evident from the numbers seen. After refuelling, away we went again in a southerly direction towards Lyons and one extra advantage of having Peter Dolleymore in the crew was that he was also a pilot and so we took turns to drive. The intention on this leg was to stay overnight in Nice but low cloud and heavy rain lay ahead and so we opted for Lyons which was clear. Even so there had been considerable rain there and the low cloud was still hanging about so we were happy to get down and stay for the night. Needless to say we all enjoyed the French cuisine in the legendary good food area although for me the expression applies equally all over La Belle France. Having altered the flight plan, we now discussed how to set about the next leg and examination of our maps showed that we could comfortably get to Ajaccio, in Corsica, a distance of 330 miles. This would mean making the Mediterranean crossing in two hops on successive days. Already the pattern of our journey was becoming clear. Although the Stinson was comfortable and pleasant to fly, its average speed (judging by results so far) was a disappointing 100 mph in round figures. Translate this into a reasonable three-hour flight as a fair run – after all we were not trying to break records – and you find that progress in terms of distance run is no more than that of a modern car on a good road. The only difference lies in being able to fly in a straight line but in France the roads are mostly like that anyway.

In the morning the bad weather had cleared nicely. We returned to the Stinson, checked everything out, and after clearance from the Tower we were airborne. The first part of the route took us over the high Departments of Haute Provence and Alpes Maritimes; it is all spectacular to look at but no place for forced landings. (It's my nervous system again at work!) Once we reached the coast, still flying nice and high up, we overflew Nice and headed out to sea and settled down to maintaining course for Corsica. Everything was working well; the Lycoming radial engine was running like a sewing machine as I sat back comfortably and waited for the minutes to pass. There was a moment I confess when I looked back for the last time and announced that we were now beyond gliding distance to the coast. After a seeming eternity but in reality about an hour we arrived over the Corsican seaport town of Calvi with another forty miles to go to Ajaccio. Corsica looked just as wild and mountainous as expected, all brown and black in colour; I was reminded of a colourful character called Gins, one of my air gunners in 88 Squadron who came from the island and not surprisingly he was called 'the Corsican Bandit'. On the final run in, once clear of the high ground, we descended down to Ajaccio and made a landing on the airstrip. It lies in the wide plain about ten miles from the town and the area looks like a desert. We had now completed the first part of the Mediterranean crossing; so far, so very good.

An elderly taxi driven by a purposeful Corsican took us into Ajaccio. The town was attractive enough in its fashion, but mostly brown and beige in colour and very little green to gladden the eye. The small hotel that we arrived at looked quite presentable but I do not recollect the name. The big surprise was going inside and starting to say my piece in hesitant French – only to discover that Madame la Patronne was English! She told us that she was expecting another party from England and almost as she said it they arrived. The new arrivals proved to be a one-armed ex-RAF Lancaster pilot who was flying a de Havilland 'Rapide', and he was ferrying his aeroplane to Kenya with passengers who were on the payroll of the company that owned the aeroplane. I recollect that there were two women, one small child, and one husband.

As the time was about 3 pm I tentatively asked our hostess if we could perhaps have something to eat, however simple, because we had not had a bite since an early breakfast at Lyons. Right away she agreed and she asked us if scrambled eggs and coffee would do. We three were delighted with her suggestion as after all it was out of normal mealtime hours and anything was welcome. Not so, I have to relate, with the passengers from the Rapide. Quite obviously they had never been abroad before and equally obviously and disagreeably they were so damned ungracious. One good lady said firmly "I don't like eggs" and the other one asked "Why can't we have tea?" (tea in Corsica? – heavens!) They were still mentally back home in Britain and refused to adapt to changed circumstance. They even complained strongly about the heat, the flies, the food, the people, the language, in fact everything. I wondered why the devil they had bothered to leave home at all but having done so they were to my mind so inflexible in their outlook as to be completely unsuited to a new way of life. I feared that this was going to be the pattern of the new post-war generation of people leaving Britain for overseas jobs. Unlike the Services and the bigger commercial companies that select carefully and then brief personnel accordingly before they go overseas, all the sound work of the past – the way in which to behave correctly in someone else's country – was about to be lost.

The flight from Ajaccio to Tunis took us across the bigger and much greener island of Sardinia. The one hundred-and-thirty mile sea crossing to a landfall at Bizerta was now thankfully behind us, and the final forty miles to Tunis was uneventful. We were now in the right continent and after a day or two we would be overflying my old stamping ground, the bit of North Africa starting roughly at Bengazi and running all along to Cairo. After that it was up the river Nile to Khartoum and then on to Nairobi; 'just down the road' as my Australian friends would say.

Tunis instantly brings the sights, sounds, smells and the insects. It is all very North African, and I could now try out my rusty Arabic but with only limited success as the language varies in style and pronunciation from one area to the next. The airport people refuelled us, and as we had time in hand we pressed on to Tripoli and the route in our kind of aeroplane took us south for an hour after which we turned left after passing the edge of the Gulf of Gabes and so on for a landing at Tripoli aerodrome.

Tripoli to me has the seaside resort look about it reminiscent of an arab-style Brighton but the population and the climate of course is quite different. We were accommodated quite well in one of the smaller hotels and I began to get the feeling that we were well on our way, especially on the following day when – '*Inshallah*', – God willing, we would be in Cyrenaica.

Unhappily this proved not to be the case. A nasty gremlin was about to haunt the three of us, and a particularly elusive gremlin at that. Soon after leaving Tripoli and when climbing up to the planned altitude of 5,000 ft the engine speed fluctuated. As it seemed to be a fuel problem I changed from the Port wing tank to the Starboard one and the engine settled down for some minutes before the same symptoms happened again. This was distinctly unsettling and prudence advised a return to Tripoli. As soon as we landed Bobby Snowden got to work. He checked the fuel system, and that was OK; he checked the propellor pitch-changing mechanism, and that was OK as well. As nothing else untoward was found, we topped up the two fuel tanks and set off once again. This time as a precaution we climbed up first of all to a safe height above the aerodrome and as all seemed well we then headed east and followed the coastal road.

By now all of us were very alert and listening to every beat of the engine and I climbed up higher still to get as much altitude as possible in the event of another partial failure – or worse. For some time all went well and then the damned business started up all over again. The engine fading could still be temporarily cured by switching from one fuel tank to the other but this was a makeshift arrangement; it was very mystifying and distinctly worrying. One thought came to my mind and that was 'thank God all this did not happen over the Med!' Eventually, with careful handling we landed at a wartime airstrip with the unlikely name of Marble Arch. The name in fact was given by the 8th Army to Mussolini's fancy archway built to celebrate his hoped-for triumphal arrival in Cyrenaica and thence into Egypt but it was now no more than a useful landmark in an otherwise desolate area of desert.

After landing Bobby Snowden got cracking again. The fault had to be found and the only clue we had to work on was that there was some kind of a common factor between the outside air temperature readings (from a thermometer that I had taken off an old Liberator) and air density. Just as soon as the outside air temperature reached 18° Centigrade at 6,000 feet the fuel mixture entering the cylinders gradually leaned out and the needle of the exhaust-gas analyser slowly moved across until it touched the red-line danger mark with the mixture-control lever still in rich setting. Within moments the damned engine fading happened again and it was only cured by changing to the other tank. Problems, problems! Poor Bobby, he took the fuel system apart all over again and each time he undid a union the petrol gushed out. After a while I said "Let's leave the bloody thing alone for a bit, sit under the wing, and collect our wits". We discussed all aspects of fuel flow, gravity feed, engine-driven pumps, temperature and altitude factors and other technicalities. Our anxieties were not allayed by the thought that Marble Arch with desolation everywhere was no place to be with an unserviceable aeroplane. I lit a cigarette to give me inspiration and even a little comfort.

Bobby suddenly said "I have just had a thought. I had this kind of thing happen once before on a Tiger Moth". With that he stepped onto a wheel and clambered up high enough to look on top of the wing. For the life of me I hadn't a clue what he was looking for. Then a voice called out "You know what? Some clot has fitted the air vents on the tanks back-to-front!!" That clever fellow discovered that instead of air pressure being forced into the top of each fuel tank with the open end of the curved pipe facing forward, both air vent pipes were facing backwards and of course 'sucking' instead of 'blowing'. What had been happening was that under North African conditions the depression created inside each tank was enough to slow up the fuel flow sufficiently to weaken the mixture to the point when a power loss would occur. Switching to another tank only gave temporary relief and the process was bound to happen again. Well, thank the Good Lord for Bobby Snowden; once again I had learned something new.

Before leaving Marble Arch, the fuel system now reassembled, I left a note, optimistically, in the little hut. It said who we were, the type of aeroplane, and where we were going – which was to El Adem. I added the date and the note ended by saying that if by some extraordinary chance anybody passing by could read English – well, would he please tell somebody what had happened in case we disappeared. I wonder after all these years if the note is still there? Marble Arch landing ground was not exactly like a service station on a motorway.

We got the engine started (with the self-starter I'm glad to say) and off we went using minimum power and coasted along at a reduced speed. All was well and the 280 mile flight to El Adem (near Tobruk) took three hours, so even with a slight following wind the ground speed was not exactly breath-taking. The RAF was still operating a staging post there with overnight accommodation and to us it seemed like a return to civilisation. The following day we traversed the old familiar route to Mersa Matruh for refuelling and then to Almaza Airport, Cairo. All along the coastal area could be seen the relics of the desert war in great profusion; tanks, trucks, field guns, crashed aeroplanes and of course at El Alamein the biggest graveyard of all.

In Cairo we stayed two nights where Peter met up with his Shell Aviation people and Bobby carried out maintenance work after thirty hours flying. It was good to have a breather and enjoy the attractions of the Gezira Club, Groppi's famous cakes, and the general Cairo scene. By now the non-Egyptian resident population had virtually disappeared with the departure of thousands of uniformed men and women of the Middle East Forces.

After the Cairo rest period we set off once more on the long haul up the river Nile to follow the familiar route to Luxor, Wadi Halfa, Atbara, Khartoum, Kosti (where the *Dinkas* live), Malakal, Juba, Soroti in Uganda, and then to Kisumu. We were now at last in Kenya after crossing seven countries.

The last lap of two hours flight to Nairobi was the best of all. Once again the splendour of the Kenya Highlands, the farms, the homesteads, the wisps of smoke from cooking fires; it was all looking just as attractive as ever. As we circled Wilson Airport and waited our turn to come in and land I could see a small cluster of people outside the Aero Club and guessed that it was the reception committee. The wandering boy had returned; Alec Noon and Stan Pearce together with some well-wishers greeted us enthusiastically although I seem to remember a voice saying "What kept you?" Dammit – we had done our best! With good fortune I was able to find a nice place to live in Nairobi. It was a small bungalow in the grounds of a senior member of the Kenya Government and it was just the right accommodation for a bachelor and suited the purpose admirably.

Before starting the job of being a commercial pilot I had to acquire a Kenya licence from the Civil Aviation Department but this presented no problems as my British equivalent was acceptable. The document authorised me to fly the Stinson 'for hire and reward' but the principle advantage that I had was to be very familiar with the Kenya scene and probably knew more aerodromes and landing grounds in that part of the world than anybody else, Alec Noon and Stan Pearce excepted. Those two were the most experienced pilots in East Africa and their uncanny skills in sniffing their way about in weather that other pilots would think twice about was remarkable. It was sheer local knowledge coupled with a sixth sense of what was possible and what was not and it was all done on pilotage and not on navigation aids yet to arrive in Africa.

Of the jobs that came my way, the best one was to take two men from the Crown Film Unit to Tanganiyka (now Tanzania) to make a publicity film about the new ground-nut project that the British Government had initiated. The concept was to grow ground nuts (or peanuts) on a vast scale to augment the family larder in Britain with cooking oil, peanut butter and other by-products. The two camera men were Robert Kingston-Davies and Stewart McAllister and we loaded up the filming equipment and left Nairobi in the Stinson to head for our destination. On the way Mount Kilimanjaro could be seen quite clearly as it is 19,000 feet above sea level and stands majestically in a vast plain inhabited by all manner of game. First stop was Moshi, and after refuelling we went on to Dar-es-Salaam on the coast. Twenty miles away is the island of Zanzibar where once a Sultan reigned until recent times; a pity as the romance of the name has now gone. Zanzibar produces more cloves than anywhere else in the world and when flying at 2,000 feet overhead the strong aroma is quite noticeable.

Unfortunately McAllister had to take to his bed in Dar-es-Salaam with a fever, and Robert and I had to leave him in good hands and fly on for some two hundred miles to get to the 'peanut country'. It was in an area called Kongwa but the name is of no consequence as the chosen place was really pure African bush country. After locating the small camp and air strip we landed and whilst looking around we began to wonder why this particular part of Africa had been chosen in the middle of nowhere: it could so easily have been 'the man from the Ministry' putting a pin in the office wall map with his eyes closed. The camp had a splendid bunch of ex-soldiers working on the site. With wartime excavating equipment scraped together from the Far East, would you believe, they were uprooting all trees and scrub so that millions of acres could be cleared for the great project to get going. In the process the soil turned into inches of deep red powder and when the rains came the poor fellows wallowed ankle-deep and more in a vast sea of mud. Without Robert or I knowing anything at all about agriculture, we wondered if the pundits knew what they were doing; to us the project seemed to be a hurried undertaking at the tax-payers expense with no preliminary research to prove its worth.

Robert set about his film work and I became his assistant which was great fun. When he had finished the job, (especially the shots of brawny boys in action with their huge mechanical devices so that folks at home could see their labours) I turned to Robert and said, "There is one important aspect that we have not yet covered; back home people will probably want to see pictures of peanuts actually growing. I doubt that they know what they look like and neither do I for that matter". Robert, ever the professional, stopped in his tracks. "By thunder, I clean forgot about that!" So we went off to see if there were peanuts growing near a local village and we were lucky because we found what we wanted, complete with the African who owned the plot. The patch I suppose was about two acres at most in area, and to lend authenticity to the scene Robert made me act the part of the expert examining the crop whilst the owner pretended to be the farmer. The camera whirred, my black friend and I walked along the rows stopping every now and again for him to lift a plant for inspection and this provided close-up shots for showing back in Britain. For the reader who does not know what a peanut plant looks like, it is similar to the potato and grown in raised rows in a similar manner. Instead of potatoes below ground the plant has long thin roots with the nuts at the extremities. For lifting you grasp the plant firmly, shake it from side to side and then pull it gently out of the ground. The particularly interesting point about the talk with our African friend was when Robert (who spoke *Swahili* fluently) asked him what he thought about the English b'wana's plan to grow groundnuts in such a huge way. Our friend shook his head; "*Hapana misuri*" (not good) was his answer. "It is much too big and the rains will wash it all away".

Robert and I returned to Dar-es-Salaam, giving a lift to two men from the site, and poor McAllister had to be left behind until his fever went away. Robert and I returned via the coastal route to Mombassa. The safari had taken seven days and it had been a most interesting trip that entailed some thirty hours flying. The sad aftermath was the British Government's announcement a few years' later that the ground-nut scheme was going to be abandoned 'for technical and climatic reasons.' The cost of not producing even one per cent of planned production was three hundred million pounds sterling. The pundits should have consulted our African friend. He knew a damned sight better than they.

The days in Kenya passed pleasantly and I enjoyed the job and my good companions. I considered myself lucky to have found something to do that many other post-war pilots would have jumped at, given the same opportunity. Just the same there were times when I got the feeling that I was living in some kind of vacuum with a curious sense of detachment from the rest of the world. It is a dangerous situation and it is one that requires examination because like a balloonist you may drift along in silence where the wind of chance takes you downwind on a path that leads nowhere. I was beginning to feel the need to take stock and explore the possibilities of making a change; however, making an appreciation of a situation clarifies the problem but does not solve it. Stage two is the difficult one, that of deciding what is the best option and the best way of tackling it. Having decided that something had to be done I cast about for ways of making it happen and it proved to be a dispiriting affair. Plenty of people pat you on the back and say nice things but there is always some kind of an excuse or reason produced at the end which means that your efforts draw a blank.

A new major factor meanwhile had now influenced my life and it had begun in London during the time that Peter Simmons and I were at school learning to become commercial pilots. Peter was about to abandon the bombed-out flat in London and I had the luck to meet a man called Gordon Kellow with a mews flat at the back of Chester Terrace. He had a vacant bedroom for me and I accepted his offer gladly. On one ever-to-be-remembered Boxing Day, 1946 upon returning to the flat I met the wonderful Irène, girlfriend of Iris Johannessen from Hong Kong. The extraordinary thing was that the moment that I set eyes on her some sixth sense immediately told me who she was despite the fact that I had no idea at all what she looked like. Now everything in my life changed. Suddenly there seemed a purpose, an ambition, a new horizon, a conviction that she was the girl who was destined to enter my life. Quite apart from the euphoria, her strong personality and statuesque beauty was such that I even allowed her to drive the pride of my life, the ex-Bernard Rubin 4½ litre Bentley that the famous Bentley boys used as the shopping car at Le Mans! Darling Irène just slipped into the driving seat and drove with the greatest skill out of London and onto the Bath Road, cruising effortlessly at 70 mph towards Newbury. Today the Bentley is in Capetown; she will still make 'the ton' and has clocked up well over 250,000 miles. WO Bentley made them to last.

The situation soon after we met was that I flew away to Nairobi in the Stinson and Irène had to go back to Bombay. Parting was one of those dreadfully hard decisions to make but it had to be and later on she made the crossing of the Indian Ocean by boat to Mombassa where I went to meet her. (The famous American author John Gunther once said that the road that I travelled along was the only one in the world from the Capital to the main seaport with grass growing down the centre; and it was true.) It was a wonderful reunion in Mombassa and my Ford V8 took us north along the coast to the idyllic Malindi where the attractive Lawford's hotel provides thatched-roof 'shambas' for guests and the Indian Ocean laps the white sands invitingly a few paces away.

Things for good or bad often come along in pairs, like turtle doves or magpies, and now that fortune had been pleased to smile on us my optimistic streak awaited the second harbinger of good tidings. Within days a letter arrived from the Air Ministry and it told me that I had been offered a permanent commission in the Administrative Branch of the RAF – the organisation that has nothing to do with aeroplanes and flying. Although initially I was delighted to think that I now had a career of substance on offer I still hankered to stay with aeroplanes and I wrote at once to Sir Basil Embry, my wartime boss. I hoped that he would support my wish to return to the General Duties (pilot) Branch. Almost by return of post that excellent leader replied and told me that he had persuaded the Personnel people to accept me back as a pilot; but there was the proviso that I had to return to Britain at my own expense and pass the medical examination. It was all very exciting news and I was quite delighted but there was still one tricky hurdle to cross. At the time that I was 'demobbed' I had had great difficulty in getting my commercial pilot's licence because X-ray photographs showed scars on my lungs the size of fifty pence pieces. Having cajoled the RAF Central Medical Establishment that the scars were a relic of my childhood and therefore of no consequence anymore, now I had to start all over again. If the specialists had passed me fit on the first occasion, well they could do so again.

I flew out of Kenya in a Vickers 'Viking' of Airwork Air Services to visit the Air Ministry and persuade the charming RAF medical consultant Sir Allan Rooke to say 'Yes' for the second time. Meanwhile darling Irène had to remain behind in Nairobi for the time being. It must have been a great strain for her but fortunately our good friends Jim and Elizabeth Cooper (who owned a coffee estate) took very good care of her. She found herself a job in Nairobi with Thomas Cook the travel agents and within days I was able to send her a telegram to say that I had been given a permanent commission in the General Duties (pilot) Branch. The battle had been won, but not without a struggle. Sir Allan conceded that if I had survived flying Wellesleys at over 20,000 feet without oxygen there was not much wrong with my lungs. Fortunately he was the rule-maker; and (as Douglas Bader used to say), he was also the rule-interpreter.

I was now back again where I belonged and I counted my blessings. I was almost in the mood to forget that earlier letter from the Air Member for Personnel, but like the elephant, I have a long memory. Irène returned to England at the earliest opportunity and on October the first, 1949, we were married in London. It was the happiest of occasions and the party at the RAF Club afterwards was memorable with so many old friends like John Crampton and Jim Lee enlivening the scene. The pieces in the jig-saw puzzle had now fallen neatly into place and the sun was shining brightly. For me life was beginning in earnest at the age of thirty-eight. It had been a long time coming.

Chapter XXIV

A Trio of RAF Appointments

It was very good to get back into uniform again. I had returned to the RAF as a Squadron Leader, cut down to size now that the Royal Air Force had reverted to a peacetime role, but it was better to be a 'struggling leader' (as they say) then nothing at all. The Air Ministry sent me to RAF Hornchurch to re-learn how to write letters, address an audience convincingly, maintain good relations with the public, the art of administration, security, Air Force Law, in fact re-learn everything except about aeroplanes. As most of us were old warriors of some kind or another, not unexpectedly thinly disguised yawns prevailed; we had forgotten, our lecturers said, that what happens on the ground enables aeroplanes to fly.

After the course I regained one rank and was sent off to RAF Syerston, near Newark, to be the Wing Commander Administration. The Station had just changed from being a Bomber Command wartime base to a Flying School for the Fleet Air Arm and the training was carried out on the famous American 'Harvard' and the Percival 'Prentice'. At first it seemed unusual that 'crabs' were going to teach the Senior Service to fly (although there were also some naval flying instructors) and I wondered how it was going to work out. In the event everybody got off to a good start and it was apparent that the dark and light blue uniforms harmonised very well and we all got on splendidly with each other. Commander Ed Walthall, DSC, RN the senior Naval Officer and Wing Commander Peter Broad AFC, the Chief Flying Instructor (who was followed later on by Wing Commander Alan Rogers, AFC) had the blending touch.

The Station Commander was Group Captain Hugh David, OBE. He was an ex-Cranwell cadet and well experienced as a commanding officer. His stern authority demanded-and got-a spick-and-span Station but unhappily he had an unpredictable and very wild temper which made my job in the adjoining office difficult to the point of impossibility. When in sheer desperation I bared my heart to our Headquarters Personnel officer and said that I wanted to leave, he blandly told me that I had been specifically given the job because of my even temperament. So I soldiered on and was considerably helped by my discerning spouse who had to listen to all my grumbles.

After withstanding the rigors of working for the most trying boss that I have ever encountered – truth to tell, he was his own worst enemy – when my tour was over and the next posting came along it proved to be something completely new and a very rewarding and enjoyable appointment. It was with the RAF Personnel Selection Board, based at a country mansion called Ramridge House (near Andover) and the job was to be a talent spotter for candidates suitable for permanent commissions. (This really made me smile, after my own difficult experience!) The applicants came basically from two categories. On one week the candidates were recommended RAF personnel and on the next they were schoolboys and of the two the more fascinating by far was the latter group because they were much more difficult to assess.

We were blessed with Air Commodore David Roberts, AFC, as President of the Board. He was a boss who had great insight into potential and that certain style of management without undue interference. Equally his wife Ruth was a fine example of a Service wife who ably supported David in a number of ways, so unlike civil life where the boss' wife only occasionally participates in her husband's extra-mural activities. The other members of the Board consisted of about a dozen officers including the specialist doctor and we made up a harmonious team; it was a complete change from my previous job.

The selection system, (which was roughly the same in the navy and army,) was based on a Country House setting where thirty two candidates divided into teams of eight spent four days of informal tasks, discussions, and interviews. The outdoor jobs for them were fun – like trying to think of ways to cross the 'crocodile-infested river' with only three planks, an oil drum, and some rope; some of the antics they got up to were wonderful to behold. The indoor programme was intended to be just like a week-end house party with prescribed subjects to talk about; some of the latter were called 'individual situations' and they very revealing where character was concerned. Candidate No 8 for example – numbers only, no names – would happily leave poor injured Jones to be killed by natives on the Amazon river bank rather than carry him to safety. "But suppose you were Jones yourself" I would say, "How about that?" Slight pause, "Ah, that's different; the expedition would rescue me!"

The interviews were always informal affairs and sometimes it was hard to establish a rapport with a young and nervous candidate until he realised that you were trying to help him to be successful. Although those already serving in the RAF were straightforward enough because their openness was manifest, all too often the schoolboy would want to ask questions about pensions, promotion prospects, marriage allowances, leave periods and so on. The directing staff noticed this modern trait and the new approach was not so much 'I want to join, come what may' as 'what have you got to offer me?' Clearly, times had changed.

It was a most fascinating insight to personalities, and the system was obviously designed by clever people to show up in a short time – as indeed it did – everything about a candidate; good, bad and indifferent. We had regular visits from outside agencies with similar personnel selection work to do and the idea was to exchange ideas for improving the system to suit the requirement. All of us at Ramridge House were very conscious of the great importance of the work because if we made bad decisions the future RAF would suffer and with that in mind we used to be particularly meticulous, sometimes suffering agonies of indecision about border-line cases at the final reckoning. In essence the job was really a question of saying to oneself 'what kind of chap is the RAF looking for?' During one intake of candidates we had a visit by the three senior personnel men from the Shell Company, and you cannot go much higher than that. I asked one of them what their own formula was, given that the applicant was educationally acceptable to a given standard. His answer was just one word – character. It said it all.

During gaps in the selection board work it was very interesting to visit the RAF College at Cranwell to check up on how the new cadets that we had chosen were getting on. Looking along the row of cadet photographs on the wall of the Commandant's office it was easy to remember faces, the kind of people they were, and how we had assessed them. Invariably our analysis was correct and every cadet proved to be exactly as written up after the four-day session at Ramridge. It illustrated two things. The first was how remarkably clever the system was; the second was that the selectors need only be reasonably discerning people with common sense and an appreciation of the great importance of getting the right answers. It proved to be one of the most satisfying non-flying jobs that so far had come my way. The expression non-flying was not really the whole truth for by good fortune the Communications Flight at Andover (with a nice old fashioned grass aerodrome) provided us with the Anson, Proctor, and Rapide to keep our hands in practise. We used to go to Andover regularly, sometimes making trips to places like Aldergrove in Northern Ireland. The Rapide was my favourite machine; with its wide-vision pilot's enclosed cockpit, the highly tapered biplane wings, the remarkably slow approach speed and finally the wheeley touch-down to stop the porpoising, it was a very special aeroplane.

The third posting after my return to the RAF was completely different again from the first two. It is one of the attractions of Service life to move from one job to something usually quite different somewhere else; it makes for great flexibility in a service career. In this instance I had put in a bid (like all good officers with a permanent commission) for the RAF Staff

College Course. It was said that only Staff College graduates ever got high up the promotion ladder because what the great ones at the Air Ministry wanted were thinkers and planners; in their judgement anybody could drive an aeroplane. The weakness of this principle is that all too often the clever staff officers get so far removed from the realities of ever-increasing development in aircraft and air warfare that they lose the vital connection between theory and practise. In my book a good senior officer is both a thinker and a practising pilot and he should not despatch the squadrons off to battle unless he has a very good personal experience of what it's all about. In that situation the squadrons trust and admire him and it generates a commodity called leadership. The bid for a Staff course had a very unexpected result, for instead of Bracknell I was sent to attend the second course of the NATO Defense College in Paris. (It was later moved to Belgium because France no longer wanted NATO Forces on her soil). When I went home to our charming thatched cottage in the village of Appleshaw to give Irène the good news, she exclaimed, "Goodness! I cannot possibly go – I haven't a thing to wear!" It seems that all women visiting Paris assume that haute couture is the pre-requisite to being acceptable in that fascinating city.

When the excitement of the news had died down we prepared to leave. At the time we had just bought a splendid little 1931 open tourer Morris Minor; it looked for all the world like an animated perambulator but it did us proud and was called 'Thumper' after the bunny rabbit mascot on the radiator. We paid the princely sum of £70 for it and as it was our pride and joy we decided that Thumper had to go to Paris too. We left Appleshaw with the car loaded up with our personal possessions and set off for the Dover-Calais sea crossing and then had to cope once again with the intricacies of driving on the wrong side of the road. Upon arrival in Paris – Irène was driving because I was chicken, as they say – we located the small and inexpensive hotel that a friend had kindly organised for us. It was a start; but, oh dear, it was awful. All the camions – the trucks – delivering their market wares to Les Halles went thundering past unceasingly through the night and bright Neon lights proclaiming Gauloise cigarettes penetrated the flimsy curtains. We moved at the first opportunity to a very small apartment near the Etoile (Arc de Triomphe) and this was a considerable improvement but the main snag was that we had to cope with what the French call a bastard double bed. To make it a little more bearable we turned it through ninety degrees to get the desired width and in order to accommodate legs and feet (we are both quite tall) we put American Army foot-lockers at the head, padded them up with travelling rugs and then a chair each at the bottom end as a final touch. It was hilarious. Fortunately soon afterwards we moved into a really nice apartment higher up in the same building.

Le Collège du Defense, OTAN (to give it the correct title) was located in a favoured section of the French Ecole Militaire, Place Joffre, a splendid and impressive complex situated on the left bank of the Seine. The French Government had been very generous in providing such excellent accommodation and it was appreciated. The directing staff was headed by US Army 2-Star General Paul Caraway with a blend of French, American and British staff officers all handpicked and the students came from all the NATO countries and included civilians amongst the military men of navy, army and air force. There were about sixty of us all told and there was thus a wide spread of nationalities and professions.

The routine as expected was along the usual lines of lectures, discussion, working groups, and sundry visits to places of military interest like aircraft factories and seaports. It was a particularly interesting course and the whole affair was made very colourful by its international NATO flavour. We British were lucky in that English and French were the official languages even if we all had to learn American, both spoken and written. The Europeans were fair as linguists but some were not and they were helped considerably by highly professional interpreters during lectures with the listener selecting the language of his choice. The interpreters were quite amazing and even made the appropriate gesticulations literally as the speaker said the words. The visiting lecturers were all Top Men from the Alliance countries and this put the whole college on a high-level basis.

The six-month course apart, (thank heaven we were not subjected to exams which are my most unfavourite hobby,) the time in such a beautiful and civilised city was a wonderful way of life and Irène and I loved every moment because there was so much to do and so many places to visit. There is an electric air prevailing in Paris, even on a day-to-day basis, and we had the opportunity of exploring some excellent little bistros recommended by French friends and made many sorties to the theatres and the night clubs. With an overseas allowance to add to my Wing Commander's pay it was surprising how well we lived; provided that is that you knew your way around. A special bonus was that Air Commodore John Elton (from whom I took over 47 Squadron in the Sudan) was the Air Attaché in the Embassy and he and his colourful Italian wife Francesca soon got us into circulation. A little later on Air Commodore Mark Selway became the Air Attaché with his wife Pat to support him. Yet another bonus was Air Vice Marshal 'Black Mac' MacDonald, my one time Wellesley commander in the Sudan, who was ably supported by the talented Moppy. Black Mac was now the Inspector General of Air Training Western Union Defence Organisation, and inevitably Mark Selway dubbed him the IGAT of WUDO. It all seemed like the old RAF Sudan gang now operating very happily in Paris.

At the end of the course I was given a posting to Supreme Headquarters, Allied Powers Europe. In those days it was based near Versailles, and SHAPE was that part of NATO land and air forces set up to protect

Europe. I was particularly lucky to be put into the Plans, Policy, and Operations Division so I was one of the clever boys – or so it was said. It was a fascinating job and one that entailed all the complexities of so many nations trying like the devil to make it all work despite so many diverse national attitudes, characteristics, customs and even prejudices. The American element naturally was predominant and as they were the biggest shareholders by far this was not surprising. Thus SHAPE was geared to the American style of military management and groaned with vast amounts of staff administration; the result was that everything took forever to materialise and in the process everything had to be translated into Americanese. Unlike the British Services (where for example you yourself normally decided to visit a unit), in SHAPE you had to get special authority first and when at last you were free to go you were loaded down with a fistful of authorisation papers to submit as you went along. American-style staff work invariably produced mountains of paper-work and Winston Churchill's dictum that he would only read a single piece of Foolscap paper would have appalled them. One day I tackled an American colleague about the need to churn out so much bumph; the Colonel said that it was essential to impress the General – it was good for promotion!.

One of the advantages of living in Paris was that it was so convenient to travel anywhere in Europe. For example we made a wonderful tour down to the South of France and another to Trieste where Irène's step-father and mother lived and we later returned to Paris by another route. Another subtle advantage was the psychological feeling that we were not visitors from England but were Parisians speaking French and Italian so we were like them, temperament and all. One evening at a cocktail party I was in conversation with three Frenchmen and we were talking about life in La Belle France and how things were settling down after the war. I commented that having lived in their attractive country for a number of months a thought had occurred to me that the French national motto could perhaps be brought up to date. After some moments one of them fixed me with a beady eye and said, "In what way, *mon Colonel*, do you propose a change?" Smiling happily to suit the little tilt at French lifestyle, I replied, "*Monsieur*, how about 'Liberty, Equality and twenty-percent for Service'?". The air became, as they say, electric; then one of them commented, "You are wrong, *mon Colonel*; twenty-five percent". At least I had made my point, but Gallic humour it seems is not the same as ours.

The French way of life certainly had it's interesting aspects and was based in some measure on their particular kind of logic. During my travels in overseas countries some pointers to the character of the indigenous people was to read their newspapers and observe the manner and style in which they drove their motorcars; in this way one could get a good insight into national traits and attitudes. In this diagnosis the Germans were meticulously correct, the Italians excitable with their car horns in constant use and the French had a dead-pan expression on their faces and never looked to their left because they were only concerned with vehicles to their right that had priority. They were quite ruthless in their parking habits and it was normal for them to shunt furiously either to make room to park or to provide a space for driving away after shopping, dining out, or whatever. As a large majority of the cars were Citroën types with identical bumpers it could only be supposed that French drivers were using them for the purpose intended and the result was that most of them showed ample evidence of regular use. French horn-blowing was more of an insurance and alibi than anything else but there were moments when the habit was triggered off by frustration. On one occasion a massive log-jam at going-home time developed on the very wide sweep around the Etoile and in no time at all a cacophony of tooting horns assailed my ears with the driver behind me at his best in the contest. I thought it would be amusing to participate in some way and so I left my car and walked towards the man behind me. "*Monsieur*", I said gravely, "if you are in a hurry to go home – as indeed you seem to be – I will be happy to let you pass as soon as possible." At this my friend got out of his car and shaking me warmly by the hand protested that in no way was he going to be so ungracious as to do that. "Why then are you using your Klaxon so much?" I asked him. The Frenchman replied with that most expressive of motions, the Gallic shrug of shoulders accompanied by arms half-raised as in supplication, shook my hand again and got back into his car. It was a great day for Paris (despite the forebodings of multiple accidents by all of the press) when the Prefecture introduced a law prohibiting the use of motorcar horns in toto except in dire need. Beautiful and elegant Paris recovered its charm and everybody was delighted.

The opportunity of getting some flying in France was not forgotten because an enthusiastic RAF officer called Sq Ldr Jones and I contrived to form the SHAPE Flying Club. With the willing and very welcome help from the French Government we were delighted to accept two 'Stampe' Belgian-constructed aeroplanes for as long as we needed them. The 'Stampe' in appearance is similar to the Tiger Moth and in some respects it was a better aeroplane if for no other reason than that it had full top and bottom wing ailerons, (thus making it more manoeuvrable,) and a fuel system that enabled it to fly upside-down for as long as pilots like myself could endure. The two aircraft were based at the military aerodrome at Villacoublay and as hangarage was provided, as indeed was maintenance, effectively all that we had to do was to pay for the fuel. The two Stampes registered F-BCQE and F-BAMY gave the members a lot of flying and by paying only for aviation fuel the cost was minimal. It was a very generous gesture on the part of the French Government and we appreciated it enormously. *Vive la France*!!

Following a visit to Le Mans, where we stayed overnight at the Hotel 'Le

Lion d'Or' at Bonnetable after driving around the track of the famous *Vingt-quatre heures du Le Mans* at all of fifty mph, my darling Arleen – a pet family name – some weeks later tentatively mentioned that something unusual was happening because she was feeling a bit off colour. Colonel Tony Crook, RAMC, who was senior medical officer, British Forces in SHAPE, soon gave her the glad tidings that she was, as the French say, enceinte. Yes!, she was pregnant. This was wonderful news and nature proceeded on its way but not without some complications. Irène was sent to the RAF hospital at Ely where the problem persisted but her determination and morale so impressed the specialists that they decided to let nature take its course. On one ever-remembered morning whilst slaving away at SHAPE to plan the defeat of the hordes invading NATO Europe, a telephone call from England told me that a son had been safely delivered. Jonathan had arrived into this world on the third of January, 1954.

When I had partially recovered from this most exciting news I walked in a dream-like daze into my boss's office to tell him because I just had to tell somebody and he was a helluva nice guy to share the news. General Al Donnelly, USAF and six-foot-five tall, grinned broadly as he thumped me on the back with a large hand. "Ar gee, kid" he said, "Well done! just forget the goddam Russian hordes today and go away some place and get drunk". As a good staff officer of course I did my best to carry out what the general instructed me to do and I enjoyed every moment of the special occasion. A week later mother and son returned to Paris. Our American friends Joe and Anne Scott of the US State Department, (Joe was a fellow student with me at the NATO Defence College) took their big Buick to Le Bourget aerodrome to collect them because I was stricken with 'flu at the time. It was snowing, and on the way to our apartment his lordship began to bellow loudly. Mother was distressed but not so Ann for she said in her charming southern accent "For gawd's sake girl, he's hungry – feed the little fellah". Thus it was that Jonathan had his first meal in France; and I have to say that it was provided from the cutest of containers!

Some weeks before our son-and-heir was born I had a requirement to make an extended tour of the Northern area of NATO Europe to call on the Air Forces in my particular area of interest. At the time Reidar and Iris Johannessen had left Hong Kong on holiday and they were staying in their Norwegian home in Bergen. It was a very fine property alongside a fjord and included a twin boathouse, landing stage, and a swimming pool for good measure. I had been told in a letter from Iris that Arleen (as Iris called her) should not go driving about in her condition in our silly little Morris so would I please go to Bergen for a night or two and return to Paris in their Allard car so that Irène could travel in much greater comfort. This was done and we now had two cars in the family.

After three years of a blissful life in France – work and playtime included – the time was approaching to go back to England and we wondered if we would take our faithful Thumper with us or look for a buyer amongst the British contingent. A sergeant in the RAMC was looking for a car and he and I made a deal which was seventy pounds, the same as our original purchase price. To help him with the problem of spare parts for a car that was over twenty years old I gave him a contact in South London and he later elected to replace some components in the differential drive to the back wheels although in my judgement it was not necessary. However, he obtained the parts, did the job himself, and then (so I was told) called out to his wife to go for a trial spin with him. She got in and he started up the engine and put the car into bottom gear for take-off. To his considerable surprise Thumper began to move backwards; he had the only motorcar in the world with four speeds backwards and one speed forwards. Oh well; back to the garage. . . .

The motorcar situation (after the Thumper was sold and the Johannessens arrived in Paris to recover the Allard) was resolved in a wonderful way. We were on leave in England at the time and I was travelling one day in a borrowed car along the Bath road between Reading and Newbury. At the Half Way Garage I happened to spot a Bentley in the showroom as I passed and the car had such unusual body-work that I went back to have a look. It was a 3-litre 'Red Label' open tourer model but I was still curious about what seemed to be non-standard bodywork in the style of 1935–36. As it was for sale I expressed my interest and then contacted my Bentley friend Tony Townshend who fortunately lived nearby. He and I returned to the showroom and he at once declared it to be one of the rare RC Series Bentleys that had been assembled by Rolls Royce in 1936 five years after the Bentley Company had been purchased.

I fell in love with the car and after scraping the barrel I bought her for £250. I must not bore the reader unduly with technical details, but to the aficionado I now owned a special Bentley tourer that was one of a batch of ten only and was numbered RC 32. We drove her back to Paris and used her constantly including a run down to Cap Martin, Monte Carlo, where the Johannessens had a splendid villa originally owned by the Prince of Montenegro. Such was the fame of Bentleys in France after their many successes at Le Mans it was so heartening whenever we stopped to hear Frenchmen say admiringly, "*Alors – quel chance – Le Bont-lee! Quel voiture*"!

Our happy days in France came to an end with a drive to Boulogne on a distinctly chilly and snowy January, it was Jonathan's 1st birthday. The Channel crossing was postponed by bad weather and after an overnight stop in a comfortable hotel the three of us and the Bentley embarked on the ferry and then had to endure a dreadful sea crossing. Poor Irène with her baby to care for was not allowed to lie low, but I confess that I did. Eventually we reached Dover, and set off to stay with friends. I was given some leave and we moved into a holiday apartment at the Ifield Golf Club and later on briefly shared a nice house near Horsham called Farthings with Elizabeth Whytock and family. We were once again in the vacuum of waiting for the next posting. I visited the RAF Club, hoping to glean something about my future on the grapevine and there met up with Air Vice Marshal 'Black Mac' MacDonald who was able to tell me what was in store for us. Over a drink – I enjoy chatting up nice AVMs! – he said that I was destined to be an Air Attaché but the precise country had to be secret until I had been accepted by the host country, a formality of protocol that is observed in diplomatic circles.

I returned to my family and told Irène what was afoot but as I was unable to say which country it was to be we made all manner of wild guesses. In the meantime, I was free of commitments and put in a bid to try my hand at some more jet flying after the brief encounter in Meteors and Vampires two years earlier at North Weald (with Peter Wykeham-Barnes' help) had whetted my appetite. On a spring day in 1955 the Bentley thundered down to RAF Western Zoyland in Somerset and the twelve hours of flying Meteors that followed was just like a holiday; but goodness, these new-fangled flying machines certainly do take up an awful lot of sky. One moment you are careering down the runway and in no time at all you are at forty thousand feet. The week spent earlier at North Weald was not without its exciting moments with my Polish flying instructor Flt Lt Kotlarz. On one of the sorties he told me to climb to forty thousand feet to practise stalls; on the second stall and after kicking the rudder as instructed the Meteor flipped upside-down and began to spin alarmingly. My inability to recover from this uncomfortable and frightening situation (due to complete loss of orientation) was not helped at all by the Polish voice which said in matter-of-fact tones, "Very interesting, eh?" He rescued me when the Meteor had lost about five thousand feet and after landing he commented "In the Meteor never use the rudder, especially near the stall". I now fully understood the reason why, and his practical demonstration was easily the best way of proving the point. Polish people are so direct in everything they say and do and if only for that reason I admire them enormously.

Soon after I returned from the Meteor flying I was told that the appointment of his Britannic Majesty's Air Attaché designate was to the Embassy in Teheran, Iran. I prefer to say Persia as it sounds so much more romantic. Once again another fascinating prospect was around the corner and we began to get organised for a completely new way of life.

A postscript to the happy days in France and the acquisition of the Bentley must be that the splendid product of WO Bentley is now in the caring hands of Dr Cy Conrad who lives in La Jolla, California. Heaven knows how many tens of thousands of miles she has travelled since she was new in 1935; Mr Bentley, take another bow!

Chapter XXV

The Land of the Peacock Throne

Now that we knew which country we were destined to go to we both admitted that apart from cats, carpets and caviar our knowledge of Persia was abysmal except perhaps that a poet called Omar Khayam wrote the Rubaiyat. There were of course the fabled Shahs of Persia who through the ages had been recorded in history books but the image was more of a fairy tale than anything else. The prospect that we might actually see the reigning shah one day was sufficiently far-fetched as to be dismissed as yet another pipe dream.

As a start we got out our well-thumbed Australian world atlas and gazing at the single page of Iran we had a geographical starting point. The factual information told us that the country is over 600,000 square miles (1.5 million square kilometres) in area and on that score alone it was well over half the size of the whole of Europe. So once again we were in for a big surprise. With a population at the time of some twenty million compared to fifty million in the United Kingdom this meant that human beings were much thinner on the ground out there and the map explained in part the reason why because of large areas of desert. The other reaction to the geography lesson was that Persia was something of a gap-filling remote area situated between the Middle East and the Indian sub-continent; the top end had the huge Caspian Sea as a significant frontier with Soviet Russia and the bottom end stretched the entire length of the Persian Gulf. The country looks rather like a broody hen in outline and is dominated by two massive mountain ranges, the northern one forming part of a two thousand mile stretch all the way from Turkey into Afganistan and beyond to the Himalayas. Judging by the altitude shading on the map (which went from green at sea level right up to the white of mountains above 15,000 feet,) the major part of Persia seemed to be around 5000 feet above sea level and this height included the capital city of Teheran. Once again we were destined to live high up and both of us liked the idea because it was the Kenya pattern where the air is good and makes one feel healthy.

The new requirement was to get to know the ropes of the new appointment. I spent some days in the Air Ministry attachés department and in between travelled around the country visiting the aircraft industry, the idea being that I would not only be up-to-date on current aviation developments but could relate what I learned to the possible requirements of the country that I was accredited to. The visits were naturally of considerable interest to me, but it has to be said that all the senior men who I called on damped my enthusiasm because without exception from the chairmen down they said that so far as they were concerned Persia was a forgotten country. Uncle Sam had gained a complete monopoly of both military and civil aviation interests so they certainly did not expect any changes in the existing situation. Ever an optimist, I hoped one day to be able to announce some moves in our favour.

The man in London who was uncle to all air attachés was a remarkable civil servant called JB Hogan, known since his early days as 'JB'. As he had been the administrator to air attachés for many years and knew precisely all the requirements and the special quirks of the appointment he was invaluable both as a guide and a father confessor. With his slightly portly figure, balding sandy hair, and a down-to-earth manner of speech he told us precisely what was expected of us. In particular he warned us against any thoughts that we might have of being a special breed of RAF officer destined to live in exalted style and probably 'above our station' as the saying goes. Specifically, he warned us that the extra allowance was intended to be used solely for carrying out diplomatic duties and should be neither under-spent or (worse still) overspent in a euphoria of high living. So far as he was concerned the appointment was just another professional job to be done, the difference being that it was quite specialised and it included the services of a wife and the official residence as platform from which a lot of the diplomatic activity would be conducted. It was no surprise therefore that JB invited Irène to accompany me one day to his office, the ploy being that he needed to discuss with her the finer points of her part of the job, but I suspected that in the process he was vetting her to see that she matched up to the requirement. Judging by the way that she and JB soon established rapport with each other I concluded that she had passed with flying colours; and that was no surprise to me at all.

There were two important factors concerning our domestic situation in Teheran. The first was that for some unexplained reason a temporary residence only was available; the second was the advice from the Foreign Office to take with us as much in the way of household furnishings and stores as possible because they were not available in the local shops and the small embassy shop only stocked basic items. It was too tricky to send anything by sea because apart from the time factor of delays at the only port of Khorramshahr, all too often the goods suffered subsequent losses in transit. On the evidence provided it looked as though we were going to have some work to do but fortunately both of us had a fair amount of experience to fall back upon in these matters and were not in the least dismayed. As Irène commented, "Persia cannot be more out-in-the-sticks than Kashmir, so I expect that between us we can cope!"

Although the house problem could only be resolved after our arrival 'en poste' at least we could now prepare a comprehensive shopping list and in this regard Irène was at her best. She ended up with a requirement list as long as one's arm and where better to shop under one roof than the excellent establishment in London called Harrods? We called at the office of one of our contacts there and he made the necessary arrangements for the purchases to be suitably crated for onward transit. On the basis of taking a pessimistic view, Irène seemed to do her best to empty the store and we armed ourselves with all manner of items like a complete canteen service of stainless steel (with no handles in bone or china to get damaged by careless kitchen staff,) a dinner service to match of crockery and glass, the usual run of domestic software, bedding and sheets; she even included items like bathroom toiletries sufficient to last for months. I gazed in wonderment at the variety and the quantities, fearful of the bad news when the account would be produced later, but her only comment was "Well, if you are accustomed to furnishing an Indian maharaja's palace from scratch as I have done – this is peanuts!" We left Harrods, now almost deserted as most of the staff had departed, and returned to our temporary home. We could now say with confidence that we would be equipped with the trappings of diplomatic and domestic life-style and so would not be obliged to invite the guests to eat with their fingers. The whole affair was hilarious until I had to pay for the purchases which ended up not far short of a four-figure sum; a lot of money in 1955.

The next task was to determine the manner of our going to far-away Persia and taking with us what the Romans so aptly called our impedimenta. We called at the overseas movements department in the Air Ministry to find out what they proposed and this was where the fun started. I explained to the civil servant fellow that the requirement was to transport three adults and one child to Teheran. In addition there was personal heavy luggage and a big number of packing cases containing a quantities of household items. I explained that this was occasioned by the fact that the British Embassy had been empty for more than two years during the Mossadek affair and so the new staff had to bring with them virtually all the items that normally would have been available as in previous years.

The Air Ministry Movements Officer apparently had already got wind of my appointment and had made plans for us to fly from RAF Lyneham as far as Habbaniya and thereafter onwards by Iraqi Airways from Baghdad to Teheran. Although I would have preferred to fly by civil airline all the way from England I accepted the fact that we were RAF personnel and so could not reasonably contest his proposal; it might prove to be less comfortable but at least it would be well organised and very professionally carried out. Where the heavy baggage was concerned he amazed me by saying that he would arrange for it to go by sea to Aqaba in Jordan and then onwards by overland means to Teheran. The idea was so preposterous that as soon as I had recovered my senses I asked him politely how he had arrived at that decision; his answer was that he had looked it up in an atlas I told him that I had personal knowledge of Aqaba and could not only assure him that no ships from Britain ever went there but it had no port facilities anyway. As for the journey overland, this was something that even Lawrence of Arabia had never attempted; and he travelled on a camel. With no camel track, let alone a semblance of a road, the prospect of making an expedition of well over a thousand miles across Saudia Arabia and Iraq before reaching even Kuwait was quite ludicrous. After other and almost equally silly proposals had been propounded, the fellow relented and agreed that the whole consignment could go by RAF air transport to Habbaniya and thereafter at the discretion of the Movements officer there. In that way at least we could ensure that our precious possessions would be cared for during the greater part of the journey and beyond Habbaniya we would cross our fingers and pray. After the visit to the Air Ministry I could not but wonder how a man like that in government service kept his job. Aqaba indeed!

I arranged for the cargo (which indeed it was) to go in a Vickers Valetta from RAF Benson and to ensure that no snags arose I went in person to see that the heavy luggage together with the Harrods consignment arrived safely and that someone in authority received it and knew precisely whose it was and where it had to go to.

Having got our cargo into safe hands, the next move was to go to RAF Lyneham in Wiltshire where a Handley Page 'Hastings' would take us to Iraq. The plan was to get to the overnight stopover point at Cliffe Pipard nearby where the RAF had accommodation for Service families prior to departure. Tony Townshend my expert vintage Bentley friend, very kindly agreed to travel in convoy with us in his own Bentley so that he could take over our own car and his passenger could drive the other one back to his home near Hungerford. We met at the planned rendezvous and in due course the party arrived at Cliffe Pipard where we made a fond farewell to both Bentley and Tony; he drove away and left us to our fate. Tomorrow would be the start of another adventure and this time it was to be in the kingdon of the Shah of Persia. The name alone made our pulse-rate quicken and we hoped that this was going to be the best posting of all, as indeed it proved to be.

The Handley Page 'Hastings' that took off from RAF Lyneham was not a particularly beautiful aeroplane but it was a well-tried cousin of the 'Halifax' and although somewhat austere inside suited the purpose well enough. The crew were very professional and caring and they could not have done more for the passengers, most of whom were Services personnel with families going to postings overseas. The hot summer of July 1955 was not the best time to fly across France and thence to El Adem in Cyrenaica and when we eventually stepped down onto the Libyian desert it was like walking into an oven. To add to our discomfort the RAF catering organisation thought fit to provide a hot meal such as one would have enjoyed on a cold winter's night in England. Roast pork, vegetables, and a hot pudding was the menu least desired in the circumstance and there was nothing remotely suitable for young children. It seemed almost incredible that the RAF Catering Branch could have been so unimaginative and as a result most of us ate only a sparrow's portion. After the overnight stop in adequate comfort – at least it was cooler after sunset – we were thankful to get away in the early morning and the Hastings trundled along the entire length of my old stamping ground of North Africa. As the sun got higher inevitably it became a bumpy ride because in the unpressurised cabin the maximum permitted height was 10,000 feet. I thought back longingly for the beautiful Mosquito which flew the same route at twice the speed and double the altitude. After what seemed like a lifetime we descended to Habbaniya in the late afternoon and the sight once again of the big air base in the Iraqi desert with the river Euphrates on one side and Lake Habbaniya on the southern side was a very welcome one. It had been a long day and thank heaven it was the end of our journey by Hastings. Admittedly Habbaniya was very hot and airless but the compensations of cool brick buildings, a shower bath, and a long gin-and-tonic with a slice of lime and plenty of ice cubes was reward enough; equally so the second one that also slipped down my throat without even touching the sides.

On the following day our journey continued and it consisted of a short sixty mile ferry flight to Baghdad in the Station Communications Flight Percival 'Prince' and we arrived in time to connect with the scheduled service to Teheran. This was in the Vickers 'Viking' of Iraqi Airways and operated by British staff headed by Captain Tom Walters, the Chief Pilot. The Viking took off and climbed away in a north-east direction and then headed for the Persian Zagros mountains that commence at the frontier and rise in places up to 13,000 feet above sea level. This of course was our first sighting of Persian country and although there is not a lot that can be seen from the cabin, the fleeting impressions were of very rugged black mountains with few trees and little vegetation. The valleys were occasionally dotted with green patches where small villages could be seen. Cabin staff told us that small holes like bomb craters in a straight line spread across the desert indicated the location of inspection points of the unique underground water supply system. The only town of consequence that we spotted was called Hamadan and this meant that we were more than half way on our 450 mile flight to Teheran. We were getting closer.

Our interest by now was beginning to intensify in the final minutes and after losing height we joined the circuit at Teheran Airport and the skipper made a thistledown landing. As we taxied in there was a good sighting of some impressive mountains to the north – the Elburz range as we learned – and the sprawling capital city of Iran appeared to be situated on a slope at the foot of them. One disappointing feature was that Teheran was a drab brown colour and from a distance there did not seem to be any white (or even off-white) buildings to brighten the scene. One of the curiosities of towns and cities in that middle eastern part of the world is that despite the climate no attempt is made to have white rooftops; this at least would make summer room temperatures bearable but the simple idea seems to have escaped the notice of the inhabitants. The Viking now arrived alongside the main airport building, the cabin door opened and we set foot for the first time on Persian soil.

We were now about to be initiated in to the characteristic ways of the British Foreign Service overseas; awaiting on the apron was a small posse of people looking for all the world like the reception committee that they proved to be. The leader was the tall, colourful, and expansive British Consul Max Perotti; he was accompanied by the Military Attaché Colonel John Maclean (Royal Garhwal rifles) and his wife Peggy together with sundry other Embassy people. The contrast to anything that we had experienced before was very marked and right away we felt as though we were being welcomed by old friends who in truth we had never met before. It was the pattern of the embassy style of operating and the staff were meticulous in endeavouring to make every visitor as welcome as possible; as we saw subsequently, nobody was left to his own devices and apart from assisting in every way where business facilities were concerned the process continued after the working day ended. In this way nobody was abandoned in their hotels and whenever possible they were farmed out to families who made life as agreeable for them as circumstance permitted. I only wish that I could say the same subsequently of other appointments in foreign places where I was obliged to endure the boredom of kicking my heels and wondering how to pass the time before moving on to the next assignation. It is fair to say that in later years when British embassies became hives of activity, particularly in regard to commercial affairs which almost took precedence over diplomatic work, the staff could no longer find time for the social niceties of the past. It was the price to be paid for the realities of having to keep pace with intense competition from foreign rivals in the world's markets.

With no more than a friendly nod from Max Perotti to the immigration and customs officials we were whisked away into town and taken to the Embassy. It is situated in a large compound in the middle of the city (exceeded in size only by the much bigger and well screened Soviet mission), and contained the Chancery, the Ambassador's handsome residence, Consular offices, the Commercial section, the Service Attaché's offices, the transport section, and some half-a-dozen residential homes of the diplomats and others. Tall chinars (plane trees) and other varieties were nicely positioned in the grounds which provided much needed shade in summer. In a central location amongst the lawns and flower beds was a small swimming pool that doubled effectively as a water supply for emergency fire-fighting purposes. Both the general lay-out and the style of the buildings was reminiscent of what used to be called the British Raj pattern in the Indian sub-continent and it was apparent that the architectural inspiration came from that source. The impression was heightened by the sight of Pakistani guards at the main gate, causing Irène to comment that she might well be in Karachi or Rawalpindi.

The accommodation initially provided for us was available because the press attaché Reggie Burrows was on home leave and this gave us about two months in which to find something for ourselves. The Gul Hak compound, much higher up and six miles away, contained the ambassador's summer residence and a number of houses for embassy staff. In recent months the Foreign Office Works Department had sent experts to Teheran to check all the buildings, (possibly the aftermath of the British evacuation after the Mossadek oil debacle three years earlier), and these gentlemen in their wisdom declared that some of the houses were structurally unsafe and so not to be used. The result was that accommodation was at a premium and the hapless Air Attaché and his family caught the brunt of it. Now we understood why it was that before leaving England we were told that we would soon have to fend for ourselves. It was not the best of ways to begin an entirely new job overseas but the situation had to be dealt with quickly and we were assured that Max Perotti's staff would continue to search for something suitable. For the time being we had a house (for which we were grateful), and Irène, Gillian Laurence (our 'au pair' and good friend), young Jonathan and I moved in and unpacked our luggage. The regular domestic staff fortunately was available and the cook and the *barjee* – a female housemaid-cum-laundry lady – were there to care for us admirably.

Our first impressions of Teheran were that it was a mixture of old and some new buildings with a somewhat Indian look about it all. Most of the government buildings were grandiose, there were a few comparatively modern multi-storey office blocks, and the rest consisted of drab brick structures that had neither style or charm; it was out of character with our visions of Persian elegance. The few shops that we saw were set up in haphazard array with window-dressing a jumble of goods of many varieties and it was evident that one had to spend some time to find something that you wanted. Western presentation and display was not for them, but on the other hand someone with an eye for spotting attractive items would find that the chase had added incentive. One unique feature of the Teheran scene was that the roads running north and south had gullies on either side about one metre wide with running water flowing from the mountains and this provided the citizens with a supply for all purposes, filtered tap water being a refinement yet to be introduced. The better houses (including those of the embassy) did at least have an internal piped system but the water tanks had to be constantly replenished from outside means. Carts delivered water to the embassy houses with a large bucket swinging crazily between the back wheels and this arrangement of course meant that water suitable for drinking had to be boiled before putting it into empty gin bottles and then placed in kerosene-operated refrigerators. The other facilities of electricity and telephones were available after a fashion to those who could afford the luxury but the service was not exactly to Western standards and when we saw the cats-cradle of wires adorning the telegraph poles in the most haphazard way it was not surprising. This then was the start of the Persian experience for us and we were learning fast.

Apart from the first introduction to the domestic scene in a day temperature of 100°F for several weeks, the settling-in process to the new appointment consisted of the new Air Attaché doing the rounds with Colonel Mac (who filled the Navy post as well as his own) to meet the Iranian Forces senior personalities and the Liaison Office staff who were the official links with all Service Attachés. The army and air generals and colonels, as also the admirals and navy captains, seemed well disposed to us and the political reasons why the British had been absent for so long seemed to be none of their making; quite the reverse in fact. Colonel Mac told me that they were all very much the Shah's men, a mixture of loyalty and keeping an eye on the main chance because what His Imperial Majesty did and said was paramount, I enjoyed my first encounter with my new associates despite having the language barrier in many cases to contend with. Some sixth sense told me that I was going to get on well with these men and that they would feel the same way about me; time would tell if my hunch was right. In the meantime I decided that I would play it cool initially and let them make the running. For her part, Irène was taken well in hand by embassy wives who went to no end of trouble to show her around and one of them was Aliki (wife of John Russell the Counsellor) dutifully presented her to Lady Stevens. Later at lunch she and I compared notes, she about Constance Stevens (who she found somewhat forbidding) and I who enthused about meeting the ambassador, Sir Roger Stevens.

As the days passed we began to get the measure of the job, and the numerous cocktail and dinner parties enabled us to meet a lot of people both diplomatic and otherwise. This gave us a good background from which to begin the process of integrating into the appropriate level of society that is an essential part of the job. Apart from the good spread of personalities that we met, the most numerous was undoubtedly the American element that boasted a fair-sized diplomatic team. The Americans also had a big Military Mission of some 3,000 advisors and instructors with an all-American provision of everything from jet aeroplanes to bootlaces. No wonder that the aircraft industry in England was so pessimistic about sales to Iran – Uncle Sam was well entrenched and could afford to give away the hardware if necessary.

All the while we continued the daily search for a home of our own and despite all efforts we had no luck and became distinctly restless as the spectre of having to move within a few weeks came ever closer. The problem was not made easier because of the dreadfully hot summer and there were some nights when we found the house so hot and airless that we preferred to sit in the swimming pool to cool off and then sleep in deck chairs as best we could. Poor little Jonathan, aged eighteen months, and Gillian (who was making her first visit to the Middle East) also had to endure the heat and we feared that they might get heat rash or some other unpleasant ailment. We prayed for the summer heat to end, and we prayed even harder for a nice cool home that would give us all a break from discomfort and anxiety.

The Good Lord must have heard our pleas because suddenly fortune smiled and our troubles vanished in a remarkable way. Irène heard through the gossip network that Hadji Namazee had returned from Hong Kong at the bidding of the Shah and was now Minister without Portfolio in the Government. She knew him well from her Hong Kong days and pdq – pretty damn quick – she was taken to his office by our driver Abdul Majid. She opened her heart to him and said that he was seemingly the only man who could help us to get a house before we had to move into a hotel, a prospect that was awful to contemplate. Dear Hadji, the immensely rich Persian Teddy bear straight out of Alice in Wonderland said in his quiet way that he would take steps and let her know as soon as possible. Within a day or two he telephoned and gave the gladdest of tidings by saying that he had arranged for us to have a house in Gul Hak owned by the Shah's ex-brother-in-law. We made contact with the charming Ali Gavam, our prospective landlord, and met him at his property to view our probable new home. It was a handsome villa not far from the Gul Hak embassy compound and situated 6000 feet above sea level in a small side road called Kouche Yakchal, the 'street of the ice' so named after a small cold store constructed of mud and stones containing ice blocks brought down from the mountains in winter. The villa was graced with a charming Persian-style garden that contained cherry trees, many varieties of shrubs, roses (naturally, as that is where they originated), huge pansies of many colours which lay under eight inches of snow for weeks only to pop up later as fresh as the proverbial daisy and other flowers so dear to the hearts of Persians. We began to get the message about the romantic and idyllic Persia so well expressed by Omar Khayam; the garden is the key to it all and as a rule they are not visible to the passer-by because they are well secluded with high walls to keep away prying eyes. To enhance the setting further, we could see high above us to the north the fantastic backdrop of the Elburz mountains, totally snow covered in winter and stretching for a thousand miles east to west. Two other desirable features consisted of a good swimming pool, (a wonderful asset in summer), and a gardener called Ali Baghbahn who soon became Jonathan's close friend as he used to operate the jubes, the water supply rivulets for irrigating the orchard and the flower beds with water straight off the mountains. At last we had found a lovely home, thanks to Hadji Namazee, and it would have been appropriate to call out 'Allah be Praised' with feeling.

Ali Gavam became a good friend and landlord and we saw him on many occasions. He told us that the name Persia had been changed to Iran because the former was a derivative of Pars, the Province lying along the Persian Gulf which seafarers who only knew the coastal area adopted as the English name many decades ago. He agreed with me that Persia though technically inaccurate had a far greater evocative meaning and sounded so much more romantic. The name Iran lacked impact and anyway was very similar to Iraq – a country that Persians used to describe disdainfully as the land of the lizard-eaters. The interesting thing was that a lot of western educated Iranians preferred to use the word Persia themselves and I hope that the habit persists.

The villa was not furnished, so we began to investigate the business of where and how we could get what was wanted. After a discussion with the embassy housing officer the recommendation was that the best plan would be to go to the RAF at Habbaniya and get what was suitable from the Depot Stores. Irène took on the job, but as her telegrams seemed to be falling on stony ground she flew down more than once to see the Works Department people herself. It was apparent that they had not the remotest idea about the specialised needs of service attachés and most of the cast-off furniture that they had on offer would not have been acceptable under any circumstance. Once again she was up against the civil service system whose minions follow the path laid down in the book of rules that applied to normal RAF practise. Anything so unusual as the supply of household furnishings to someone five hundred miles away in another country for official diplomatic usage confused them to the point of her exasperation. Eventually she banged their heads together and declared that she would go to Bagdad to get what she wanted, particularly items for the principal rooms including hard-to-obtain carpets large enough to cover the floors of the principle rooms that she purchased in the Baghdad Bazaar. One fine piece of furniture that she ordered was a dining room table made to her specification with a solid top with six legs only and able to accommodate sixteen guests seated in comfort. (It proved strong enough for her to dance on, solo!) JB Hogan was right, she was the right girl for the job; she operates at speed and in great style.

The ambassador Sir Roger Stevens was the epitome of what I imagined to be the ideal envoy. With a tall and distinguished stature he towered both physically and intellectually amongst his contemporaries who he addressed invariably as 'mon cher collègue'. He had an incisive mind, a special intuition about Persians and great speed of perception in grasping the technicalities of matters like my specialised field of aviation. To add to his undoubted abilities he had abundant energy and enthusiasm and effortlessly carried his staff with him by taking the greatest interest in all that they did. In retrospect he was probably the best boss in all respects that I was privileged to serve under and he made my job so pleasant because although most supportive he allowed me to get on with it without hinder. All the embassy staff, particularly those of diplomatic status, were obviously hand-picked for Teheran after our long absence and they had to begin the delicate process of renewing the contacts that Britain had enjoyed in the past. Without exception they were a pleasure to be with even though their talents and panache often left me mentally breathless. Denis Wright was the Counsellor who earlier in 1953 led the team sent by the Foreign Office to reopen the embassy after the Mossadek oil crisis. He remained at the post until 1959 when he became ambassador to Ethiopia and was knighted by HM The Queen. Thus to him must go the credit of being the pathfinder – and a very successful one – of our subsequent good relations with the Persians. It was a foundation that he continued to build up on when ten years later he returned as ambassador; an appointment that was to last exceptionally for eight years. It was not surprising that his successor multi-lingual John Russell, equally fitted the part admirably and he and his gorgeous wife – I use the expression deliberately – made such a deep impact. Aliki Russell's style of official entertaining was scintillating and it was an education to see the tall host and hostess in effortless overdrive all the while talking as appropriate in any one of five languages. No wonder that the Russells later were given ambassadorial appointments in Addis Abbaba, Rio de Janerio and Madrid for which Her Majesty the Queen bestowed a knighthood on John during her official visit to Ethiopia.

As the weeks passed Irène and I began to love the job more and more and the big country that we took to so much. With such a pleasant home to operate from we went about our activities (separately and collectively) with much enthusiasm; the way of life suited our temperaments and personalities and every day brought a new experience and another interest. I was reminded of the often-repeated comment during my days at Heliopolis as a young officer when I used to say "Amazing – I love every moment of my job and the government is actually paying me to do it!" One special bonus in the appointment was that as Service Attachés of Counsellor rank Colonel Maclean and I automatically fitted into the bracket of associating with the top strata of diplomatic and social activity. This made the job even more fascinating as it meant that we got to know everybody of consequence; the very influential, the very rich, and the very talented. The contrast made us aware of the huge gulf between the so-called thousand top families of

Persia and the rest of the population. Unlike Western countries where the backbone of a nation is the all-important middle class (as with Senior NCO's in the Forces) the old East of Suez formula still persisted with the middle part missing; you were either very rich or very poor. One day Ali Gavam and I were travelling on horseback whilst he was making an inspection of one of his properties. After visiting yet one more village I was tempted to say "Ali, which exactly *is* your bit of Persia around here?" With a smile and a wide sweep of his hand across the countryside, he said simply, "If you can see it, it belongs to me". He also owned estates around Rasht on the shores of the Caspian Sea where the best rice in the world is grown.

A few weeks after our arrival in Teheran the news arrived that my official car had been unshipped at Khorramshahr and an embassy driver flew down to the Gulf port to collect it and return along the 500 mile unpaved road to Teheran. The vehicle was a Standard Vanguard, and apart from its unsuitability for the job in some respects, to my dismay it was black, the official colour. The summer climate would have made it unbearably hot to travel in and so the first thing to do was to get it repainted in a cool air force blue. I protested to London that it would not last long on the very rough country roads when on tour and what I really needed was a Landrover. To my surprise one was flown out to me in a Hastings freighter some weeks afterwards. Things were looking up, but there still remained one more item to complete the set up – an aeroplane. At an appropriate moment I put my proposal to Sir Roger Stevens and he responded with enthusiasm. He made strong representations to the Foreign Office giving cogent reasons why it was essential for his air attaché to be able to carry out his job properly in such a large country and I in my turn wrote to the Air Ministry and pressed home my request with pungent emphasis.

The two-pronged thrust unfortunately fell on stony ground. Both the ambassador and I received replies from our respective London offices which said that although the proposal was valid and acceptable, (the point was taken that prior to the Mossadek affair the previous air attachés had been provided with an aeroplane so the precedent had already been established), the situation had now changed for the simple reason that the Treasury would not sanction the cost. Britain could not afford this kind of expenditure because of the economic recession and only essential requirements could be funded. This decision was reflected in the whole of the overseas expenditure of His Majesty's government and it was difficult to the point of embarrassment to try to maintain the erstwhile standing and prestige of Great Britain with foreign countries. It was the start of gradual decline, and it has to be said that it made the task of diplomatic activity very difficult for many years to come. In Teheran we had to keep up the pretence of representing a nation famed for its prominent place in world affairs but in reality our activities of a practical nature was a facade; all that we had to offer was style and the ability to offer wise counsel if and when it was asked for. The situation overseas, particularly in Middle East oil-producing countries, was now of Britain going broke and by contrast our friends becoming ever richer entirely thanks to Western expertise. That hackneyed expression *nouveau riche* was abundantly evident and with all the overtones associated with its thinly veiled uncomplimentary meaning. Our job now was to try to keep up appearances, a variation of the 'keeping up with the Joneses' formula except that the Persian name was often unpronounceable. One casualty of the economic squeeze was that no aeroplane was available for the Air Attaché; not yet anyway. Time would tell if this omission would be corrected.

All of Iranian life was dominated by one man; His Imperial Majesty Shah Mohammed Reza Pahlevi, King of Kings, Emperor of Iran, and a man of immense power. He inherited the Peacock Throne from his dynamic father Reza Shah who started life in the Imperial Army as a soldier and by sheer thrust rose so rapidly that he eventually disposed of the Royal family and the reigning Shah and took on the mantle of monarchy himself. This dramatic move was not unusual in Iranian history as in the preceding two-and-a-half thousand years since Cyrus the Great there had been many turbulent years during which the Imperial Crown had changed hands from one dynasty to another. The present Shah had succeeded to the throne as a young man and to begin with he had to tread cautiously. As maturity and experience developed he began to assert himself and during the time of the writer's tour in the late fifties there was no doubt whatever about his profound influence. All this occurred at a time when there were a large number of developments under way which were inevitably bringing radical changes in lifestyle that pushed the country from a medieval posture into the early 20th century. Thus it fell to the lot of the Shah to monitor and control this development and as he was the sole referee of everything of consequence it was apparent that he not only had many problems to solve, he needed all the energy and skills that he could muster.

It was fascinating to be a close observer of the scene and on a number of occasions my contacts, particularly in the military field, showed that almost every new project had to have the seal of approval from the Shah. Not for the Persian generals the very lengthy and cumbersome process of endless sub-committee meetings, committees, and interminable paperwork. On more than one occasion in my experience a chance remark or a suggestion made in reply to a discreet enquiry produced rapid results. The general would nod approvingly, he would say that a decision might be reached within twenty four hours, and almost before I had time to sit back and await developments the answer frequently was that the project had been given the stamp of royal approval! Iran was a good country for getting something done quickly, but you had to know the right people at the top who trusted your judgement and your integrity.

A good example of the way that it happened was an occasion at a reception when I was talking to the chief of staff of the Imperial Iranian Navy. I mentioned that England had very recently produced a remarkably clever amphibious craft and in my opinion it would be ideal for his purposes, especially anti-smuggling patrols in the Persian Gulf. I said that it was called a hovercraft and would he please dispense at that stage with the technicalities of the idea but just remember the name and keep an eye open for its development. Admiral Shaheen nodded approvingly and thanked me for my suggestion. Within a few years and without all the panoply of sales teams visiting Teheran armed with briefcases full of convincing data I was pleased but not surprised to learn that the Imperial Iranian Navy was now equipped with the biggest hovercraft fleet in the world. It all began with a calculated remark to the right person at a good moment. In effect only two men were involved at the decision-making level – the Shah and the Admiral.

Twenty years later, after delivering a Range Rover to Michael Simpson-Orelbar in the Teheran Embassy (a splendid ten-day journey across Europe into Turkey and beyond), Ahmed Shafic and his Italian wife invited us to dinner before we flew back to England. We met their son Captain Shafic of the Imperial Iranian Navy and he told us that he was based at Bandar Abbas and in command of the big hovercraft fleet. He spoke with enthusiasm of the craft and how suitable they were for operations in the Persian Gulf. I doubt that he ever knew the background story of how it all began by a chance remark to Admiral Shaheen at a cocktail party. The important thing was that he as the customer was delighted and it brought a darn good order to British industry – something that in Britain was as welcome as it was very unexpected.

The other interesting coincidence at the dinner party was to meet the Duke D'Aosta, a charming and good-looking Italian whose late father had been the Governor General and Commander-in-Chief of Ethiopia during the days of the Mussolini war. Little did he realise that he was talking to the Englishman who led the first air attack on his father's East African Empire when within hours of the declaration of war the Wellesleys swooped down on the biggest air base in the country.

The work of the diplomats, including as it did regular contacts with Government officials, office activities, and the constant receptions and official dinner parties was fortunately interspersed with tours away from Teheran. It is an essential ingredient of the job to travel regularly and see how a country manages its affairs for only in this way you can evaluate that much better. In the case of the Service Attachés it is particularly valuable because you can observe the military scene at operating level, meet the commanders of each area, and discuss when possible their tasks and responsibilities. In my particular field I decided to include civil aviation in my portfolio and in this regard I was very lucky because the two top men of military and civil aviation were brothers-in-law. General Gilanshah commanded the Air Force and General Isa Studakh was Director General of Civil Aviation and both men seemed well disposed towards me. In normal circumstance anywhere the personality factor is important but the Iranians seemed to have a special intuitive sixth-sense about foreigners and possessed wheeler-dealing skills almost to the extent that you had the feeling that they could read your thoughts. You were either acceptable or you were not, and I flatter myself that they approved of me. On many occasions they not only provided facilities well beyond normal protocol but were happy to implement suggestions that I made. I began to get the notion that I had become a friend and confidante, a situation out there that is difficult to achieve and rarely happens. The fact of the matter was that they knew all too well that I genuinely interested myself in all that they did and wanted to apply my experience to improve and develop aviation in their country. It made my appointment absorbing and interesting as a result, and there was never any vacillating; decisions were taken promptly and swift was the action thereafter. Compared to my earlier aviation career it was breathless in its application.

My initial travels (or tours) were made by road to cities with romantic names like Isfahan and Shiraz, both of which came fully up to expectations with their fairytale-like beauty and the exquisite mosques with tiled mosaics much too detailed to take in by eye in one visit. In normal circumstance I am not much of a sightseer, content just to absorb a token impression, but the Persian cities seemed to have a certain magic about them which was compelling.

For longer tours one such journey in the Landrover was made to Julfa, north west of Tabriz and situated on the river Araxes which forms the frontier with Soviet Russia. Julfa's only claim to existence is that the one and only single-line railway system between the two countries crosses the river at this point, and more out of curiosity than professional interest I asked the Service Attaché's liaison colonel if he could arrange a trip. He expressed considerable surprise that anybody would be so crazy as to want to go to Julfa voluntarily but said that he would advise the area army commander of the tour.

Irène, Jeremy Watkins-Pitchford, Abdul Majid and I set off on a cold winter's day in January and the weather became worse and worse as we traversed the four hundred miles of unmade snow-covered road to Tabriz. We eventually arrived in a blizzard and made our way to the Persian Army barracks, our first night stop. Jeremy was an Army officer who was continuing his studies of Farsi (Persian) after a language course in London and I thought it was a good idea to take such an agreeable and useful companion with us. His uncle Rupert had been my trout fishing partner in

Kenya and Jeremy followed the family traits of loving the outdoor life. The night stop as guests of the army gave us a good insight into life at working level and it was enlivened by Irène telling us that the hammam (bath) was a beautiful copper tub filled with warm water by a friendly soldier who thought that his duties included pouring water over her from a large copper jug!

After a bitterly cold night (such that I doubted that Abdul would get the Landrover's engine to start) we set off on the eighty mile run to Julfa. If the previous road surfaces had been considered rough we knew better because it was now like a farm track. We passed through the small town of Marand (where the main road goes to the Iranian-Turkish frontier post of Bazagan) and we continued due north towards Julfa. The speedometer reading eventually warned us that we should be getting close to our destination and suddenly in the falling snow a lonely figure waved us to a stop. It proved to be the general himself and he had elected to meet us in person outside the town; a charming if unusual custom that we appreciated. I thanked the general for his kind thought, but mindful of the appalling weather I had to ask him if his vigil under the tree had been not unduly long. He replied that he had been waiting there for three days. Poor fellow, his headquarters in Teheran had issued instructions about the visit but had not told him when to expect us. Such is the way of things in Persia. We followed the general's jeep for about a mile and on arrival at the army barracks the next surprise was to see a 16-man guard of honour lined up in frozen immobility. Dressed as I was in full winter clothing, including my old full-length Hebron sheepskin coat, I was not exactly looking the part of Her Britannic Majesty's Air Attaché. I walked quickly past the front rank and then asked the general to dismiss his troops before they keeled over like ninepins. It was a bizarre experience.

Julfa was a singularly uninspiring place and on the pretext of something to do I persuaded our host to take us for a walk by the river with Irène providing the family outing atmosphere of a pretend picnic. The realities of political geography were all too obvious because on the other side of the river were Russian observation towers and no doubt the soldiers inside were watching us closely with binoculars. I wondered what they made of us and what they reported to their superiors? For the life of me I could see no reason at all for those Soviet observation posts as what on earth was there to see – or even to worry about – on the Iranian side of the River Araxes?

The return journey, now that I had satisfied my curiosity and had seen a very dreary bit of the Soviet Union for the first time, was made by a westerly route that took us into Kurdistan. This is the very large area which unfortunately for the inhabitants is divided up into three parts politically and controlled by Iran, Turkey and Iraq. It is a singularly wild and beautiful country notable for its mountains and spring flowers in great profusion, particularly black iris and jonquils that cover the ground by the acre. We halted at a small town called Saqqez, after traversing the ninety mile western side of Lake Rezayieh, and the air was festive with colour and music because a wedding was in progress. Abdul made friends with one of the locals of substance who invited us to his house and from the balcony we had an excellent view of the Kurds in their baggy trousers, loosely arranged turbans, and curved knives at the waist who were dancing a form of slow motion Morris dancing. The music was provided by bagpipe-like noises from wind instruments and other minstrels were beating tambourines rhythmically. It was quite charming and the general atmosphere was carnival but unhappily in complete contrast to the other side of the coin when the serious business of fighting for independence would break out again. Here we had the situation of a Kurdish nation at odds with three occupying countries and today no one is the better for all the ugly business that continues interminably. Humans are such contrary beings in their relations with each other and although not directly applicable to this case it has to be said that the vital element called religion that should provide a common denominator of tranquility all too often is at the root of conflict. It was ever thus.

Another Landrover journey took us to an equally wild area of North East Iran and the holy city of Meshed was the aiming point. It is over five hundred miles from Teheran and not far from the huge plains of Soviet Russia which lie fifteen hundred feet lower down along the frontier of a steep escarpment five hundred miles long. It is thus a natural political dividing line akin to the Andes of South America. Accommodation on the road to Meshed was no better than barely adequate, one resting place for the tired travellers necessitated the fumigation of our beds to rid them of very unwelcome tenants. Some eighty miles short of Meshed we passed through Nishapur, and nearby is the mausoleum of Persia's most famous poet and intellectual Omar Khayam whose Rubaiyat had been ably translated by Edward Fitzgerald. The ornate resting place was adorned appropriately with a good measure of phallic symbols, thus illustrating one facet of the Persian's love of wine, women and song.

Meshed is a holy place of great repute in the moslem world and the dome of the principle mosque is completely covered in gold leaf. The city houses the remains of many martyrs, most of whom were done to death savagely in past ages. Their commemoration (in common with many other holy men elsewhere sacrificed to religious fervour in similar fashion) had produced a plethora of public holidays. Each time yet another one was announced I would ask the circumstance and almost invariably the answer followed a similar pattern; "Oh, it was because Ali the son-in-law of the Prophet was stoned to death in the streets of Qum". Having heard the sad tale it was difficult not to comment "Surely therefore it should not be a holiday so much as a day of mourning?" and this usually produced the typical Persian-style nod of the head backwards, this meaning "Not for one moment" or even "You must be joking" depending on the desired emphasis.

We were accommodated in Meshed on a makeshift basis using our own camping gear in the abandoned British Consulate; it was sad to see such a handsome property in varying stages of disrepair and with a solitary Pakistani as the caretaker. The reason for its demise was not so much lack of usage but one of economy, so once again there was evidence of the decline of the British where the citizens were concerned. The Consulate did at least give us a clean place to stay and from there we explored the holy city and made some purchases. Meshed is close to the famous turquoise mines of Niashapur and we visited a dealer in a back street who sat impassively in a sparsely appointed room and produced gems by the handful for us to make our choice at prices that shoppers in Paris or New York would not have believed possible. As it was the right season, a special attraction in Meshed was to enjoy the delicious large black cherries and pistachio nuts of the locality. Other very good fruits and vegetables were grown in the area but the primitive method of packaging at the time was such that the products were rarely sent to Teheran and when this was done the condition on arrival was predictable.

The two days in Meshed were followed by making the return journey by a northern route and it took us in the faithful Landrover over high ground to Bujnurd where there was a large army base. The landscape was greener, (due to Caspian Sea influence producing the rainfall), and the tall poplars in the town situated 5000 feet above sea level gave a beautiful elegance to the scene. The army accommodated us for the night in Persian style and the hospitality included a delicious evening meal of chicken kebab and that superb long-grained rice from Rasht nicely washed down with local red wine. The next place of interest on our Westerly journey was Gombad-i-Kabus, one hundred and fifty miles away and situated at Caspian Sea level. It's name is derived from the Tower of Kabus and most surprisingly this is a quite remarkable brick structure looking for all the world like a fluted and sharpened pencil some 150 feet high. It was constructed in AD 1006 to receive the body of the Ziyarid Ruler Shams el Ma'ali Kabus who died in 1012. Legend has it that he was suspended in a glass coffin high up in the tower with a small East-facing window to simulate the open door of a tent, the conical tip giving an optical effect. Despite it's stark simplicity it is very impressive and must be regarded as one of the great buildings of the world. A little to the south of the town (which it has to be said had little charm) there is a hundred-mile-long stone-built wall running from the south east corner of the Caspian Sea to the hills nearby. It was built by Alexander the Great to contain the warrior horsemen of Turkestan.

Gombad-i-Kabus had no suitable accommodation (to put it mildly) and we decided to move out into the countryside where after a search we found a charming site to camp out for the night. It was a typically Persian setting of poplar and willow trees growing alongside the banks of a running brook of fresh cold water. It was so much better than the best that Gombad-i-Kabus had to offer and camping out under such an idyllic setting was delightful. Whilst we were busy setting up the camp a horseman was seen galloping towards us at speed and when he was quite close he reared up his mount and vaulted out of the saddle in a way that a circus performer would have envied. With Abdul as interpreter he said that he was the chief of the tribe in the area and wanted to seek the advice of the 'Khanoum hakim' (lady doctor) about his young wife who poor girl had endured a second miscarriage. Irène soon discovered that she was a teenager and the fact of the matter was that this young girl needed a rest from her husband's attentions. She thereupon told the wild-looking chief in no uncertain terms to leave his wife alone for some months and in the absence of anything better she produced a dozen aspirin tablets for her to use as necessary but to take no more than one tablet per day. With the advice now received and clutching the small packet in his hand the huge fellow lept onto his beautiful stallion with a cry of thanks and galloped away in a cloud of dust as rapidly as he had come. Irène was curious about the unusual circumstance and said to Abdul "Why did he think that I was a doctor?" Abdul looked at her knowingly; "When we arrived at Gombad-i-Kbaus I told the people in the town that you were a doctor; therefore you were an important person and when we decided to camp nobody would try to rob us or attack us; the news reached the chief who came specially to see you and now everybody knows that the English doctor has done good things for their chief and they will remember".

After a good night under canvas we set off in the early morning to visit the famous tented bazaar that is set up every week right on the border with Soviet Russia. This is where beautiful Turkoman tribal rugs and other attractive hand-made items can be obtained, and we were anxious not to let the opportunity pass. As we neared the site on the edge of the huge Russian steppe to our chagrin nothing was to be seen and so sorrowfully we retraced our route. Abdul made enquiries and we then realised that we had foolishly chosen the mohammedan sabbath day. Very reluctantly we had to leave empty-handed and it was not possible to return later. We greatly regretted our mistake; it would have been fun back in England to be able to say with the casualness of intrepid travellers "Yes, we picked up some Turkoman rugs when visiting the tent of the woman who made them; she lived in Russian Turkestan, of course".

The last stages of the long journey took us to Gorgan and then along the Caspian coastal road to Babul Shahr where the holiday resort hotel at last provided us with very welcome creature comforts. After the first bath in many days we sat down to enjoy a Persian style dinner that included Beluga caviar straight from the Caspian fishery at Bandar-e-Pahlevi and local vodka to compliment it. Who could resist such a feast? In the morning, now nicely refreshed after a good night's sleep in proper beds, the final leg of 100 miles entailed a steady climb up over the Elburz mountains with the railway track disappearing into the mountain side at different places to keep the gradient as gentle as possible. We stopped every now and again before reaching the highest point at 10,000 feet and as a train was ascending at the same time it was entertaining to guess where the very remarkable Swiss-designed rail track would emerge from each tunnel. I have to admit that nearly all our guesses were hopelessly wrong.

When the Landrover arrived back home after the ten-day safari we concluded that it had been by far the best tour of all. It had not been done in any degree of comfort, but that was of secondary importance. What it had taught us was something of the huge size of the country, the varied terrain and climate, and not least something about the kind of people who lived in such remote places. We loved what we saw and our affinity to the country increased with the experience.

An equally pleasant but different assignment was occasioned by the visit of a party of some sixteen students from the Imperial Defence College in London. Led by Evelyn Shuckburgh of the Foreign Office, they were on a fact-finding tour of Middle East countries and it had been arranged with the Iranian Government that the itinerary included a visit to Teheran. The ambassador asked me to think of something useful for them to do after they had made formal calls on the senior military personages; I made a plan accordingly. The proposal was a very simple one, and it was that rather than escort them around the city like a party of tourists or make boring courtesy calls on the lower echelons of the military I would take them by road across the mountains and down to the Caspian Sea for a night stop in the Babul Shahr Hotel. In this way, and with suitable stops en route, they would get a much better impression of the country than any amount of meetings and discussions would give. Furthermore they could regard the outing as a bit of a busman's holiday and so get away from the interminable and often useless programmes that all too often were laid on by zealous if unimaginative organisers.

The convoy of cars set off in fine order from Teheran and I was delighted that one of the students was the redoubtable Air Commodore Fred Rosier of Fighter Command and Desert Air Force fame who invariably injected his special style of entertaining personality into everything that he did. The first stop for a picnic lunch was at a very charming Persian setting alongside a small stream of ice-cold water babbling past. Our guests had their first experience of sitting on tribal rugs under willow trees whilst iced vodka-and-tonics were served prior to a real Persian-style meal. The more erudite of the students began to quote passages from Omar Khayam's Rubaiyat and it only needed ladies present like the beautiful hostess Irène to complete the idyllic scene. When we reached the summit of the Elburz mountains we stopped again and the students began to appreciate the military problems of an invading force trying to emulate Hannibal with his elephants crossing the Alps. From the summit we made the steep descent down countless hairpin bends to the coastal plain and eventually arrived at Babul Shahr. It was a telling experience for them to see at first hand what geographical problems would be encountered in any military activity and it was all learned under the pleasant conditions of a holiday outing. The Persian hotel manager was an excellent host and the party enjoyed the relaxation from constant travel to the extent that a second night-stop was made; on the third day we retraced our steps back to Teheran. The party now knew much more of the country than they had ever imagined and the overall impression that they received was judged most valuable. The final bonus on the eve of their departure back to England was an outdoor party laid on by John and Aliki Russell; and who better to do justice to the occasion than they? The members of the Imperial Defence College had good cause to remember the Persian visit; and so did the Air Attaché and his wife.

Chapter XXVI

Persian Tales

The second part of the three-year appointment in the magic land of legend and contrast proved to be even more varied and interesting than the first; it was occasioned by a mixture of gathering experience and events that seemed to arrive in an ever-increasing crescendo. By now we were coming to understand the rhythm of life of the Iranians, (that is as far as it is possible for foreigners to do so), and it was helped because we had a curious affinity for them despite their reputation for deceptive ways and customs and not least the language barrier although this was slowly being broken down to some extent. All this enabled us to go about our affairs with greater confidence and so proficiency and enjoyment went hand in hand. The Iranian language is called Farsi and resembles Arabic only in the sense that it looks similar on paper to a Westerner's eyes and is also written from right to left 'backwards'; on the other hand numerals are written from left to right and although different in speech are almost identical to Arabic. To add to the mixture, words like *hakim* (meaning doctor) are common to both. It is a natural language for left-handed people to write and flippant people used to say that 'writing in Farsi is all arsy-tarsee!' Persians speak with less of a throaty rasp than Arabs and the spoken word has a pleasant lilt to it not unlike Welsh and delivered articulately with each syllable clearly pronounced.

The process of integrating with them much more enabled us to range far and wide, and one example was to meet a charming lady called Princess Safia Firuz whose family had been part of the previous Qajar dynasty so today she was only an honorary princess. Safia Firuz had a charming country house about one hour's run out of Teheran; it was set on a hillside 6000 feet up from sea level and it provided a green oasis in an otherwise barren landscape. The swimming pool (which as usual doubled for a water supply) was very deep and the first plunge into it almost took your breath away, so cold was the water. All around were the typically Persian poplar trees together with many shrubs and flowers, and the lunch was of course in Persian style and quite delicious. It consisted of lamb kebab cooked on charcoal, that superb Rashti rice, and local wine followed by fresh fruit and finally coffee served in small cups not unlike the Arab style. Curry and other hot spices used in everyday life further East (so it was said, to disguise the basically poor quality of meat) were never used in Persia and so with my kind of palate I could taste everything with great enjoyment. Persian cooking however includes delicious additions like cardomon seed, cinnamon, dill, garlic, mint, and fresh walnuts properly skinned. One memorable dish in summer is called mast, and it is basically yoghurt with cucumber, dill, and raisins with a touch of mint to taste and served chilled with ice cubes. In private homes all the meals were served conventionally, but it has to be said that at official functions although the quality was excellent everybody had to endure the sight of magnificent platters of food sometimes laid out on the driveway outside the cook-house before being served and thus getting cold; by the time that we had helped ourselves and then eaten it standing up most of the enjoyment had gone. As with Meshed but in less profusion there are any number of fruits and vegetables available in Teheran. One of the former is called 'tutti farangi' – the fruit of the foreigner – which in fact is the strawberry and no doubt imported into Persia many years ago by an enthusiastic Briton from the Consulate. They were delicious and eaten with relish with thick cream to your taste from a herd of cows imported from Jersey by Safia's family.

Another new experience was to be invited to visit the state-run caviar fishery at what used to be called Bandar Pahlevi on the Caspian coast and of course to-day inevitably given another name to erase every reminder of monarchy. Very big sturgeon are to be found at the southern end of the Caspian because the water is much deeper and fed from clean rivers cascading down from the Elburz mountains. The caviar is quite excellent, both the Beluga and the second quality Sevruga comparing very favourably with the Russian variety. To some, caviar is the epitome of pleasure for the gourmet but its reputation as a dish only for the rich is due in large measure to the small output. Even in the country of origin the cost was quite high but it bore absolutely no comparison to astronomic prices charged in Western capitals. It was interesting to see the big fish (some ten feet long and more) being processed and the roe extracted, washed and slightly salted before being put into somewhat primitive flat tins and then sealed – so to speak – with a wide elastic band! As with a visit to a chocolate factory, the strong aroma was such that we could not for a moment accept the kind offer to taste the product; that pleasure was to come later with friends or under home conditions and with a small glass of Persian vodka for good measure. Today, with the excess of religious fervour predominating in the country, one can only assume that the wine and vodka produced in the Shah's day is just a happy memory. Admittedly they were not as good by any means as those of European origin but I have a nice memory of a red wine that answered to the undistinguished description of Number Twelve. I wonder what Baron Phillipe de Rothschild's vineyard would have made of that?

Any account of life in Iran must inevitably include a reference to that desirable commodity called oil. It is of course available in untold quantities around the top end of the Persian Gulf and for the record it was explored for and developed as a major industry by Western geologists and engineers. The bonus to the peoples of the area has been of immense proportions, something that it might be fair to say has been as unmerited as it has been remarkable in changing the politics and the immense wealth of the few who live there. Who at the turn of the century would have given a damn about such a hot and unpleasant part of the world, except perhaps those seeking pearls from the sea? My own professional interest in the oil business was perfunctory but all the same there was a certain fascination that attracted my attention and on more than one occasion I was able to see at first hand some of the operating procedures during visits to the fields. Oil men are a breed unto themselves – I suppose they have to be – and on my first introduction to the complexities of it all my simple request to see crude oil, perhaps only in a glass jar, was not possible because there was not one single tap to turn on anywhere to satisfy my curiosity. However one day I saw more than enough to dip my finger into because the dreaded spectre of all oil men happened; there was a blow-out.

When the news reached Teheran we learned that the gusher was not far from the holy city of Qum and therefore sufficiently accessible for John Russell and myself to motor down and have a look for ourselves. It was a memorable experience. On arrival in the area our Persian oil-man took us in his car across the desert and said that the famous American trouble-shooter Myron C. Kinley had been engaged to do his hazardous work and even before his departure from the States he was getting a fee of $10,000 per day. Very fortunately the gusher had not caught fire as can so easily happen, but all the same his task was formidable because he had to employ special techniques and heavy equipment to plug the hole and later control the flow via another outlet. Before leaving the car (which stopped short one mile away) we had to empty our pockets of items like matches and put on rubber-soled shoes against the possibility of sparks. Even at that distance the black fountain rising up 500 feet into the air was impressive enough and the nine-inch hole with 12,000 feet of drill still inside had a pressure of over 10,000 pounds per square inch at the surface. At a distance of about five hundred yards our guide stopped; apart from the impossibility of speech due to the tremendous roaring noise it was very dangerous (and pointless) to get any nearer in case the oil caught on fire by stones striking what remained of the toppled derrick. When we had retreated back to the car and could speak again without shouting we were told that what had happened was that the drill-bit (hired incidentally from the Howard

Hughes company) had punctured the dome of the oil field allowing high-pressure gases to escape and taking crude oil with it high into the air.

Kinley's first job was to erect a big fire-screen with water in abundance playing on it whilst he and his team got to work; as the location was in the desert the water supply alone was a major undertaking. Having got his protective screen into position the next job after dragging away the twisted gantry was to lower a very heavy metal box over the gusher by crane, the box having a vertical hole in the centre and the contraption was then anchored very securely to the ground. That done, the next task was to drill a second hole at an angle in such a way that it joined up deep underground with the first hole but before actual contact the second hole was fitted with a massive tap. With correct timing and everything prepared, the two holes were connected up underground whereupon both exploded oil. The final stage was to turn off the No 1 tap and then after slowly turning off the No 2 tap, god willing the precious oil would stop gushing. It must have been an extraordinarily dangerous and difficult operation technically and we both marvelled at it all. Before John and I left we walked to a shallow depression in the desert where the crude oil from the huge fountain was collecting and had formed a small lake. The liquid was running like water and I had my first sighting of crude oil; it was black and looked and felt in my fingers somewhat like dark engine oil from a motorcar. Interestingly enough the oil in the lake was not lost because a wax skin forms underneath which prevents seepage and it is straight-forward enough to pump it away into tankers. As we drove back to Teheran I commented to John that I marvelled at the huge costs and complexities of the oil business, particularly when something goes wrong so dramatically, but I concluded that I was happy to stick to aeroplanes; it was a sentiment that he endorsed.

According to our visitor's book (now showing signs of age and much travel), there is an entry for November 1956. We had an unexpected guest and his name was Group Captain Peter Townsend. The story begins some years earlier when my old friend and inheritor of the equerry's job at the palace had to endure all the traumatic circumstance of being one of the best known names in the World's newspapers. The story of his romance with a princess inevitably produced all manner of rumour, conjecture, and gossip. They had to withstand the awful business of being constantly in the headlines; nothing was allowed to stop the penetrating thrusts of the gentlemen of the press. Once their decision not to marry had been made, Peter went to Brussels to become the Air Attaché at our embassy and so reverted to the RAF after an absence as a courtier of a number of years. In Brussels it was hoped that he might gain a degree of privacy that most of us enjoy, but it was not to be. Peter therefore decided to retire from the RAF and he made a plan to make the Grand Tour around the world by Landrover and with any luck escape from the interminable and thrusting attentions of the media.

When I heard about his plan I concluded that in all probability he would have to pass through Persia. On that assumption, and bearing in mind that his route would be quite a rugged one with wild country and few creature comforts across Turkey and then into Persia, I wrote to him and reminded him that I was in Teheran. When his reply came back, he said that although he was delighted that I had contacted him he knew that I would understand when he said that he had made up his mind to steer clear of friends and officialdom; that spelt danger from the press. I could not but sympathise with his decision, and wrote and said so. Two months later, very early one morning the Pakistani guard at the embassy telephoned to me to say that a sahib with a Landrover was asking for me. I did not have to ask who he was and said that Abdul Majid would go at once to meet him and navigate him back to our house in Gul Hek. Poor Peter, when he arrived at seven-thirty in the morning he looked dreadful; he had obviously picked up an influenza bug or something similar. Irène took one look at him and she said "Peter, what you need is a cup of tea, a hot bath and after that into bed pronto; please stay there for as long as you like". He did what the lady said; so in the event Peter Townsend had come to stay. We now planned the next stage of his enforced visit and the essence of it was that he had for all practical purposes disappeared from sight; he could relax in our home for the time being until he was well enough to continue his very long tour.

For the next few days Peter hid-up and we cared for him like a member of the family. It was just as well that he had contacted me because during the long haul across eastern Turkey he had been feeling miserable and it is certainly not the place to be unwell on your own with no friends and no place to sleep except in your Landrover. I was surprised that he had managed to reach Teheran at all. When he eventually arose from his bed I told him that not a soul knew where he was except the ambassador and the Press Attaché Reggie Burrows who had to know so that he could fend off any probings from the world's press. Our distinguished guest's health improved rapidly and he just could not believe his luck in being so easily left alone from clicking cameras and tape-recorders. Young Jonathan, now rising three years of age, thought that he was super because he had a Landrover. Anybody with a Landrover was special and the two got on famously.

Although we made a point of avoiding any reference to recent events in his life, one day I tentatively asked him if he ever had thoughts of telephoning to a certain young lady in London. When he replied that he would welcome it I said that I would try to arrange something but the call had to be made from the Telephone Company's overseas exchange in the city. Peter told me that if the call was at all possible, success depended entirely upon which telephone operator was on duty 'at the other end'. There was only one that mattered, someone who was sympathetic and discreet. The call was booked, and we went into town the following evening to try his luck. I sat in the car and Peter with Abdul as escort went inside the telephone building. It seemed a long wait, and when he reappeared he got into the car and looked pensive as we drove away. After some moments I said "Peter; any luck?" He shook his head. "No James, it was not the right operator at the palace so I just hung up". The silence as we drove up the hill was painful. I sensed that he felt that the world had ganged-up on him and there was nothing that he could do about it. The tension was only broken when we returned to the house and had a damned good whisky-and-soda. Life plays the strangest tricks sometimes; and so often it hurts dreadfully.

Inevitably the grape vine in Teheran somehow leaked the news about Peter and the ambassador told me that we had been summoned to Princess Ashraf (the Shah's twin sister) for dinner on the following night. There was no escape despite the fact that Peter and I were due to leave in the Landrover very early the next day, the plan being that I would accompany him as far as Isfahan and return with Abdul in the Vanguard. So there was no option but to attend at the princess's palace, but previously Sir Roger and Constance had invited some of the embassy staff for a drink at the Residency. One guest was Gillian Laurence, known as Gigi as that was how Jonathan pronounced her name. Some of HE's guests were lady secretaries and when they saw the three of us they naturally asked who was at home looking after Jonathan. She smiled happily; "Oh", she said, "the babysitter is an awfully nice chap called Group Captain Peter Townsend!" What a splendid throw-away line!

The royal command proved to be a singularly boring affair and it was obvious that after the initial curiosity of meeting such a world-famous person had worn off our hostess and her entourage lost interest. When the buffet dinner was over, we had to endure watching the film 'Moby Dick', with the projector constantly stopping with breakdowns. Eventually Irène, Peter, and I made our excuses and thankfully we left the palace. At 3.30 am we arose, collected our kit, and set off for Isfahan. It had been a long night of little sleep and nothing to commend it.

The six-hour run to Isfahan produced one of those incredible situations of Peter at last opening his heart to me about the events of the past years in his life. Poor fellow, he obviously needed to say it to an old friend, and where better than when travelling in the night together across central Persia? I must confess that from time to time I fell asleep; and to think that all the world's newsmen would have given their eye-teeth to have been in my seat even for five minutes!

On arrival at the hotel in Isfahan I tried to perpetuate the illusion of anonymity by saying that Peter was an old friend who was passing through and wished to be left alone. However the manager knew otherwise when he looked at his passport (which was triple thickness to accommodate all the visas), saw his name on the cover, and smiled knowingly. In the morning our paths diverted. Peter set off on the very long desert run down through Southern Iran into Baluchistan and so to Pakistan and beyond. If he feared any pressmen on that section of his round-the-world journey, well he would be delighted to know that it was an area where they would not show up. Camel men perhaps, but certainly no camera-wielding news vultures. Abdul and I retraced our steps to Teheran and I resumed my diplomatic duties.

The land of contrast continued to bring fresh surprises and interest. There was skiing to be enjoyed in winter at a place called Ab Ali (over an hour's run by car from Teheran up into the mountains) and the fact that the Shah was fond of winter sports ensured that essential facilities like road access and a ski-lift were available. With equipment provided by the embassy sports club it was an excellent day's outing whether one was a skier or not – and I was not. It was somewhat optimistic to become even a nursery slope person without any previous training, but with the exuberance of the cold clear air and the company of experienced enthusiasts I could not resist trying my hand at the exhilarating sport. The start from somewhere up the slope was not particularly difficult but after that I invariably suffered from the almost total absence of rudder and brakes. When disaster seemed imminent the best that I could do was to fall over into the snow and disappear in a flurry of white and pray that I did not hurt myself unduly. It was the greatest fun and the picnic that followed was always enjoyed. One of my few regrets is that I never had a chance of learning to ski earlier in my life; starting at the age of forty-five has distinct disadvantages.

Another surprise was much more in my line of earlier experience and that was to participate in the joys of the embassy summer camp at a superb place called the Lar Valley high up in the Elburz mountains, 8000 feet above sea level. The camp was accessible only by a six-hour pony trek from the nearest point that vehicles could reach and it then entailed crossing two high ridges before getting to the valley. One of the embassy concessions of long standing was that the Iranian army provided horse and mule transport to get everybody and everything there; but for this handsome gesture the camp site would have been inaccessible. The camp consisted of a mess marquee and sleeping tents and was set up in the same place each summer alongside the Lar river; it was possible to accommodate about one dozen people at a time. Two embassy servants provided all the cooking and domestic requirements, such as they were, and so we were singularly lucky to be able to have ten days of bliss in the cool air and away from city life. Apart from walks and some mountain climbing of a simple nature, undoubtedly the great attraction was the river flowing down to the Caspian because it contained brown trout that were the greatest sport to fish for and then cook for breakfast soon afterwards. The camp site had a carpet of green grass occasioned by spring water emerging from a rocky hill known as Chuh-Chehel-Chehesme, the hill of forty springs; it was perfectly safe to drink because pollution was non-existent. All around were wild and mostly barren mountains, inhabited by Ibex and there was sufficient grazing close to the river for nomads to come with their sheep. Where they came from and how they got there remained a mystery. Camels occasionally invaded the camp, causing mild upsets to say the least.

My family soon made a booking to stay at the camp for the standard ten-day period and I happened to mention to my friend General Isa Studakh that we were looking forward to it very much. He said, "Group Captain, why don't you fly up there? There is a small strip nearby that His Majesty uses occasionally and I can arrange for you to go in a Beaver from the Air Force". It was the teddy bear picnic big surprise yet again and I accepted enthusiastically. Irène preferred on the first occasion to go by Landrover and horseback for the experience (thus recapturing the style of her beloved Kashmir) but I decided that an aeroplane was for me. The flight up from Doshantapeh aerodrome took twenty-five minutes and it was quite spectacular to see the mountains all around us and then descend down to the unmarked landing area about one mile from the camp site. As I opened the door and stepped down onto the ground my nostrils took in the unmistakably strong perfume of wild thyme, sage, and clover growing in the greatest profusion everywhere. It was quite wonderful; and to add to the physical impressions there were innumerable grasshoppers jumping about all over the ground. As the Lar valley is completely snow-covered in winter I wondered how on earth life returned so easily with each successive springtime.

The army ponies arrived at the strip to pick us up, the kit (including of course the fishing tackle) was removed from the Beaver, and John Russell and I rode like Marco Polo to the camp. It was a fascinating start. For me the trout fishing was the best thing of all and two or three times a day I would walk along the banks of the ice-cold river, often to cross it at shallow spots where a gravelly bottom permitted, and I invariably returned with trout for the frying pan. It was Kenya happiness all over again. In the evening it was wonderfully cool and after meals that only a fresh-air life can fully appreciate we slept under blankets and woke as soon as the sun rose over the mountain tops. In the distance to the East could be seen Mount Damavand, eternally snow covered, and at 19,000 feet the equal of Mount Kilimanjaro. My first experience of getting to the Lar Valley so easily, thanks to the Iranian Air Force, naturally produced a number of subsequent requests from people who for one reason or another could not travel on horseback. So with new-found confidence in the relationship that I had established with my Persian friends I approached General Gilanshah and asked him if he could help. Typically, he replied, "I will tell Major Rafat to arrange as many flights as you ask for". A whole series of flights to the Lar

Valley were laid on and many people both from the embassy and their friends were able to take advantage of an almost unique air service provided by His Imperial Majesty's Air Force. Where else, I wondered, would that have been possible?

One subject that frequently cropped up at the ambassador's Monday morning meetings (known as 'prayers') was the problem of how Britain could usefully contribute anything of a practical nature towards the development of Iran. Admittedly the thin top layer of society was well placed, it had been that way for centuries, but there were many facets of life for the majority that needed attention. An obvious requirement for example was to introduce piped water to the cities and a water tower in each village instead of the primitive kanats (underground water tunnels) that were inefficient and required a lot of maintenance. The problem was the usual matter of cost; Britain was having an economic recession and overseas aid had been cut drastically. How then could we help without a big expenditure of Sterling? Our American friends were not handicapped in this way; they contributed millions of dollars, as witness the Armed Forces where everything was provided by the Rich Uncle.

In my own field of activity nothing seemed to come to mind; anything to do with aviation was becoming excessively costly and anyway there appeared to be nothing outstanding that was not already set up by the Americans. Supplying technical advisers was pointless if there was nothing in the way of British aviation equipment to advise about. One day however – to be more precise, one night – the hand of chance played a card that was to prove to be a heaven-sent inspiration.

In recent weeks I had been listening to the faint sound of aerial activity high up over Teheran; as I have an acute sense of hearing I began to wonder what or who was making regular night flights in this way. Whenever I checked up with the men in the airport control tower the answer was invariably that no aircraft movements had taken place. Well now, what to do about it? I decided to see my good friend General Isa Studakh, the boss of civil aviation. I had formulated an idea in my mind and now was the time to test it out.

The General was most interested to hear of my account of high-flying aircraft by night that were unaccounted for and said that he would advise his brother-in-law General Gilanshah although the reality was that nothing could be done of a practical nature. I then came up with a proposal that I would try and persuade the Air Ministry in London to send out a Tactical Air Force Mobile Radar unit. I explained that these units were self-contained, they had their own specialised vehicles, and were manned by a handful of technicians and operators. It was by far the easiest way of introducing a radar facility into Iran. A Mobile Radar Unit could arrive under its own steam, so to speak, and needed no costly setting up. The general was delighted. At last I had thought up an idea that was not only a practical solution for checking up on those mystery flights, it could be accomplished for a small outlay.

Immediately after my talk with the general I reported to the ambassador and he thoroughly approved of the concept and would pursue it through his own channels. I told him of a later extension to the idea; and that was to investigate the possibility of a training scheme whereby specially selected airmen from the IIAF would go to Britain for a course on electronics. This however might present problems as I doubted that the students would cope with such sophistication; perhaps a straightforward radio course to begin with would do initially.

Surprisingly, the idea caught on quickly in London and action was taken immediately. It was decided to move a TAF Mobile Radar Unit from NATO Europe complete with personnel and ship it out to the Persian Gulf and then the vehicles would travel overland up to Teheran. Despite a mild warning from me that the mountainous route in winter could be fraught with problems I was certainly not going to over-emphasise it and so postpone the arrival date. The unit duly arrived at Khorramshahr and we sent an embassy transport man down to lead the convoy back. It was on Christmas Day 1957 when the three large vehicles arrived and were located at Doshantapeh military aerodrome. As I remember there were two officers and four NCO's plus drivers so it was a compact team and for the first time in history Radar had arrived in Iran. Although the road journey was quite dicey at times they completed the trip safely. It was a very satisfactory conclusion to the long journey from somewhere in Germany and everybody was pleased. Now we could get down to business.

Right away the Unit was operational and the RAF airmen were hard at work feeding the data received to the control tower. The controllers no longer had to look out of the window to try and track aircraft movements – the RAF was doing the work for them. To me, the curious thing was that radar surveillance had never been thought about earlier. At my suggestion the Iranian Air Force sent twenty of their best men to England to take a radio course at an RAF School and I thought it prudent to warn our Signals people not to expect too much from them. In particular I asked them to be zealous and understanding during the training period because the Iranians would be in a strange country trying to cope in an unfamiliar language. After a struggle, some of them passed the course (if only marginally), and so no real problems arose. Meantime the Radar Unit ticked away happily and the RAF men found time to give selected senior Iranian Air Force personnel some initial training in operating procedures. I have to confess that I was pleased; Britain had made a worthwhile contribution and the Chief-of-Staff of the Armed Forces was quick to thank us. The night skies over Teheran no longer produced faint noises that previously I had been so suspicious about.

In 1956, when I was attending the SBAC Air Display at Farnborough as an essential part of my Air Attaché work, the very glad news came to me that the Air Ministry had decided that the de Havilland 'Devon' based in Ankara could be shared with Teheran. After some discreet investigation I discovered that this unusual compromise was the result primarily of Treasury threats to take the aeroplane away altogether, the reason given was that the winter weather in Turkey was so bad that without adequate radar navigation aids my opposite number in Ankara was limited in the amount of flying that he could carry out. The Persian weather factor fortunately was much better. So far as I was concerned it was exceedingly good news as half an aeroplane was better than none and on return to Teheran I waited to be told when to go to Ankara and claim my winter share. The plan was made easy because my opposite number was Group Captain Gilbert Howie; we had both been in 216 Squadron together and it became an amicable arrangement between friends. I was quite elated that at last my request was to be granted and I had visions of flying all over Iran during the final part of my tour. There was however a requirement to get back to sound flying practise but fortunately Gilbert was a qualified instructor and so he was the man for me. In early January 1957 I flew to Ankara to stay with Gilbert and begin my refresher flying course before returning in triumph to Teheran with my latest – and let's be honest – my prized possession.

The final and the most exciting piece of the jig-saw was at last to become a reality; I had gone to a strange country to do a job well removed from normal RAF life and had been obliged to build up both the professional and the domestic aspects of it from scratch. In two years I had succeeded in making a lot of progress; Irène and I had made friends with the Persians and we had a very good home, a growing son splendidly looked after by Gillian, two vehicles, a staff of six, and now the prospect of an aeroplane together with an RAF engineer to look after it. All the evidence pointed to the happy thought that the latter period of the tour would be concluded in a euphoria of happiness and perhaps some success to justify the decision (and not least the cost) of my appointment as an Air Attaché. The final and last year of the tour was beginning and I was determined that it would be the best and the most profitable of the three. An aeroplane to complete the set-up was about to become a reality and I looked forward eagerly to taking it over, if only for the winter months.

Alas! the joyful expectations were short lived and disaster struck in a singularly embarrassing way. Gilbert took me to Ankara airport and showed me the beautiful aeroplane in pure white with all the appropriate livery of the Royal Air Force markings and 'HBM Air Attaché' proudly showing on the fuselage below the cockpit. The instructor and pupil then got aboard and after take-off I began to get my hand in again after an absence from regular flying of four years. She was a delight to fly and Gilbert showed me the technicalities of operation and demonstrated how nice she was to fly on one engine. Then he said "Whilst I'm at it, I had better show you a single-engine landing – a piece of cake in the Devon". He took control, got clearance from the tower and descended to the long runway and explained the finer points of approach speed and so on in a flying instructor's style. Just as we were about to touch down I heard a sinister scratching sound outside and before we could even gasp in dismay the Devon arrived on her belly and stopped abruptly. Yes, two experienced pilots of senior rank between them had committed the unforgivable sin of forgetting to lower the landing gear. Sorrowfully we walked away with heads down and I returned to Teheran as an airline passenger.

In due course the Devon was repaired but in the meantime I had lost my winter share and so had to wait for my turn to come round again. Just before that was due to happen the Air Ministry decided that only a qualified ferry pilot with navigator was good enough to ferry the Devon to Teheran so I was not given the pleasure of collecting my own aeroplane. I was eventually checked out in Teheran and at long last the story ended with one lovely Devon in my charge and the excellent Flight Sergeant Bob Goody to care lovingly for it. The team, and the correct equipment that any self-respecting Air Attaché should be blessed with, was now complete. With a well-run office with Flight Sergeant Ralph Grey (followed later on by Warrant Officer Charles Giles) to hold the fort there was no more need to keep badgering the Air Ministry for more. We were now in business. The first manifestation of success came within a day of the Devon's arrival because Sir Roger told me that all his associates had been congratulating him upon his new acquisition and even the Shah had commented favourably. It is in matters like this that in some subtle way a country is judged overseas and the cost is very difficult to assess accurately in terms of real profitability. It is called showing the flag, and despite outbursts from socialists forever complaining about the principle, the system is magical in its application. It was now my good fortune to be the private owner of an expensive aeroplane and I had every intention that it would show dividends. It was an exciting prospect, and as events were to show it was totally rewarding. I felt that I also had adopted (as with Casano of armoured cars fame) the mantle of Oliver Cromwell's russet-coated captain who knows what he does and loves what he knows.

Chapter XXVII

More Persian Tales

Three years had passed since Her Majesty's Government had returned to Iran and re-occupied the embassy. After a cautious start the handful of career diplomats, hand-picked for the job, were now settled in and things were going smoothly. There were no problems and our relationships with the Iranians at all levels were very satisfactory almost to the point of being excellent. We continued to maintain the momentum and at each 'prayer meeting' the ambassador received heartening accounts of continued progress. However there still remained the need to continue the means whereby Britain could at least appear to be contributing to the recovery of Iran after the earlier setbacks. The two Service Attachés were at a disadvantage in this regard; anything substantial that we might be able to offer cost a lot of money and the radar unit was not exactly contributing to the wellbeing of the people; something commercial was wanted, and I began to explore the options open in the aviation world. The choice narrowed to airline activity and it focussed on the fact that the British Overseas Airways Corporation had not resumed flights to Iran for three years. I put this to the ambassador and he reacted favourably with the result that I went to see General Studakh, and asked him for his opinion. He responded enthusiastically and encouraged by his approval I wrote to BOAC in London to say that the airline's return would be welcomed. Apart from the prospect of increased business there was the added advantage that Iran lay on the shortest route from the UK to the Indian subcontinent and beyond.

Fortunately my letter arrived on the desk of Basil Bamphylde, in charge of Far East routes; his reaction was favourable but I had to convince him that the traffic would sustain a change of route. My reply must have impressed – perhaps even startled – the Board members because I supplied figures for Teheran overall air traffic movements in detail; I even gave very confidential information of each airline's activities, something that is not at all easy to acquire. BOAC was quick to respond and proposed to use the outdated Argonaut airliner for an initial weekly service. My reply was swift; I said that if that was the best that they could do they had better not come at all. The counter-proposal of using the new de Havilland 'Comet' jet airliner was turned down because of non-availability; agreement however was reached to use the turbo-prop Britannia, an excellent airliner with a good reputation for its quiet and smooth performance.

Having agreed on the policy and the type of aeroplane to be used, the next stage was to make a proving flight, the standard airline procedure to check out all the operational matters before commencing scheduled services. Before that took place BOAC decided to send out the Senior Pilot and Manager of Flight Operations to make an inspection and Captain Norman Robb arrived to find out if Teheran Airport was acceptable. He and I discussed the whole business at length and the Devon was put to work to good effect; we made a thorough inspection flight and he got valuable practical experience from the cockpit of the facilities that were available. Admittedly the navigation aids were pretty basic (which made him wince) but he was reassured when I told him that from personal observation the bad-weather factor was very small and also very predictable.

The proving flight was then discussed and in order to get the maximum impact the suggestion of making a non-stop flight (and with luck creating a new record) was agreed. With the cooperation of my Control Tower friends the operation was to include the Devon as a radio link so that I could relay messages between the Britannia and the tower and by so doing speed up the time of arrival and ensure a priority landing. It all smacked of wartime operations with Bostons and Spitfires twelve years before. Where else but in Iran would this kind of military-civil aerial exercise on an international air route have been possible?

As soon as news of the Britannia's departure from Heathrow was known, Bob Goody and I took off in time to make the rendezvous point one hundred miles to the West of Teheran. Having checked that Meherabad Tower was still in contact with us on the VHF radio frequency in use I began to transmit "RAFAIR 532 calling SPEEDBIRD – do you read?" After two similar transmissions were made, SPEEDBIRD replied and it was Norman Robb's voice. The Britannia was somewhere within R/T range and flying much higher than the Devon so we never saw each other. I passed the information to the tower and gave the Britannia's ETA (estimated time of arrival) and the tower replied "Clear to come straight in on Runway 08" which I relayed to the Britannia. With that Bob and I sped back to Teheran but by the time that we reached the airport the Brit had already landed; I followed suit and parked alongside. To our astonishment there were no less than six Captains on the apron. Captain Norman Robb had brought a big team of four-stripers with him to get to know the airport and its facilities and he also brought two very charming and attractive air-hostesses as well. With that kind of a start BOAC was about to make an impact on Teheran in a spectacular way and the press coverage laid on by Reggie Burrows was comprehensive and effective.

The Britannia stayed for four days and a large number of VIP's were given flights over the top of Mount Demavand, a sight that I doubt that any of them had seen before. All the Captains took turns to fly and thus became familiar with the airport and its facilities; finally, by way of a public relations boost, Irène and I laid on a big reception. With Norman Robb's concurrence he closed a good eye (like Admiral Lord Nelson) and the whole BOAC team attended in uniform. Inevitably they were identified and surrounded like film stars – not least the air hostesses! It worked like a charm. I was able to complete the impact on the guests by announcing that the Britannia had flown non-stop from London to Teheran, a distance of some 3,500 miles, in less than seven-and-a-half hours; a new record. British Overseas Airways had returned in style.

In late 1957 a letter from Cyprus arrived from the Commander-in-Chief of the RAF forces in the Middle East area. Air Marshal Sir Hubert Patch, (known as Sam to his contemporaries), wrote to ask my reaction to a proposed goodwill visit. Although Iran was beyond his normal sphere of activity he thought that it might be acceptable to the Iranian authorities and such a visit could well be beneficial to both countries concerned. The suggestion appealed to me very much for a number of reasons and I went to speak to the Ambassador to get his reaction. He was equally enthusiastic and said that he would get the Shah's blessing before anything could be done by way of a programme. Soon afterwards Sir Roger said that he had seen the Shah who not only gave his royal assent but went further by saying that he would be pleased to meet the Air Marshal himself.

With that encouraging starting point I began to make preparations. There were a number of factors to take into account; suitable accommodation; which senior military personages to call on, other than the Shah; the length of the stay; the means of travel from Cyprus to Teheran; and of course the kind of diplomatic party to lay on in his honour. The accommodation element was soon resolved because I said that Sam Patch was a particularly well-liked Air Marshal which prompted Sir Roger to say that he himself would be his host. I persuaded the C-in-C not to travel by RAF Comet, as he at first proposed, but said that he should fly in a Canberra light bomber and I would explain the reason later. The C-in-c agreed, and about a fortnight later three Canberras arrived very punctually in impeccable formation over Mehrehabad Airport and carried out a neat stream landing one behind the other. The Royal Air Force of Great Britain had made an impressive arrival and the Ambassador, Colonel Maclean, technician Bob Goody and I felt great pride to witness what perhaps was the first RAF official visit by air to Iran in living memory – or ever, for that matter.

The Air Marshal stepped out of the first Canberra and departed with His Excellency in the ambassadorial Rolls Royce and then Bob Goody and I organised the rest of the party. Bob carried out the entire servicing of the three Canberras single-handed and how he managed so well was a testimony to his undoubted talents; he took it all in his stride. So the first day's work was successfully carried out, the three aircraft were neatly parked and made secure, and our distinguished visitor and his fellow airmen were all suitably cared for. It was the embassy style once again and the RAF crews took note!

The next day began with the C-in-C's formal call upon the Shah. Acting as his ADC and in our best uniforms (with medals jangling together plus aiguilettes and ceremonial swords to complete the ensemble) Sam Patch and I stepped into the Rolls and were driven to the palace. The audience with the Shah of Iran was about to begin, and I thought that we looked the part of suitable emissaries from Britain. As the car drove into the Saadabad Palace driveway with the Royal Guard saluting smartly as we entered, Sam turned to me and said "Pelly, what's the form?; How long are we supposed to stay?" I replied "Sir, I'm told that visitors to His Majesty come in two categories. Most of them are ten-minute ones but exceptionally a few are two-hour people. I have a notion that you are in the second bracket". We stepped out of the Rolls under a white colonnaded portico rich with beautiful Persian mosaics and were taken to a waiting room by the Palace Chamberlain and awaited our turn to be taken to the Shah's drawing room. Within a few moments we were ushered in and after being presented to His Imperial Majesty we were invited to comfortable chairs and were served coffee. The audience had begun and I sat back and waited to see what would happen.

The Shah's first question after welcoming the Air Marshal to his country was the natural one of asking about his journey and the means of getting to Teheran which he presumed was by air; had he travelled by commercial airline? "No, your Majesty, I flew in one of a flight of three Canberras based in Cyprus". I could see the Shah's immediate reaction and as a practising pilot himself he naturally asked how long the flight had taken. Sam Patch smiled at the question and replied "Not long, sir; it was exactly two hours and thirteen minutes". I could see the Shah's mental reaction and it was apparent that His Imperial Majesty quickly appreciated the military implications; for better or worse his country was not so remote as it had been in the past. Sam looked at me knowingly; now he knew why I had advised him to use Canberras. The impact was exactly as I had hoped and it was a good start to what followed.

The two men soon found each other's company most agreeable and subjects of mutual interest were discussed as though they were friends sitting in a London club. With the distinguished visitor taking a keen interest in a country that he had never previously visited, the Air Marshal asked a number of question ranging from the Iranian system of government, the armed forces, education, communications, the oil industry, irrigation, power sources, national economy, political geography, and many others. On every subject the Shah was particularly well informed, not only in outline but in considerable detail. Who would have expected a reigning monarch to know precisely the output of all the new power stations, completed and projected, and not only their locations but details of construction and cost? On each subject he gave a text-book summary in articulate English that was not only a delight to listen to but illustrated his remarkable memory and his obvious deep interest in the progress of his kingdom into the twentieth century. He even went so far as to say that he hoped that history would show if he had been successful or not in setting the right pace of development; some of his senior men were asking him to press on; some were not, and in this regard he made a veiled reference to the religious element, the leaders of which were extremely difficult to convince. The Shah's anxieties in this regard were so prophetic indeed. After almost two hours, the audience – if indeed that is the appropriate word – was concluded and we left the Palace with the Shah pointedly showing his pleasure and expressing a wish that the Air Marshal would make another visit to his country. As we drove away Sam Patch commented "What an extraordinary man! His detailed knowledge is quite amazing and he was such a charming person to have had such a long and interesting conversation with – and without any formality at all". I agreed wholeheartedly; Sir Hubert Patch was a two-hour man as forecast.

On the same day, an evening reception in our villa was given in his honour and all manner of personalities numbering some two hundred and fifty arrived to meet him. Initially our guest-of-honour dutifully stood with Irène and myself at the entrance whilst she effortlessly rattled off name after name of the visitors; it is something that she had an incredible facility to do and her retentive memory always amazes me. Particularly in that kind of appointment it is an invaluable asset and always adds a nice touch because people like to be instantly identified. Having launched our very charming Air Marshal, I suggested that he waste no more time shaking hands with so many people, (some with almost unpronounceable names), but circulated to talk to everybody and in this way get yet another impression of the Persian scene. It was a very good evening and particularly enjoyable for the host and hostess who for once did not feel constrained by formal duties that sometimes make these occasions dreary rather than a pleasure. After the party Sam Patch went back to the ambassadorial residence for dinner; for both of us it had been a fascinating day to remember.

The following morning, whilst shaving (when most of my thought processes seem to be at their best), I ruminated about the events of the previous day and in particular wondered how we could usefully follow up the obvious good-will that had resulted from the C-in-C's visit and the remarkable audience with the Shah in particular. I was anxious to suggest some practical ideas that he could think about and if possible present them to him before he returned to Cyprus in mid-morning. One idea in particular appealed to me and I decided to tell him about it; it had the merit that it was quite straightforward to carry out and would benefit both Britain and Iran in equal measure.

Sir Roger Stevens elected to attend the departure of the Canberras in person and a small team from the embassy was there to say goodbye and so end what had been a very successful sortie in furthering friendly relations with Iran. Whilst the RAF party were getting into their flying kit I thought it prudent to sound out the ambassador to begin with, and as expected his reaction was positive and enthusiastic. Sir Roger said "It's your idea and so you tell the Air Marshal yourself". With that encouragement I walked up to him and said "Sir, how would you react to the notion that your Canberra squadrons make goodwill training flights to Teheran? Sir Roger is enthusiastic and I think I can set it up at this end provided you do not send too many aircraft at one time". Sam jumped at the idea and said that it was an excellent opportunity for his crews to get some valuable experience in the mountain conditions that he had seen for himself. Both politically and operationally he saw every advantage; the snag was that the Iranians might baulk at the idea if only because they had never done this kind of thing before. I said that I would explore the possibilities by taking a sounding at top level in my own fashion. "Do not be surprised, sir, if you get a telegram from me within a couple of days – and I'll bet that it will say 'Go ahead' " With that thought he climbed into his beautiful Canberra and within minutes the three aircraft took off in quick succession and headed west back to Cyprus.

That afternoon I called on General Hedayat, Chief of Staff of Iranian Armed Forces, and I put the proposal to him. I told him that it was entirely my own idea and only my ambassador and the Air Marshal knew about it. I assured him that there were no political implications or overtones at all and I had certainly not been instructed to call on him. If the idea was unacceptable, well it would not matter as at this stage there was no need for any official action and nobody would be any the wiser. The General was normally a reserved and unsmiling man but this time he was relaxed and friendly; he told me that he would give me an answer very soon and of course I knew precisely what that meant – the Shah had to decide. When I called on him the next day he said "Approved". I thanked him warmly for his favourable decision and before leaving I took the opportunity of asking if it was necessary to have anything in writing between the two countries. I also asked to what extent the RAF could send training flights to Teheran. His reply was typical; "Colonel, no need for letters; send a thousand aeroplanes every day if you wish."

I returned to the embassy with the news and Sir Roger was really pleased – as indeed was Sam Patch when he received the telegram which said 'Approval granted; letter follows.' Once again an important policy decision had been made without any fuss or complication at all. During later correspondence with Air Headquarters in Cyprus about the best way to set up the Canberra training flights, my suggested formula was agreed whereby a flight of three aircraft arrived once a week and this arrangement worked out admirably. The six aircrew were accommodated overnight in a nice hotel run by a German lady on a contract basis and all the servicing was done as usual by Bob Goody in addition to his task of looking after the Devon. To begin with I was able to keep an eye on the weekly flights, even to the extent of regularly entertaining the crews, but once the pattern was set and no snags arose they were able to fend for themselves. Reports soon reached me that the 'Teheran run' had become more popular than the one to Nairobi; and that was very satisfying to hear. The concept was proving a success in every way; my Iranian friends approved and it was the beginning of further co-operation with them. Later on nearly all ferry flights from Britain to India and beyond by Service aircraft (both Naval and Air Force) took the shorter route through Iran rather than via the Persian Gulf.

Stage two of the Canberra plan now had to be tackled, and that was to try and initiate a reciprocal arrangement whereby the Imperial Iranian Air Force made a visit to Cyprus. This was going to be more difficult; I was about to tread on new ground because to my knowledge they had never undertaken this kind of thing before. At a propitious moment I mentioned the idea to General Gilanshah, and after a cautious reply he agreed and even undertook to go himself. This was exceptional because he was not a practising pilot and I was only able to persuade him on the score that the Air Marshal would be very upset if he did not make a return visit in person. Three days before the General and his squadron of six Lockheed T.33 jets were due to leave I suddenly had the awful thought that he had no previous experience of flying at 30,000 feet, even as a passenger, and what would happen if he passed out – or even died, as could happen? Brother! whose fault would that have been? That dammed British Air Attaché of course. The only way round this knotty problem was to contact his brother-in-law General Isa Studakh, and he discreetly passed on the suggestion that Gilanshah make a test flight as a passenger with his pilot going up in stages to operating height to check how he was coping physically. In the event all was well and I breathed a sigh of relief. On the appointed day I went to see the squadron depart and asked the Colonel in charge to be meticulous in all aspects of airmanship and to put on a really smart exhibition of flying as I had told the Royal Air Force how dammed good they were. He smiled and said that he would not let me down. He was as good as his word and a report came back afterwards to say how impressed the RAF were with the flying and the pilots themselves. The personnel at RAF Akrotiri pushed out the boat and my Iranian Air Force friends were loud in their praises of the hospitality that they received during their stay. It was all very satisfying.

The Imperial Iranian Air Force consisted of some five or six squadrons equipped with American and Canadian aircraft. The front-line machine was the Lockheed T.33 trainer-cum-fighter two-seat jet and the balance consisted of Douglas DC3 and Canadian de Havilland Beavers, the latter an excellent single-engine five-seater very suitable for the job in a big mountain country with only a few airfields and the rest primitive airstrips widely dispersed. All aircraft were Teheran based either at Merehabad Airport or Doshantapeh (which was all-military) and also housed the Flying Club which was General Gilanshah's pet baby and so enjoyed facilities that flying clubs normally do not have. The ground maintenance was given overall supervision by American technicians and as most (if not all) the pilots were trained in the United States the standard was high. One of the natural characteristics of Persians is that they are good horsemen and to them handling or piloting a flying machine is just a change of mount but it does tend to make them somewhat reckless. On Air Force Day the pilots put on a performance that is wonderful to behold, especially the very low-level attacks on a target with jets streaking in from all directions in a way that would make the RAF blanch with anxiety. The show always made my hair stand on end; it must have been Allah who was protecting those pilots.

The de Havilland Devon became a very important element in my life and as soon as I had accumulated enough flying practise in the Teheran area I began to range far and wide with an enormous territory to cover. It was a most satisfying situation and it was coupled with the realisation that it was productive because I could now see my job through the eyes of a practising pilot and could evaluate Iranian aviation from a cockpit rather than from an office chair.

Apart from trips to get to know Persian conditions, an opportunity arose to make a long tour that would take us on a big sweep around the south and eastern part of the country up to the Afghan frontier. Commander Peter Needham, DSC, RN, had recently visited Teheran from Baghdad to advise the Iranian navy about setting up an underwater diving school in the Caspian on similar lines to the one that he had already established in Iraq. One of the curiosities of his appointment was that it was very much a one-man affair; he had no office and no staff and as neither the Baghdad embassy or the British Military Mission took him under their wing for administration purposes his allegiance was to the Naval Commander-in-Chief Far East based in Singapore. He was obliged to travel each month to Bahrein to collect his naval pay from the Senior Naval Officer Persian Gulf (SNOPG) and this crazy arrangement meant that the air fare was more than his pay! When planning the aerial tour that included the entire length of the Persian Gulf it seemed very appropriate to invite Peter to join us and he timed his next visit accordingly.

The Devon set off from Teheran one sunny morning with Irène and Peter on board and of course my second-pilot-cum-engineer Bob Goody made up the fourth member. We landed at Isfahan and after a brief stop we flew on south again to the romantic city of Shiraz where we stayed overnight and took the opportunity of visiting Persepolis, the ancient city where Alexander the Great had rested during his conquests and left his mark during a celebration one night by setting fire to the magnificent palace. It must have been quite an evening. Shiraz is situated 5000 feet up in Southern Iran and is perhaps the most beautiful city in all Persia. Apart from Omar Khayam's resting place in Nishapur, Shiraz can claim to be equally distinguished because it is the eternal home of two other famous men called Hafez and Firdozi, Persian poets of great repute. The Devon pressed on the next day towards the coast and after overflying the now abandoned port of Bushire we flew along the Gulf coast towards Bandar Abbas, our intended night stop. This was where the captain of aircraft was faced with his first major problem; the new aerodrome that he had been advised to use before leaving Teheran had not yet been constructed. All that I could see was a very small strip that would accept a Beaver but it was certainly not suitable for a twin-engined aeroplane. After flying over the area and looking at the special map provided, allegedly showing where the aerodrome was located and finding nothing, the problem was where next to go. It was an awkward situation and Bob and I checked on another map to find a suitable alternative. Jask was at least one hour away further along the coast; it was an option but as the sun was setting at the end of the four hour flight it would have meant a night landing. This was not a wise proposition because Jask was not manned and it was no more than a relic of early days when Imperial Airways used to stop there. The Persian map that we had, sketchy though it was, did at least have sundry dots on it to represent the location of a number of airstrips so I decided to make for the nearest one thirty miles away inland and have a look; this on the assumption that I would find it. In the meantime the two passengers in the back were trying to look relaxed although (as I learned later) they were somewhat concerned about getting down somewhere – and desirably in one piece!

We flew north, and after fifteen minutes a likely area in the desert showed up; with my earlier desert experience I sensed that this should be the place that I was looking for. My hunch was right because faint tell-tale wheel marks were seen on the sand; after a good look around to get the measure of everything I lowered the landing gear and landed safely. We were down, but what to do next? The fact of getting down safely was sufficient in itself and if necessary we could sleep in the aeroplane, but this would not solve the problem of being able to tell anyone where we were. The major anxiety therefore was that when Teheran got news of our disappearance it would cause a lot of worry. Whilst we were stretching our legs and discussing ideas about the situation we saw in the distance the dust being thrown up by a vehicle which was heading in our direction. This really was a heartening sight, particularly as we never expected it. When the truck stopped two occupants got out and they proved to be a Dutch husband and wife team engaged in petroleum exploration; they were as surprised to see us as we were of them. They took three of us into Bandar Abbas and Bob stayed behind to make the Devon secure and he followed later in another car sent out to collect him, together with all our overnight gear.

By good fortune and applying our limited Farsi we located the man who had been instructed to receive us – he was the mayor as it turned out – and he led us to a building with a large rectangular room where we sat in a row facing some dignatories on the opposite side. Tea was provided and we did our best to try and explain what had happened and why we had arrived from the desert in such an unusual way. Bob eventually arrived with the gear and then to our surprise more men appeared who were also officials of some kind and a splendid meal was laid on for guests and hosts to sit down and enjoy. Without our interpreter Abdul Majid we had for once to cope on our own and it was surprising how well we managed to communicate with some simple words and a lot of sign language. When the meal was over the reception committee departed and in the same room we took to our camp beds. It was just like sleeping in a school dormitory with the added attraction that many dark-eyed young women constantly peered at us through the windowless apertures, curious to see the *farangis* (foreigners) going about their domestic occasions. Despite the March heat (Bandar Abbas is one of the hottest places in the Gulf and the summer climate is dreadful) all of us slept soundly. In the morning we were taken back to the aeroplane and we took off for Jask to refuel after the long flight of the day before.

Jask landing ground is no more than a flat sandy area on a peninsular and at the water's edge the concrete shells of the old Imperial Airways buildings were standing as a mute reminder of bygone days of eighty miles per hour air travel in the Handley Page 'Hannibal' class. We parked alongside and after a while a Shell Petroleum Company man arrived and we began to refuel by using those old-fashioned four-gallon cans, one after the other, almost interminably; I really thought that those tins had gone for evermore but it was not so. Whilst the laborious work was going on a truck arrived loaded with men looking like Afghans with baggy trousers and loose turbans and they stopped to watch the proceedings. After a few moments Irène said "They're not locals – they're Italians!" They were oil exploration men and very pleased to talk in Italian to Irène, the first European woman that they had seen in months. We ended up by accepting a box of rather small hens' eggs and in return I produced a copy of 'Playboy'; the reaction was predictable. Eventually the refueling was finished and we had a refreshing swim before getting ready to leave for the next stage of the tour. This was to be Zahedan, five hundred miles inland and situated right alongside the frontiers of Pakistan and Afghanistan. I hoped that this time there really was an aerodrome to land on, particularly as the nearest alternate was over two hundred miles further away; touring by air in those parts of the world can spring unexpected surprises! I was prepared to cope with the same bush-flying conditions as I had encountered when flying over the Sudan and Ethiopia but this time at least there was the comfort of a twin-engine aeroplane fitted with an extra fifty gallon tank to give extended range. Normally it was impossible to communicate with anyone by radio – there was nobody to communicate with anyway – but by a fluke of radio reception I heard the tower at Karachi Airport three hundred and fifty miles away talking to an aeroplane on our frequency. I was able to call the tower myself and relay our position to the friendly Pakistani controller. Our identity and position was now known even if it was only by a man in another country; it was better than nothing.

Close to the Pakistan frontier at Chah Bahar I turned the Devon away from the Arabian Sea and we headed north for the three hundred mile run across hilly and very desolate country towards Zahedan. The view after traversing the entire length of the Gulf (including a good sighting of the 7000 foot mountains of Oman on our right-hand side) was one of a complete wilderness and we wondered how any humans could manage to survive at all. They do however, and every now and again we could see little brown villages dotted along the route. What do the people of Baluchestan do and how do they eke out an existence under such conditions? Perhaps the Shah knew; for that matter I wondered if whoever was down below bothered to find out that there was someone called the Shah as he would have meant nothing to them.

The three hour flight eventually took us to Zahedan; and to the relief of everybody on board there was not only an aerodrome to alight on but it was a surprisingly big one with a long runway. The town from the air looked so drab and featureless (apart from the usual mosque) that we wondered what was in store for us. It lies 5000 feet above sea level, the common denominator for the hinterland, and from its location we concluded that its sole claim to existence was that it was on the old trading route between Iraq and the wild area between Isphahan, Yazd, Kerman, (famous for carpets), and so to Zahedan and beyond. A railway system following the same route had been constructed (it was a great feat of engineering) and it carried on into Pakistan. However today the Kerman-Zahedan section has been abandoned but whether for political or economic reasons is difficult to establish. What was painfully clear to us was that Zahedan was a singularly unattractive place hundreds of miles from anywhere and even in springtime was uncomfortably warm with temperatures in the high eighties.

My charming Indian Military Attaché friend in Teheran, Colonel

'Jimmy' Vakil, had arranged for us to be met by the Indian Consul in Zahedan and this gentleman very kindly took us to his home for an overnight stop. This was a great pleasure for us and but for his hospitality I do not know where we could have stayed other than camping out alongside the aeroplane. His kindness was even more appreciated when we realised that we had arrived on the very day when he should have been enjoying a special Indian holiday, evident because he and his small staff were decked out in the formal national costume that Irène quickly identified. After a pleasant evening meal Indian-style (when for once I enjoyed the curry) we all slept well and rose early in the morning to begin the return journey across central Persia back to Teheran. We had now entered the fifth day of the tour and apart from the adventure of the missing aerodrome at Bandar Abbas we were doing well with no technical problems at all. All you need in this regard is a dammed good aeroplane and ditto engineer to match; we were blessed with both, so what more can an airman wish for?

Our host took us back to the aerodrome after an early breakfast and we set off to fly to Yazd to refuel and then on again to the magic city of Isfahan where we stayed the night in hotel comfort. Peter Needham, ever the enthusiastic photographer, arose at dawn in order to take pictures of the Shah Abbas mosque facing the one-time polo ground but now graced with ornamental lakes and fountains. He wanted to photograph the mosque with its image mirrored in the water before the fountains started up, but it was not to be; the Persian whose job it was beat him to it by a very short head! So he had to be content to record his visit with fountains playing and photograph the mosque in the oblique rays of the early sun. All of us would have loved to be able to put the clock back and witness Persian-style polo being played with the Shah and his entourage sitting in the Royal balconied grandstand. After hundreds of years the goalposts, consisting of rounded stones like pepper-pots about three feet high, can still be seen; a reminder of past glory.

The final run back to Teheran was an eighty minute flight and as the date was March 23rd it coincided (give or take a day to adjust to the Persian calendar) with Nauruz, New Year's Day. The remarkable feature of the Persian new year is that it is invariably the signal for nature to burst out into all its spring glory. Yesterday all is barren and no birds sing; today the new shoots are out, the flowers and rose-buds appear, the snow begins to melt at the lower levels, the sun brings its spring warmth, and everything and everybody come to life. It is very agreeable indeed.

The excellent Devon continued to play an important part in embassy activities and out of the blue an unexpected bonus for me happened because the Turkish Government banished all diplomatic aircraft of foreign missions because the French Air Attaché had been so indiscreet as to fly over a prohibited area. Gilbert Howie's loss became my profit and instead of returning the Devon to him in the early spring I retained her until the end of August 1958 when Group Captain Bill Swift took over from me as the air attaché. There were all manner of jobs to be done in the final months of my tour and as I had now accumulated some 200 hours on the Devon under 'bush-flying' conditions I considered myself proficient as a pilot based in Iran. However I must record that when my ambassador asked me to fly him and a senior Minister of Her Majesty's Government, who was due to visit Iran on an official tour, the bright boys in the Air Ministry vetoed it because, so they said, I was not a VIP pilot. Sir Roger Stevens was incensed. "James, of all people you are easily the best qualified pilot for the purpose; what's the point of getting someone from England who has never experienced the difficulties of flying out here?" Sir Roger added that if I was good enough to take him and five other ambassadors on tour, well that passenger list was a total VIP affair and not just one politician. In point of fact my flying log book records a number of VIP passengers that includes ministers, commanders-in-chief, ambassadors, a Persian princess, and might well have included King George VI who wanted me to give him a flight in a Mosquito. In the event the Minister travelled by other means and so the valuable services of a fancy pilot from Britain never materialised; I could not resist the thought that whoever it was as likely as not he was still at school when I was a VIP pilot in 216 Squadron.

The Devon with it's extended stay in Teheran continued to be in the air with great regularity and one of its useful tasks was to make a reconnaissance of an earthquake near Kermanshah in southern Iran where virtually all the inhabitants of a village were killed. Earthquakes are very unnerving experiences, especially when they are unexpected, and one closer to home woke me up in the small hours when fast asleep on the terrace. My bed rocked violently and such was the force of it that it partially emptied the swimming pool with the water surging from end to end in an alarming fashion. Gillian's reflexes must have been singularly quick on this occasion because as soon as the tremors started she leapt out of bed and picked up Jonathan before going to the strongest part of the villa to shelter underneath a stout doorway. Although not trained as a child specialist she had a certain touch and had organised a play-group for other embassy children and taught Jonathan the alphabet and rudiments of reading when he was not even three years old. When she had to return home for family reasons we were lucky to replace her with my god-daughter, the petite and entertaining Ann Milligan whose parents were Freddy and Mollie from Heliopolis days. The contrast in stature from Gillian to Ann was marked, but apart from that young Jonathan was wonderfully cared for and the transition was smooth.

Another episode when the Devon came into its own is almost unique in the telling and an experience that I have good cause to remember. In mid-July 1958 my household was preparing for the day's activities. I noticed that Abdul Majid had not reported for duty and when he showed up at 7.30 am I lightheartedly gave him a wigging for oversleeping after a party in town. "No sa'ab, I am late because I have been listening to the Baghdad radio. Very bad things have happened and the King has been killed." Abdul was fluent in Arabic and knowing him well as I did I saw no reason to doubt what he told me. Even though it was so early in the morning I decided to telephone the ambassador and told him what Abdul had said; Sir Roger knew nothing at all of the dramatic story but said that he would call me back. Half an hour later he did so and told me that one of his fellow ambassadors confirmed that a rebellion led by an Iraqi General had in fact taken place and King Feisal had been assassinated together with all of his family and staff. Apart from the dreadful nature of the news which inevitably would have repercussions right across the Middle East, the extraordinary thing was that it was my chauffeur who was instrumental in providing the news. As I remember, we were the first to tell London.

Immediately after work started in the embassy Sir Roger called a meeting to inform his staff and discuss what, if anything, we could do. The problem of course was in a reverse sense in that our contingency plans were based on British people having to evacuate Iran, not now to rescue them from a neighbouring country. It was additionally complicated because we had nothing to work on and thus it was extremely difficult to determine what could be done and by what means. I contacted the Iraqi military attaché for something of value to work on but I have to say that he seemed so vague and elusive that I concluded that he was sitting on the fence and hedging his bets by not showing his hand. For us the only practical thing to do was to set up a pipe-line of road communication from the frontier to Teheran and make provision for items like medicine, tinned food, warm clothing, blankets and baby food in the event that families succeeded in escaping from Iraq. Most of us doubted that it would be possible for anybody to get away, knowing all too well what happens when situations like this occur, but we set about organising a rescue system all the same. The Devon now came into its own because it was the only means of going down south quickly to assess the situation on the spot.

We took off early next day for a reconnaissance and with John Hardman our language specialist, Bob Goody and myself on board we began by flying along the frontier road from Baghdad, including a run into Iraq in case we saw anything of value. Nothing was seen; the route was deserted and we landed as planned at Kermanshah, 100 miles from the frontier. In the meantime Abdul Majid had driven 300 miles non-stop overnight in the Landrover to meet us on arrival, an invaluable facility that I often used because without road transport we would be immobile. He had first of all driven to the frontier and had seen the Devon overflying Khrosovi and entering Iraq; upon our return machine-guns opened fire noisily and he feared for our lives but he did not know that I was high enough to be out-of-range. The four of us discussed the situation after the land-air reconnaissance and concluded that the only useful move was to go to the Anglo-Iranian oil company rest house on the off-chance that there was somebody there with up-to-date news. It was a fine establishment, as one would expect, and as we entered a man appeared who I recognised at once as General Batmanquilich, ex-Army Chief of Staff and currently the Iranian ambassador in Baghdad. He had succeeded in escaping from Baghdad only hours previously. The account of his experiences after the uprising by the Iraqi army was horrific and the disgusting habits of a Baghdad mob in full cry made us blanch. The General saw Crown Prince Abdul Illah's corpse being towed through the streets behind a jeep and it was being hacked to pieces by the mob as it passed. Charming people.

The general succeeded in making his escape, not so much because of diplomatic immunity so much as by plain bribery. He moved from one road-block to the next, handed out the cash, and repeated the process again and again before eventually crossing the frontier and saying a prayer to Allah for his safe delivery. He was dammed lucky to have survived. At every hold-up his car was searched quite thoroughly for anything of value, but one item escaped the scrutiny of the Iraqi soldiers; underneath the driving seat was a thin brief case taped to the underside and so out of sight. The General told me that it contained very secret and important documents for His Imperial Majesty's eyes only and as it was imperative that they were delivered as soon as possible would I please take it back to Teheran? I was most flattered that he was prepared to trust me and when accepting it I asked him to nominate one other man only to whom I could deliver it in the event that the Shah was not available. He named the palace Chamberlain and this was fortunate because I had met him on the occasion of Air Marshal Sam Patch's visit.

We returned to Kermanshah aerodrome soon after the meeting and flew direct to Teheran. As soon as we were in radio contact with the tower I asked the controller to telephone the embassy for a car to take me to the palace and to advise the Royal Chamberlain that I was coming to give him a special package. Immediately after landing I set off to deliver the briefcase and my Persian friend was waiting to receive it. Whether or not he was ever told what it was all about I will never know but for my part I could claim to have been the only foreigner ever to have been a special air courier to the Shah of Persia.

In the succeeding days of the Iraqi rebellion the Devon made a number of trips down south and the passengers included Colonel Desmond Phayre, (the new Military Attaché,) sundry other specialists, and Irène who accomplished miracles of organisation by setting up a trail of stopover points along the route and left appropriate supplies at each one for those lucky enough to have escaped from Iraq. All our efforts were to no purpose as it turned out; not one single vehicle arrived and it was just as well because it was much safer for foreigners to lie low in Baghdad and wait for the dust to settle. It must have been a very nasty time for them but it is one of the hazards of working in that unstable part of the world. You do so at your peril – as witness the Lebanon today.

In the context of expatriates, we were very lucky to have a number of excellent friends in Teheran who in various ways were promoting business energetically in what was steadily becoming a rich country thanks to oil and the Shah's driving force. The Bloomfields, the Checketts, the Webbers, the Hollingsworths, the Venthams, and not least John and Sheila Caldwell (who were close friends and neighbours) were only a few who did sterling work for British interests. John Caldwell had great talent, and to see him skiing on one leg (having unfortunately lost the other in childhood) was brilliant. He probably knew more of Persia and the people than anyone else as his business interests took him far and wide. Another was Tim Mayne, ex-RAF and an architect in the big-time Taylor Woodrow building construction business. He had visited Teheran purely on an exploratory basis for a few days and I persuaded – perhaps bullied – him to stay on. He did so and was still there when we left for England. His company profited considerably as a result. Once again it was the personality factor that counted, something that Persians lay great store by.

The last few months of the three-year tour were now passing all too quickly and I began to take stock of the position and look back on what had been the best job that had ever come my way. In personal terms it had been quite fascinating, and judged by conventional standards Irène and I had been living handsomely and at a level that even the Managing Director of a large industrial complex would have been very happy about. As the key to success was productivity, what had we accomplished? Well, there were four good marks on the score board. Number one was successfully to cultivate such a good relationship with both civil and military top men that they accepted me as a friend and in every case they were anxious to go out of their way to be helpful. Some of their kindnesses bordered on embarrassement, as witness providing the Shah's royal pavillion on his polo ground for top people to watch a demonstration of a Scottish Aviation 'Pioneer' with a 200-strong army team to clear the snow away beforehand. In Iran I could come and go as I pleased – including trips in the Devon to RAF Habbaniya to replenish stocks from the NAAFI without any question of foreign travel clearance in either direction.

Number two was the unquestioned approval for the RAF to use Iran virtually at will, something that was frankly greeted with incredulity in London as it had never happened anywhere before. It was simplicity itself; one man said 'yes' and that was that.

Number three was equally simple – the return of British Airways to Iran just on the nod from one man. He even created 'at a stroke' a completely new Airway across Iran for Qantas to use; something that the Australian airline had completely failed to accomplish at Ministerial level after months of fruitless correspondence. My Australian friends were quite amazed because it took just one personal visit to the right man lasting five minutes!

Number four was a purely commercial success – the real accountable yardstick as opposed to fringe activities that are difficult to quantify, particularly by the United Kingdom Treasury ever seeking cuts in government expenditure. In spite of the complete pessimism shown by the British aircraft industry before I left for Iran (and, I have to say the subsequent need to jolt some companies into action when success was no more than just a Persian handshake away by it's Managing Director on a flying visit). I maintained my ambition to succeed and ended up by being personally credited with the sale of millions of pounds sterling worth of British aviation equipment. It was accomplished not by high-pressure sales teams but by one air attaché who said the right thing to the right man at the right time. A classic example of not what you know but who you know. I was singularly lucky; I was liked and I was trusted. I concluded that I had justified my existence working for HM Government in an overseas appointment and in the process had thoroughly enjoyed the experience.

In the late summer of 1958 I returned to England in time to attend the Farnborough Air Show; my family followed soon after with a stop in Trieste en route so that Irène and Jonathan could visit her step-father. Then came confirmation of my worst fears – the Personnel Department at the Air Ministry told me that I was due to retire because the system prescribed that I had reached my age ceiling related to rank and as promotion was apparently not coming my way I waited for the days to pass before my next birthday. For the second time I left the Royal Air Force with the greatest regret. I was now considered to be too old; I was forty-seven.

Chapter XXVIII

Going Back to Square One

If nothing else the air attaché appointment in Teheran had ended my RAF career on a high note; it had been the best job of all, but all over again I had to go through the tedious process of looking for a job in civil life. The same old problems arose, with the added snag that I was now seemingly in the wrong age bracket. Whenever I called on my contacts in the aviation world I was greeted with the same happy smile and a warm handshake, but that was all. All the old excuses were trotted out of being too senior, a bit on the old side, and it would upset other men on the payroll because I would be judged as someone who held up their promotion prospects. The view of contemporaries in the same boat as I was that they sensed that potential employers often baulked at taking on an ex-service man not so much because he was unsuited as the fear that his ability and wide experience might embarrass even the boss himself. I believe that there is a lot of truth in this. If one follows the logic of this attitude of rejection, how then does one account for the fact that, for example, a politician, a retired admiral (or whoever) gets appointed to the board of a big company, perhaps even becoming it's chairman?

In my case I had a lucky break because I heard of an overseas job with the Ministry of Aviation and I was advised by the Air Ministry to report to a Mrs Munro in Shell Mex House. The man at the desk in the big marbled entrance hall directed me to a top floor and when I enquired of the secretaries in a big office which of them was the lady that I was looking for they all laughed and said "Mrs Munro is not one of us – she is the Under Secretary!" I was about to meet the first lady boss in my life. Alison Munro was no ordinary person; not by any manner of means. She had been private secretary to Sir Robert Watson-Watt (of radar research fame) during the war and after joining the civil service was promoted rapidly to her appointment of being in charge of world-wide civil aviation interests entailing complex dealings with foreign and Commonwealth governments. She was very articulate; she had a keen brain; and she had an incisive clarity of thought and speed in getting to the point. After a brief conversation she enrolled me on her staff and I went on my way rejoicing. Once again it was selection at a stroke without any of the preliminary processes. Alison subsequently became the High Mistress of St. Paul's School for girls in London and was later very appropriately made a Dame Commander of the Order of the British Empire by Her Majesty.

The appointment in practise was to be Civil Air Attaché in Australia and New Zealand although the official designation was Civil Aviation Adviser to the High Commissioner; and of course in my case to two High Commissioners. The office from which I was to operate was based in Melbourne rather than Canberra or Wellington and this was convenient because the Australian Department of Civil Aviation was in Melbourne and so the location was an obvious choice. The domestic aspect also suited as Melbourne would be as good a place as any to find somewhere to live and schooling for Jonathan, now rising seven years of age, was no problem. A return to Australia appealed to me and it was in a way prophetic because many of my Australian friends said that in some way or other I would be back. Evidently I was the kind of Englishman that appealed to them and this compliment was reciprocated because I got on well with them and liked their open-faced and frank personalities. Australians say precisely what they mean and so do not resort to a choice of words that imply what is in their minds without actually coming to the point. The new appointment was going to be very different compared to the job that I had done in Australia previously when I was in the RAF and in effect running an airline. Now I was going back as a civilian in charge of nothing at all and the only worthwhile comparison was that it was still to do with aeroplanes. That in itself was good news and my family was delighted. We thought that it was going to be an extension of our Persian experience in that the job would be much the same and with the diplomatic tag to suit. Once again we were in for one more of those familiar surprises.

The air journey to the Southern Hemisphere by British Airways was uneventful and we arrived at Essendon Airport Melbourne to be met by the man who had been successfully holding the job for a number of years. Air Vice Marshal Robin Willock was an experienced airman and very popular and this meant that I had to be on my mettle to follow in his footsteps. One disappointment was to find that the small office on the ground floor of noisy Burke street seemed more like a second-rate mens' hairdressing parlour rather than something appropriate to one of Her Majesty's diplomatic servants. It was a priority job therefore to look for something better. Robin took me to meet his civil aviation friends, both at senior government and airline level, and so right away I met the top men in Australia who controlled the industry. It was apparent that they knew very well what it was all about and it confirmed my earlier experience that Australians have an innate sense that the aeroplane is an essential requirement; they accept flying in the same way that we in Britain take to the sea.

The Australian overseas airline is Qantas – an acronym of Queensland and Northern Territories Aerial Services – and is based in Sydney whereas the two major domestic ones called Trans Australia Airlines and Ansett have their headquarters in Melbourne. The Government had introduced the clever idea of making both TAA and the private enterprise Ansett-ANA airline operate with exactly equal opportunities and the result was that competition was fierce and the customer benefited. In the case of all three major Australian airlines, the centralised organisation of each made for maximum efficiency and the managements knew perfectly well what was going on both with respect to personnel and to operations; each airline was therefore compact but big enough to need some 300 pilots on average. The Federal organisation of civil aviation was in the hands of a splendid government minister called Shane Paltridge and his right-hand man was the Director General, Donald Anderson. He in turn had four deputies and every time I winced when one of them, Dr Harold Poulton, invariably used to refer to the boss as 'the Dai Jai'. Dr Bill Bradfield was in charge of airfield construction and coincidentally nephew of the architect of the Sydney Bridge; he was an excellent engineer and a charming person. Without exception Don Anderson's men were highly professional and dedicated in specialised fields and woe betide the man from Britain arriving to do business with them who could not match their expertise. My old friend Captain (ex-RAF Wing Commander) Reg Bailey DSO, OBE, DFC, was Director of Operations for TAA and arguably the most competent airline operator in the Southern Hemisphere; with full current airline pilot qualification and considerable flying experience it was not surprising that he was greatly respected by everybody.

Another Australian airman of note was a dynamic young personality called Richard Cavill. He had recently returned to Melbourne after completing a Short Service Commission with the RAF and enthused about Fighter Command, an organisation that he loved for its style and competence. He arrived one day in an Anson that he had flown from England and for a time he was one of Reg Bailey's pilots. However the routine work was not in keeping with his character and he turned to sundry flying jobs like charter work and crop dusting. Irène and I feared for his prospects in such a dead-end and limited career, but we were not to know that fate was to take a hand and change everything. Some months after we had returned to England after my appointment ended Reg Bailey came to see us and I said "How is poor old Dick getting on?" Reg replied "Haven't you heard?", a question that made me fear the worst. "No, he hasn't killed himself crop-dusting; his father died recently and left him a fortune." Rather than become a rich young man with nothing to worry about, he decided typically to press on and using his inheritance to excellent purpose he trebled his wealth within a few years. The tables later turned when erstwhile employer Reg Bailey was enrolled as one of Dick's men. Now both of them career around the world endlessly hunting for opportunities and I have no doubt that they are meeting with success. Dick's new property outside Adelaide has been purpose-built and has an airstrip from which the owner (when time permits) can fly about very happily in either of two rebuilt Tiger Moths; something that would appeal to me in equal measure.

Although the general nature of my new job was along the lines of being an air attaché observing the aviation scene overseas, the manner of going about it where the High Commissioner's office was concerned was in an entirely different setting. The moment of truth came when I flew to Canberra to make my first pre-arranged visit and on arrival found that I would have been left standing in the roadway but for a rescue by the Chief of the UK Military Services Liaison Staff. Air Vice Marshal Eric Stapleton had sent his PA to meet me and when I asked later why this was so, Eric replied "Those High Commission people haven't a clue about the niceties of operating, compared to the Foreign Office. If I had not sent my PA to collect you you would still be there as taxis only arrive to order". After a good dinner party in my honour and a comfortable night with my unexpected host and hostess I was taken next day to what was in reality my own headquarters but where nobody seemed to be in the slightest bit interested in me. I eventually found myself in Keith Matthew's office, senior man after the High Commissioner, Lieutenant General Sir William Oliver, and when I commented unfavourably about my treatment (or lack of it) he said "My dear chap, please don't think I'm a Commonwealth Office man – I'm seconded here for my sins from the Foreign Office!" No wonder that I rarely visited Canberra again and my contacts were confined to correspondence or telephone calls. Teheran and Canberra had entirely different ways of operating and when later the Foreign Office and the Commonwealth Office amalgamated I wondered how it would work out in practise as it was evident to me that the personalities concerned had little in common. A posting to Canberra had nothing to attract anyway because the new Federal capital was still so undeveloped that amazingly it only boasted one restaurant. So far as I was concerned Canberra was not for me; they could keep it.

By contrast Melbourne reminded me of Guildford with a similar country town atmosphere and the upper levels of Melbourne society trying to maintain a high standard and the top ladies did their shopping wearing hats and gloves. One of the chief yardsticks of success was to be a member of the prestigious Melbourne club that has no affiliation at all with any other club anywhere in the world. I had the rare experience of being invited to become a temporary member and it was fascinating to be able to rub shoulders with the elite of the State of Victoria. Unlike Sydney, Melbourne did not judge a man primarily by his wealth; something else was wanted and if in the process you were rich, well that was an extra bonus. Hostesses vied with each other to give dinner parties and a high score was to be the first to entertain famous visitors. A good catch was the occasion when the very talented American actress and author Cornelia Otis Skinner arrived to take a leading part in her own brainchild 'The Pleasure of His Company'. A friend in America had earlier written to ask me to greet Cornelia and her husband Alden Blodgett on arrival and this was unwittingly a godsend because our house became a bolthole for her to escape from some of the numerous dinner-party invitations that inevitably came their way. Cornelia's relaxation after the theatre was to kick off her shoes the moment she walked in and tuck into my scrambled eggs in the kitchen whilst Alden enjoyed his sole tipple of scotch whisky and water. They would tell us some of the happenings of the previous dinner party in a very amusing way and Cornelia's acting ability enabled her to quote verbatim. She loved the acquired Melbourne accent and how some women used to say 'littol' when they meant 'little'.

Soon after our very charming American friends left Melbourne at the end of the theatre season we gave up the house in Armidale because we were invited to occupy (on a caretaker basis) an apartment in Amesbury House whilst the owners Tristan and Marie Buesst were away in Europe. This really was moving up in social status because South Yarra is the Belgravia of Melbourne and Amesbury House in particular was a very select address. It was from this charming home that Irène used to lay on receptions in honour of visiting aviation VIP's, so now we were back to the style and standards of Teheran. Tristan's interests included rare first-edition books and paintings by famous Australian artists like Percival and Sidney Nolan which alone made the contents of the apartment worth a fortune. We could not have had a better platform from which to operate and it raised the style of social activity in a city that took note.

As in other parts of the world with its own customs and habits, Melbourne was no exception and we learned by experience. For our first cocktail party we issued invitations on printed cards that gave the basic details and the wording said 'At home; 6pm.' The guests arrived and all went well until we realised that in Australia invitations at cocktail-time presupposed a meal and a long evening! Subsequently we wrote '6 pm to 7.30 pm'. Another trick to learn was that if we invited people for tea they usually assumed that to mean supper; the secret was to ask them for a 'cup of tea'. The most difficult task at our cocktail parties was to try and break up clusters of males at one end of the room and get them to mix with the unfortunate ladies who were abandoned at the other end. Habits die hard and our efforts invariably met with failure; we might as well have had two separate parties for men and women on succeeding days. I asked a lady guest one evening why this segregation happened and her answer was that it was a relic of early days when men predominated, especially on farms, and whenever a get-together happened it was the women who instinctively gravitated together because they saw so little of their own sex. I suspect that her reason was an alibi in defence of the system as it was apparent that Australian women liked the way that the English mixed enjoyably with everybody. The 'wingeing poms' could now score a good point with the ladies but the Australian men persisted in their old ways.

A new office was a top priority and after a hunt I was able to find good accommodation in the new office block of the New Zealand Bank. Denys Riley, my assistant soon got to work and all the tired old furniture was disposed of and superb hand-made replacements arrived from two expert Polish carpenters that I tracked down. This exercise was another Habbaniya situation because initially the Works Directorate in London proposed to ship cast-off furniture all the way from Hong Kong! When the Works inspector from England arrived sometime later to see what the Civil Aviation Adviser had been up to, he had the dammed nerve to say that the set-up was much too good for me; I commented that if I had waited for his organisation to act the result would have been abysmal and cost three times as much as I had spent anyway. Needless to say he was not one of our guests at Amesbury House. As the Devon had raised the prestige of Britain in Teheran so did a good office and a splendid official residence greatly enhance Britain's standing in Melbourne. It became a pleasure to carry out our duties and Irène was almost tempted to please the pillars of society by saying 'littol' from time to time.

Alison Munro visited Melbourne on special occasions to represent HM Government at conferences with Don Anderson and his team. The meetings invariably centred on tricky bi-lateral horse-trading agreements in which the Australians wanted to improve their overseas route network (probably at our expense) but Alison was such a tough and successful negotiator that Anderson in desperation used to refer to her afterwards as 'that bloody bitch'. Coming as it did from the most uncouth man in high office that I have ever encountered I concluded that his epithet was almost flattering. On Alison's second visit, whilst waiting dutifully on the apron to greet her at Sydney Airport, an admonishing finger was wagging as she descended from the airliner. "James, you are being naughty and it's got to stop." After enquiring what was amiss, she said. "You have been telling the Australians that I'm your mistress; well, I'm jolly well not!" What could I say but that as she was not my master, well she must surely be the other thing? Point taken! She had a nice sense of humour.

Visits to Sydney were usually occasioned by calls on QANTAS, and after business it was often the signal for Cedric Turner the Managing Director to summon his men to entertain the pom by opening the grog locker. The heavy sessions may not have improved my waistline but by thunder I kept up with them; the Aussies were not to know that I have hollow legs, an attribute acquired in Service life as a young officer. On each occasion I won the contest – if only just – and with a smug smile walked back to the Union Club to recover. Cedric subsequently received two awards but for different reasons; he was knighted for sterling work in airline operations and he hit the jackpot in the national lottery to raise funds for the Sydney Opera House. Sir Cedric was now a millionaire, a double success that could not have been better timed. As with me, Irène also used to fly the 450 miles from Melbourne to Sydney but her sorties were for a very different reason; like the Baron Empain in Egypt she preferred a Sydney hairdresser and she would go by air and return on the same day. Apart from these trips it was unfortunate that she could not make longer journeys with me to places like Tahiti, Fiji, Darwin, Brisbane and Alice Springs; the office could not pay her fare and in any case she insisted on staying at home to care for Jonathan herself rather than accept offers from friends. He was now attending Grimwade House, the preparatory school to the famous Melbourne Grammar and he not only became top of his class (although over two years younger than the others), he also became bi-lingual. 'Good on yer, sport!'

The New Zealand scene was different in a number of ways compared to Australia. The country is of course much smaller and New Zealanders are not so forthright or thrusting. The pace is more leisurely and nobody seems to want to press on as in Australia. My visits were conditioned in practice by requirement and I suppose that the need to go only infrequently was well balanced because Group Captain John Blount and Captain Angus Turnbull RN (who were Sir Francis Cumming-Bruce's Service advisers, jointly with Colonel Sir Tom Butler) kept me in the picture on civil aviation affairs. I found that New Zealanders at government level were cautious and conservative in their attitudes and decision-making, the result I supposed of national character and a desire to avoid making mistakes. It produced amongst other things a parochial mentality as evidenced by the newspapers that devoted only a token space to international affairs. The department of civil aviation people were charming but nevertheless they tended to be inflexible in their attitudes and kept strictly to the book. Whenever an important meeting like the annual South Pacific Air Transport Conference took place (for example) in Fiji, the New Zealand civil servants refused to travel on Sunday to attend a Monday start and so all the rest of the delegates lost a working day. Geographically New Zealand is so far removed from the rest of the world that one gets a sense of isolation, particularly so in South Island which although very spectacular and looks like a huge version of the Scottish Highlands seems psychologically to be next door to the South Pole. Nevertheless I enjoyed the beautiful country but all the time the sense of remoteness persists and this may explain why New Zealanders were so resilient and self-sufficient. These were the qualities that made them a natural choice for the Long Range Desert Group in the North African war. Perhaps it is an unkind and ungracious story, but I heard tell of an Australian airline captain on his way to Auckland who is alleged to have said to his passengers "Folks, we are now approaching New Zealand; put your watches back thirty years".

Overall, the impression that I got of Australasia was that there was still a great deal to be done and very many more people were needed for the purpose; a corollary to this was that unless they did something about it a political situation would arise whereby a vastly overpopulated South East Asia would be hammering on the door to get in. One day in Melbourne after an international civil aviation meeting I met the Air Minister from Indonesia who angrily aired his views to me on the subject. I could not resist the comment that only 300 miles separated his country from the Australian continent and for thousands of years his forbearers had made no attempt at all to move in. He was not amused. I imagine that he had never heard of the saying 'First come – first served'. The white man's burden in modern history is to set everything up overseas and then hand over a going concern only to see it all fall apart soon afterwards.

Apart from the absorbing and interesting job of observing at close hand the aviation scene ranging from top level government activity to private flying – including some Cessna trips myself that kept my hand in adequately – the occasional upset marred what otherwise would have been an uneventful tour. The worst was the tragic accident to racing driver Ron Flockhart who was killed in a P51 'Mustang' just before his second attempt at the Australia-England air record in a propellor-driven aeroplane. The first one ended at Athens when ridiculous and quite unnecessary argument about payment for fuel just as he was about to take-off on the last lap forced him to abandon the attempt. On his next visit to Australia for another season of motor racing he bought a second Mustang and as the sole representative of British civil aviation I again attended to all the administration including the transfer of the aeroplane from the Australian register to the UK list. Ron had been staying with us at Amesbury House and set off very early one morning to fly to Sydney for a new radio to be installed just before the record attempt. Alas! he crashed in the Dandenong Hills within minutes of take off and all the miserable aftermath had to be dealt with as a result. Flying is a tough mistress but on this occasion it was almost certainly insufficient instrument flying practise that caused the crash.

Our off-duty activities were very varied and all manner of diversions came our way like cruising on the Hawkesbury river. Another was flying with Dick Cavill over one of those very frightening bush fires on reconnaissance whilst Irène took Anthony, (son of an old RAF friend Wg Cdr Peter Williams) to their home in our 'CD' diplomatic registration car, passing through raging fires on either side of the highway. Another was to attend the big social event of the Australian racing calendar called the Melbourne Cup. We were lucky to be invited and went in style to

Flemington race-course but poor Irène was forced to accept local custom and join the ladies in a separate enclosure. She hated it and quickly made her escape. It was yet another manifestation of the attitude of some Australian men to women who they invariably described as 'Sheilas'. All too often we had to say to a prospective guest that if his wife could not attend, well neither could he; the wives were so often much nicer than their spouses.

A great discovery was to locate my long-lost first cousin John Boyd-Moss and his Australian wife Nancy. John had joined the British army at an age when he should have still been at school and the happy association with the Aussies in Mesopotamia in World War One prompted him to follow them back to Australia. He loved what he called 'the black' – the whisky that was unobtainable except to diplomats and the subject of one of Jonathan's schoolboy literary masterpieces at Grimwade House School. After being told to write a sentence in his school-book that had to include the word black, our six-year old startled the teachers by writing 'My daddy is very fond of Johnnie Walker Black Label scotch whisky!' When I congratulated him on his spelling and handwriting but expressed concern about the subject matter, his comment was "Well Daddy it's true – isn't it?" With a delighted parental smile I had to agree.

The written word, in consonance with the spoken one sometimes had its pitfalls 'down under'. There was the story going around of an English lady author (Monica Dickens from memory) who had travelled to Sydney at her publishers' bidding and she was dutifully autographing her new book for would-be purchasers. One lady customer in the David Jones' emporium muttered something, whereupon our author wrote 'To Emma Chissit, with best wishes' and then applied her signature. The recipient looked at her autographed copy and declared in dismay that the wrong name had been written. What the good lady had intended to say was "How much is it?"! It was just one of those days.

My appointment as Civil Aviation Adviser came to an end in late 1962 and prior to departure my family and I toured New Zealand by car before they left for England so that Jonathan could go to Ashdown House preparatory school in Sussex. They loved New Zealand with its grand scenery and greenness compared to Australia and travelling as we did by road was easily the best way of choosing the routes and the stopover places. I returned to Melbourne for some weeks and after farewell calls on my associates I also departed. In many ways it was sad to give up an interesting job in such a huge area of interest and I probably saw more of Australasia and the Pacific than the inhabitants themselves. The anticlimax on my last day unfortunately was dispiriting because not one single person in an official capacity took the trouble to observe the niceties of protocol – or even good manners – to see me off. Had it not been for Bill Bradfield and Reg Bailey who showed up informally I would have departed without a single handshake. It caused me so much ill-feeling that after I got into the aeroplane I never bothered to look out of the window as we took off.

The journey home took me across the Pacific via Tahiti (which I chose in preference to Honolulu) and after staying with Cornelia's son Dick in Los Angles I made the long flight in a Boeing 707 non-stop to Heathrow. I was back again in the Northern Hemisphere and it was wonderful to return to our 400-year-old home near Chichester after so many years overseas. An added bonus was that my cousin Jane, married to Commander Ken Mills RN with their three children now lived next door to Windmill Cottage. Once again it was going to be the same old dreary business of hunting for a job in the harsh world outside the protective umbrella of government service.

The Handley Page Company fortunately came up with a proposal that I take on the special task of seeking new avenues of activity for the 5,000 employees whose work-load was diminishing steadily. This was occasioned (so the story goes) because Sir Frederic Handley Page refused to join forces with either of the two industrial giants ordained by Duncan Sandys for reshaping the aircraft industry. I travelled far and wide across NATO Europe seeking contracts for aircraft repair or overhaul but it was to no purpose because some countries had their own capability and the others were cared for by the Americans. As Dr Spooner might have said, I fell into the trap of stalling between two fools. Another avenue that I pursued was in space research work, now that a European consortium had been set up; however at that early stage in space development it was frankly chasing shadows. The only thing of substance in this activity was to attend a small private luncheon in the Savoy Hotel where I had the privilege of meeting Airey Neve who was later killed by an IRA bomb when leaving the House of Commons. After three years of fruitless and depressing effort I concluded that I was wasting the Company's money and my time and so I departed and shortly afterwards the Handley Page Company folded up. It was the sad end of a famous name in British aviation history.

The months that followed were very depressing and I reluctantly accepted some strange jobs in aviation that are best forgotten. In desperation I called on Lord Portal, the man who had chosen me for the appointment of equerry to the King and his advice was to abandon the aviation industry altogether because it was in the doldrums. As he was Chairman of the British Aircraft Corporation I followed his advice. After that depressing talk Irène and I discussed what options were open for a retired airman; one thing was certain and that was that I was not going to be away from my family and my home any more. This automatically narrowed the search geographically and in some way that even today I cannot explain we hit upon the idea of setting up a speciality food shop in Chichester. To get expert advice we went to see a friend in Harrods and he not only endorsed the idea he went further and enrolled us as unpaid trainees in the food hall. Thus a retired Group Captain (who had said goodbye to the past glory of knowing kings and emperors) was put to work cutting cheese for the cash customers. It was excellent training and it gave us the golden opportunity of meeting the food trade suppliers of exotica to the best shop in the world; a secondary bonus was a string of invitations from friends once they had recovered after seeing us so completely out of our previous environment. Any illusions of grandeur that I might have acquired in my life soon vanished and the process was good for me even though I did not care for it at all at the time.

'Epicure of Chichester' started up soon after the Harrods indoctrination and as the weeks passed we became more proficient with experience. We had super lady friends who came to assist, and best of all was Capt Angus Turnbull RN who became our full-time helper and brought his considerable ability into play by taking on the job of master storekeeper and general factotum – and all this for a pittance. Our customers flatteringly referred to Epicure as the Fortnum and Mason of Sussex and it became not only a shop well stocked with over three thousand exotic items, it acquired the atmosphere of a club and to some extent work became a pleasure. We supplied items for Her Majesty's delectation at Goodwood, for which a thank-you letter followed from the Lady-in-Waiting. We had a visit by Iranians (one of whom was a huge champion wrestler who proceeded to knock over a big stand of spice jars by accident) and when I spoke some Farsee to them as they left the shop it amazed them. One day a smartly dressed man ordered a particular commodity and said in a stage whisper "It's for the Duke". Dammit, I lost my cue on that occasion; what I should have said was "Yes sir; *which* Duke?" It was all a lot of fun but it was also a lot of hard work, particularly for Irène who had the tricky job of selecting the stock.

As touched upon earlier, one very pleasant break from routine, only made possible because Angus Turnbull handsomely undertook to hold the fort in our absence, was to deliver a beautiful white Range Rover to Teheran for Michael Simpson-Orlebar, the Commercial Counsellor at the Embassy. Equipped with all manner of gear for the very long safari, the route took Irène and I across France into Italy and thence via Yugoslavia and Bulgaria to Istambul. The long run across Turkey – it gets wilder and wilder still as one travels east in mountain country – eventually got us once again into Iran, the Persia of happy memory. Dramatic changes were immediately apparent; a fine highway, water towers in each village, new hotels, and a bustling Teheran. Thanks to the Shah the country was in overdrive. Our final run-in, listening to Glen Miller's band, got us to the Embassy gates, there to be greeted effusively by Abdul Magid and many others who awaited us all the way from England. A splendid delivery trip with no snags. Ten days later, having visited the Caspian Sea area in the Range Rover and meeting old friends, we flew back home. The self-same journey soon afterwards was repeated by our son Jonathan, his bride-to-be Anna, and John Byrne. This Range Rover was duly delivered to my old friend, Colonel (now General) Esfandiari of the Imperial Iranian Air Force. And of course with Glen Miller's wonderful tunes once again to delight them en route.

After close on ten years the time came to have a change and the result was that we sold 'Epicure' and we also sold Windmill Cottage in West Ashling, the plan being to live in the West Country. We were very sorry to go and I was certainly going to miss Chichester Harbour and the fun of maintaining Jonathan's 'Flying Dutchman' Olympic class racing dinghy. He and John Byrne used to travel far and wide across Europe to attend races and their fellow-yachtsmen envied them such a tame and willing maintenance man. The things that a doting parent will do for his son!

So we packed everything up and after seeing our household goods and chattels stored on Henry Batten's farm at Ryme Intrinseca – something that we appreciated very much – Irène and I plus our cat Maudie set off to find another home. By now Jonathan had become a student at Imperial College in London so innocently we thought that we had his term period in which to succeed. The reality was that we had no luck at all and it took 2000 miles of travel before we finally came across an attractive converted granary in Somerset and were thankful to move in after so many weeks of living out of a suitcase. The Tall House (as it is called) was located in the nice village of Kingsdon, Somerset, and as it is close to the Naval Air Station HMS Heron at Yeovilton it inevitably reminded me of my old passion – the aeroplane. This train of thought prompted me to decide that there was only one way that I could recapture my old enthusiasms, and so model aeroplanes returned into my life. It was back to the drawing board and then to the workshop to construct what I had dreamed up; it was just like old times and I applied myself enthusiastically. Eventually a ten-foot span sailplane came out into the sunlight and in addition to being radio-controlled it was fitted with accurate scale-type wing flaps and also working wing-tip slots as used on Tiger Moths. David Parker and John Crampton were the test pilots and after launches from White Sheet Hill in Wiltshire the model behaved impeccably. As a compliment to Yeovilton and a reminder of a model of pre-war times it was called 'Heron'. Later I fitted a small engine and the model's slow flying capability was so good that to verify it I designed and constructed a recording air-speed indicator that fitted into the nose of the model. The Heron can fly so slowly that you could walk briskly alongside it, thus demonstrating that those true scale flaps and slots really worked on a model as well as on a full-sized machine. It was very satisfying.

The Tall House in Kingsdon proved in practise to be much too big for us and amazingly within days of putting it on the market we literally exchanged houses with an ex-Army family. We moved into their smaller home in the charming village of Fivehead, near Taunton, where everybody smiles and the nice village shop (so well run by Bill and Agnes Robertson) is regarded as a meeting place. My custom-built workshop overlooks the garden; it has the sun streaming in and birds sing away in the trees to delight the ear and eye. The second model project after the 'Heron' was I confess pure nostalgia coupled with the wild optimism of an old aeromodeller armed with schoolboy skills but no experience at-all of flying models remotely controlled by radio. It is a one-tenth scale version of 'Boston 111A' RH-A that was my personal aircraft in No 88 Sqdn. There is something very special about the way that it taxies out and takes off down the Merryfield runway and climbs away with the landing gear disappearing as if by magic. What looks like a real Boston flies around the circuit and after about fifteen minutes the landing gear reappears, the flaps are lowered, and the Boston makes a smooth touch-down and taxies back to David Parker, the test pilot.

The third model is also a one-tenth scale (90 inch wing span) replica Wellesley AO-A of NO 223 Squadron, the trusty aeroplane in which I made my first operational sortie into Ethiopia against Mussolini's men. As with the Boston its realism in the air faithfully follows the prototype's style of flight and for me it is another emotional experience especially when British champion Brian Taylor is the pilot because his flying is faultless and completely realistic.

The current project under way is a one eighth scale, 86 inch span, version of the de Havilland DH104 'Devon' that I had the greatest pleasure of flying when I was Air Attaché in Teheran. Apart from my first love, the Tiger Moth, these three splendid aeroplanes together with the de Havilland 'Mosquito', claim top places amongst the seventy very varied types recorded in my pilot's log books. None of this activity would be possible and not one model would fly but for the invaluable help and engineering skills of David Parker, master craftsman on the lathe and in many other trades that modelling demands. In between making his own-design and constructed model aero engines he will happily spare time to make components like engine cowlings and fuel tanks for me and follow it up by flight testing the completed model with all the background experience of an ex-Naval test pilot to call upon. In my sentimental way I like to think that his early training with the de Havilland Company provided the starting point of our close association because de Havilland's will always be remembered with affection as the producer of the Tiger Moth, the wonderful flying machine in which I learned to fly in 1933.

Today, after a wealth of aviation and other experiences around the globe the wanderer and his superb wife have come to roost in Somerset. Our home is very comfortable, the view looking south across rich farmlands to the Blackdown Hills is splendid, herons fly down to the streams to fish and old friends from around the world come to visit us. Typically, Irène plunged into village life energetically and contributed her skills and that certain style by helping to run the Women's Institute, Meals-on-wheels, and (her favourite activity) a member of the team that decorates the village church with superb flower arranging. Our dearest son Jonathan, delicious Anna, and the two grandchildren Rebecca and Claire give us endless pleasure and happiness. The workshop claims my undivided attention – lawn mowing and other chores permitting – and despite sundry incidents inherent to flying them, all the models are serviceable; for the moment anyway! Naval pilots streak past overhead in their Sea Harriers and helicopters grunt their way on training exercises. The occasional Hercules (possibly of my old No 47 Squadron from Sudan days) can be seen on runs across Sedgemoor, on the other side of the ridge. All this aerial activity is a nostalgic reminder of my aviation life.

The wheel has turned full cycle. I have been cut down to size and am back with my aeromodelling friends just as though it was Wimbledon Common, sixty years ago all over again. Today it is the Royal Naval airfield of Merryfield, just three miles away in the faithful Citroën 2CV. No wonder that I am a very contented old airman. Heavenly days indeed!

Appendix 'A'.

Order of the Day by 'Bomber' Harris

(copy of original as posted on the HQ Notice Board at RAF Holme-on-Spalding-Moor; May 1945).

Headquarters Bomber Command. — Serial No 52.
ROYAL AIR FORCE. — Dago No 1.
Date 10.5.45.

COMMAND ROUTINE ORDERS.
BY
AIR CHIEF MARSHAL SIR AT HARRIS. KCB., OBE., AFC.

A.52. *PART I. ADMINISTRATIVE.*
SPECIAL ORDER OF THE DAY.

Men and Women of Bomber Command.

More than 5½ years ago, within hours of the declaration of War, Bomber Command first assailed the German enemy.

You were then but a handful. Inadequate in everything but the skill and determination of the crews for that sombre occasion and for the unknown years of unceasing battle which lay beyond horizons black indeed.

You, the aircrews of Bomber Command, sent your first ton of bombs away on the morrow of the outbreak of war. A million tons of bombs and mines have followed from Bomber Command alone. From Declaration of War to Cease Fire a continuity of battle without precedent and without relent.

In the Battle of France your every endeavour bore down upon an overwhelming and triumphant enemy.

After Dunkirk your Country stood alone – in arms but largely unarmed – between the Nazi tyranny and domination of the world.

The Battle of Britain, in which you took great part, raised the last barrier strained but holding in the path of the all-conquering Wohrmacht, and the bomb smoke of the Channel ports choked back down German throats the very word 'Invasion': not again to find expression within those narrow seas until the bomb-disrupted defences of the Normandy beachheads fell to our combined assault.

In the long years between much was to pass.

Then it was that you, and you for long alone, carried the war over deeper and ever more furiously into the heart of the Third Reich. There the whole might of the German enemy in undivided strength, and – scarcely less a foe – the very elements, arrayed against you. You overcame them both.

Through those desperate years, undismayed by any odds, undeterred by any casualties, night succeeding night, you fought. The Phalanx of the United Nations.

You fought alone, as the one force then assailing German soil., you fought alone as individuals – isolated in your crew stations by the darkness and the murk, and from all other aircraft in company.

Not for you the hot emulation of high endeavour in the glare and panoply of martial array. Each crew, each one in each crew, fought alone through black nights rent only, mile after continuing mile, by the fiercest barrages ever raised and the instant sally of the searchlights. In each dark minute of those long miles lurked menace. Fog, ice, snow and tempest found you undeterred.

In that loneliness in action lay the final test, the ultimate stretch of human staunchness and determination.

Your losses mounted through those years. Years in which your chance of survival through one spell of operational duty was negligible. Through two periods, mathematically Nil. Nevertheless survivors pressed forward as volunteers to pit their desperately acquired skill in even a third period of operations, on special tasks.

In those 5 years and 3 months of continuous battle over enemy soil your casualties over long periods were grievous. As the count is cleared those of Bomber Command who gave their lives to bring near to impotence an enemy who had surged swift in triumph through a Continent, and to enable the United Nations to deploy in full array, will be found not less than the total dead of our National Invasion Armies now in Germany.

In the whole history of our National Forces never have so small a band of men been called to support so long such odds. You indeed bore the brunt.

To you who survive I would say this. Content yourselves and take credit with those who perished, that now the "Cease Fire" has sounded countless homes within our Empire will welcome back a father or a son whose life, but for your endeavours and your sacrifices, would assuredly have been expended during long further years of agony to achieve a victory already ours. No Allied Nation is clear of this debt to you.

I cannot here expound your full achievements.

Your attacks on the industrial centres of Northern Italy did much toward the collapse of the Italian and German Armies in North Africa, and to further invasion of the Italian mainland.

Of the German enemy two to three million fit men, potentially vast armies, were continuously held throughout the war in direct and indirect defence against your assaults. A great part of her industrial war effort went towards fending your attacks.

You struck a critical proportion of the weapons of war from enemy hands., on every front.

You immobilised armies, leaving them shorn of supplies, reinforcements, resources and reserves, the easier prey to our advancing Forces.

You eased and abetted the passage of our troops over major obstacles. You blasted the enemy from long prepared defences where he essayed to hold. On the Normandy beaches. At the hinge of the battle of Caon. In the jaws of the Falaise Gap. To the strongpoints of the enemy-held Channel ports, St Vith, Houffalize and the passage of the Rhine, In battle after battle you sped our armies to success at minimum cost to our troops. The Commanders of our land forces, and indeed those of the enemy, have called your attacks decisive.

You enormously disrupted every enemy means of communication, the very life-blood of his military and economic machines., railways, canals and every form of transport fell first to decay and then to chaos under your assaults.

You so shattered the enemy's oil plants as to deprive him of all but the final trickle of fuel. His aircraft became earthbound, his road transport ceased to roll, armoured fighting vehicles lay helpless outside the battle, or fell immobilised into our hands. His strategic and tactical plans failed through inability to move.

From his war industries supplies of ore, coal, steel, fine metals, aircraft, guns, ammunition, tanks, vehicles and every ancillary equipment dwindled under your attacks.

At the very crisis of the invasion of Normandy, you virtually annihilated the German naval surface forces then in the Channel, a hundred craft and more fell victim to those three attacks.

You sank or damaged a large but yet untotalled number of enemy submarines in his ports and by mine-laying in his waters.

You interfered widely and repeatedly with his submarine training programmes.

With extraordinary accuracy, regardless of opposition, you hit and burst through every carapace which he could devise to protect his submarines in harbour.

By your attacks on inland industries and coastal ship yards you caused hundreds of his submarines to be still born.

Your mine laying throughout the enemy's sea lanes, your bombing of his inland waters, and his Ports, confounded his sea traffic and burst his canals. From Norway throughout the Baltic, from Jutland to the Girondo, on the coasts of Italy and North Africa you laid and relaid the minefields. The wreckage of the enemy's naval and merchant fleets litters and encumbers his sea lanes and dockyards. A thousand known ships, and many more as yet unknown, fell casualty to your mines.

You hunted and harried his major warships from hide to hide. You put out of action, gutted or sank most of them.

By your attacks on Experimental Stations, factories, communications and firing sites you long postponed and much reduced the V.weapon attacks. You averted an enormous further toll of death and destruction from your Country.

With it all you never ceased to rot the very heart out of the enemy's war resources and resistance.

His Capital and near 100 of his cities and towns including nearly all of leading war industrial importance lie in utter ruin, together with the greater part of the war industry which they supported.

Thus you brought to nought the enemy's original advantage of an industrial might intrinsically greater than ours and supported by the labour of captive millions, now set free.

For the first time in more than a century you have brought home to the habitual aggressor of Europe the full and acrid flavours of war, so long the perquisite of his victims.

All this, and much more, have you achieved during those 5½ years of continuous battle, despite all opposition from an enemy disposing of many a geographical and strategical advantage with which to exploit an initial superiority in numbers.

Men from every part of the Empire and most of the Allied Nations fought in our ranks. Indeed a band of brothers.

In the third year of war the Eighth Bomber Command, and the Fifteenth Bomber Command, USAAF from their Mediterranean bases, ranged themselves at our side, zealous in extending even mutual aid, vieing in every assault upon our common foe. Especially they played the leading part in sweeping the enemy fighter definitely from our path, and, finally, out of the skies.

Nevertheless nothing that the crews accomplished – was much, and decisive – could have been achieved without the devoted service of every man and woman in the Command.

Those who tended the aircraft, mostly in the open, through six bitter winters. Endless intricacies in a prolonged misory of wet and cold. They rightly earned the implicit trust of the crews. They set extraordinary records of aircraft serviceability.

Those who manned the Stations, Operational Headquarters, Supply lines and Communications.

The pilots of the Photographic Reconnaissance Units without whose lonely ventures far and wide over enemy territory we should have been largely powerless to plan or to strike.

The Operational Crew training organisation of the Command which through these years of ceaseless work by day and night never failed, in the face of every difficulty and unproductive call, to replace all casualties and to keep our constantly expanding first line up to strength in crews trained to the highest pitch of efficiency: simultaneously producing near 20,000 additional trained aircrew for the raising and reinforcement of some 50 extra squadrons, formed in the Command and despatched for service in other Commands at home and overseas.

The men and women of the Meteorological Branch who attained prodigious exactitudes in a fickle art and stood brave on assertion where science is inexact. Time and again they saved us from worse than the enemy could ever have achieved. Their record is outstanding.

The meteorological reconnaissance pilots, who flew through anything and everything in search of the feasible.

The Operational Research Sections whose meticulous investigation of every detail of every attack provided data for the continuous confounding of the enemy and the consistent reduction of our own casualties.

The scientists, especially those of the Telecommunications Research Establishment, who placed in unending succession in our hands the technical means to resolve our problems and to confuse the every parry of the enemy. Without their skill and their labours beyond doubt we could not have prevailed.

The Works Services who engineered for Bomber Command alone 2,000 miles of runway, track and road, with all that goes with them.

The Works Staffs, Designers and Workers who equipped and re-equipped us for Battle. Their efforts, their honest workmanship, kept in our hands indeed a Shining Sword.

To all of you I would say how proud I am to have served in Bomber Command for 4½ years and to have been your Commander-in-Chief through more than three years of your Saga.

Your task in the German war is now completed. Famously have you fought. Well have you deserved of your country and her Allies.

(Signed) AT HARRIS.
Air Chief Marshal,
Commanding-in-Chief,
BOMBER COMMAND.

Appendix 'B'

Survival Chances

Statistics worked out by the Air Ministry in November 1942 showing aircrew losses sustained – and thus survival chances – by type of operational role.

Type of Squadron	*Percentage chance of survival*	
	One tour	*Two tours*
Heavy & medium bombers	44	19½
Light bombers	25½	6½
Day fighter	43	18½
Night fighter	39	15
Long-range fighter	59½	35½
Torpedo bomber	17½	3
Heavy General reconnaissance landplane	71	50½
Light General reconnaissance landplane	45	20
Sunderland flying boat	66	43½
Catalina flying boat	77½	60
Fighter reconnaissance	31	9½
Bomber reconnaissance	42	17½

Index